MENLO PARK
REMINISCENCES

Volume One

BY
FRANCIS JEHL

NEW INTRODUCTION BY
WILLIAM S. PRETZER

Published in association with

HENRY
FORD
MUSEUM
&
GREENFIELD
VILLAGE

by
DOVER PUBLICATIONS, INC.
NEW YORK

Introduction copyright © 1990 by Henry Ford Museum & Greenfield Village.
All rights reserved under Pan American and International Copyright
Conventions.

Published in Canada by General Publishing Company, Ltd., 30 Lesmill Road,
Don Mills, Toronto, Ontario.
Published in the United Kingdom by Constable and Company, Ltd., 3 The
Lanchesters, 162–164 Fulham Palace Road, London W6 9ER.

This Dover edition, first published in 1990 in association with Henry Ford
Museum & Greenfield Village, is an unabridged republication of the 1937 edition
of the work as published by The Edison Institute, Dearborn, Michigan. For further
details see the new Introduction by William S. Pretzer, prepared specially for this
edition. The original text is completely unaltered.

Manufactured in the United States of America
Dover Publications, Inc., 31 East 2nd Street, Mineola, N.Y. 11501

Library of Congress Cataloging in Publication Data

Jehl, Francis, 1860–1941.
    Menlo Park reminiscences / by Francis Jehl ; new introduction by William
S. Pretzer.
        p.   cm.
    Reprint. Originally published: Dearborn, Mich. : Edison Institute, c1937.
    Includes indexes.
    ISBN 0-486-26357-6
    1. Edison, Thomas A. (Thomas Alva), 1847–1931.   2. Inventors—United
States—Biography.   I. Henry Ford Museum & Greenfield Village.   II. Title.
TK140.E3J4   1990
621.3'092—dc20   90-3669
    [B]   CIP

INTRODUCTION

In 1876, the prolific inventor Thomas Alva Edison established a research and development laboratory at Menlo Park, New Jersey. Edison obtained over 400 patents during his six years at Menlo Park for inventions that included the phonograph, the telephone transmitter and the incandescent electric lighting system. Francis Jehl joined Edison's team in 1879 as a teenaged laboratory assistant. Looking back on Menlo Park as an enthusiastic veteran in the 1930s, Jehl wrote *Menlo Park Reminiscences*—three volumes of historical research, anecdotes and reminiscences that today are still frequently quoted sources of information about Edison.

Jehl's *Menlo Park Reminiscences* does more than illuminate the activities of Thomas A. Edison at his laboratory in Menlo Park, New Jersey, between 1876 and 1882. It reminds us of our changing attitudes toward technological innovation and our need to assess those attitudes critically. Many people who read Jehl's work today will question his uncritical endorsement of technological progress; his simplistic, hero-worshipping attitude toward Edison; his naive championing of Edison's business and personal dealings; and his affirmation of his own importance in the work at Menlo Park. However, in criticizing Jehl's attitudes, today's readers will have the opportunity to ponder changes in the image and the reality of industrial research and development since the 1880s.

Menlo Park Reminiscences was first published in three volumes by The Edison Institute between 1934 and 1941. The Edison Institute is the official name of Henry Ford's innovative educational institution founded in 1929 in Dearborn, Michigan, and composed of Greenfield Village and Henry Ford Museum. Francis Jehl compiled his *Reminiscences* while he served as caretaker and guide at the reconstruction of Edison's Menlo Park laboratory at Greenfield Village.

Greenfield Village was conceived by Ford as an outdoor museum containing a variety of homes, schools, stores and workplaces illustrating the everyday experiences of ordinary and extraordinary Americans. Most of the buildings in the Village show how typical eighteenth- and nineteenth-century families and tradesmen combined traditional and ingenious methods to solve everyday problems. Other installations were set up to venerate men whom Ford idolized as innovators: Orville and Wilbur Wright, George Washington Carver, Luther Burbank, Noah Webster, William Holmes McGuffey and, with the large Menlo Park reconstruction, Thomas Alva Edison.

Henry Ford and Thomas Edison had been friends for several years when Ford approached him in 1928 about resurrecting the old laboratory as a museum piece. Edison and his company, Thomas A. Edison Inc.

(which still maintained a large research and manufacturing operation in West Orange, New Jersey), agreed to help in the search for material. The Edison Pioneers, an association of former Edison employees dedicated to perpetuating the inventor's memory, became involved as well. Abandoned by Edison in 1882, the buildings had almost totally disappeared from the New Jersey landscape. Ford's associates salvaged as much material as could be found in the ruins of the original complex. Fragments of demolished buildings were retrieved, and used in replicating them. Only two intact buildings were found: a glassblowing shed, which was no longer on its original site but was found instead at a General Electric Company employee park in Parsippany, New Jersey; and the dwelling of Sarah Jordan, which served as a boardinghouse for some of Edison's Menlo Park employees. Both of these buildings were moved to Dearborn.

Francis Jehl, then one of the few living veterans of Menlo Park, was an obvious candidate for recruitment into Ford's reconstruction project. He was Vice President of the Edison Pioneers and, when approached by Ford, had been publishing reminiscences of the Menlo Park days in a trade periodical for a few years. Jehl agreed to help Ford, and began by recovering some laboratory equipment and providing information to assist Ford's architects in reconstructing the buildings. Then, in late 1928, Jehl was invited to visit Dearborn and soon became the semi-official "keeper of the flame." He and his wife decided at that point to make their home in Dearborn, where he devoted himself fully to the reconstruction of Menlo Park buildings, the arrangement of museum displays and correspondence with other Edison Pioneers who could provide more artifacts and information relating to Edison's work. He also gave tours of the Greenfield Village installation to dignitaries, scientists, electrical-industry executives, entertainment celebrities and groups of schoolchildren. Jehl was publicly associated with Greenfield Village from the day of its dedication, October 21, 1929 (the fiftieth anniversary of Edison's successful light-bulb experiment). At the time of his death on February 9, 1941, his work at Greenfield Village as an advocate of Edison's memory was recognized nationwide.

Francis Jehl was born of immigrant parents on September 6, 1860, in New York City. At sixteen, he became an office boy for the law firm of Grosvenor P. Lowrey, an associate of Thomas A. Edison. Jehl was especially interested in the mechanical aspects of electricity, a burgeoning new technical field. He took night classes at Cooper Union, an engineering school in Manhattan, and worked a year in the Western Union Telegraph Company workshop headed by George M. Phelps, a prominent electrical engineer. In early 1879, Jehl induced Lowrey to write a letter of introduction to Edison for him.

Jehl began work as a general laboratory assistant at Menlo Park in

February of 1879. At first he spent much of his time performing menial chores around the lab: maintaining batteries, running errands and cleaning up. By the fall of 1879, he was assisting one of Edison's more prominent collaborators, Francis Upton, with a series of experiments on mercury vacuum pumps that were used to evacuate lamp globes. Later responsibilities included testing a variety of incandescent lamps and working on the chemical meter, a device for measuring electrical consumption.

When, in 1881, Edison moved his base of operations to Manhattan from Menlo Park, Jehl followed him for the opportunity to work in the testing room of the Edison machine shop at 65 Goerck Street. The workers at the Goerck Street shop built the dynamos used in the Pearl Street Central Station and the "Jumbo" dynamos installed at the Paris International Electrical Exposition and at the Holborn Viaduct in England. The next year Edison sent Jehl to the Holborn Viaduct to set up a meter department for the English Edison company. For Jehl, this was the beginning of a long career as an electrical engineer in Europe. In 1883 he prepared a demonstration of the electric lighting system for the Vienna Electrical Exposition. After that he helped install lighting systems in France, Austria and Hungary. He chose to settle in Hungary for a long time, spending seventeen years as chief engineer of the Budapest electric company. Shortly after the end of World War I, he returned to the United States.

Upon returning from Europe, Jehl became active in the Edison Pioneers. This was an extraordinary and very partisan group whose avowed purpose was to promote the image and heritage of their mentor. His membership in this group gave him opportunities to exchange memories of working under Edison with former colleagues. As early as 1924 he began writing about his experiences with the inventor, publishing short autobiographical sketches in *The Edison Monthly*, a publication of the New York Edison Company. In October 1928, Marie Goucher Greene, an associate editor of the *Monthly*, wrote to Henry Ford suggesting that he sponsor Jehl's efforts to publish a full account of his work with Edison in time for the fiftieth anniversary of the electric light, to be observed in 1929. *Menlo Park Reminiscences* was the account Jehl finally published. This project was sponsored by Ford, but not published in time for the anniversary Marie Goucher Greene suggested.

The Ford Motor Company publication, *The Ford News*, began serializing Jehl's reminiscences in 1930. In 1931, Ford's publicist, William A. Simonds, published *A Boy With Edison*, a biographical account of Jehl's years with Edison at Menlo Park. This book included much of the material from the *Ford News* articles.

Finally, in 1932, an initial, incomplete version of the first volume of *Menlo Park Reminiscences* was published by The Edison Institute. Subsequent editions of Volume One, issued in 1934, 1936 and 1937, contained several more chapters. Volume Two appeared in 1938 and 1939; and Volume Three was completed and published in 1941, shortly after Jehl's death. Each subsequent edition of each volume contained minor alterations and emendations. Chronicling all the different versions of the three volumes of *Menlo Park Reminiscences* would certainly be a nightmare for a bibliographer!

Volume One, reprinted here exactly as it appeared in 1937, covers Edison's early career and his experiments at Menlo Park. In the first half of this volume, Jehl introduces us to the Menlo Park laboratory and describes Edison's inventions through 1878. Individual chapters deal with such inventions as the stock ticker, the motograph, the quadruplex telegraph, the electric pen, the telephone transmitter, the phonograph and the tasimeter. Jehl's narrative includes his own recollections of Menlo Park, cites newspaper and magazine accounts about Edison and other scientists published in the 1870s and reflects on what it was like for him to encounter the inventions again at Dearborn in the 1930s. The second half of Volume One is taken up with a lengthy discussion of the experiments on incandescent electric lighting. It ends with a description of the successful public demonstration of the lighting system on December 31, 1879.

Volume Two continues the discussion of the development of the electric light and extensively treats its first applications. It provides further details on work and social activities at Menlo Park and more biographical information on many workers employed there. Volume Two also includes an important nine-page reminiscence written by Charles L. Clarke, who joined the Menlo Park team in February 1880. This additional perspective provides useful details about the working atmosphere around the laboratory. The volume ends with Jehl's instructions from Edison in May 1881 to pack up his equipment and move his work to 65 Goerck Street in Manhattan.

Volume Three opens with a discussion of the post-Menlo Park commercial introduction of Edison's lighting system, the growth of Edison's electrical manufacturing plants and the development of the General Electric Company in the 1890s. The narrative then leaps to the year 1928, when Jehl revisited the ruins at Menlo Park, and concludes (in a chapter finished by William A. Simonds) with Jehl's participation in the re-creation of the light-bulb experiment as part of the dedication ceremonies for The Edison Institute.

As a historical document, Jehl's *Reminiscences* should be used with great care, for all three volumes are full of inaccuracies and unsubstantiated opinions. Jehl writes convincingly of events of which he had no firsthand knowledge, and embellishes his descriptions of events with details that cannot be verified. He includes page after page of dialogue with no documentation to prove that the conversations took place just as he recalls them, or that they even took place at all.

Yet there is still much of value in the *Reminiscences*. Jehl exultingly depicts a Menlo Park laboratory full of social interaction, personality conflicts, camaraderie, competitiveness, challenging tasks and simple pleasures. His intimate remembrances of events and personalities provide a taste of what it must have been like to work in the small community of Menlo Park. His impressions of Edison's associates, competitors and adversaries are instructive. Many (but not all) of the artifacts noted in the *Reminiscences* as being "in the restored laboratory at Dearborn" can still be viewed there. Jehl quotes at length from publications contemporary with the events he recalls (such as *Scientific American*, *Scribner's Monthly* and *Journal of the Telegraph*), and provides many illustrations from the same sources. His technical descriptions are often inaccurate or incomplete, but some of these inadequacies serve to illustrate the limitations of knowledge about electricity that were common in the 1880s.

Jehl's enthusiastic, almost filiopietistic adulation of Edison in the *Reminiscences* was encouraged by several factors. Writing in the 1930s, his positive view of Edison was influenced by the general tenor of the times, his association with the Edison Pioneers, his correspondence with other Menlo Park veterans and the support given to him by the electrical industry and Henry Ford, the greatest promoter of Edison's image. Earlier, while still in Europe in 1913, he had expressed an entirely different opinion of Edison in a long memorandum to Francis Upton, the university-trained mathematician who served as Edison's close associate. In this memorandum, Jehl was openly critical of Edison's technical and managerial abilities, going as far as to call Edison "a shrewd, witty business man without a soul, an electrical and mechanical jobber. . . ." At that time, Jehl also credited Francis Upton with being the real brains behind the successes at Menlo Park.

By the time Jehl was preparing his *Reminiscences*, he had been for years an active member of the Edison Pioneers. The group worked closely with the electrical industry, specifically with the New York Edison Company and with the industry's national trade association, the Edison Lighting Institute. In 1929, Francis Upton was president of the association. Upton had always given Edison credit for the work at the laboratory and was not inclined to claim glory for himself. Jehl's *Reminiscences* reflects this type of thinking, in spite of the doubts he had about Edison early on. Jehl and Upton, in fact, shared the unofficial but generally held belief of the Edison Pioneers that Thomas Alva Edison deserved personal credit for all the inventions at Menlo Park. The Edison Pioneers also credited Edison with the development of the modern electrical industry (despite the important contributions of George Westinghouse, Nikola Tesla and others).

Jehl's *Reminiscences* was the product of a collective memory of events that had occurred forty or fifty years previously. His memory was reinforced by contact with Menlo Park veterans. For example, Charles Clarke, who after Menlo Park remained in the electrical industry as an engineer, wrote Jehl numerous letters between 1928 and 1941 congratulating him on publishing the *Reminiscences*, providing more anecdotes, chiding him on errors of fact or judgment and encouraging him to focus on Edison's achievements. Jehl's most immediate audience were members of the electrical industry; his work was made possible by the Edison companies and by Henry Ford. For his fellow Edisonians, Jehl provided reminiscences—not calculated fabrications, and not rigorous history.

It should also be remembered that Jehl began writing during the Roaring '20s and completed his work during the Great Depression. According to Wyn Wachhorst's *Thomas Alva Edison: An American Myth* (Cambridge, Massachusetts, MIT Press, 1981), Edison's popularity in the years surrounding his death in 1931 was based on the image of his personal enthusiasm and energy. In a society that feared losing its productive energy, confidence and sense of individualism, Edison symbolized, for Jehl, progress brought about by individual perseverance and enterprise.

Readers who wish to understand more about Menlo Park, or do their own research on the subject so that they might be able to evaluate Jehl's *Reminiscences* critically, should consult the following works:

Friedel, Robert, and Paul Israel, with Bernard S. Finn, *Edison's Electric Light: Biography of an Invention*. New Brunswick, N.J.: Rutgers University Press, 1985.

Jenkins, Reese V., et al., eds., *The Papers of Thomas A. Edison: Volume 1, The Making of an Inventor (February 1847–June 1873)*. Baltimore, Md. and London: The Johns Hopkins University Press, 1989. (Subsequent volumes of this multivolume scholarly edition of Edison's papers will deal directly with the Menlo Park years and undoubtedly augment, perhaps even challenge, some of the impressions left by Francis Jehl.)

Pretzer, William S., ed., *Working at Inventing: Thomas A. Edison and the Menlo Park Experience*. Dearborn, Mich.: Henry Ford Museum & Greenfield Village, 1989.

WILLIAM S. PRETZER
Curator
Henry Ford Museum & Greenfield Village

MENLO PARK

Reminiscences

By
FRANCIS JEHL
Former laboratory assistant of
Thomas Alva Edison

VOLUME ONE

Written in
Edison's restored Menlo Park laboratory

Published by
EDISON INSTITUTE
DEARBORN, MICHIGAN

Copyright Nineteen Hundred and Thirty-Seven

TABLE OF CONTENTS

PART ONE—The Years Prior to 1879

TABLE OF CONTENTS (*continued*)

PART TWO—Invention of Electric Light, 1879

PREFACE TO SECOND EDITION

IN THESE pages is presented a picture of Menlo Park as it was during the great years of Thomas A. Edison's achievements. The purpose is twofold: To convey to our readers information about those events and to give visitors at the restored Menlo Park a better understanding of them.

In doing this, we have sought to make plain the uses to which the apparatus in the laboratory was put and the methods whereby the inventions were accomplished.

The narrator of these facts is Francis Jehl, who alone survived of that little group in the research laboratory which assisted Mr. Edison at the time of his invention of the incandescent electric light.

Mr. Jehl erected the testing department in the Edison Machine Works in Goereck Street, New York City. In 1882 Edison sent him abroad to work with the English, French and Italian Edison companies. He assisted Batchelor in establishing the French Edison Company's lamp factory near Paris, and as a special engineer for the French Edison Company, set up the Edisonian standard in many parts of Europe. He assisted Rathenau at Berlin before the German Edison Company was founded.

Returning home after forty years, he became associated with the Edison Historical Collection. When the Menlo

Park group was restored at Dearborn, Michigan, he was asked to assist and at the re-enactment of the invention of the first practical lamp October 21, 1929, again played a part as on the original occasion.

Edison spoke of Jehl as 'one of my old associates and fellow-workers . . . one of my assistants in the experimental work pertaining to my invention and development of the incandescent electric lamp and lighting system . . .'

—The Editors.

To Francis Jehl
Pioneer of Incandescent Lighting
Orange USA from Thomas A Edison
Oct 5 1904

PART ONE

(CHAPTERS I TO XXVI INCLUSIVE)

*The
Years Prior to 1879—
Early Inventions of
Edison*

ACKNOWLEDGMENT

I DESIRE to acknowledge my indebtedness first to my old chief, Thomas A. Edison. Then to his friend Mr. Henry Ford, who has opened the kaleidoscope of the past and restored Menlo Park at Dearborn, reviving memories of those days when Edison did his work for humanity. Next, to the first pioneers of the Edison system of incandescent lighting and the distribution of electrical energy: Charles Batchelor, Francis R. Upton, John Kruesi, Sigmund Bergmann, Edward H. Johnson, Charles L. Clarke, Edward G. Acheson, Dr. Herman Claudius, Wilson S. Howell, Martin Force, William J. Hammer, Ludwig Boehm, William Holzer, James Hipple, William S. Andrews, John H. Vail, James M. Seymour, John Hood, David Cunningham, James Holloway, James Bradley, H. A. Campbell, John W. Lawson, John F. Ott, and others. These colleagues of mine helped to make the first 'camps,' dig the first 'water holes,' set down the first 'marks and bearings' and build the 'lonely cairns' through which so many others have been instructed. At home and abroad they raised the first Edisonian standard.

Then to those able men who followed in the path thus thrown open I make similar avowal: John W. Lieb, Samuel Insull, Charles L. Edgar, Alex Dow, John W. Howell, Louis Rau, Professor Guiseppe Colombo, Emil Rathenau, Oscar von Miller, Philip Seuble, Stephan von Fodor, W. N. Stewart, Robert A. McCarty, Charles Hortsek. And to those energetic veterans whose names have filled the roster of the Association of Edison Illuminating Companies and are still identified with the development of the art. Their voluminous minutes are the encyclopedia of the 'great electrical revolution' down to the present and constitute the codification of Edison's work. Pioneers and veterans make up this association and their assiduity and perseverance keep green the transcendent genius of their chief's name. To them, as well as to the Electrical Testing Laboratories and its president, Preston S. Millar, I express my thanks for much assistance.

To John W. Lieb, Arthur Williams and Frederick W. Jesser, past executives of the New York Edison Company, and Norman Maul, past editor of the Edison *Monthly*, I desire to express my special gratitude for encouragement and help given on my return to America after forty years' sojourn abroad. Through them I was started on the task of writing my reminiscences. Last, but not least, to William A. Simonds, editor of *Ford News*, for extended help in editing my voluminous notes and writings of the past.

Francis Jehl

Menlo Park Reminiscences

I. Introduction

IT IS not an easy task to roll back the curtain of Time and after a lapse of half a century recall the events and circumstances which at that period filled our lives. There are certain things which engrave themselves on the memory of a youth and which neither Time nor Distance can blot out; but the broad picture of life as it was and of the world as it was known before the discovery of all that makes this age so wonderful requires the touch of a master painter.

If you will bear with me briefly, I will introduce you to that world—to New York City, if you please, in the year 1878. I choose that time because it was the year before the discovery of the incandescent light and of power distribution by Mr. Edison, and marked the last hours of darkness before the dawn of our present era.

Mr. Edison was a frequent visitor in New York City, coming from his headquarters at Menlo Park, New Jersey. Two years previous he had gone down there from Newark, seeking a quiet, secluded spot where he could erect a laboratory. Menlo Park, a straggling hamlet in the rolling hills of northern New Jersey, offered him privacy and plenty of room. He bought a large rectangle of ground and built a two-story clapboard structure, long and unpretentious but exactly what he wanted in the pursuit of his unusual profession—that of inventor.

Nobody in that day had ever heard of such a thing as a professional laboratory in which experiments were carried on toward practical ends. The experiments of the research laboratories of the scientists were all made to add to the sum of human knowledge, but the practical application of that knowledge was for other hands. Edison in boldly launching out as an inventor was unique. Whatever he did was questioned severely by the savants of that day.

I knew him as a caller at the law office on Wall Street where I was employed as an office boy. One of my duties was to operate the electric pen, a device we had to make many copies of a single letter, and since it had been invented by

Mr. Edison I wanted to seek and know the maker. During his early days of inventing, he had brought out various improvements on the telegraph which were patented, of course, but were constantly being infringed. As the Western Union Telegraph Company had acquired his patents of that nature, they often called him as an adviser or witness in enforcing their rights. My employer, Grosvenor P. Lowrey, was general counsel for the Western Union, which ex-

Thomas A. Edison in 1878.

plains the reason for Mr. Edison's frequent visits to our office.

At that time he was thirty-one years old, and was already world famous as the inventor of the speaking phonograph and many other devices. He was described in a New York City newspaper as rather under the medium height, about five feet six or seven inches tall, and had thick, soft chestnut brown hair and clear, bright, grayish blue eyes.

'His forehead,' said this writer, 'is round and moderately full, but not high; nose prominent; mouth large but possessing a pleasant expression, and his chin is of the purely executive type—square and prominent. His manner is modest and retiring, and exhibits a total lack of egotism or self-assurance, a quality as rare as it is marvelous in one whose name and reputation are world wide and his achievements among the most astounding of the age.'

The Drexel Building, on the third floor of which was our office, was an imposing building at the corner of Wall and Broad streets. Its exterior was fashioned of white marble and it was looked upon as the most stately and ornate business structure in all Manhattan. On the ground floor were the offices of Drexel, Morgan & Company.

My desk or table where I operated the electric pen and the intercommunicating telegraph—a device by which it was possible to send messages from one office to another as we do today by means of the telephone—was by a window facing Wall Street and just opposite the Sub-treasury.

Edison's electric pen was used almost universally in business and professional offices during the late '70's and early '80's.([1]) He invented it while still in Newark before moving to Menlo Park, and perfected it at the latter place. (His other office inventions, the Ediphone, for use in dictation

(1) One of Edison's electric pens, with wet battery as here described, may be seen on one of the tables on the second floor of the restored Menlo Park laboratory at Dearborn. It may be operated today as it was in 1878.

Wall Street as it appeared about the year 1878. On the left is the Drexel Building, on the third floor of which was Mr. Lowrey's office, frequently visited by Edison. Across the street is the Sub-treasury, and in the distance is Trinity Church.

of letters, and the mimeograph for making stencils, did not come until later. (See chapter XIV).

In operating the electric pen, I got my current from a Bunsen battery consisting of two glass jars, capped at the top and controlled by a plunger with which I lowered the plates into the acid solution or drew them up when the pen was not in use. Thus the life of the battery was prolonged.

The pen had a needlelike point which darted in and out of the writing end so rapidly that the eye could hardly detect it. This was operated by a miniature electric motor small enough to be attached to the upper end of the pen. The shaft containing the needle was given its motion by cams on the rotating engine shaft so that when the current was turned on, and I wrote with the pen, holding it in a vertical position, it made innumerable tiny punctures on the sheet of paper, tracing the words that comprised the letter.

After the master copy of the stencil had thus been made, I took it to the 'press,' where it had to be spanned in a frame before the copies could be made. A plain sheet of paper was placed on the press, the stencil was laid on top and an ink roller passed over it. The impression of the handwriting was marked on the under sheet by the ink through the holes made by the needle. It was said that 5,000 copies could be made from a single stencil.

Its widespread use is indicated by the fact that, within three years after Edison brought it out, it could be found in the government offices in Washington, D. C., in city and state offices, and in such far-away lands as Australia, New Zealand, China, Brazil, Russia, and elsewhere.

Beyond our office railing was the desk of our other office employe, a young man who acted as bookkeeper and stenographer. Yes, we had a form of typewriter; it had been given to the world a short time previously. Mr. Edison is known to have lent his assistance to Mr. Sholes, its inventor, who came on from Milwaukee for that purpose.[2]

One day my companion asked me if I knew the name of the man who had just gone into Mr. Lowrey's office. I replied that I did not, and he informed me it was Mr. Edison.

When I learned that this great man was actually in our midst, I hovered about the door until he emerged, and watched

[2] An early patent office model of the typewriter may be seen on the long table at the south end of the second floor of the restored laboratory. Edison's connection with it is described in Chapter XI.

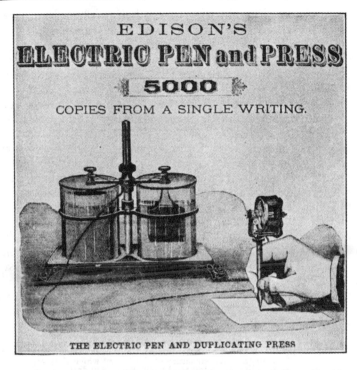

Excerpt from an old advertisement telling about the Edison electric pen and press. Note the Bunsen battery of two glass jars, the plunger by which the plates were lowered into the solution when current was desired, and the tiny motor attached on the upper end of the pen.

him until the outer door closed behind his back. I was surprised to find him so young and pleasant-faced, so different from our conception of great men.

In almost every way Mr. Edison was different from the accepted standards of greatness and even of science. It was unheard-of to start a large private business laboratory and it was charged that he was creating a specialty of inventing as a new profession, although he had never attended a regular school or college.

He was regarded by scientists as a sort of intruder, a revolutionist of an inferior stamp far below themselves. He set the old school aghast by his methods of research wherein, instead of following the traditional technique, he went direct to Nature and asked her the questions he wanted to solve.

Many persons still living will recall the fact that science

was quite conservative during the era before 1880, dominated by a dictatorial spirit which imposed terms and usually refused to discuss them. A few men far above the general average, such as Sir Humphrey Davy, Faraday, Henry, Volta, Ohm, Weber, Ampere, Becquerel, Regnault, Poggendorff, Kohlrausch, Helmholtz, Maxwell, Wheatstone, Thomson, Bunsen and others, were so illustrious that mediocre men were encouraged to dabble in science, although they possessed little except the means.

Clubs and societies were formed such as Dickens has satirized so cleverly in the *Pickwick Papers*. They seldom if ever engaged in real or progressive research. Their members were well-educated, graduates from universities who had taken many higher degrees. It was considered gentlemanly to while away half a lifetime at a university or about some round table. The business of trade or manufacturing was too plebian for such leisured classes and they looked with scorn on any one audacious enough to attack a problem without previously spending years in study.(³)

The sad thing about it all was that they built up countless theories which seldom had any practical value. One society

(3)   Macaulay describes these savants thus:
'These writers showed so much acuteness in arguing on their wretched data that a modern writer is perpetually at a loss to comprehend how such minds came to such data. . . . Not a flaw in the superstructure of the theory which they are rearing escapes their vigilance, yet they are blind to the obvious unsoundness of the foundations. . . . How it chanced that a man who reasoned on his premises so ably should assume his premises so foolishly, is one of the great mysteries of human nature.'

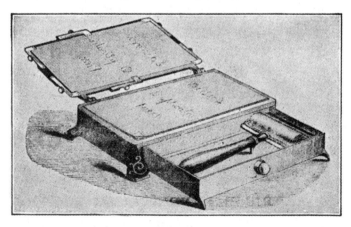

Hand press in which stencil was placed after the electric pen prepared it. Note ink roller.

attacked the theories of another and protracted discussions about nothing continued *ad nauseam*.

A good example of this came a few years later when Mr. Edison announced his perfecting of a successful dynamo in which only one-tenth of the power was lost in the machine and nine-tenths was available for use, instead of but four-tenths then obtainable from dynamos. Some of his critics generously tried to show him by simple algebraic equations that he was wrong and knew nothing whatever of the subtleties of electrical science.

Others sought to convince him that it was more economical to have the internal resistance of his generator equal to that of the external circuit, thus making the dynamo fifty per cent efficient.

At first he was astounded by their absurdity but after a time his common sense asserted itself and he replied that he would make his dynamo even more efficient.

Many men, if they had been buffeted, jeered, scoffed at and criticized as Edison was, would have lost heart, but he was superior to any arguments that were against common sense. He kept at his work and before long his critics saw that he was right even if they didn't know why. Some of his most ruthless critics afterward apologized to him and became his adherents.

:: :: ::

Francis Jehl writing with electric pen in restored laboratory at Dearborn.

Front of Menlo Park laboratory as it looked in 1878, showing hickory tree where bear was chained. In lower right-hand corner is a sketch of the bear drawn by Mr. Jehl.

II. Arrival at Menlo Park

A Bear Story

THE study of electricity engaged the attention of most scientists as well as the public in general during the time of which I write. Everyone seemed to feel that we were on the verge of great discoveries but just what they were to be no one could guess.

For nearly seventy years it had been known that electricity could produce light either through carbon rods or by heating metal or other substances to incandescence, but how to adapt that knowledge so that it might be used in the home was apparently beyond man's reach. The few arc lights which blazed up here and there convinced the public that they were suitable for outdoor illumination but not for domestic lighting.

Since the time of Faraday, men had known that a current could be generated by revolving coils across a magnetic field, but the efforts to harness that discovery and put it to practical service were pitifully inadequate. It was known, of course, that more power was required to turn the dynamo than could be obtained from it, but the loss was still so great that it was a failure commercially.

It was believed impossible to generate a current and use it to produce light, heat and power at the same time.

The period of which I am speaking was only two years after the Centennial Exposition in Philadelphia, which marked the 100th anniversary of the signing of the Declaration of Independence. As is well known, the first practical telephone receiver was introduced to the world at that exposition by Dr. Alexander Graham Bell. By 1878 it was still limited in use to short distances and small units, and such offices as that wherein I worked still used a sort of dial telegraph to communicate with other offices.

We shall find that it was Edison who contributed to make the telephone useful beyond the wildest dreams of that time, speeding the occasion when it could be used universally.

My interest in electricity was like that of many other youths; we wanted to be abreast of the very latest ideas just as boys of today devote themselves to flying, radio and the automobile. I read every scientific paper I could find and when

Mr. Lowrey saw how much I was interested, he graciously opened the way for me to pursue that study.

Electrical shops for experiments and the manufacture and repair of telegraphic equipment were maintained by the Western Union Telegraph Company in New York City, and as its general counsel he was able to arrange to get me a course of training in them. The superintendent in charge was an inventor named G. M. Phelps who had evolved several improvements on the Bell (or magneto) telephone. My first job was on his so-called 'pony' telephone. (See chapter XVIII)

During my apprenticeship I was keeping up my night classes at the Cooper Union school, studying chemistry, natural philosophy and higher algebra. So eager was I to learn about electricity that I took over the chore of cleaning the chemical apparatus and the glass jars holding the wet batteries, in order to be on the stage during the lectures and assist in the work.

One day Mr. Lowrey sent word that he wanted to see me and I learned, on responding, that it might be possible for me to join Mr. Edison's staff at Menlo Park. A young chap was needed to act as an assistant and apparently I had the qualifications. I accepted the chance with much eagerness and was given a note to present to him, introducing myself.

At the same time Mr. Lowrey gave me a token which I still possess and which I have always treasured very highly. It was a copy of Kempe's *Electrical Testing*, published in 1876.

Early one cold dreary November morning I left New York City by train and journeyed by ferry over the Hudson River and thence down to Menlo Park. I got off at a small way station, and stood there with my satchel in hand as the accommodation train chugged away. A flight of wooden steps led up from the tracks and I climbed to the top to look about.

It was, I discovered later, the highest point between New York City and Philadelphia, an eminence commanding a view of the surrounding country and not far distant from the buildings which Mr. Edison had erected. A footpath offered me a short cut across the field and soon I reached the picket fence surrounding the rectangle.

A new two-story red brick structure marked the corner of the dirt street but it seemed to be unoccupied, and so I directed my steps around it to the side gate admitting to the yard. Beyond was a long, grayish-white clapboard building which I knew must be the laboratory.

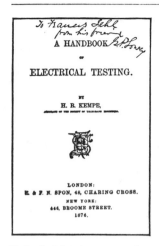

A HANDBOOK

OF

ELECTRICAL TESTING.

BY

H. R. KEMPE,

LONDON:
E. & F. N. SPON, 48, CHARING CROSS.

NEW YORK:
446, BROOME STREET.
1876.

Flyleaf of book presented to Francis Jehl by Grosvenor P. Lowrey.

As I passed through the gate my thoughts were excited and confused and in somewhat of a turmoil. Chained to a hickory tree near the east side of the laboratory was what seemed to be an unusually large dog, apparently asleep. I stepped aside to bestow a friendly pat upon its head, but as I came nearer suddenly the head turned and you can imagine my astonishment to find the creature was not a dog but a shaggy bear.

Without stopping for a second look I made a bee line for the front veranda of the laboratory and dashed up the steps. Nor did I stop until I had rushed inside and closed the door behind me.

Later I learned that this 'pet' had been given to Mr. Edison by an admirer who had been in Canada, and was being kept in the yard for the entertainment of the workmen and discomfiture of the visitors. It did not take me long to become good friends with it. I bought sweets for it frequently—sticks of peppermint candy and sometimes lumps of sugar surreptitiously removed from Mrs. Jordan's dining table.

One day the bear had vanished and we never saw it again. Some of the men thought it had escaped, but we could never trace a rumor as to whether it actually did or had been put out of the way because it was too rough and becoming vicious. At any rate, I never heard anyone admit having eaten bear steak for dinner; nor boast of a nice bear rug adorning the parlor floor.

The disappearance of Mister Bruin was one of Menlo Park's unsolved mysteries, and has remained so even to this day.

Menlo Park buildings as they appear today restored to their original form. The laboratory is the clapboard structure in the center.

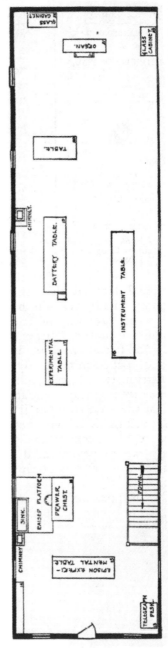

Plan of the second floor, Menlo Park laboratory (as restored). The experimental table where Mr. Edison sat on the day described here is on the left. The table which held the glass jars for the Bunsen battery cells was on the right of the center of the floor.

III. An Interview With
Mr. Edison

LET me give you the picture of Thomas Edison as I saw him on the second floor of the Menlo Park laboratory on that day in November, 1878, when, as a youth of eighteen, I came to work for him.

You can imagine how thrilled I was to be in Menlo Park, that mite of a hamlet that had been placed on the map by Mr. Edison and already was known in every part of the world. Even now he was hailed as 'The Wizard,' and to me, at least, that nickname was no exaggeration.

Much to my surprise and somewhat to my discomfiture, I found things in the clapboard building topsy-turvy. The floor of the tiny office on my right was littered with books and papers, as if desks or other furniture had already been carried out, leaving the corner quite bare. From the rear came sounds of heavy trampling and dragging machinery.

It was Moving Day. The little office was being installed in the handsome new structure that I had observed on the corner of Christie Street. The machinery in the back room of the laboratory was being carted out the rear door and across a narrow space into another new brick building, the machine shop.

I was considerably bewildered and stood just inside the entrance looking about for someone to act as a guide. Finally the office boy, Johnny Randolph, spied me and inquired what I wanted, and I showed him the letter of introduction to his chief which I brought with me. It seemed to break the ice.

'Mr. Edison's upstairs,' said he, motioning toward a flight of steps just beyond the deserted office. 'Go up and hang around until he sees you.'

So I left the disorder behind me and climbed to the quiet second floor, the scene of so many of Mr. Edison's greatest discoveries, a single room running across the entire length of the laboratory. At the far end stood a small pipe organ, the intervening space being well filled with long rectangular tables on which stood instruments of many varieties. The walls were lined with rows and shelves of bottles and jars, all containing chemicals. Mr. Edison was seated at a table which stretched across the south end of the floor, with

Charles Batchelor near by acting as assistant, and they were deeply engrossed in a platinum lamp with which at the moment they were experimenting.

Mr. Edison had already commenced his intensive search for a practical household electric light and I was, in fact, the first of several employes whom he was adding to his force to assist in that work. He was so busy that he didn't notice me when I arrived and I halted diffidently, awaiting a sign that he was ready to talk to me.

On one side of the table I saw his wonderful phonograph, the mechanical contrivance that recorded voice and sound. It was still in the form of a cylinder mounted on a stand and joined to a flywheel, and the indentations were engraved by its stylus on a sheet of tin foil wrapped about the cylinder.

Crude as it was, it was the marvel of the world. There it stood and here, close by, sat the man who had invented it. To the eighteen-year-old youth waiting, hat in hand, for an interview, he was the greatest figure among living men. The very chair on which he sat was a throne and the materials with which he worked were history-compelling.

At length he saw me and an expression of friendly interest replaced the intense concentration.

'Hello,' said he, 'what do you want?'

I stammered my answer and covered my confusion by handing him the letter of introduction. As I have said, it was from Mr. Lowrey, general counsel for the Western Union Telegraph Company, who was a trusted adviser of Mr. Edison's.

'Oh, yes, Mr. Lowrey spoke to me about you. What experience have you had?'

I told him how I had worked in the Western Union shop in New York City where Mr. Lowrey had placed me after I had been advised by him to go into electrical work, and how I had studied chemistry, natural philosophy and higher algebra at the Cooper Union night school. He already knew of what I had done in the law office, operating the inter-communicating telegraph and how I kept the Edison electric pen in order.

'When can you start?'

'Right away.'

'Well, I need the cells of my Bunsen battery cleaned and filled, as I will want to use some current tonight. I'll show you how to do it.'

I have already mentioned the practice I had on that job at Cooper Union, and as soon as he found out about it he let me go ahead. The storage battery was not yet invented and there were not more than six current generators in the whole country. Mr. Edison derived his current from a group of fifty or more glass jars or cells, each having in its center a porous cup holding a carbon plate in a solution of bichromate of potash. Around the cup was a zinc plate resting in a solution of diluted sulphuric acid. The task of filling and cleaning all of these was tedious, for it meant moving the heavy oblong glass jars one by one, to the sink, emptying them, scraping off the carbon, rubbing the zinc plate with mercury and then rinsing it off again. The mercury was kept in a bottle in a cupboard underneath the sink.

Large crocks near the sink were used for making the solutions. First, I had to obtain the chunks of orange-yellow bichromate of potash from a large bottle at the far end of the laboratory behind the organ, grind them into a powder in the mortar that stood on the corner of the chest of drawers in front of the sink, then put the powder in a crock and, after adding water, stir the solution with a paddle that hung close by. As in the case of the sulphuric acid, the solution contained about nine parts water to one part bichromate. The final step was to

Chest of drawers. On the right near the corner is the mortar described in this article as it appears today.

Mr. Jehl shows how current was derived from a group of fifty or
more glass jars or cells which made up the 'battery.'

scoop off the top layer and fill the porous cup with the solution and then fill the other part of the jar with the diluted acid.

After I had done all this Mr. Edison inspected my work,
especially the binding posts on the cells. In those days, loose
connections caused a lot of trouble.   But I had them all
tightened. At length he was satisfied.

'Well, I see you know the ropes,' he commented, briefly.

The mortar, used for holding the pellets of bichromate
while they were being ground, was finally smashed and found
its way, like so many other broken receptacles used by us, to
the dump heap near the glass house.   Half a century later
Henry Ford, while arranging to restore Menlo Park as a
memorial to Mr. Edison, recovered the pieces. Taking them
to his home, he fitted them together, finding all except one
small fragment. That was supplied; the mortar was cemented
together once more, and then replaced on its old perch on the
chest of drawers facing the sink.

At the time of the dedication of the Edison Institute in
October, 1929, while Mr. Edison was inspecting the restored
laboratory, Mr. Ford took the mended bowl and laid it on

Mr. Edison's lap. The great inventor immediately recognized it.

'Why, where in the world did you get that?' he exclaimed. 'That's our old mortar!'

He picked it up carefully and placed it on the corner of the chest.

'There it is,' he said, 'where it belongs, where it always was and where it did its duty.'

And there it rests today, with the cracks still visible showing where it was mended after its recovery from the dump heap.

The hole which marked the dump heap has been faithfully reproduced near the east fence between the glass house and the office building. Just beyond it is a long glass case containing many other relics which were recovered here. Another case with relics of laboratory apparatus, like the mortar, may be seen on the lower floor of the restored laboratory.

:: :: ::

Long glass case in yard of restored Menlo Park quadrangle, containing actual relics of Menlo Park days.

Looking south across second floor of laboratory. The table at which Mr. Edison sat is beyond the stove. The phonograph flywheel is just visible on the left edge. In the right foreground is the battery table.

IV. Mrs. Jordan's Boarding House

MY FIRST task—that of cleaning and charging the Bunsen battery cells—took most of the day and the November dusk was already gathering when Mr. Edison finally checked it over, as I have related, and discovered that I knew 'the ropes.' Then he asked:

'Where are you going to stay?'

Now, I had come directly to the laboratory from the depot and had made no effort yet to find lodgings. I told him so.

'Then you can have the rest of the day to yourself,' he suggested. 'Perhaps you can get a room over there.'

As he spoke, he led me to one of the windows on the south side of the second floor and pointed past the office building to a drab-colored frame house with green shutters, a short distance down Christie Street.

'Go over there,' he told me, 'and talk to Mrs. Jordan.'

I picked up my satchel and made my way downstairs and out the front door, inwardly amused at his reference to the 'rest of the day.' Already it was nearing the hour when Christian folks had supper and went to bed. But I remembered that the passing of time meant nothing to Mr. Edison—which explained the seeming inconsistency of his remark.

There was a path leading to a side gate in the rear of the office building. Beyond it stretched Christie Street([1]) running north and south past the picket fence on the east side of the compound. I crossed the street diagonally and found myself in front of the first of two dwellings which were alike in appearance and construction. The second proved to be the one that Mr. Edison had indicated to me. The first was occupied, I found later, by a mechanic employed in the Menlo Park machine shop([2]), Charles Dean.

I turned in at the far gate and set foot for the first time on the porch of the Jordan boarding house which was to become my home for more than a year and which during that period was to achieve fame as the first dwelling house ever lighted by electricity.([3])

---

(1)   The dirt street along the east side of the restored group of buildings bears the same name.

(2)   Subsequently Charles L. Clarke lived here also, after he came to Menlo Park to assist Mr. Edison.

(3)   The same house, restored exactly as it was in those early days, stands today in its proper location with reference to the Edison group of buildings, and forms part of the memorial to the master inventor.

An interesting group on the front porch of the boarding house about 1879. Left to right they are—Dr. A. E. Haid, Mrs. Jordan, Miss Jordan, Major Mc-Laughlin, S. L. Griffin, Mrs. S. Van Cleve, Miss Van Cleve, Francis R. Upton, Thomas A. Edison, Miss Alice Stillwell (in window), Charles Batchelor, John W. Lawson, and Francis Jehl.

In a few moments I was introducing myself to a slight, frail little woman who was the proprietress. Business was not yet brisk and she was glad to see a new lodger. She escorted me up the narrow winding stairs and into a large room at the front of the house.

Although I did not know it at the time I came later to the conclusion that the room she gave me was the best she had. It looked out over the porch and had an additional window on the far side, making three windows in all. The furnishings were plain but ample—large, clean bed, commode with wash bowl and water pitcher, bureau and a few chairs.([4]) Board and room, I learned, were to cost five or six dollars a week.

I accepted the room at once and after unpacking my satchel by candlelight and hanging up my clothes, went downstairs and took a seat in the dining room where two or three men were already at the table. By that time darkness had fallen and a coal-oil lamp furnished the light for our supper.

One of the men seemed to be a sort of 'star boarder,' a large, stout individual, jolly and friendly. Ere long I discovered that he was 'Griff,' Mr. Edison's secretary.([5]) After we had become acquainted, he asked me how I happened to get my job there.

'Through G. P. Lowery,' I told him.

'He's a good card to have,' commented the secretary, dryly.

Supper was a bountiful meal with meat, vegetables and fruit forming the main dishes. The big meal of the day—dinner—was at noon when soup, potatoes and the pies, for which Mrs. Jordan was noted, were served.

After the meal we sat for a time in the living room while Mrs. Jordan and her little ten-year-old daughter did the dishes in the kitchen just beyond. Mr. Edison's home, I learned, was down the road a ways, and embraced not only a good-sized residence but also a stable and windmill. He had at that time two youngsters, known to the Menlo Park residents as 'Dot' and 'Dash,' after the Morse alphabet. 'Dot' was about five years old and a lively child([6]), fully capable of chaperoning her younger brother, whose true name was Thomas Alva Edison, Jr.

---

(4) In this same room in the restored boarding house was born the first child to have his birthplace in the early American village. In honor of the event, he was named James *Jordan* Humberstone. The date was May 26, 1929.

(5) Stockton L. Griffin.

(6) Now Mrs. Marion Edison Oser.

Opposite the Edison home near the road junction stood another house not quite so large as the former but of more than usual size. John Kruesi, the head mechanic and assistant, lived there, as did Charles Batchelor whom I have already mentioned. Beyond their home was an excellent highway that disappeared among the woods and fields in the distance. It was the main-traveled road between Philadelphia and New York City and led from Menlo Park toward the little village of Metuchin about two miles distant, thence to New Brunswick, Trenton and Philadelphia.[7]

Leading down, as it did, from the Edison laboratory to the main highway, Christie Street was the real center of the village. Along its length was installed the first electric street lighting system in the world. Edison was a familiar figure on the plank walk that ran from his laboratory to his home. He generally wore a skullcap or farmer's wide-brimmed straw, walked with both hands in the front pockets of his trousers (as was the style at that time), and never seemed to notice the beauties of nature on all sides of him. When he went to New York City he always donned a high hat, and on his return to Menlo Park, brought it to the laboratory with him.

In later years, the boarding house bore a painted sign 'Lunch Room.' Many of the distinguished visitors who called to see Edison were served there.

Perhaps a brief explanation about the plan of Mrs. Jordan's boarding house might not be out of place here. It comprised two separate apartments, each a unit in itself. One was shut apart from the other and the communicating doors were usually kept locked. In one half lived Mrs. Jordan and her daughter and the other was given over to the boarders. Occasionally the door between the two front rooms downstairs was unlocked and that on the family side was made available to lodgers or visitors as a sitting room. The influx of lodgers taxed the capacity of the little dwelling and it was necessary to use the original sitting room as an overflow dining room to make possible a second table at mealtimes.

Mr. Edison used to walk down the street past the house when he returned home after the long hours at the laboratory. Frequently at night after I had retired in my room I heard his footsteps on the walk as he trotted homeward. On such

---

(7) The present Airport Drive occupies a corresponding position with relation to the restored group of buildings as did the road mentioned. The latter is now known as the 'Lincoln Highway.'

Mrs. Jordan's boarding house as restored today in Greenfield village.

occasions as he passed the house during the day, he stopped to chat with Mrs. Jordan, or with those of us who happened to be loafing on the stoop when the weather was nice.

Within a few days after my arrival, Francis R. Upton, who was to serve as Mr. Edison's mathematician, came to the boarding house and was assigned to the small room at the top of the stairs adjoining mine. From then on until he was married, he and I were fellow boarders.

Upton was a keen young chap, who had studied at Princeton and later under the great Helmholtz in Germany. He had taken a postgraduate course at Johns Hopkins University, and was well versed in the sciences.

It was Upton who was destined forty years later to become the first president of the Edison Pioneers. During a speech delivered by him on February 11, 1918, he described briefly how he began his work at Menlo Park.

'I joined Mr. Edison in November, 1878,' said he. 'At that time he had done some work in arc lighting and was going thoroughly through the art. The first time I worked with him was downstairs in the old laboratory in the small room just back of the front door. His intuition was then clearly marked, for his first line of calculations was on the general proposition if you double the resistance of the electric light,

This view was taken in front of the Menlo Park laboratory shortly after the invention of the electric light. On the left edge of the picture is the corner of the brick office building. Beyond is the Charles Dean house, and next door is Mrs. Jordan's boarding house. In the distance are the barn, windmill and home of Mr. Edison, facing what is now the Lincoln Highway.

you would need only one-half the copper to feed the light.'

The whistle, calling the mechanics and workmen to their tasks in the machine shop, blew at seven o'clock in the morning. Those working in the laboratory with Mr. Edison did not follow its summons for they were likely to remain long after hours; but no matter how late they worked the night before, they usually rose early in the morning to be on hand for breakfast. The first who got to the table had the choice helpings and sometimes could squeeze in a second helping before the late comers arrived.

It was still dark when I stepped forth from the boarding house to go across to my first day's work at the laboratory, and a cold rain was falling. I put up my overcoat collar and breasted the wind along the board walk to the point nearest the side gate where we splashed across and raced into the compound.

The long gray building loomed up through the rain like a ghostly palace, its flickering gas flames already blazing a welcome in the black windows. Solitary gleams marked the low brick machine shop at the far side of the rectangle, but the office building on our left was still shrouded in gloom.

:: :: ::

Menlo Park

ON this site, half a century since, the searching brain,
The patient hand, began their work to find and wield
The latent powers Nature still held in store.
Today, a million men, at rise of sun
March to the workshops of the world, their tread
A pean to the Chief, whose wizardry
Made live the whirring wheels, the vibrant wires,
And woke new powers of service for the world.

RICHARD ROGERS BOWKER

V. The Telegraph Table
in the Corner

I SOON found the second floor of the laboratory was to be the principal scene of my labors. It was filled with objects which constantly attracted my attention and fascinated me. If my new chief was the 'Wizard' of Menlo Park, this second floor was the abode of wizardry. On every side were strange things not known to the world at large—some of them not known outside the walls of this building.

To be a part of the inner circle among those who were associated with him in his researches, explorations, and discoveries, was an extraordinary assignment, especially for a lad eighteen years of age. Although Edison was only thirty-one at this time, he was already the leading inventor in the United States, if not in the world.

My first recollections of this scientific treasure house are, of course, somewhat hazy, for I had so much to learn and almost everything was new to me. But almost immediately I found myself performing regular duties, cleaning the battery cells and operating the hand vacuum pump. I was at Mr. Edison's disposal at all times and soon became familiar with his methods of working.

Around the building were many models of the inventions that had been made by him, and during odd moments I

Telegraph instruments used by Edison at Menlo Park. These identical instruments, a sounder and sending key, may be seen on one of the shelves in the southwest corner of the second floor of the restored laboratory.

studied them so that I might know something of his earlier work.

Already, he had to his credit such astonishing devices as

(a) Vote recordograph

(b) Gold and stock tickers

(c) Quadruplex telegraph

(d) Automatic telegraph

(e) Electric motograph

(f) Electric pen

(g) Carbon telephone transmitters

(h) Phonograph

J. U. Mackenzie seated at writing shelf near window on east side of second floor of laboratory. This picture was enlarged from a photograph showing Edison and a group of his associates taken on February 22, 1880.

These were only a few of the many which he had perfected and patented. The microphone, wireless spark (¹), megaphone, messenger call system, and mimeograph were other discoveries on which he had labored; he perfected many models; chemical, Roman character and acoustic telegraphs and different kinds of perforators.

Of these, many notable ones had been invented in this laboratory and on the very floor where now I was to work. It was like a wonderland to me, wherein the objects about which I had been studying and dreaming had come to life.

This laboratory had been in existence but two brief years, Mr. Edison having transferred his headquarters here from Newark in 1876. Menlo Park offered him seclusion with plenty of room to set up the sort of equipment that he desired —a laboratory where he could experiment to his heart's content.

Most of his inventions prior to Menlo Park had been made in the field of telegraphy, for he had become an inventor chiefly through that field.

(1)   Called by Mr. Edison 'etheric force.' (See Chapter XII.)

I soon had plenty of proof that he was both an experienced telegrapher and a privileged one. A small table stood in the southeast corner of the second floor and on it rested a battery of telegraph instruments which gave him a direct connection with Western Union lines. That table had been brought from Newark by him to Menlo Park and after all these years now occupies the same corner in the restored laboratory, just as it did when I went to work for Mr. Edison in 1878.

The Western Union appreciated Mr. Edison's ingenuity in devising so many improvements of the telegraph, and whenever they had any serious mechanical or electrical troubles they always consulted him. It is easy to understand why he was so helpful to Mr. Lowrey and why a direct telegraph line was arranged between Mr. Edison's Newark office and New York City. For one thing, he was enabled to use real lines in his experiments instead of artificial ones.

I recall him sitting here at this old table and making the sounder spin for half an hour at a stretch while conversing with some distant point. Six loops came into the Menlo Park laboratory for his use. Upstairs and downstairs under many of the tables were stored condensers which often he hooked up with his instruments during his experiments.

The original telegraph table used by Edison at Menlo Park, and before that at Newark. It now occupies the same corner in the restored laboratory and is connected by wire with the Western Union lines as it was in the old days. 'That table has followed me all through my life,' Edison once told Henry Ford.

'Griff' was an ex-telegrapher as well as a secretary, and Mr. Edison commissioned him to send messages now and then when too busy himself.

This southeast corner of the second floor was a favorite spot of Mr. Edison's whenever one of his friends of the old telegraphic days came to visit him. Here they sat and swapped reminiscences. I can still see our chief, with his feet cocked up on the old table, enjoying a chat with Johnson(2) or some other crony. Perhaps the telegraph instruments brought back fond memories and gave this corner a familiar atmosphere.

Above the table were shelves on which were kept rows of bottles of chemicals, just as you see them today. Among them were many common medicines such as may now be found on the topmost shelf. Edison was a great hand for concocting homeopathic remedies from these bottles whenever one of the men associated with him complained of some disorder. He would come over to this table, take down a bottle or two, compound a dose and hand it to the sufferer with the words: 'Here. Take this.'

As we had no telephone connection between the laboratory and the outside world, the telegraph often proved to be an invaluable help, particularly in times of emergency. Whenever he wished to communicate with one of his financial backers, with Mr. Lowrey or some of the company officials in New York City, he had but to sit at this table, reach out his skilled hand, and make his own connections.

It was also useful in experiments which required a longer wire than we could string around the laboratory. The carbon telephone transmitter was tested over it from this table, with Edison in Washington, D. C., at one end and Batchelor in the laboratory at the Menlo Park end.

When our chief made his first electric light demonstration, he tested the insulation of the lines strung between the machine shop and the houses in Menlo Park, with this same sounder, to see whether there were any faulty connections.

Another man associated with his early telegraph days whom we came to know and love was J. U. Mackenzie. A frequent visitor, he was very popular with every one because of his congenial disposition, ready smile and quick wit. He soon took an interest in me and we became a strangely assorted

---

(2) E. H. Johnson. He was selected by Edison to introduce the phonograph to the public, but was not a permanent resident of Menlo Park. See Chap. IX and XXIII.

pair of pals. Often I heard him tell the story of how Edison saved his child's life.

Sixteen years previously, he had been station master on the Grand Trunk railroad at the town of Mt. Clemens, twenty miles northeast of Detroit on the Port Huron line. Edison, then a youngster of fifteen, was news agent on the train, at the same time publishing a little newspaper in the baggage car and carrying on early experiments with chemicals in another corner of the car that was rigged up as a laboratory. The train usually lay over at Mt. Clemens for thirty minutes at least, to permit switching and shunting of cars destined for transfer to side roads. One day while he was standing on the platform waiting for this work to be finished, young Edison was able to save the station master's infant son from being crushed to death by one of the moving freight cars.

The event has been described thus:

'In August, 1862, while at Mt. Clemens station, he saw the infant son of J. U. Mackenzie, the station agent, crawling on the tracks . . . He made a dash, picked him up and took him to the father. He did not risk his own life and he was not even grazed by the car, but he did save the child's life. Out of gratitude the father taught young Edison the elements of telegraphy.

'The boy picked it up very quickly and soon was an expert operator—one of the best, if not the best, in the country, and able to send or receive with anyone. The operator's job which eventually took him all over the country was only a means to an end, but it directed him into electricity and diverted him from first making his name and fame as a chemist. Rescuing that child from the tracks was the start of that section of Edison's career which gave us the incandescent light and that whole new system of electrical power which has brought in modern industry.'[3]

(3) From 'Edison as I Know Him,' by Henry Ford. In collaboration with Samuel Crowther. *Cosmopolitan Book Corporation*, page 27.

The youthful Edison saves little Jimmy Mackenzie from oncoming freight car at
Mt. Clemens depot. As pictured by artist.

The youthful inventor's crude, hand-whittled model of his first invention, the vote recordograph, made by him for the patent office. The marks of his jack-knife are still visible on this historic relic. It may be seen in the case of instruments on the lower floor of the restored laboratory at Dearborn, on the west side. As Mr. Edison once said, 'To become a good inventor, you must first know how to use a jackknife.'

VI. Ticker and Telegraph

AS MACKENZIE'S name implies, he was a Scotchman, and he kept us roaring with laughter while he spun his yarns. On those occasions when he visited Menlo Park, he lived near the railroad tracks at the boarding house of Davis, who was also a Scotchman. He kept a bar known as the 'Lighthouse.' Mackenzie limped as he walked, due to a lameness from which he had never been entirely cured, and I have but to close my eyes to see him go limping across the field between the laboratory and the tracks, on his way home for a game of billiards with Davis.

As the man who had first taught our chief how to operate the telegraph instruments, he was always welcomed at Menlo Park by his former pupil, as well as by us. Indeed, the latter became the teacher, in turn, and the old telegraph instructor learned something new from the man who had not forgotten him, even after world fame came.([1])

---

(1) It may be of interest to note that years afterward, in 1886, when the Edison activities were being moved from Menlo Park to Orange, Edison was too busy to undertake an invention that had been referred to him, and he asked his old teacher Mackenzie to do it for him. 'But I am no inventor,' Mackenzie demurred. Edison reassured his old teacher, and persuaded him to tackle it. Within thirty days he had solved the problem, that of sending two or more fire alarms over the same wire, and before he died had taken out six other patents. Thus the old-time teacher became in later life the pupil of his former pupil.

One of the interesting characters whom I noticed on the second floor of the laboratory soon after I began my work there was an elderly gentleman who toiled quietly by the window that stood between the old telegraph table and the head of the stairs. His name, I discovered, was Patrick Kenny, and he had been engaged by Mr. Edison to work out a system of facsimile or autographic telegraphy. Mr. Kenny lived in New York City and came down to Menlo Park each day, bringing his lunch with him. For that reason, I never saw him at the boarding house.

I mention this because it shows how interested our chief was, even at this late day, in his first love, the telegraph. Besides the table in the corner with its instruments there were many other evidences of that affection about the place. Indeed from it came much of his inspiration, and practically all of his earlier inventions centered about it.

In a case on the lower floor of the laboratory were stored models of those early inventions. They had been piled on the shelves in no particular order, and about the only time their creator visited them was when he wanted a connection or part of some kind and knew he could find it on one of

Edison's first patented invention, the electrographic vote recorder. This was evolved by him in Boston in 1868, when he was but 21 years old, and patented the next year.

Models of Edison's inventions of the gold and stock
ticker, or printing telegraph, as they now appear in
the glass case that stands near the foot of the stairs
on the first floor of the restored laboratory at Dearborn.

those models.   Of course, I made it my business to become
familiar with these inventions as soon as opportunity permitted.([2])

Among the objects which interested me intensely was a
model of his first patented invention, the electrographic vote
recorder, which was really an adaptation of the telegraph.
Edison invented it in 1868 in Boston when he was but 21
years old and patented it the following year. It fascinated me

_____

(2)   On the lower floor of the restored laboratory may be seen two such cases, one
against the east wall and another opposite it, housing the models of Edison's earlier
inventions.

Printing telegraph, or ticker, invented by Edison in 1869 as an improvement on the Laws instrument. This is listed as Edison's third invention, his second having been a form of the same instrument.   Patent No. 96,567.

because it was the product of the genius of Edison when he was only a few years older than I.([3])

The purpose of this particular device was to permit a vote in the National House of Representatives to be taken with dispatch.   When a member of the legislative body closed a switch at his desk, the machine would record and count the vote.   Edison took the vote recorder to Washington, D. C., to exhibit it before a committee of the House. His attorney was Carroll D. Wright, later director of the eleventh census and for twenty years United States Commissioner of Labor.

The machine worked to perfection, but the politicians saw that it would interfere with some of their practices.   As Edison said:

'The chairman of the committee, after seeing how per-

------

(3)   A working model of this first invention stands against the west wall on the second floor of the restored laboratory.

fectly it worked, said to me: "Young man, if there is any invention on earth that we don't want down here, it is this. One of the greatest weapons in the hands of a minority to prevent bad legislation is filibustering on votes, and this instrument would prevent that." '

As a press operator on the telegraph, Edison had taken miles of Congressional proceedings, and knew how much time was wasted during each session of Congress during votes, in calling member's names and in recording and adding their preferences. The whole operation could have been simplified by merely pressing a button on each desk as each member voted 'Yea' or 'Nay' but Edison's idea was not wanted, and even to this day has not been put in use.

One lesson it taught him was to turn his efforts toward inventing things that not only were needed but were wanted as well.

Second in chronological order was his gold and stock ticker, models of which rest in the east case downstairs. The story of the ticker is intensely interesting, for it gave Mr. Edison his first real start in life and provided him with the funds with which he was able to set up his shop in Newark.

By accident—or led by destiny—when he arrived in New York City penniless from Boston he found shelter in the battery room of the company which operated the 'indicator' service on Wall Street. He was waiting for a job with the Western Union and took advantage of his opportunity to study the workings of the 'indicator.'

Most of you doubtless are familiar with the story. He was still a telegraph operator. On that exciting day in 1869, when he went into the office of the 'Laws Gold Reporting Telegraph Company,' he found everything in a state of wild commotion and Dr. S. S. Laws, the inventor of the reporting indicator, was almost in a frenzy because the master transmitting instrument was out of order.

Curiously, Edison had edged himself in to see what it was all about and with his sharp observing eyes soon discovered what was wrong. Without hesitation he stepped forward and volunteered to fix it. Dr. Laws and his assistants looked over this callow youth pityingly, but something in his face must have persuaded them to give the stranger a trial. They were entirely helpless and were ready to seize upon anything to end this bombardment of messengers from the bankers and brokers of Wall Street, who were upset because the gold quotations had halted. That precious metal bobbed up and down and fluctuated so swiftly that the market was in a pandemonium when the ticker reports ceased.

Edison went about his task calmly and soon had the instrument working again. As a result he was immediately engaged at the stupendous salary of $300 a

Printing telegraph as improved by Mr. Edison, working with Frank L. Pope, Patent No. 102,-320. It was Edison's second ticker and his fifth invention in order of listing. His fourth was an electrical switch for use on the telegraph.

month to take charge of the operation of the system. This sudden elevation swept his breath away but he recovered speedily and turned his active brain to the problem of improving the 'reporting telegraph.' He suggested several innovations which were adopted, and, meanwhile, he tackled the problem of creating a new ticker.

A patent for this was applied for August 17, 1869, and related to 'an electrical printing instrument,' which was but another name for a gold and stock ticker. He assigned the patent subsequently to Dr. Laws, and this ticker is one of the prized relics now to be seen in the restored Menlo Park laboratory.

With all its original parts, it has been rejuvenated in the machine shop at Menlo Park and operates today as smoothly as it did in 1869.(⁴)

Within one month after the patent was applied for, he sought a patent on another printing telegraph which embodied another important improvement. 'The nature of the invention,' he wrote in his application, 'consists in arranging the parts of a telegraphic printing apparatus so that the same is not only capable of receiving and recording communications

(4) See picture on page 41. This instrument may be seen on the second floor of the restored laboratory.

in automatically printed cnaracters at a much greater speed than has been found practicable by the instruments in common use, but the same result is accomplished by the use of one wire, without local battery, which has heretofore required the use of two or more wires or a local battery, or both, in connection with each instrument.'(⁵)

Like the instrument previously described, this one also may be seen on one of the shelves of the restored laboratory at Dearborn.

(5)   Patent No. 102,320, applied for September 16, 1869. Issued April 26, 1870, to Thomas A. Edison and Frank L. Pope. See picture on preceding page.

:: :: ::

How Mr. Edison averted a gold and stock ticker panic on Wall Street.
(From an old print.)

N. M. BOOTH,
Superintendent.

'POPE, EDISON & CO.,
ELECTRICAL ENGINEERS,
AND
GENERAL TELEGRAPHIC AGENCY,

OFFICE:

EXCHANGE BUILDINGS,
Nos. 78 and 80 BROADWAY, Room 48.

A necessity has long been felt, by Managers and Projectors of Telegraph Lines, Inventors of Telegraph Machinery and Appliances, etc., for the establishment of a Bureau of Electrical and Telegraphic Engineering in this city. It is to supply this necessity that we offer facilities to those desiring such information and service.

A LEADING FEATURE

will be the application of Electricity to the Arts and Sciences.

INSTRUMENTS

for Special Telegraphic Service will be designed, and their operation guaranteed.

CAREFUL AND RELIABLE TESTS

of Instruments, Wires, Cables, Batteries, Magnets, etc., will be made, and detailed written reports furnished thereon.

CONTRACTS

for the Construction, Re-construction and Maintenance of either Private or Commercial Telegraph Lines will be entered into upon just and reasonable terms.

VARIOUS APPLICATIONS OF ELECTRICITY.

Special attention will be paid to the application of Electricity and Magnetism for Fire-Alarms, Thermo-Alarms, Burglar-Alarms, etc., etc.

TELEGRAPHIC PATENTS.

We possess unequalled facilities for preparing Claims, Drawings, and specifications for Patents, and for obtaining prompt and favorable consideration of applications for Patents in the United States and Foreign Countries.

EXPERIMENTAL APPARATUS.

Attention will be paid to the construction of Experimental Apparatus, and experiments will be conducted with scientific accuracy. Parties at a distance, desiring Experimental Apparatus constructed, can forward a rough sketch thereof, and the same will be properly worked up.

DRAWINGS, WOOD ENGRAVINGS, CATALOGUES, Etc., prepared in the best and most artistic manner.

PURCHASING AGENCY.

Telegraph Wire, Cables, Instruments, Insulators, Scientific and Electrical, and Electro-Medical Apparatus, Telegraph Supplies of all descriptions, Telegraphic and Scientific Books, etc., will be purchased for parties favoring us with their orders, and forwarded by the most prompt and economical conveyance, and as cheaply as the same could be purchased by our customers personally. Our facilities for this business are unexcelled.

Letters and orders by mail should be addressed to

Box 6010, P. O., NEW YORK.

The first advertisement ever published announcing a firm of 'electrical engineers.' Published in *The Telegrapher*, October 1, 1869.

VII. Forty Thousand Dollars
The Start at Newark

ONE of the men who occupied a somewhat important position in the field of the telegraph and stock ticker at the time of which I am writing was Frank L. Pope. Before Edison went to work for Dr. Laws, Pope had been superintendent of the Laws company and he was quick to recognize the natural abilities of the newcomer from Boston. The two young men decided to organize a partnership and open an office.([1])

Although I came onto the scene more than eight years later, long after the partnership had been dissolved, I was fortunate enough to become acquainted with Pope. He called occasionally at Mr. Lowrey's law office in connection with business or social matters and even after I began working at Menlo Park I saw him when I had occasion to go to New York City.

My mental picture of him is of a stocky man of medium height, wearing a straw hat and loosely fitting clothes. Like so many others of that same period, he had a handsome black beard.

They announced their partnership in an advertisement which they published in a trade paper, *The Telegrapher*, in its issue of October 1, 1869. It was the first card ever issued by a firm doing business in the new profession of 'electrical engineers,' as they styled themselves.

The firm was known as 'Pope, Edison & Company.' Their office was in Room 48 of the Exchange Building, at 78 and 80 Broadway. Edison was to serve as the inventor while Pope handled all the office details and labor of promotion.

During this period Edison boarded with Pope in the latter's home at Elizabeth, New Jersey, and carried on his experiments in the private shop of Doctor Bradley, an electrical experimenter in Jersey City. Later, J. N. Ashley, publisher of the paper named above, was taken into the firm.

After the Laws enterprise was absorbed by the Gold &

---

(1) Pope later became a distinguished technical writer and was elected President of the American Institute of Electrical Engineers in 1886. In 1860 he was a member of the *Scientific American* staff and later he was editor of *The Telegrapher*. It was in that paper that the advertisement announcing the firm of Pope & Edison appeared. After the partnership terminated he became connected with the Western Union. He is best known as Franklin L. Pope, which name he adopted in later life.

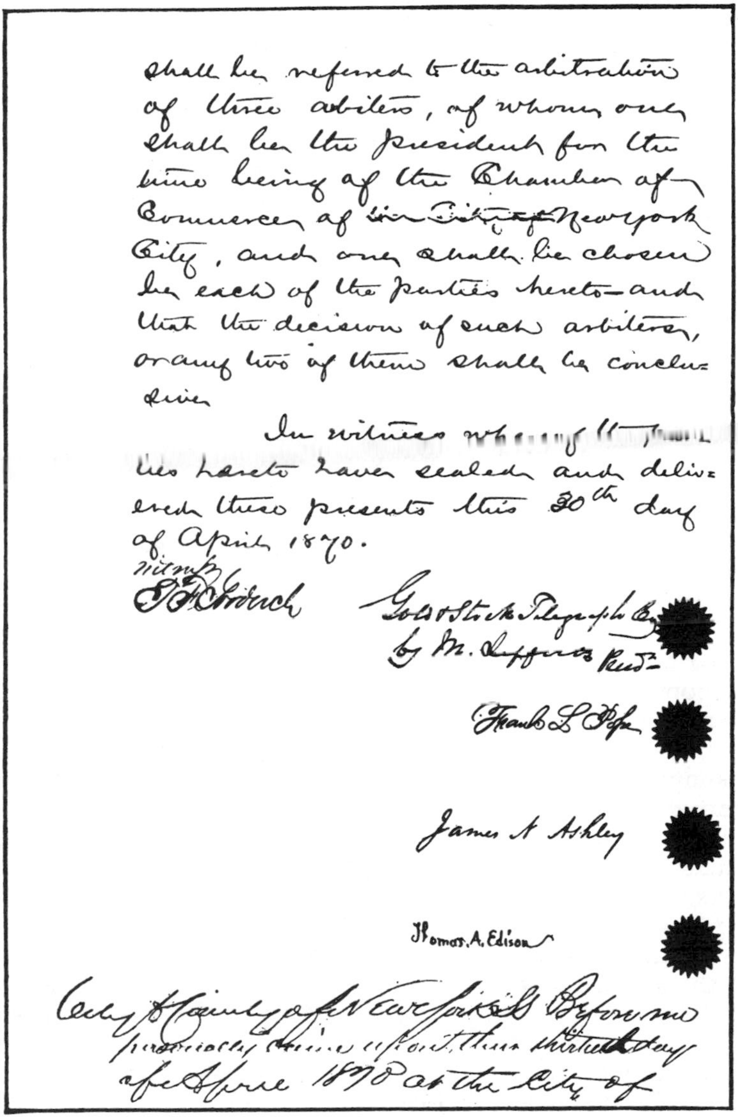

shall be referred to the arbitration of three arbiters, of whom one shall be the president for the time being of the Chamber of Commerce of ~~the City of~~ New York City, and one shall be chosen by each of the parties hereto—and that the decision of such arbiters, or any two of them shall be conclusive.

In witness whereof the parties hereto have sealed and delivered these presents this 30th day of April 1870.

Witness
[illegible]

Gold & Stock Telegraph Co
by M. Lefferts Presd.

Frank L. Pope

James N Ashley

Thomas A. Edison

City & County of New York ss Before me personally came upon this thirtieth day of April 1870 at the City of

Last page of contract dated April 30, 1870, between the Gold and Stock Telegraph Company (by M. Lefferts, president), and Frank L. Pope, James N. Ashley and Thomas A. Edison.

Stock Telegraph Company, Edison and Pope invented a one-wire printer which confined itself to the recording of quotations on gold and sterling exchange only. This, too, was taken over by the larger concern, and then the Western Union acquired a majority of stock in the latter, so that once more Edison was associated with the telegraph company.

General Marshall Lefferts, who had been an outstanding figure in the development of the telegraph, was elected president of the Gold & Stock Telegraph Company and he set Edison at work improving the stock ticker, patents of which were now held by his company. Edison applied himself to the task and brought out the 'Universal' which, as its name indicates, enjoyed almost universal popularity in the years that followed.

He also invented a simpler ticker for use outside New York City in communities where electrical experts were few or almost unknown. His instrument was used on the London Stock Exchange.

Perhaps you have wondered why I have devoted so much space and time to Edison's early efforts with the printing telegraph and the

Mr. Edison's shop and laboratory at 10–12 Ward Street, Newark, as it was in 1873. Here he invented the gold and stock ticker, printing telegraph, chemical and automatic telegraph systems, quadruplex telegraph system, electric pen, messenger call system; discovered the motograph principle, likewise etheric force. While here he took out 96 patents. He operated this shop between 1870 and 1876, between the ages of 23 and 29.

Gen. Marshall Lefferts.

stock ticker. I have two reasons, aside from the natural desire to explain to you clearly the significance of these historical relics which are to be seen in the restored laboratory at Dearborn.

In the first place, that work paved the way for him to set himself up in business in Newark, furnishing the funds with which he started his shop. Secondly, as I shall point out shortly, it foreshadowed his unmistakable genius.

The story of how he got the money to start the manufacturing business at No. 10-12 Ward Street reads almost like fiction. Only a few years ago I walked along that street in the New Jersey city and tried to visualize the old building as it was when it formed the center of his activities in the early seventies. A lodging house now, no trace remains of the Edison occupancy.

General Lefferts was anxious to secure from Edison the rights to the improved tickers, for he felt they should be owned by the company. One day he called the young man into his office and asked him how much he thought he should receive for them. Edison felt that five thousand dollars would be a suitable sum, but was prepared to accept as low as three thousand. Even that amount was so large that he hesitated to name it.

'Well, General, suppose you make me an offer,' he replied.

'How would $40,000 suit you?'

Forty thousand dollars! The mere mention of such a staggering sum nearly caused young Edison to faint. He stammered out finally that he thought it was fair, and so it was arranged to have a contract drawn to that effect.

Three days later Edison came in to sign the documents and get the money. Even yet he could scarcely believe it was true; it seemed too unreal. So, when the general handed him a piece of paper drawn on the Bank of New York for the sum named, Edison was still unconvinced. It was the first check he had ever received and he would not believe it was true until he got the actual cash.

Ignorantly he handed it in at the bank teller's wicket without endorsing it. The teller with a smile handed it back and tried to tell Edison what was wrong. In his deafness and excitement, Edison failed to understand, and walked out of the bank in a cold sweat, ready to believe he had been cheated.

The only thing to do was to go back to the general and he did so, to tell how the check was turned back. His account of his experience caused much hilarity in the office. A clerk was sent back with him, the check was properly endorsed, and forty thousand dollars in small bills was paid over. The teller thought he would continue the joke by making the bills as small as possible, and as a result Edison had to stuff them into the pockets of his overcoat and in all his other pockets, also.

Thus laden down with currency, he crossed the Hudson on a ferryboat and went to Newark where he sat up all night, guarding his wealth. In the morning he returned to New York and sought the aid of the general who introduced him to a bank account.

It was this money that enabled him to open up his manufacturing shop in Newark. He secured large orders for tickers from General Lefferts and soon had a crew of men at work, meanwhile setting up a laboratory in which he could continue his experiments.

His improvements on the ticker led to forty-six patents, but that was only a part of his

Franklin L. Pope.

work in Newark. It was here that he brought out his marvelous inventions in telegraphy, and at the same time evolved so many others.

Now for my second reason. In his tickers we are able to detect elements of coming greatness. The ticker school which he himself inaugurated gave him advantages in practical experimenting far more helpful than any college could have offered.

A superficial glance at these early instruments will reveal some of the knacks which he was employing so dexterously as to place him above the average in ingenuity and conception. You will note how they lead up progressively, step by step. You can see with what refinement he devises compound-wound electromagnets, and how he creates local circuits through relays; and with what nicety he solves the problem of shifting mechanism and unison regulation.

He displays cunning in the way he neutralizes or intensifies electromagnets, in applying strong or weak currents or in using polarized magnets; and with aggressive certainty commands either negative or positive directional currents to do his work. You can see his natural talent shaping the resistance of the electromagnets to a certain ratio as regards that of the line.

The Edison Universal Printer as it appears today in the restored laboratory at Dearborn. It has been entirely restored and rejuvenated, and the ticker tape unrolls just as easily as it ever did. Ordinarily, a glass case enclosed the upper part. (Patent No. 123,005, applied for July 26, 1871, granted January 23, 1872.)

VIII. No. 10-12 Ward Street
Newark

THE fact that one of my kindly superiors at the laboratory, Charles Batchelor, Edison's assistant, and John Kruesi, boss of the machine shop, had both come from the Ward Street factory to Menlo Park gave me a strong desire to know more about those Newark days.

All about the laboratory were evidences of that period— stock tickers, printing telegraphs, and instruments that bore the firm names of 'Edison & Unger' and 'Edison & Murray.' But that was not all. There was a little black box on a table, a fascinating mystery, which had come with him from Newark. Inside it he could create a spark which baffled the scientists and which we know now to have been wireless.([1])

There was a model fire alarm system with call-boxes and complete circuit, another product of his Newark days. Near it was the model of a messenger call system, likewise invented there.([2]) On the west wall was a telephone box which was connected elsewhere in the laboratory, and the principle by which it transmitted the sound of the human voice was not that of Alexander Graham Bell's. It used the motograph principle, discovered by Edison at Newark.([3])

In addition to these things, there were models of his multiple telegraph circuits, which some regarded as the crowning feature of all his work on Ward Street. Among so many reminders of those years between 1870 and 1876, I could not help discovering much about them.

I have mentioned the names of Batchelor and Kruesi. Besides those two there were many other skilled mechanics with him at Newark. Bergmann and Schuckert were there; so were Charles Dean, Thau, Herrmann, Ritter, Wendelbon, Hinze, Muller, Bradley, Ott, and others. First-class toolmakers who had been with Brown & Sharp or Pratt & Whitney, well-known makers of precision instruments, served in the Ward Street shop.

Occasionally at Menlo Park the men would talk over those earlier days, recalling incidents of an interesting or humorous nature, and I was always an eager listener. One of them illustrated how the young manufacturer had to teach himself

---

(1) See Chapter XII.   (2) See Chapter XI.   (3)   See Chapter X.

business methods.
'Over his desk
were two large
wire hooks. On
one he would hang
bills as they came
in; and on the
other he would
hang those that
had been paid. By
that arrangement
it generally hap-
pened that the bills
which came in first
remained on the
bottom of the pile
and had to wait a
long time before
they could be paid.
'One day a cred-
itor who had sent
in his bill quite
some time pre-
vious remonstrated
with Edison,

This might be called a typewriting telegraph, since it had finger keys for each letter in the alphabet. It was invented by Mr. Edison at Newark in June, 1872, and patented September 17, of that year, No. 131,343. The operator was able to transmit messages by strik-ing the keys instead of using the Morse code, the same keys being struck in unison on other instruments that were connected with it. When this photograph was taken the model had been restored. It may be seen in one of the glass cases on the first floor of the restored laboratory at Dearborn.

and told him this arrangement was not fair, since he always selected the bills to be paid from the top of the pile, although they were always the last to come in. He suggested that Edison, whenever he wanted to pay bills, turn over the file and take from the bottom. As soon as this argument was presented, Edison saw its justice and agreed to follow it.'

During the six years at Newark, Edison took out forty-six patents on the printing telegraph or stock ticker.

Most prominent among the men who were associated with him in those days were Batchelor, Kruesi, Bergmann and Schuckert. Their names are all interwoven in the later history of electric lighting, and his teachings, no doubt, laid the foundations of their subsequent successes.

I have already told you something of Batchelor. He was an Englishman by birth and had been sent over to this country to help install machinery in the Clark Sewing Thread Mills in

Four famous graduates of the Newark shop.
Upper left—Johann S. Schuckert; Upper right—
Sigmund Bergmann; Lower left—John Kruesi;
Lower right—Charles Batchelor.

Newark. When that job was finished, he sought out Edison and soon demonstrated his ability as a top-notch mechanic with more than average patience and intelligence.

Kruesi has been mentioned, also. He came from Switzerland and was a mechanic of the highest order. He understood work in the drafting room and could decipher one of Edison's sketches no matter how crude it was. I soon found that he had a keen mind for machine construction work and a congenial, pleasant disposition.

Johann Sigmund Schuckert came to America from Nurnberg, Germany, possessed of a varied experience gained in machine work in Munich, Stuttgart, Hanover, Berlin and Hamburg. It was in 1869 that he visited Baltimore and Philadelphia, and the following year he joined Edison's pay roll at Newark. His name played an important part in the development of electric lighting in Germany.

I met Herr Schuckert in Munich in 1882 during a celebration. The name of Edison was mentioned and he told me that the experience he had gained in the Ward Street shop was the most valuable lesson he had ever received. There he had learned the true meaning of courage, resolution and honest conviction. Edison's work in electricity led him (Schuckert) to resolve to enter the field himself. He did so through the arc light which was then to the fore, and after saving $1,000 went back to Nurnberg and started his first arc lamp and generator experiments.

All the world knows how he rose to eminence and founded one of the greatest electrical industries of those

This, I think, will be sufficient to your inquiries, but, no doubt, Mr. Edison will remember the names given and corroborate.

The time working at Newark was the most valuable and interesting in my younger days, and it was a great luck for me in my starting in life to come together with Edison.

It may be possible, as I told you before, that I may come over some time in March or April, and then I will call on you.

With best wishes,

yours very truly,

Bergmann

Part of a letter from Bergmann to Jehl.

days, later merged with Siemen's. Siemen's-Schuckert has a world-wide reputation because of its tremendous growth and excellent products.

Sigmund Bergmann was a frequent visitor at Menlo Park so that I came to know him almost as well as those whom I saw daily about the place. When I joined the staff he was engaged in manufacturing the phonograph in a factory in New York City, having been assigned by Edison to undertake that important work. Bergmann had started this plant after the Newark days ended. Later he was to become prominent as a maker of general electrical products.

Like Schuckert, Bergmann has never ceased to pay tribute to the training he received at Newark. His career reads like a romance. Arriving at Ward Street in 1870 a poor young man, hardly able to speak English, he made a friend of his boss through his fine work. One of the foremen complained to Edison because Bergmann was hard to understand. 'What difference does it make?' retorted Edison. 'His work speaks for him.'

In 1876, when Edison came down to Menlo Park, Bergmann went up to Manhattan to launch his humble shop. At first he manufactured alarm bell systems and subsequently took over the making of phonographs, carbon telephone transmitters and the motograph, or chalk telephone.

His shop was located at 104 Wooster Street, New York

City. It was in this shop that Edison, appreciating the exactness and reliability of Bergmann's work, entrusted him with the manufacture of the first commercial lot of his recently invented tin foil phonographs and telephone apparatus, together with telegraphic and other electrical devices.

The first phonograph ever made, aside from the experimental one made by John Kruesi at Menlo Park in 1877, was made by Bergmann.

In a letter which Bergmann wrote me about one year before he died, he added with a touch of wistfulness: 'I wish I could live those years over again.' Of him Edison said, after Bergmann's success had been assured, that it was all Bergmann's own doings; and that all he (Edison) had done was to give him the opportunity.

In the next few articles I will explain some of the other products of Newark with which I became acquainted. Edison's crowning achievement in the Ward Street shop has been said to have been the quadruplex telegraph, whereby four different messages could be sent over the same wire at the same time; but there were many others that appealed to my boyish mind.

Many of these may now be seen in the form of patent office models or working instruments in

Compact type of printing telegraph invented by Mr. Edison at his Newark shop. 'My present invention,' he wrote in his application covering this instrument, 'consists of a printing telegraph instrument in which the type wheel is revolved and the printing and feeding mechanism operated by a movement communicated from the same armature of an electro magnet.' The patent was applied for on November 13, 1871, and granted May 7, 1872, as No. 126,530. The above model may be seen in one of the glass cases on the first floor of the restored laboratory at Dearborn.

the restored laboratory at Dearborn, and practically everything I will describe has its place on one of the shelves or tables.

With Edison, it was only a step from the telegraph key to the printing telegraph and stock ticker; from the stock ticker to the automatic telegraph. From the experiments with the automatic telegraph, it was only one more step to the phonograph.

That is why I am devoting so much time and space to his early activities, for I realize that out of them came all his later greatness that we were to share at Menlo Park.

It may be of interest to you to hear that the Edison stock ticker is still being made sixty years after the first one, and that the principles on which the modern tickers operate are the same as those utilized by him.

Another point that may be of interest is that, of the twenty-one presidents of the Society of the American Institute of Engineers, two were associated with Mr. Edison in the days of which we are now writing, namely, F. L. Pope and Norvin Green; and six of the later ones were at one time or another in his employ.

:: :: ::

House in which Edison was born at Milan, Ohio.
(From an old photograph.)

On the anniversary of his invention of the incandescent electric light, October 21, 1929, Mr. Edison sat for a moment at his old telegraph table in the southeast corner of the second floor of the restored laboratory at Dearborn, just as he sat there in the old days at the same table.

IX. A Telegraph That Would Write

ALTHOUGH my first meeting with the ex-telegrapher, Ed Johnson, took place at Menlo Park, I subsequently learned that he, like Batchelor, Kruesi, Charles Dean and several others, had come in contact with Edison first at Newark. To me he was the man who introduced the phonograph to the world, but Edison's first acquaintance with him came about in connection with the automatic telegraph, between the years 1870 and 1873.

Edison was busily engaged in the manufacture of the stock ticker when some New York City capitalists asked him for his opinion on a so-called automatic system of telegraphy that had been imported from abroad and which had interested them sufficiently to lead them to make some investments. A Pennsylvania Railroad official, to whom the idea had been submitted, had turned it down because of its inefficiency. It was then that they realized they needed help.

Edison's name was mentioned to them as that of a 'young fellow who was doing some good work for General Marshall Lefferts, and who it was said was a genius at invention and a very fiend for work.' He was invited over from Newark and, on his arrival, was placed in charge of Ed Johnson. Because of his telegraphic experience, the latter had been brought east from Colorado on what was supposed to be a three months' leave of absence, to aid the capitalists.

This automatic system operated on a simple principle. The message was perforated on a narrow strip of paper with holes which corresponded to the dot and-dash of the Morse code. The tape was then placed in the transmitting machine. Electrical contact was made wherever the holes occurred, and the message was recorded at the receiving end by a stylus on a strip of chemically prepared paper.

It was possible to repeat the same message many times; but the chief value of the system

Model of machine devised by Mr. Edison for perforating holes in strip of paper. The patent was applied for on August 16, 1871, and granted December 5 of the same year, as No. 121,601. This was one of the earliest machines made by Mr. Edison in connection with the automatic telegraph and now rests in one of the glass cases on the first floor of the restored laboratory at Dearborn.

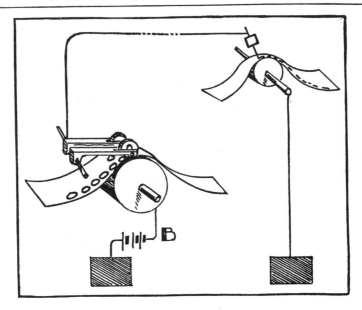

Diagram showing operation of automatic telegraph.

was that messages could be dispatched much more rapidly than with the sending key.

The trouble with the system was that electrical impulses became sluggish when extended over a long distance, due to self-induction. High speed was impossible except over very short lines.

Edison's method of overcoming this defect was simple and effective. He made a shunt around the receiving instrument with a soft iron core, and caused the current at the end of each impulse to reverse itself just for an instant, enough for each signal to be defined sharply even between distant points.

Edison and Johnson succeeded in transmitting and recording one thousand words a minute over wires between New York City and Washington; and three times as many between New York City and Philadelphia. The usual rate at which telegraphers of the old school were able to send or take in the ordinary way was not over fifty words a minute.

Next he turned his inventive faculty to the machines used for perforating the holes. If you will examine the glass cases on the lower floor of the restored laboratory, you will see models of some that were improved by him. Pictures of them are reproduced elsewhere in this chapter.

The style of perforations used to transmit messages by the code were described by Edison ([1]) thus:

'The machine is made with keys that perforate either a single *dot*, or three openings to form a *dash*, one of the three openings being larger than the others so as to produce a longer pulsation.

'The paper is fed the proper distance each perforation, and word spaces, pauses, and sentence spaces are produced by keys. These keys are arranged in a small compass and the instrument is compact, cheap and adapted to local offices or to individual use.'

Edison was not satisfied with the dot-and-dash and persuaded his backers to let him find a way to transmit over the wire actual letters of the alphabet; in other words, Roman

---

(1) From Mr. Edison's application for patent No. 132,456 filed March 15, 1872, and granted October 22, 1872, entitled 'Improvement in Apparatus for Perforating Paper for Telegraphic Use.'

Above is shown Mr. Edison's patent-office model of the automatic telegraph, renovated and now housed in one of the glass cases on the first floor of the laboratory at Dearborn. From this model and the diagram on page 60 the reader can gain a better understanding of this device. The small metal discs serve as contact points and complete the electric circuit when they pass over the perforations in the strip of paper. At the receiving end, a stylus makes blue marks on a strip of chemically prepared paper, whenever the circuit is closed.

characters. They set up a complete new shop for him in N e w a r k, equipped it with about $25,000 worth of machinery, and gave him full charge. Here he achieved his aim, perfecting the system whereby he was able to send 3,000 words a minute in New York City and record them in Philadelphia, using alphabetical characters instead of the dot-and-dash of the Morse code.

Machine devised by Edison as an improvement on that on page 59. Patent was applied for March 24, 1873, and granted February 10, 1874, as No. 147,-312. This model may be seen in one of the glass cases on the first floor of the restored laboratory at Dearborn.

His application for a patent covering this improvement described it in his own words, as follows:

'In the Morse system of telegraphy, the operator frequently receives the message by sound, and writes the same out as received.

'In the printing telegraph system (as, for example, the stock ticker), the printed strip itself is usually delivered as received.

'In the ordinary automatic system, the paper has to be punched or composed; at the receiving station, the message on the chemical paper has to be translated and written out by hand, or printed by a key printing instrument.

'Each system has its defects or disadvantages. The Morse system is slow, and requires a large number of wires. The printing telegraphs are expensive, liable to inaccuracies and injury, and limited in speed to the fingering of the keys. The automatic system is rapid on the line, but the composing of the message and the writing of it at the receiving station are comparatively slow operations.

Edward H. Johnson

'The object I have in view is to print the message chemically. Thereby, the message, as received upon a strip of paper, is ready to be folded and sent to its destination; and the rapidity is equal to any automatic transmission.

'I accomplish this object by perforating the strip of paper used for transmitting with groups of holes, representing by each group a letter or character, the perforations being arranged to produce, as nearly as possible, the block or Roman letters or characters.

'The transmission of the message by the wires may be in the usual manner by a roller or stylus and a wire to each row of perforations, so that, if there are five rows of perforations there will be five stylus points, each connected to a wire, and, at the receiving instrument, there will be five pens or stylus-points near together; and the letter received will be in dots corresponding to the position of the perforations in the transmitting paper. By their aggregation in groups, the letters will be clearly delineated, and formed almost as perfectly as printed characters, so that the strip of chemical paper can be delivered, and the rewriting or printing of the message dispensed with.

'The message as received being the counter-

This specimen of tape shows the small individual holes used to represent 'dots' (on the right), and the groups of three holes used to represent the 'dash.' The holes were perforated on the tape by one of the machines shown on page 59. (Reproduced from Edison's application for patent No. 132,456.)

These letters were perforated by the Edison machine shown on page 64, and thus made ready for transmission over the automatic telegraph. (Reproduced from Mr. Edison's application for patent No. 151,209.)

Mr. Edison's patent-office model of his Roman-character perforator is shown here as it appears today in the glass case on the first floor of the restored laboratory at Dearborn.

part of that transmitted, the perforated paper at the transmitting station becomes a perfect record of the message, and the line can be worked up to its utmost capacity, because the paper can be perforated for transmitting about as rapidly as an ordinary printing-telegraph can be operated, and as many perforating operators and machines can be used as are necessary for the work that is to be done on the lines.'

The completed machine in use. Mr. Edison's patent was applied for September 2, 1873, and granted May 26, 1874. Patent No. 151,209. May be seen in restored laboratory

Here is a model of Mr. Edison's motograph relay, as it appeared after it had been constructed in the restored Menlo Park machine shop from Mr. Edison's original pattern. In the right center is the round cylinder of chalk, on top of which rests a metal arm, or strip. This connects with an upright metal post in the middle of the relay. The latter vibrates at its top between two points, whenever contact is made with an electric circuit. The making and breaking of circuit makes this instrument a telegraph able to receive signals without the use of the electromagnet. The instrument may be seen on one of the tables on the second floor of the restored laboratory at Dearborn.

X. A New Scientific Discovery—

The Motograph

I HAVE told you something of Edison's labors with the automatic and chemical telegraph, and now I want to describe an amazing scientific discovery that grew out of those labors. One day as he was watching the strip of moistened paper pass under the stylus, or pen, transcribing a message, he noticed that the tape ran more quickly whenever the current passed from the stylus through the paper, than when no current passed.

In other words, *the paper became slippery.*

([1])You will recall that this paper had been chemically pre-

(1) The paper was kept moistened by some chemical solution, such as ferrocyanide of potassium, which produced a blue mark by means of electrolysis when the current was passed through the stylus.

pared so that it would receive the writings of the stylus. The stylus was controlled by the transmitting instrument, at which point a strip of paper containing the perforated message was passed under a number of tiny revolving discs. These were made of metal and acted as contact points, and every time one of them dropped into a perforation, it closed the circuit of the line.

Many persons had worked and experimented with similar systems as far back as Bain in 1848, prior to the time Edison undertook it, but among them all he was the first and only one to notice this apparently innocent phenomenon. His inquiring mind compelled him to provide some explanation, and in his search he came upon the interesting principle, which he called the motograph and which he, subsequently, put to practical use in many different ways.

By means of it he was able to transmit telegraph messages *without the use of an electromagnet relay.* He was able to construct a telephone receiver which introduced a method of communication *entirely different from that developed by Bell.* For it he received the eighth patent ever awarded by the government for an original discovery.

Incidentally, for his application of this discovery to the telegraph, he received one hundred thousand dollars! By his application of it to the transmission of spoken words, he received thirty thousand pounds, or about one hundred and fifty thousand dollars! A quarter of a million dollars!

In his first experiments to utilize it, he attached a spring to the stylus and found he could obtain a small amount of mechanical motion. Also, the action was exceedingly rapid, far more sensitive than that of an electromagnet.

He demonstrated it

THOMAS A. EDISON.

Picture made from an old print dated 1877

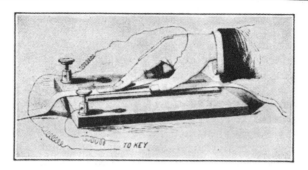

In demonstrating his motograph discovery, Mr. Edison laid a strip of paper, chemically prepared, on a metal plate, as shown above, and passed a bent strip of metal over the paper. When an electric current was introduced, the friction of the metal strip on the paper was noticeably diminished.

simply as follows: He laid a strip of paper on a metal plate, moistening the paper with a solution. Over the paper he passed a bent strip of metal, and friction resulted. Then he tried the same experiment introducing an electric current. One wire from the battery was connected to the plate while the other was attached to the moving metal strip. Now the friction was noticeably diminished.

The amount of friction varied according to the current (within certain limits). The stylus would ring a bell while the current was passing through it; or it would act as a relay, sending a current mechanically, and repeating the signal in other circuits.

About that time the well-known New York financier, Jay Gould, had secured the rights to a patent granted an inventor named Page, which threatened to compel all companies using the telegraph to pay it a royalty.([2])

The president of the Western Union, William Orton, turned to Edison and assigned to him the task of discovering some new means of sending telegraph messages which would not require the use of the electromagnet as in a relay. Before returning to Newark Edison promised to go at the problem that very night. He solved it by adapting his motograph discovery.

'I substituted a piece of chalk rotated by a small electric

(2) The Page patent related to the use of a retractile spring to withdraw the armature lever from the magnet of a telegraph or other relay or sounder and thus controlled the art of telegraphy except in simple circuits.

motor for the magnet,' he said, 'and connected a sounder to a metallic finger resting on the chalk. It made the claim of Page worthless.'

He applied for a patent on August 13, 1874, which was granted him January 19, 1875, as No. 158,787.

Edison's description of his discovery, as set forth in his application for the patent covering it, was as follows:

'In electric telegraphs motion has been obtained at a distance by a galvanometer and by an electromagnet. Both of these are comparatively slow, and hence chemical decomposition has been resorted to for recording the characters sent from a distant station.

'Heretofore there has been great difficulty in obtaining any means for repeating messages at high rates of speed, and magnets or galvanometers in an electric circuit always produce more or less disturbance by the secondary or induced current, and act to reduce the speed.

'My invention is dependent on mechanical motion and electrical action, and responds to the most feeble currents when properly adjusted and with very great rapidity; hence I term my invention the "electric motograph."

'The principles of its operation are that, when a moving surface is in contact with a slightly yielding substance, the tendency is to move the latter by and with the former. If the circumstances of contact are varied the adhesion of the surfaces will be sufficient to cause the moving surface to move the yielding substance, or else to cause the yielding substance to slip more freely, and by its spring to go in the opposite direction to the moving surface.

'I have discovered that the passage of electricity through the surfaces in contact

On one of the tables on the second floor of the restored laboratory is this motograph apparatus, used by Mr. Edison to demonstrate the principle. Its use is illustrated in the diagram at the top of the preceding page.

The instrument was taken to Paris, France, in 1881, and used by Charles Batchelor to demonstrate the motograph principle to European scientists at the International Exposition.

will change the frictional adhesion, making it more or less according to the substances employed; and by balancing the mechanical forces so that when the surfaces in contact are not electrified the moving surface carries with it the yielding surface, and when electrified the yielding surface slips back over the moving surface or vice versa, a mechanical movement is produced that is dependent on the electrical condition of the surfaces in contact. Hence mechanical motion is obtained, first one way and then the other, as unlimited in its speed as the pulsations of electricity that pass, unobstructed by magnets or other hindrances, over the telegraphic lines.'

Two or three instruments using the motograph principle were constructed, and found to work so successfully that Orton bought the rights to it at once. He agreed to pay one hundred thousand dollars at the rate of $6,000 a year for seventeen years. That arrangement was at Edison's request.

On one of the tables on the second floor of the restored laboratory is a working model of Edison's motograph relay, constructed in the Menlo Park machine shop after the pattern devised by him. Large numbers of visitors have viewed this interesting instrument and learned for the first time of the principle and of the fact that, by means of it, Edison was able to transmit telegraphic messages.

When the cylinder of chalk is turned slowly, the tick-tick-tick of the dot-and-dash is plainly audible. Amplified with a sounder, it fills the entire room. We have connected it with a single cell dry battery, and found it to operate on as weak a current as 1/1000 part of an ampere. That was one of its features—ability to work on weak currents. Another was its speed. If you will listen to its operation, I think you will agree that it is much faster than the ordinary Morse relay.

If you will turn to the files of the *Scientific American*, you will find in its issue of September 5, 1874, a letter signed 'T. A. Edison, Newark, N. J., August, 1874,' in which Edison related an interesting story in connection with his discovery of the motograph.

'I had a long message received over the Automatic Telegraph Company's wire from Washington (this wire runs into my laboratory at Newark) and recorded the same on ordinary chemically prepared paper. The speed with which the message was sent from Washington was about 800 words per minute, and the colorations forming the dots and dashes were rather faint.

One of Edison's motograph relays ready for use as telegraph instrument in place of Morse instrument. On base may be seen words, 'T A. Edison, Menlo Park, New Jersey.' This instrument now is in restored laboratory at Dearborn.

'I then passed the strip into the electromotograph (I use this name for want of a better one), the colorations being in a direct line with the lead point.

'On rotation of the drum, and when no coloration was under the lead point, the lever was carried forward by the normal friction of the paper. But the moment a coloration passed under it, the lead point slid along the paper as upon ice, the friction was greatly reduced, and the lever moved in an opposite direction to the rotating drum.'

You can easily test this phenomenon for yourself on the motograph relay which we have reconstructed here. As you turn the cylinder of chalk (or drum, as Edison called it), you find a certain amount of pressure is required to move it

Interior of motograph relay. Note cylinder of chalk on left.

past the lever. As soon as a current is sent into the cylinder, it moves smoothly without friction and slips around so easily as to be almost dumfounding.

Edison described it as an entirely new system of telegraphy. In the issue of the *Scientific American* just mentioned, the editor states that he has a sample of the apparatus under practical operation in the editorial office, where it was being examined and tested.

'It promises,' he wrote, 'to result in the creation of an entirely new and advantageous system of telegraphy. The salient feature of Mr. Edison's present discovery is the production of motion and of sound by the pen, or stylus, without the intervention of a magnet or armature.

'By the motion thus produced, he works any of the ordinary forms of telegraph printing or sounding instruments or relays, and is enabled to send messages by direct transmission over thousands of miles of wire at the highest speed, without rewriting delay or difficulty of any kind.

'More than this, his apparatus operates in a highly effective manner under the weakest electric currents, and he is able to receive and transmit messages by currents so weak that the ordinary magnetic instruments fail to operate or even give an indication of the passage of electricity.'

The story of how this principle was applied by Edison to the telephone does not come properly until after his invention of the carbon telephone transmitter, so with your indulgence we will leave it until that time. Meanwhile, let us turn our attention to what has been pronounced his most wonderful invention at Newark—the quadruplex telegraph.

Old-time jack plug telegraph switchboard for plugging in an additional line on any one of six lines or on all of them.

About the time he moved to Menlo Park, Mr. Edison perfected this improvement on the telegraph and alarm apparatus. Application was filed May 18, 1876, and granted January 23, 1877, No. 186,548. The present system for summoning messengers is based on Mr. Edison's ideas, which were developed by the Domestic Telegraph Company. The object of this apparatus, said he in his application, was 'to provide a cheap and reliable alarm adapted to small cities and towns for giving fire alarms or other signals. I make use of a central station with one or more lines running to the respective signal instruments.' This model of the system is now in one of the glass cases on the first floor of the restored laboratory at Dearborn.

XI. Four Messages Over A Single Wire

A LINE using Edison's automatic telegraph system was placed in service between New York City and Washington and he was sent to England by the financiers to introduce the system. After overcoming many difficulties he demonstrated it successfully but was never able to realize any financial benefit from the trip.

From the automatic telegraph, Edison turned his efforts to the duplex and quadruplex systems. In one of the glass cases on the first floor of the laboratory you will find patent office models of the former. The work on the quadruplex started while Edison was still wrestling with the typewriter, helping out a Mr. Sholes of Milwaukee. At that time he was bossing other shops in Newark as well as carrying on his experiments.

The typewriter promised to make things easier for the transmission of alphabetical characters over the telegraph. Mr. Sholes, who was striving to perfect it, came to Newark to consult Edison, and the latter worked many nights over

One of the products of the Newark shop and of Mr. Edison's inventive genius was a fire signal alarm apparatus. The patent office model shown above now rests in one of the glass cases on the first floor of the restored laboratory at Dearborn. It was filed December 3, 1872, and was granted January 27, 1874, as Patent No. 146,812. The clockworks which Mr. Edison used in this device bear the name of 'Seth Thomas.'

the first model seeking to make it commercially practicable.

'This typewriter proved a difficult thing,' said Edison. 'The alignment of the letters was awful. One letter would be a sixteenth of an inch above the others; and all the letters wanted to wander out of line.'(¹)

After the toil on the model ended, several machines were built by hand and used in the office of the Automatic Telegraph Company. By the time I went to work in Mr. Lowrey's law office in 1878, it was in common use among the leading firms, and even I knew how to operate one after a fashion.

Among the many improvements on the telegraph, the quadruplex still stands as a striking illustration of Mr. Edison's powers of ingenuity and the mastery of his subject. It was completed in 1874 when he was only 27 years old, and made possible the sending of four different messages at the same time over a single wire. In cheapening the cost of sending messages for the public he saved literally millions of dollars, stretching three phantom wires alongside the actual wire in use.

Mr. Reid of the Western Union called it 'the chief product

(1) *Edison, His Life and Inventions*—Dyer & Martin, Vol. I., p. 146.

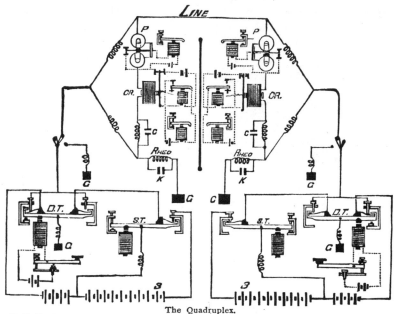

The Quadruplex.

D T, Double Transmitter; S T, Second or Single Transmitter: P, Polarized Relay; C R, Common Relay; C, Condenser; G. Ground; 1 and 3 Batteries.

Diagram of the Edison quadruplex system of telegraphy. Its distinguishing feature consists of combining at two terminal stations of two distinct, unlike methods of single transmission, so that they may be carried on independently upon the same wire and at the same time without interfering with each other.

of Mr. Edison's genius . . . by which already the equivalent of fifty thousand miles of wire have been added to the capacity of our lines.'

Years later Mr. Edison remarked that the problems in incandescent electric lighting were relatively simple compared to the complex and tantalizing ones that came up during the period when he was laboring with the solution of quadruplex telegraphy.

The quadruplex system consists of a complicated system of circuits in which relays, neutral and polarized; keys, plain or pole changers; sounders; condensers and batteries are employed and operate either on a differential or Wheatstone bridge principle.

Currents of different strength and different polarities are employed. Thus, each of four sets of instruments is so con-

With this device, made by Mr. Edison during his experiments in acoustic telegraphy it is possible to reproduce the human voice, as by a telephone. It may be seen on the second floor of the restored laboratory at Dearborn.

structed and adjusted that it will respond only to an increase or decrease of current, or to one polarity or its reverse.

Edison's rights in the quadruplex were bought by Jay Gould for $30,000, after a demonstration of its operation between New York City and Albany. During two months of arduous drilling, Edison had schooled a detail of eight operators, four on each end of the single wire over which they were to send or receive messages; and they 'put on' the demonstration.

Through General T. T. Eckert, Edison was approached to sell his interest and he arranged to show the invention to the prospective purchaser the next day in the shop at 10 12 Ward Street. General Eckert arrived at the appointed time, accompanied by Gould himself. After an inspection of the apparatus, they left, and next day Edison was called to Gould's home in New York City.

At that time Gould was seeking control of the Western Union and was afraid some one would recognize Edison. He had General Eckert bring the inventor in by way of the servants' entrance. Edison's description of what followed is interesting:

'Gould started in at once and asked me how much I wanted. I said: "Make me an offer." Then he said: "I will give you $30,000." I said: "I will sell any interest I may have for that money," which was something more than I thought I could get. The next day I went with Gould to the office of his lawyers and received a check for $30,000, with the remark by

Gould that I had got the steamboat *Plymouth Rock*. He had sold her for $30,000 and had just received the check.'([2])

Shortly afterward, the company of which General Eckert was president, the Atlantic & Pacific Telegraph Company, bought out the Automatic Telegraph Company. At Newark, Edison made automatic apparatus for his new bosses, and it was during this period that he also spent so much time working on the district messenger call box system.

He organized the Domestic Telegraph Company to install the system in New York City and, after signing up about 200 subscribers, sold it to the Atlantic & Pacific Company.

At the time of the transfer of the Automatic Telegraph Company, the purchasers had agreed to increase their capital to fifteen million dollars and give four million to the men who had worked and made possible its development. Edison was appointed electrician of the purchasing company, but when the agreements were not carried out he returned once more to the Western Union banner.

In 1906, the Federal court in New York handed down a decision on a bill filed nearly thirty years previous, ordering an accounting under the old agreement. The master who made the accounting set the damages for the wrongful appropriation of the automatic telegraph patents at one dollar!

(2) Ibid, p. 159.

Some idea of the complicated nature of the electroharmonic multiplex telegraph with which Mr. Edison was experimenting when he invented the carbon telephone transmitter, may be obtained from this picture of the patent office model submitted by Mr. Edison on August 16, 1876. Four months later a patent was granted, No. 185,507. Note the tuning forks. This model as well as others may be seen in one of the glass cases on the first floor of the restored laboratory at Dearborn.

This embossing telegraph was said by Mr. Edison to be the father of the phonograph. A working model of it may be seen on the instrument table near the head of
the stairs on the second floor of the restored laboratory. (Patent No. 213,554.)

You may be interested to hear that this same automatic
telegraph of Edison's was recommended for an award at the
Centennial Exposition in Philadelphia in 1876. The juror
making this suggestion was none other than the famous
English physicist, Lord Kelvin. With the aid of Ed Johnson,
Lord Kelvin made exhaustive tests of the system and carried
back to Glasgow University records of the tests for use in
that institution.

The ultimate fate of this fascinating instrument did not
seem to justify Edison's hopes and labors, although it was still
in use in 1879, one year after I went to work for him at Menlo
Park. If you will look in Reid's historical work on the telegraph, published in 1879, you will find reference to the Atlantic and Pacific Telegraph Company, together with the
following statement: 'The instruments used are those known
as Edison's American Automatic Telegraph.' You will also
note that the method was being used only as an auxiliary
and 'had nowhere shown itself practicable as a separate
system.'[3]

Nevertheless, the through business of that company was
transmitted solely by this process from January, 1875, to July,
1876, to twenty-six stations, from New York City as far
west as Omaha. The President's message on December 5,
1876, composed of 12,600 words, was filed in Washington,
D. C., at 1:05 p. m. and was sent by the Automatic Telegraph
to New York City in one hour and two minutes.

Before leaving the fascinating subject of Edison's researches into telegraphy, I must mention two fields which he

[3]   Reid—*The Telegraph in America.*   (p. 588)

explored with astonishing results. Much of what I am going to tell you now happened here in this laboratory, for it was after he removed from Newark to Menlo Park that he pursued most of these two studies.

One of them had to do with what was known as 'harmonic' or 'acoustic' telegraphy, and during his experimenting with it he had the secret of the telephone in his grasp, had he but known it. It began at Newark and in 1875, one year before Bell and Gray gave their ideas to the world, he had an acoustic telegraph over which it would have been possible to talk.

Perhaps you would be interested in trying out the instrument for yourself. It consists of two hollow metal cylinders, fitted one inside the other like telescopic tubes, so that the length of the instrument could be increased by drawing out the inner one. The metal base of the cylinder acted as a diaphragm, and against it were two electromagnet coils, as shown above.

We have connected this instrument to a transmitter hung on the wall downstairs, and when someone talks in the latter, as over the telephone, the voice is reproduced on the diaphragm.

Shortly after Bell announced his discovery, Edison tried out this device and found that it was capable of use as a telephone. However, he has never sought to take the credit from Bell for the discovery. But it is interesting to note that he produced a device that could talk, prior to 1876.([4])

All three of those famous inventors, Edison, Bell and Gray, were seeking at the same time to perfect a telegraph system using tuning forks. The idea was extremely complicated but in general (as described by Edison) it consisted of 'combining a large tuning fork with multiple forks arranged at two terminal stations with contact springs leading to different Morse instruments, so that the synchronous vibrations of the forks would change the main line wires from one set of instruments to other sets at both stations at the rate of 120 times per second.'([5])

They sought to accomplish the simultaneous transmission of eight different messages over a single wire.

What actually happened was described by Edison himself.

---

(4)   Edison said: 'I can, however, lay no claim to having discovered that conversation could be carried on between one receiver and the other upon the magneto principle by causing the voice to vibrate the diaphragm.'—Prescott, *The Speaking Telephone*. (p. 222)

(5)   Prescott—*The Speaking Telephone*. (p. 218)

'I started in and soon produced the *carbon telephone transmitters.*'([6])

The foregoing is one of the two fields which I referred to in the preceding paragraph. The second was the embossing or translating telegraph.

On February 3, 1877, Edison applied for a patent covering an 'Improvement in the Automatic Telegraph.' By that time, of course, he was well settled here in this laboratory. It was granted to him two years later as No. 213,554 and was devised 'to indent upon a sheet of paper the characters received from a distant station, and use such sheet to transmit the same message, thus providing an automatic device for transmitting the same message more than once from one station to different stations; and for retransmitting it automatically where it has to pass through several offices.'([7])

If you will look at our working model here you will see how the two discs revolve, while the dot-and-dash of the Morse code are pricked into the surface of round sheets of paper, like phonograph records.

One day I happened to be standing looking at this instrument, when Mr. Edison came up. He saw my interest in it and told me a few things about it, one of which I have never forgotten.

'That machine,' said he, 'was the father of the phonograph.'

(6) Dyer & Martin—*Edison, His Life and Inventions.* (Vol. I. p. 179)
(7) From Edison's application for patent No. 213,554.

::   ::   ::

Cartoon in *Daily Graphic*, 1878, depicting train that
traveled between Jersey City and Menlo Park.

XII. Etheric Force
The Famous Black Box

NOT long after I went to work at Menlo Park I happened to stop at the instrument table one day and saw among its scattered articles a black rectangular box. It was surmounted by an extension eye-shade so designed that, when fitted around the eyes, it permitted unobstructed vision into the interior.

Wondering what this queer-looking contrivance might be, I leaned over and peered down into it. All I saw were two points separated by a gap. The latter was evidently arranged so it could be lengthened or shortened as desired by turning delicate micrometer screws.

At first I was puzzled as to the purpose of the machine. As it resembled a black box, I suddenly recalled that I had read about an Edison black box that had been used in Newark to show a mysterious spark Mr. Edison had discovered. He had named it 'etheric force.' I found this box to be the identical instrument about which I had heard so much.

Mr. Edison's discovery was made on November 22, 1875, while he was studying the workings of a vibrator magnet that

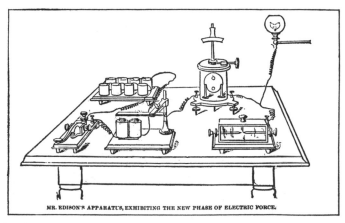

MR. EDISON'S APPARATUS, EXHIBITING THE NEW PHASE OF ELECTRIC FORCE.

Drawing from *Scientific American* of December 25, 1875, showing Edison demonstration of 'etheric force.' This is an excellent illustration of a true wireless system. The transmitting set comprises a circuit in which oscillating pulsations are developed upon opening and closing the key. The receiving circuit includes the inductance of the galvanometer, the capacitance of the wiring and the gas piping and a spark-gap receiver. Note the bar suspended above the magnet.

Page from Edison's notebook describing the discovery of the new, unknown force.

was being operated by a battery current. His sharp eyes detected a peculiar spark coming from the core of the magnet. It was unlike any spark with which he was familiar. In all his long service as a telegrapher, he had never seen a spark of similar aspect.

With him at the time was Charles Batchelor, to whom we are indebted for the notes describing this occasion. A reproduction of these appears on this page.

Thinking perhaps the spark was due to faulty instruments, he tested the connections and insulation, only to find them perfect. Here was something as yet unknown to the electrical

Binocular instrument described on page 85. Like the black box it may be seen on one of the instrument tables on the second floor of the restored laboratory at Dearborn.

world and to science, a spark which could not be explained and which was unlike the usual electrical one. It was easily obtainable as it was the product of the ordinary one. At first he got one by touching some part of the vibrator with any substance that formed a good conductor; then he attached a wire to the end of the rod that vibrated and drew a spark from the wire. Next, he got one by turning the free end of the wire back on itself.

During that fall and winter he performed many experiments seeking to determine the nature and find the characteristics of this new discovery. It was independent, he learned, of polarity; had no respect for insulation; would not charge a Leyden jar and had no effect on the electroscope or galvanometer.

In December, 1875, he brought his observations before the Polyclinic Club of the American Institute, at the same time giving a demonstration of etheric force. A battle raged about his theory, for many critics challenged and doubted him. The very name chosen by him seemed to upset them.

To all of this, Mr. Edison replied: 'I suggest that, as I have freely laid myself open to criticism by presuming to believe in the capacity of Nature to supply a new form of energy, which presumption rests upon experiment, it is but fair that my critics should back up their assertions by experiments and give me an equal chance as a critic.'

He had his champions, too. Doctor Beard, one of them, said:

'At the present time, the weight of evidence in my mind is in favor of the theory that this is a *radiant* force, somewhere between light and heat on the one hand, and magnetism and electricity on the other; with some features of all these forces.'

More significant than all others was Mr. Edison's own explanation of the 'spark' and what it promised. He was still a young man—twenty-eight years old—but his vision as published in *The Operator*, a telegraphers' journal, in January, 1876, seems highly prophetic, in the light of the development of wireless telegraphy since that day:

'The cumbersome appliances of transmitting ordinary electricity, such as telegraph poles, insulating knobs, cable sheathings, and so on, may be left out of the problem of quick and cheap telegraphic transmission; and a great saving of time and labor accomplished.'

In its editorial columns of December 2 of that year, the New York *Herald* added:

'All that the world has learned in the short life of modern science indicates that we are only at the threshold of the great secrets of Nature that are yet to be opened to us, and every step we take in this direction counts toward the grand result.'

Black box with extension eye-shade, used by Mr. Edison to demonstrate etheric force. Inside were micrometer screws with graphite points separated to form a gap, which could be increased or diminished by adjusting them. Mr. Edison discovered sparks leaping across this gap which were unlike any known to electrical phenomena and which we now know to have been caused by wireless, or, as he called it, etheric force. This box was sent by Mr. Edison to Paris where Charles Batchelor demonstrated his discovery before European scientists in 1881. It may now be seen on one of the instrument tables on the second floor of the restored laboratory at Dearborn.

THE

THE OPERATOR,

THE ORGAN OF THE AMERICAN AND CANADIAN
TELEGRAPH OPERATORS, AND JOURNAL OF
SCIENTIFIC TELEGRAPHY.

The Publishers, in announcing the Fourth Volume of THE OPERATOR, which commences with the number for Sept. 1st, 1875, desire to return thanks for the liberal support which it has hitherto received, which it is expected and believed will be continued during the ensuing year.

All the popular and valuable features of the paper will be retained, and it will continue, as heretofore, to labor for the best interests of the Telegraphic Fraternity, and the advancement of Electrical Science and the Telegraphic Art.

As heretofore, no labor, time, or expense, warranted by the patronage received, will be spared to improve its character and add to its interest, and to sustain its reputation as the only first-class Electrical and Telegraphic Journal upon the American Continent.

SCIENTIFIC NOTES

Edison's Discovery of a Supposed New Force

MR. EDISON, whose name promises to become famous as the discoverer of a new natural force, was at his laboratory in Newark last evening attended by his assistants and surrounded by a little company of interested persons, among whom were several expert electricians and a representative of the *Herald.* Mr. Edison is a young man, of about the medium height, with full oval face, a large head, and a manner that bespeaks the utmost devotion to his business. He was formerly a telegraph operator in the employ of the Western Union Company, and, during the war, was engaged in the Associated Press operating-room, serving with excellent skill and fidelity. Possessed of natural inventive genius, he began to turn his attention to the betterment of the telegraphic instruments then in use, and succeeded in making a number of additions and improvements with such pecuniary benefit to himself that he was enabled to abandon the laborious occupation of an operator, and devote his time to the study of electric science. His most important invention up to this time is that of the quadruplex system, by which four messages can be transmitted simultaneously through a single wire. It was while engaged in his occupation of experimenting that he made the discovery of what he is pleased to term, without much appropriateness, 'etheric' force.

This force or principle is the direct offspring of electricity and magnetism. The operation of an ordinary telegraphic circuit affords the simplest means of deriving it, and it is by this method that the present experiments are being conducted. When the circuit is open or broken, the electricity stored in the magnetic coil by the operation of a continuous current is withdrawn artificially, and it is in this manner of relieving the magnet that the invention consists. Hitherto the power stored in the magnet has been permitted to dissipate itself unnoticed in the air, in ignorance of the fact that it has assumed a new nature, and possessed properties more valuable than those of electricity itself. Edison noticed that the accidental contact of a wire with the core of the magnet caused the production of a peculiar bright spark when a metallic substance was applied to it. Though this manifestation has been frequently observed, he was led to investigate it to its origin, and was amazed to find that the new manifestation failed to respond to the tests applied to discover the presence of electricity, either inductive or static. The galvanometer was unmoved by it, the dainty gold

On this page and succeeding three pages is reprinted the article published by *The Operator* in January, 1876, telling of Mr. Edison's discovery of 'etheric force.' Copy of this is on second floor of restored laboratory at Dearborn.

OPERATOR

leaf of the electroscope exhibited no signs of deflection; the tongue could detect no sensation; the Leyden jar charged with it was possessed of no property that is contributed to it by electric contact. In a word, the manifestation was non-electric. It was the display, recognized for the first time, of a principle until then buried in the depths of human ignorance.

Since the moment of this discovery Mr. Edison has worked night and day to ascertain more intimately the nature of the new 'etheric' principle, and with results which are strongly confirmatory of his original theory. A voltaic battery, of several cells, is applied to an ordinary telegraph instrument. The trial of twenty-eight different metals having shown that cadmium is best adapted for the transmission of the new power, a bar of that substance (analogous in its nature to zinc) is placed across or near to the magnetic coil, either directly or with an insulating substance intervening, and from this bar a copper wire conducts the 'etheric' force to any desired point. Connected with the gas-pipe, it charges every gas fixture in the building, so that the application of metallic substance to any one of them will produce the etheric spark. A connection with the street main enabled Mr. Edison to draw the sparks from a gas fixture in his residence, some distance away. Hence, it seems that the new force is not affected by the contact of the earth, but performs its operations independent of the necessity of insulators. Herein lies its immense practical value. The cumbersome appliances of transmitting ordinary electricity, such as telegraph poles, insulating knobs, cable sheathings, and so on, may be left out of the problem of quick and cheap telegraphic transmission, and a great saving of time and labor accomplished. Ocean cables operated by 'etheric' force need cost but a fraction of the present clumsy lines. Wires may be laid in the earth or in the water. The existing methods and mechanisms may be completely revolutionized. The experiments witnessed by the *Herald* representative were of an exceedingly interesting nature. Attaching the wire upon which the etheric current is conducted to a gas fixture in the large laboratory, it was found that the peculiar sparks could be obtained from every other gas fixture in the building simultaneously by the application of a file, knife-blade, or other metallic substance. A confusing and inexplicable experiment was as follows: The current was transmitted through the gas pipes, and the experimenter proceeded to a distant burner and drew brilliant sparks by applying his knife-blade. Three feet from this burner was another burner, at which a second person was stationed with instructions to grasp it firmly, which was no sooner done than the sparks at burner No. 1 became so feeble as to be almost imperceptible. When the grasp on burner No. 2 was released the sparks were evolved from No. 1 with renewed brilliancy. Water was then placed upon the floor and a piece of iron laid in the wet spot and connected with burner No. 2 by means of a copper wire, thus furnishing ample opportunity of escape had the current been an electric one. But the brilliancy of the sparks at No. 1 was found to be unaffected by this test. The person who first grasped burner No. 2 was then made to resume his grasp, standing on the wet spot, but the former effect of diminishing the force of the spark at No. 1 was now imperceptible. Standing upon the dry floor his grasp of burner No. 2 was fatal to the manifestations at No. 1 but when the floor was moistened the interruptive effect ceased. Still another experiment consisted in grasping the gas pipe into which the etheric current was being led, the person grasping it being made to hold a knife in his other hand. Upon touching a file to the knife-blade sparks were freely drawn, showing that the human body is a good conductor of the new force. No peculiar sensation was observed by the person through whom the current passed. When the writer left the laboratory, Mr. Edison had just brought the microscope to bear upon the etheric sparks, magnifying them several thousand areas.

It has been suggested that this discovery throws new light upon the nature of the auroral phenomena. Telegraph operators are familiar with the difference between the effect of the electricity developed by a thunderstorm, and that which affects the wires previous to an auroral display. The former passes through the wire, emitting both spark and sound; it is instantaneous in action, seldom traveling far on the wire before discharging

THE

itself. But the electricity produced by the aurora passes along the wire in a continuous stream, with no sudden discharge, effecting the same result as that produced by the galvanic battery. A colored mark upon the paper is made by the positive current of the aurora as by the positive pole of the battery. When these effects have been observed the aurora follows, and so familiar have the operators become with the manifestations, that they can predict an auroral display with absolute certainty. They regard the electricity which precedes its appearance as of precisely the same nature as that of the electro-galvanic battery, which is distinguished by its voluminous current without intensity of action, differing from ordinary atmospheric electricity or the kind produced by friction, which may be dissipated by means of a wire conductor leading to the ground. Now, it is an old theory that the cause of aurcral displays is the accumulation of quantities of electricity in the earth (which may be regarded as a vast magnet) and by the liberation of this electricity, which is dissipated in the form of a magnificent display of light. But this is precisely the mechanism by which the etheric spark is produced. The core of the magnet corresponds to the magnetic pole of the earth; the cadmium and wire act in correspondence to the peculiar conditions of the atmosphere under which the earth's electricity is liberated; the galvanic battery and electric current are analogous to the vast currents of the electric fluid which encircle and pervade the earth; the auroral flame is kindred to the etheric spark. In short, the newly discovered manifestation, producing no effect but light, is believed to be a miniature of that grand and mysterious illumination which has excited the admiration and wonder of men for so many centuries.

"Mr. Edison is constructing a quantity of special apparatus for the purpose of experimenting with the new force. Guttapercha rods will be suspended so that the instruments may be more thoroughly insulated and all possibility of electric induction prevented; an 'etherioscope' will be contrived by means of graphite points, so that the etheric sparks may be more advantageously studied, and a spectroscope analysis will be made of the spark in order to ascertain the affinity of the light with that of the auroral display. The discoverer will labor unremittingly to develop the etheric manifestations until he succeeds in putting them into more tangible shapes, and evolves a force which shall be as docile and adaptable to the uses of man as those faithful drudges—steam, heat, and electricity.

Mr. Edison's theory of 'etheric' energy is as follows: 'Under certain conditions heat energy can be transmitted into electric energy, and that again, under certain conditions, into magnetic energy, this back again into electric energy, all forms of energy being interchangeable with each other. It follows that if electric energy under certain conditions is transformed into that of magnetism, under other conditions it might be transformed into an entirely unknown force, subject to laws different from those of heat, light, electricity, or magnetism. There is every reason to suppose that etheric energy is this new form. The only manifestation of its presence previously recorded with scientific accuracy is that of the German chemist Ruchenbach, who noticed that an electro magnet, under certain conditions and placed in a dark room, became luminous when the hands of peculiarly constituted persons were made to approach the poles. This phenomenon, inexplicable to Ruchenbach, is easily to be accounted for on the etheric theory.' "—*New York Herald* Dec. 2d.

In its editorial columns the *Herald* adds:

MR. EDISON'S DISCOVERY

"In another column will be found an account of a new discovery in natural science recently made in the experiments of an electrician. This gentleman observed that the spark which arises from the contact of two pieces of metal when one is in contact with the core of a battery was apparently the product of some force other than electricity, and upon the application of tests was able to prove that the principle whose existence and operation were thus demonstrated by the electrical apparatus was not electricity, but was some hitherto unknown and undescribed force. From what he has thus far learned of the nature and manifestations of the new

OPERATOR

principle, he is led to compare its operation to that operation of nature which produces the aurora, and venture the theory that he has detected the principle upon which that grand pageant of nature depends. The practical results of the discovery, as now contemplated, have regard to telegraphic manipulation, and the discovery seems to promise greatly increased facility for the transmission of signals. All that the world has learned in the short life of modern science indicates that we are only at the threshold of the great secrets of nature that are yet to be opened to us, and every step we take in this direction counts toward the grand result of the victory of man over the obstacles of matter and space and time."

Dr. John Cowen, of New York, writing to the *Sun*, says:

"I read in the *Sun* the new discovery made by Mr. T. A. Edison, of Newark. He has touched the outer limits of one of the grandest discoveries of modern times. I think I can place him, or any other electrician who will observe the following rules, on the right track: Use for the ends of the battery wires, balls of glass one inch in diameter with the insertion of the wire to the center of the ball. The balls must be exactly one inch in diameter—no more, no less. Next, place in a suitable frame a sheet of ordinary white paper one inch from the glass ball on the positive pole. Now transmit the message in any of the usual ways, operating by a key from the negative pole, and it will be received by the glass ball on the positive pole and the message transmitted to the paper placed one inch before it. No conductor of any nature is required, and in no way will the new force be affected by distance. By the use of this discovery messages can be sent to and from the uttermost end of the earth in a moment of time, the only expense being for battery and glass ball points.

"Mr. Edison errs in believing the new force has actinic power. He is right in supposing it has 'positive registering mechanical power,' and also in its being non-polar.

"Mr. Edison is on the boundaries of a new law. I give the only method by which that law can be used intelligently. I have not applied for a patent —do not intend to. Its simplicity, its cheapness, its availability, should make its use general, and It ought not to be controlled by any corporation.

"Concerning the possibilities resulting from the application of the discovery, much might be said, but there are the facts, and what more is needed?   JOHN COWEN, M. D.

NEW YORK, *Dec. 1, 1875.*"

Unfortunately, the attention of Mr. Edison was diverted by his experiments in telephony, and after a time he ceased his researches into the realm of etheric force. Other experimenters and scientists failed to carry them on and his early work was shelved, to be forgotten by many.

The first official mention that I can recall of the sending of messages by means of this new force without wires was in the *Scientific American* of December 18, 1875.

'By this simple means,' said the writer in that article, 'signals have been sent for long distances, as from Mr. Edison's laboratory to his dwelling house in another part of the city, the only connection being the common system of gas pipes. Mr. Edison states that signals have also been sent the distance of seventy-five miles on an open circuit, by attaching a conducting wire to the Western Union Telegraph line.'

At first everyone thought his new force was a manifestation of the 'weak sparks' that had been observed by Professor Reis, the eminent German electrician. Later demonstrations proved to the satisfaction of such authorities as the
Scientific American that it was actually a new discovery. Such
an announcement was made in the columns of that paper; in
fact, on December 25, 1875.

At the same time it described the experiment which is
illustrated in the drawing on page 80.

'All the parts are insulated except the gas fixture. On the
table is the telegraph key in the left-hand corner, connected
with an electromagnet on its right and with a battery on its
left. Above the electromagnet is a bar of cadmium which is
supported by an insulated stand. In the background is a
mirror galvanometer which is connected to the insulated
stand and to the box which holds common lead pencils with
their points facing each other.

'The unknown current passes from the bar of cadmium
through the galvanometer without causing the slightest deflection, and, notwithstanding the gas pipe connection—
which would drain the wire of induced electricity, if there
were any—bright sparks are visible between the graphite
points in response to the motion of the telegraphic key.

'Among its observed peculiarities may be noticed its lack
of polarity, indifference to the earth (and consequently its
capability of transmission through uninsulated wires) its
power of producing action when turned back upon itself, its
independence of nonconductors, and seeming lack of mechanical and physiological effect.'

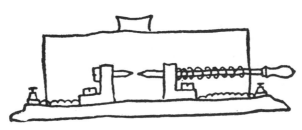

Sketch from Edison's note book for November 23, 1875,
showing how the first 'Black Box' was constructed for his
etheric force experiments.

XIII. Edison and the Wireless

CREDIT for the foundation of wireless has been justly accorded to Professor Heinrich Hertz, but it is a fact that, twelve years before him, Edison had the discovery of that new force within reach. His experiments, lacking the theoretical basis of those by Hertz, were never taken very seriously by the scientific world.

The names of those who heard Mr. Batchelor's description of them in Paris in 1881 are unknown, but it is interesting for me to look back at those days (when I also was in Europe in the interest of Mr. Edison) and see how similar instruments for obtaining a minute gap appeared at different localities. There is no doubt that some credit for stimulating interest in European researches should be given to Mr. Edison, even if it was neglected in this country because of lack of theoretical preparation.

Dr. Heinrich Hertz does not mention Mr. Edison's experiments and we have no indication that he was aware of them or even of the lectures that Mr. Batchelor gave in Paris. But it is a fact that Hertz used a similar apparatus with the same micrometer screw adjustment for detecting the same identical spark; only he called the spark 'electric force,' instead of 'etheric.'

Many of his experiments were exactly like those performed

Drawing from Mr. Edison's patent No. 465,971, showing his ideas for transmitting messages between ships at sea. Filed by him in 1885, two years before the Hertzian waves were announced.

at the earlier date by Mr. Edison, including that of turning the end of the wire on itself.

What is even more remarkable is that Mr. Edison actually sent messages without wires in 1885, two years before Dr. Hertz announced his discovery.

Although Dr. Hertz was doubtless not aware of Mr. Edison's experiments at Newark, Sir Oliver Lodge of England, who was engaged in similar research at the same time as Dr. Hertz, has acknowledged the reference to Mr. Edison. The latter's discovery was, said he, 'a small part of this very thing, only the time was not ripe; theoretical knowledge was not ready for it.'

Lord Kelvin, who acted as chairman at the meeting (held in 1889) when Sir Oliver spoke, declared that 'Edison seems to have noticed something of the kind in what he called the "etheric force." His name "etheric" may have seemed absurd to many people thirteen years ago. But now we are all beginning to call these inductive phenomena etheric.' [1]

As a correspondent wrote to the New York *Sun* on December 1, 1875: 'The new discovery made by Mr. T. A. Edison has touched the outer limits of one of the grandest discoveries of modern times.'

How prophetic that was! In the history of wireless pioneering, in the days before its practical development began, no one raked over the subject more thoroughly than did Mr. Edison. Doctor Hertz's brilliant researches and his mathematical conclusions were responsible for stirring up the interest of others and resulted in the naming of these waves 'Hertzian' in his honor. But it is at least interesting to know that Mr. Edison twelve years previously worked with those same waves.

Indeed, as we study the matter, we are convinced that his name 'etheric force' was prophetic, just as was his prediction that cumbersome appliances would be superseded in connection with the telegraph.

---

[1] Writing again in 1923, Sir Oliver Lodge in *Radio News* said: 'In or about the year 1875, Mr. Edison observed something which at that time could by no means be understood, about the possibility of drawing sparks from insulated objects in the neighborhood of an electrical discharge. He did not pursue the matter, for the time was not ripe; but he called it "etheric force," a name which rather perhaps set our teeth on edge; and none of us thought much of it.

'Silvanus Thompson, however, took the matter up in a half-hearted way and gave a demonstration to the Physical Society of London in, I believe, June, 1876, a paper which I have had a little difficulty in finding in the proceedings of the society. Nothing much came of it though his argument tended to show that the sparks could be accounted for on known principles.'

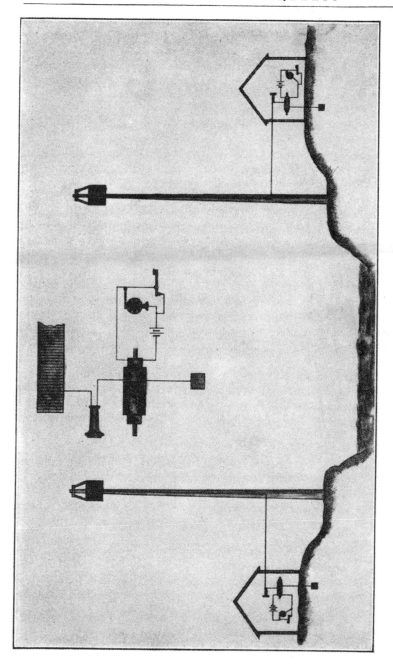

Drawing from Mr. Edison's Patent No. 465,971, sold by him to Marconi. His idea of broadcasting towers is shown.

Let us skip ahead ten years—a privilege which we may enjoy since we can look back on the panorama of more than half a century since those days of 1875. In the year 1885, we find Edison actually patenting a system of wireless *telegraphy*. And even that is before Dr. Hertz announced his discovery of 'electric' force—with its mysterious waves.

Edison's system was based on induction, instead of 'etheric force,' but it was a prophetic picture of what was in store for the near future.

Indeed, his patent (No. 465,971) which was filed May 23, 1885, contained drawings of aerials and antennas long before such things were dreamed of anywhere. ([2])

'I have discovered,' he stated in his application, 'that if sufficient elevation be obtained to overcome the curvature of the earth's surface and to reduce to a minimum the earth's absorption, electric telegraphing or signaling between distant points may be carried on by induction, without the use of wires connecting such distant points.

'This discovery is especially applicable to telegraphing across bodies of water, thus avoiding the use of submarine cables, or for communicating between vessels at sea, or between vessels at sea and points on land. But it is also applicable to electric communication between distant points on land.'

He proceeded to explain that the elevation must be increased to reduce to a minimum the induction-absorbing effect of houses, trees and intervening elevations. He suggested that ships at sea utilize their masts, and that communication between distant points on land be carried on through the use of poles of great height.

As we study this patent and observe its illustrations we must concede that Edison covered most of the elements of modern wireless transmission.

But he went a step further. In 1886, he devised a system whereby passengers could send messages via telegraph direct from moving trains. He used induction, of course, instead of wireless waves. The first railroad to use it as equipment was the Lehigh Valley Railroad.

The point to this reference, however, is that Edison was working on wireless telegraphy in advance of the first an-

---

(2) This patent was purchased from Edison in 1903 by the Marconi Wireless Company.

nouncement of the Hertzian waves, from which our modern wireless history is supposed to date.

When you link together his researches into 'etheric force,' which we know now to have been the wireless spark; his invention and patent of the aerial and antenna later sold to Marconi; and his transmission of messages through the air from moving railroad trains without the use of wires, it would seem almost as if Edison were entitled to mention, at least, in the story of the development of wireless.

But when we go further, as we shall, and learn that he invented the microphone, we find an even stronger reason for including him in it. Finally, when we discover that our radio tubes owe their origin to him, through his researches into what is now known as the 'Edison Effect,' we can no longer deny him his rightful place as one of the great pioneers in the early days of radio development.

In recent years some of that credit is being accorded him. Orrin E. Dunlap, Jr., radio editor of the New York *Times*, in his book *How Radio Works* said:

'On the evening of November 22, 1875, Thomas A. Edison observed a peculiar scintillating spark in one of his experiments with an electromagnet, and after study he proposed the name "etheric force" for the phenomenon.

'The gods of science tried to attract Edison in a radio-way again in 1883 while he was experimenting with incandescent lamps and discovered the phenomenon called the "Edison Effect," fundamental to every radio tube detector today.'

:: :: ::

XIV. The Electric Pen
The Mimeograph

AS MENTIONED in the first of this series of articles, I frequently used the electric pen while working in the law office of Mr. Lowrey on Wall Street. That invention of Edison's was the product of both Newark and Menlo Park, forming a sort of bridge between those two shops.

Edison worked out the principles of the pen while at Newark and took its manufacture with him to Menlo Park. Shortly after I went to work for him I noticed one day a large frame building not far from the Edison homestead. It stood across the railroad tracks on the way to Newark, and looked considerably dilapidated. Some one told me that this was the building in which the electric pen had been manufactured after the Edison headquarters had been transferred to Menlo Park from Newark.

During the years of 1876-77 it was a flourishing plant. Later, the manufacturing rights were bought by the Western Electric Company and the building fell into disuse. It became a roosting place for tramps along the railroad, but, eventually, I was to see the same building rebuilt and restored to use as the first commercial factory for making the Edison incandescent electric light.

To operate his electric pen, Edison used a small electric motor of the impulse type which drew its current from a wet battery of two cells. This was the first electric motor in history to be manufactured commercially and sold in large quantities, and for that reason the device has a peculiar interest to us today.

The first patent covering it was applied for on March 7, 1876, and was granted August 8 of the same year, after he had settled in Menlo Park. It was Patent No. 180,857. Before that time, however, he had brought out an 'autographic press' and what at first was called a 'magnetic pen.' If you will note the letter, reproduced on page 97 just as it was written with the electric pen at No. 10-12 Ward Street, Newark, you will see that it is dated October 6, 1875.

His first patent covered 'the method of printing in permanent semi-fluid ink by puncturing a sheet of paper or similar material with numerous small holes, filling such

A. B. Dick, of Chicago, president of the A. B. Dick Company, which purchased the right to Mr. Edison's electric pen patents from him in 1887.

holes with a semi-fluid ink and pressing the same upon the surface to be printed.'

Edison improved this during 1877, bringing out a 'stencil pen,' a pneumatic stencil pen and a perforating pen. The latter (Patent No. 203,329) was operated by the foot or other convenient power instead of by an electric current; the power was conveyed to the pen by a shaft with universal joints. The pneumatic pen (Patent No. 205,370) could be worked by air, gas or water.

We have in our possession an interesting clipping from the New York *Sun* published during 1878 in which a lecture and exhibition are described, with Edison and his inventions serving as the attractions. Three inventions were shown, of which one was the electric pen.

'A wire is attached to the pen or stencil,' said the reporter, 'and while a person is writing, a steady stream of electricity perforates the paper, making almost invisible little holes corresponding to the formation of the letters. As you write, the needle is projected into the paper at the rate of about 8,000 punctures a minute, forming a perfect autographic paper stencil.

'The stencil is then secured in a frame or press, a felt roller saturated with printer's ink is passed over the face of the stencil, and the perforations become filled with ink, which is deposited upon the paper underneath. From 1,000 to 15,000 copies can be taken from one stencil prepared with this pen.'

I am very happy to state that I regard Mr. Edison as being the father of AUTOGRAPHIC stencil duplication, and therefore he is in my opinion the grandfather of ALL stencil duplication.

Albert B Dick

Part of letter from A. B. Dick to Francis Jehl.

Many advertisements dealing with the pen or some form of it were published in magazines and journals of the time. One told of the 'Woodbury Holder,' designed to keep the electric pen automatically in a vertical position, thus relieving the operator of that necessity. It was, as I well knew, hard on the fingers to keep the pen upright while writing with it.

The Woodbury holder could be attached to any pen and was much liked 'by those who are not expert with it, as it enables anyone to write in their natural handwriting without practice.' Its price was five dollars.

Another device was the so-called 'Reed Pen,' an extremely rapid form of the electric pen devised by Mr. Edison for fast, skillful penmen. Its speed was so great that it sometimes cut the center out of round letters. Then there was the 'Music Ruling Pen,' an electric pen having five needles for the purpose of ruling music. The stencil paper had to be placed on thick, firm cloth or the edges of paper when this particular form of pen was used. Two batteries instead of one were required to supply the current.

After the Western Electric Company acquired the

In this picture the electric pen rests in its holder, which formed a part of the outfit and held the pen when it was not in use. The holder was of metal painted black and made an attractive desk ornament.

selling rights to the pen, it made quite a business of it. In one of its catalogs there was a full page showing parts prices for the pen from a bottle of ink to the complete unit, which cost twenty-five dollars.

Bought separately, a pen cost eight dollars, a wet battery was five dollars and twenty-five cents, a press ranged from eight to seventeen dollars, and a roller from two dollars and twenty-five cents to three dollars and twenty-five cents.

Perhaps you would be interested in the directions given for preparing a wet battery.

'Place the porous clay cups or cells in the glass jars, one with the flat side turned from you and the other toward you. Then attach the zincs and carbons to the rubber discs so that one zinc and one carbon will be secured to the brass posts, and one of each to the iron screws. The brass posts always rest on the rubber discs, the iron screw on the little brass strap.

'Fill the porous cups to within three-quarters of an inch from the top with red fluid.

'Fill the glass jars to within three-quarters of an inch of the top of the porous cups with

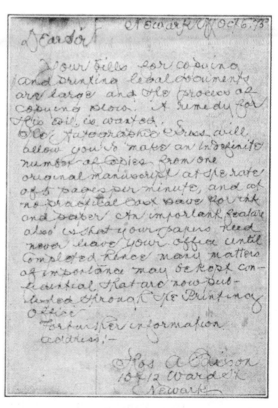

Sample letter written at Newark in 1875 with electric pen.

water, into which a tablespoonful of common sulphuric acid is then poured. Move the porous cups backward and forward in the glass jar a few times to thoroughly mix the acid and water together. If this is not done the acid, which is much heavier than the water, settles to the bottom and does not mix.

Edison Mimeograph No. 1, as brought out in 1887. One of these has been presented to Henry Ford for the Edison Institute by A. B. Dick.

'Slip the battery plates secured to the rubber discs on the upright rod in such a manner that the black plates of carbon shall lower into the porous cells, and the zincs into the water.

'It will be noticed that the zinc and carbon plates on one disc are reversed on the other, hence the necessity of placing the porous cells on opposite sides of the glass jars.

'The collar to which the two discs are secured is provided with a screw sliding up and down in the long groove in the rod, which prevents the collar from turning around, and with a catch which drops into a notch on the opposite side when the discs are lifted high enough, and holds the plates out of the liquids. If they are allowed to remain down when the pen is not in use, the sulphuric acid and water would soon eat the zincs away. To prevent this, they should always be lifted out after using.

'After considerable use the mercury with which the zincs are amalgamated becomes eaten off, and the action of the acid upon the pure zinc is more intense, causing what is termed "boiling." This can be obviated by removing the zincs from the discs, washing off all superfluous matter, and allowing them to remain in the acid and water a few moments; then remove and add a few drops of quicksilver to them, which will immediately spread over the surface, making them good as new. By this precaution, zincs will last a long time.

'The battery fluid should last from one to two weeks,

according to the amount of work it has to perform. When it is in daily use, for an hour or so at a time, it is recommended that it be changed once a week. Operators will have to be guided by experience.'

With the coming of the typewriter and the subsequent use of that machine in preparing stencils, the electric pen passed from use. At one time, however, more than 60,000 were in offices, and its use had spread outside the United States. It could be found in many government offices in Washington, D. C., as well as in the majority of such large industries as the railroads.

Exclusive licenses under the two principal patents mentioned above, No. 180,857 and No. 196,747, were sought and obtained from Edison in 1887, shortly after he left Menlo Park, by the A. B. Dick Company, of Chicago. This company, through A. B. Dick, its president, had entered into the business of manufacturing and distributing the 'mimeograph,' which embodied an autographic stencil and a method of printing therefrom.

Because of his earlier patents in that field, Edison has been called by Mr. Dick 'the grandfather of autographic stencil duplication.' Since purchasing the rights, the Dick company has served as the manufacturer and distributor of the 'Edison Mimeograph,' which of course has been greatly improved since that day.

The electric pen was not confined to circular letters and the like, but could be found in restaurants where it was used for making up the bill of fare. I well remember buying a book on 'How to Learn to Telegraph,' containing many different diagrams of sounders, relays and switches, which were all printed by the Edison Electric Pen process.

Then, there was a comic sheet, which was circulated by some sort of telegraphic fraternity. It was also prepared with the Edison pen and you would be surprised at the artistic designs which could be produced by this little device.

Among the treasures in the Edison collection at Dearborn is a scrapbook in which the letter shown on page 97 was found. The book contains pictures, calling cards, letterheads, invoice forms, menus, and many other examples of work actually done with the electric pen back in 1875. The book was located in Port Huron, Michigan.

XV. Edison and the Telephone
Introduction

BEFORE describing Edison's contributions to the telephone and his assistance in its development, if you will permit me, I would like to give you a hasty picture of the background and repeat a few of the predictions made before the day of Bell's great invention.

As I look back at the year of the great Centennial in Philadelphia, when I was still a lad in my teens, I am able to recall the world as it was at the dawn of the present age. Although Bell's telephone was then the universal theme of conversation, mankind, as in the case of other great inventions, had been expecting it for many years.

The other day I received from my friend, J. W. Schroeder, of East Orange, New Jersey, a clipping which quoted from a

Model of Bell's first telephone.

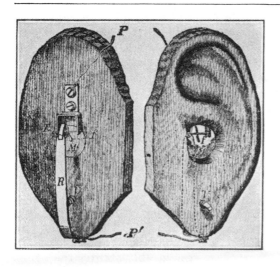

Reis' telephone receiver made in shape of human ear.

Boston newspaper of 1865:

'A man about 46 years of age giving the name of Joshua Coppersmith, has been arrested in New York for attempting to extort funds from ignorant and superstitious people by exhibiting a device which he says will convey the human voice any distance over metallic wires so that it will be heard by the listener at the other end.

'He calls the instrument a "telephone" which is obviously intended to imitate the word "telegraph" and win the confidence of those who know of the success of the latter instrument without understanding the principles on which it is based. Well-informed people know that it is impossible to transmit the human voice over wires as may be done with dots and dashes and signals of the Morse code, and that, were

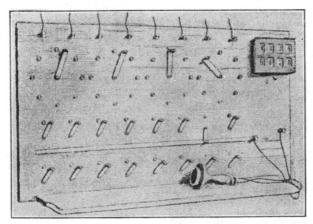

The first telephone exchange at New Haven, Conn. It had about 30 subscribers.

it possible to do so, the thing would be of no practical value.

'The authorities who apprehended this criminal are to be congratulated and it is to be hoped that his punishment will be prompt and fitting, that it may serve as an example to other *conscienceless schemers* who enrich themselves at the expense of their fellow creatures.'

The year 1865 was only eleven years in advance of the telephone. Go back to 1688 when Robert Hooke, Fellow of the Royal Society of England, published a work entitled *Monographia; or some Physiological Description of Minute Bodies made by Magnifying Glasses, with Observations and Inquiries Thereupon.* In it you will find this prediction:

'I can assure the reader that I have, with the help of a distended wire, propagated the sound to a very considerable distance in an instant, or with as seemingly quick a motion as that of light, at least incomparably swifter than that which at the same time was propagated through the air; and this not only in a straight line or direct, but in one bended in many angles.'

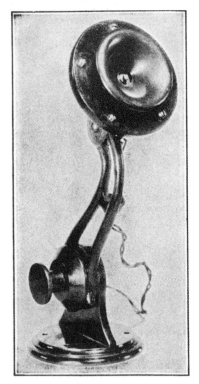

One of Edison's experimental transmitters.

The great Doctor Reis, who cleared the way for Bell and all the others, died in 1874, too soon to see the substantiation of his belief.

Perhaps the prize prophecy of all was in the address by Sir Edward Thornton, British minister to this country, at a banquet given in 1868 to Professor Morse, inventor of the telegraph. Among those present were William Cullen Bryant and a long list of notables.

'Should I have the good fortune to live to the age of the venerable professor, I still hope to see some such improvements as will enable us to carry on the *viva voce*

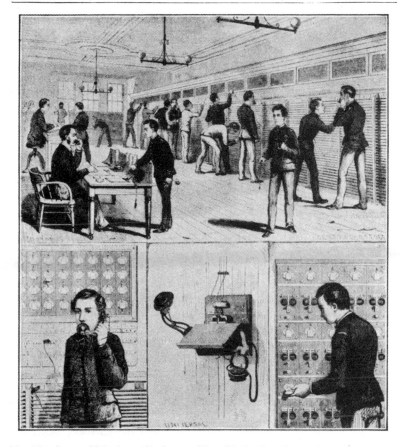

The Merchant's Telephone Exchange, New York City. Note the Edison transmitter on the left of the instrument, and the Phelps receiver hanging on the right. (From *Scientific American*, January 10, 1880.)

conversation by means of the Atlantic cable (laughter). We shall then have merchants on this side of the water discussing their affairs with those on the other at so much a minute. We shall hear, perchance, of some love-stricken youth of London or Paris whispering soft nothings along the cable to one of those bewitching sirens of New York at so much an hour (laughter), she tempting him all the while to throw himself into the gulf which separates them (laughter). We shall have statesmen, aye, and in those days of progress, even stateswomen (laughter and applause) discussing international questions across the water at so much a conference (laughter).'

Edison's most notable contribution to the telephone was the transmitter, although, as I have already told you in Chapter XI, he made a perfect magneto telephone receiver at Newark ahead of Bell, and, as I shall explain later, other important contributions. After Bell showed the world the way in which to use the telephone receiver, it was fitting that to Edison should go the distinction of supplying the almost equally important adjunct, the transmitter.

Did you ever stop to think that whenever you talk over the telephone today, you are using one of Edison's inventions? His connection with that useful instrument is seldom recalled though all of the credit for the transmitter belongs to him.

The present-day transmitter still utilizes the principle that Edison discovered. Let me describe it as it is given today in one of the publications of the American Telephone and Telegraph Company:

'A circular piece of mica forms the front end of the box-like button of the transmitter. This is a highly essential part of the instrument, since the grains of carbon which it contains alternately are compressed and loosened up as the diaphragm is vibrated by the speaker's voice. This produces a continual change in the resistance to the flow of the telephonic current, which accordingly varies in strength, thus copying the voice sounds and carrying them to the receiver.'[1]

The first central telephone exchange is said to have opened at Richmond, Virginia, on April 1, 1879. It is interesting to note that during the same year what is said to have been the first central telephone exchange in England was opened in London, using Edison instruments. In the following year a detailed description of an exchange controlled by our old friend the Gold and Stock Telegraph Company was published in the *Scientific American*, in which appeared the picture shown on page 103 and the following:[2]

'The telephone shown in the lower central figure (of the accompanying cut) scarcely needs description, its construction and the details of its operation having been repeatedly described in these columns. The adjustable arm carries an *Edison* carbon button transmitter, connected with the primary wire of an induction coil concealed beneath the desk.'

---

(1)   *Telephone Almanac*, 1931.
(2)   *Scientific American*, January 10, 1880.

XVI. Menlo Park in 1876
Early Experiments

SEVERAL reasons have been advanced why Edison moved his activities from Newark to Menlo Park in 1876. My personal belief is that he needed a more secluded place where he could pursue his experiments without so many interruptions and distractions.

The explanation which he himself gives is that it happened because of some trouble he had over his rent. He had rented the top floor of a padlock factory in Newark on a monthly basis and for a time used it as a small shop. When he didn't need it longer, he notified the landlord that he would surrender it at the end of the month.

'I paid the rent, moved out and delivered the keys,' said Edison. 'Shortly afterward I was served with a paper, probably a judgment, wherein I was to pay nine months' additional rent. There was some law, it seems, that made a monthly renter liable for a year. This seemed so unjust that I determined to get out of a place that permitted such injustice.'[1]

Menlo Park was at that time nothing more than a spot on the map. Situated several miles below Rahway on the Pennsylvania Railroad, its principal attraction was a quiet atmosphere of peace. It was selected by the inventor after an examination of several different places. One by one he visited them all on different Sundays, accompanied by two of his Newark assistants.

As I have already mentioned, the eminence was the highest point between New York City and Philadelphia. He bought the site on December 29, 1875, and then purchased another tract nearby, 150 x 300 feet, for his residence.

By the spring of 1876 he was firmly settled here and ready for his experiments. Before leaving Newark he told his friend, Dr. George Beard, the electrician, that he proposed to invent some minor thing every ten days and some big thing every six months. Beard recalled this conversation several years afterward and confessed that the prediction had seemed a 'wild one' at the time. Strange to say, Edison more than fulfilled it.

Batchelor, Kruesi, Dean, Ott, as well as other Newark

(1) *Edison, His Life and Inventions*—Dyer & Martin, Vol. I. p. 267.

Back page of folder issued by the Bell Telephone Company at Boston soon after that company was organized. Bell's name appears as its 'electrician.'

workers, came down with Edison to Menlo Park and cast their fortunes with his. Bergmann (as I have stated once before, I believe) went in the other direction. He decided to try out his luck in New York City as a manufacturer of electrical accessories. Establishing himself at 104 Wooster Street, he built alarm-bell systems, at that time a popular electrical invention.

As the fruits of Edison's labors —the phonograph, carbon telephone, chalk telephone and incandescent light—followed one another from the new laboratory, Bergmann's shop branched into an important manufacturing business and Bergmann became a famous figure in his field.

Alexander Graham Bell about time he invented the telephone.

The long gray laboratory had to serve as both office and shop for Edison, as well as experimental headquarters. Power was furnished by an upright steam engine in the rear room on the ground floor. The place was lighted by illuminating gas made from gasoline by a machine which stood in a shed back of the main building.

During the last summer at Newark much of Edison's interest had been taken up by experiments in telephony, together with acoustic and harmonic telegraphy. It was not until November, 1875, that he discovered 'etheric force,' and turned his attention for a time to exploring that strange phenomenon. But before long he returned to telephony. He had been supplied by his friend Orton, president of the Western Union, with foreign scientific papers describing the achievements of the brilliant Doctor Reis of Germany in this field.

A monument has been erected in Frankfort to Doctor Reis as the inventor of the telephone, owing to the fact that, fifteen years before the date just mentioned, he had built several forms of electrical telephonic apparatus in the German town. His apparatus was crude, of course, and was based on the make-and-break principle. Every time a sound went through it, the circuit was made and broken. The instruments could not be kept in adjustment more than a few seconds at a time, and the whole thing was not practicable; yet

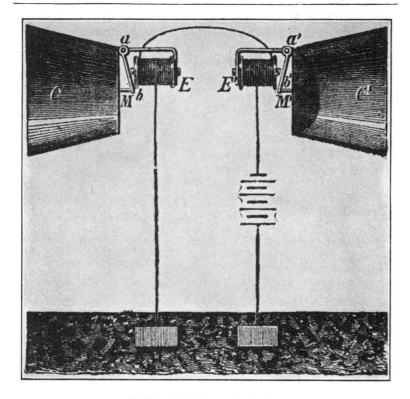

Model of Bell's second telephone.

Reis comes down in history as the first man who attempted to transmit sound by electricity.

One of Edison's first experiments was directed at curing this defect. He sought to keep the gap closed by the use of a drop of water, later several drops. However, the water decomposed and the defect remained uncorrected.

'Some time in or about the month of July, 1875,' he wrote, 'I began experimenting with a system of multiple telegraphy which had for its basis the transmission of acoustic vibrations. Being furnished at the same time by the Hon. William Orton, president of the Western Union Telegraph Company, with a translated description from a foreign scientific journal of the Reis telephone, I also began a series of experiments with a view of producing an articulating telephone, carrying on both

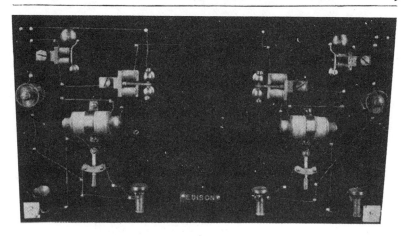

Patent office model of 'speaking telegraph,' as Mr. Edison styled his Patent No. 203,-016.   This model may now be seen on one of the shelves at the restored laboratory at Dearborn.

series simultaneously, by the aid of my two assistants, Messrs. Batchelor and Adams.'([2])

He described an early experiment with drops of water thus: 'In one of the first experiments I included a simplified Reis transmitter having a platinum screw facing the diaphragm, in a circuit containing twenty cells of battery, and the resonant receiver, and then placed a drop of water between the points; the results, however, when the apparatus was in action, were unsatisfactory.   Rapid decomposition of the water took place and a deposit of sediment was left on the platinum.'

I shall leave a narration of his further experiments to a succeeding chapter in order to record now the achievements of another young man who had also learned of Dr. Reis' discoveries.   His name was Alexander Graham Bell and he was a teacher of vocal physiology—elocution.

The Reis telephonic apparatus had been brought to America by a prominent physicist in 1868 and exhibited in Cooper Union.   Professor Joseph Henry of the Smithsonian Institution obtained a set for his exhibit and when Bell visited the institute in 1875 seeking data on harmonic telegraphy, it was shown to him.

During his visit, Bell filed an application for a patent on a

(2) *The Speaking Telegraph*—Prescott, p. 218.

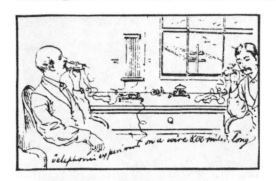
Cartoon showing telephone experiments at Menlo Park.

multiple telegraph, which up to that time had occupied his attention. Also, he met Orton, who invited him to bring his apparatus to New York City where all the facilities of the Western Union would be placed at his disposal.

Subsequently, Bell spent several week-ends in Manhattan until he had the unhappy experience of learning that his telegraph was in conflict with one which had been patented by Elisha Gray, chief electrician for the Western Electric Company.

Soon Bell's attention became riveted on the possibility of transmission of human speech by telegraph. During that year he constructed his first pair of magneto telephones and in February, 1876, applied for his first telephonic patent. In May he read a paper describing it before the National Academy of Sciences in Boston and, in June, it was shown at the Philadelphia Centennial.

Despite the furor that his invention caused, he had difficulty in getting an operating company under way and finally offered to sell his patent to Orton for one hundred thousand dollars. For once, at least, Orton seems to have been shortsighted, or else believed that the Bell patents never would amount to much. He refused the offer and, according to one story, remarked:

'What use could this company make of an electrical toy?'

It is true that the telephone up to then had not been a success commercially. During May, 1877, Bell lectured in New York City and Orton began to wonder if he had acted wisely in refusing the 'toy.' His chief electrical expert at that time was Franklin L. Pope, whom you will recall from my previous chapter on 'Pope, Edison & Co.'([3]) Orton summoned Pope and asked him to compile a report on the fundamentals

(3) See Chapter VII.

of the new speaking device, as it might have considerable value in the future.

Pope and his assistants made an exhaustive research over several months and at length recommended the purchase of the Bell patents.   Again Orton failed to go ahead, perhaps because he knew Edison had already filed an application for a patent covering his 'carbon telephone,' giving to the world the transmitter, and Edison was under a contract that had been signed in March with the Western Union.

Orton bought the rights of Gray who had filed a caveat in the patent office covering his ideas in the transmission of speech by electricity a few hours after Bell's application had been filed.   This remarkable coincidence played an important part in protracted litigation in later years.   Orton retained Gray as well as Edison in the hope of making a practical telephone which would not infringe on Bell's patents.

But we are galloping far ahead of our story.   I have tried to give you a general view of Bell's development of the telephone because, after all, he invented the first device and deserves all the credit for his achievements.   I don't want you to think, as you read the next few chapters, and find so many references to Edison and the Western Union, that I am ignorant of Bell's great work.   This narrative happens to deal chiefly with Edison and it is his work on the telephone, rather than that of Bell, that I shall describe from now on.

Birthplace of the telephone, 109 Court Street, Boston. On the top floor, Bell carried on his experiments in 1875.

XVII. The Invention of the Carbon Telephone

THE year 1877, which just preceded my coming to Menlo Park, was marked by two notable inventions there by Edison—the carbon telephone transmitter or microphone, and the phonograph.

Announced one year previously at the Philadelphia Centennial by Alexander Graham Bell, the telephone was still imperfect and was attracting the attention of electricians and scientists in every part of the world, in the effort to improve it and make it practical.

The field of usefulness of the telephone as invented by Doctor Bell was circumscribed. The same instrument was both receiver and transmitter. The person talking into it produced sound waves that vibrated the goldbeater's skin diaphragm, on which rested the hinged iron armature that

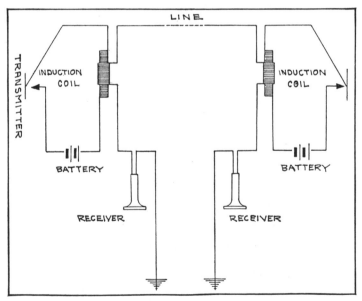

Diagram showing how Edison changed the telephone by adding the transmitter and introducing a primary circuit from an induction coil.

faced the electromagnet of the telephone.

This induced in the coil, or, rather, superimposed, very weak electric impulses which passed over the wire, according to Bell's theory, to the electromagnet coil at the other end of the line. They energized the coil and vibrated armature and diaphragm in accordance with the impulses, thus reproducing the spoken words.

At first Bell used a battery that was in direct connection with the magnet, coils and line. The superimposed currents were so faint that the sounds were almost inaudible at the other end.

If I am not mistaken, it was Professor Dolbear of Tufts College

William Orton, president of Western Union Telegraph Company and friend of Edison. It was he who enlisted Edison's aid in perfecting the telephone.

who proposed using a permanent magnet instead of the electromagnet, thus doing away with the battery. The magneto telephone receiver resulted.

There were many reasons why the magneto telephone could not be generally used as receiver and transmitter combined, and it was soon evident that a separate transmitter was required. Scientists and electricians everywhere applied themselves to telephony. It remained for Edison to find the solution and give to the instrument its practical and commercial usefulness.

Edison devised the transmitter, separated it from the receiver, and by making varying resistance possible and by use of an induction coil, extended the length of the lines for hundreds of

Edison's Carbon Rheostat. B represents base; fifty or more silken discs filled with fine particles of graphite; C plate holding down discs; D revolving screw which broadened into disc marked F; G is index scale.

miles, until today it is possible to talk over them almost anywhere.

I have already told you something of his researches into acoustic telegraphy and of how he had the telephone within his grasp, had he but known it, one year before it was announced.

Edison's carbon rheostat as it appears today in the restored laboratory. See preceding page for cutaway view.

But he did not know it and has given Doctor Bell full credit for the invention. What Edison did was to invent another instrument that was equally important. The Bell instrument is a delicate hearer, while the Edison transmitter possesses a good lung and speaks loudly, so that each does its share of the work, and, together, they have formed an ideal combination and have made the telephone a universal success.

You may not realize it, but it is a fact that, for a long time, Edison's name was stamped on telephone instruments, as was Bell's. If you are further interested, you might read the Federal court's decision in the famous Berliner patent suit, copy of which is in the restored laboratory. In it you will find the following:

Device invented by Edison for testing effect of voice on carbon transmitter. Note the mouthpiece, the connections for the current, and the adjustable screw which varied the pressure on the carbon. It may now be seen on the second floor of the restored laboratory.

'The carbon electrode was the invention of Edison . . . Edison, by countless experiments, succeeded in advancing the art . . . The carbon transmitter displaced Bell's magnetic transmitter and, under several forms of construction, remains the

On one of the shelves in the southwest corner of the second floor of the restored laboratory may be seen a wooden cup-shaped object in which the name Edison is imprinted. The bowl is covered by a thin metal diaphragm and inside are the coils of an electro-magnet. This was made by Mr. Edison for a receiver of the acoustic telegraph and incorporates the principle of the telephone receiver; in fact, it reproduces the voice perfectly. On the lid is the name of Murray, Mr. Edison's former partner in Newark, who manufactured the device. Antedates Bell's telephone.

only commercial instrument . . . The discovery of the availability of carbon was unquestionably invention, and it resulted in the "first practical success in the art." '

To understand Edison's work, you must go back to the Ward Street shop in Newark four years earlier, when he was struggling to perfect the quadruplex telegraph.

In the working of that system it was necessary to balance the electric current perfectly, and the common method of accomplishing it took too long.

To overcome this, he invented a new kind of rheostat—the carbon rheostat. The old method was to employ a rheostat containing a great length of resistance wire, of which more or less could be thrown into or cut out of the electric circuit by inserting or withdrawing plugs or keys. It usually occupied a long time, which could not always be spared.

In his new instrument, Edison embodied for the first time the principles that later he used in the carbon telephone. He screwed a hollow cylinder of insulating material upright onto a brass base, and placed within its walls fifty or more silken discs that had been well saturated with sizing, filled with fine particles of graphite, and dried.

These were packed down one above the other by a plate which could be raised or lowered from above by a revolving screw. The lower end of the screw rested on the plate, and the upper end broadened into a disc with a knife edge, which extended to a scale on the side of the rheostat and served as an index to show the degree of compression to which the silk discs were subjected.

He placed the instrument in circuit by connecting a cap (through which the screw passed) to one wire, and the base to another.

He found that the compression of this series of discs increased their conductivity; and that a lessening of it increased their resistance. Thus he could obtain any degree of resistance desired by turning the screw one way or the other. The instrument made it possible to vary the resistance from 400 to 6,000 ohms.

That discovery was utilized by him when he undertook to improve the telephone and aided him greatly in accomplishing his object. But before describing his efforts, let me rehearse briefly how he came to undertake it.

I have already told you about his friend, Orton, the president of the Western Union. An attempt to introduce the Bell telephone commercially had failed, and Mr. Orton believed that Edison could correct its faults. If so, it would enable the Western Union to enter this new field which, in some respects, threatened to compete with the telegraph. He secured reports of the experiments performed by Dr. Reis as I have already described, and gave them to Edison.

Edison had been studying acoustic telegraphy, as I have said, and was familiar with the use of tuning forks along the lines on which Doctor Bell, Elisha Gray and others had been working. By now he was settled in Menlo Park and eager to tackle the problem.

The path before him was a long, laborious one. Thousands of pages of manuscript were to be written before he hit upon

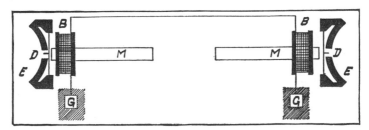

Diagram showing Bell telephone system before Edison made his contributions. Note that the same instrument is used for both transmitter and receiver. *M* represents permanent magnet which was added by Dolbear. *D* is the diaphragm and *E* the receiver-transmitter.

Apparatus devised by Edison to test materials for use in transmitter. An arm extends from the support on the right to the center, forming a cap over a cup in which the materials were placed. In the rear are different weights which were placed on the cap to vary the pressure. Note electrical connections to admit current.

the secret. He experimented with drops of water (as Elisha Gray had done), acidulated solutions, sponges, paper and felting, saturated with various solutions, placed between the discs. Knife edges were substituted for the discs.

When none of his efforts proved successful, he turned to thin films of graphite and white Arkansas oilstone, on ground glass.

'It was here,' he said, later, 'that I first succeeded in conveying over wires many articulated sentences.'

Metal springs were attached to the diaphragm and numerous other devices were made to cut in and out of circuit more or less of the film, but the disturbances which the devices themselves caused in the vibrations of the diaphragm prevented the realization of any practical result.

One of his assistants, however, continued the experiments without interruption until early in 1877, when he applied the peculiar property which semiconductors have of varying their resistance with pressure.

His first experiment along this line was in his laboratory on January 20 of that year, and was described by him during the Berliner patent suit as follows:

'It consisted of a diaphragm and three platina points immersed in a dish containing loose carbon. The talking, though very poor in quality, was of a sufficient volume that it could be heard through the teeth when an ordinary Morse relay, the magnet of which was included in a circuit, was held against the teeth.'

His notebook entry as quoted during that famous trial is interesting:

'Three platina points don't seem to work any better than

one point; get it very good on a Western Union relay through my teeth, but I think I could get it better if I had an adjustment to it, for Charley can't hold it steady enough.' ([1])

An apparatus was constructed which you may look at now, if you choose, on one of the shelves in the restored laboratory. It was provided with a diaphragm that had a yielding spring in its center, faced with platinum. Below this, in a cup of metal, he placed the substance to be tested.

Thus it lay between two metallic plates and a circuit was established with a wet battery furnishing the current. A galvanometer was also brought into the circuit to record the variations. Weights of different quantities were placed in turn upon the upper metallic plate, so that they pressed downward against the substance in the center. A corresponding deflection was at once recorded by the galvanometer needle, showing a variation in the resistance of the substance. As additional weights were added, the deflection could be measured and thus the various changes of resistance.

With this instrument he began his search for the substance which would show a resistance that varied in precise accordance with the amount of pressure applied. Such a substance would make a proportionate variation in the electric current and prove ideal in transferring human speech over wires by means of vibrations.

At first he tried solids. Finally he abandoned them all and substituted fibers which would conduct electricity, floss silk coated with plumbago, and so on. These results were better. He got a larger volume of sound, but the articulation was not as clear as over the magnetic telephone of Doctor Bell. Also, the instrument was always getting out of order.

His first application for a patent in telephony was filed in April of that year and embodied the principles of separate transmitter.

_____
(1) Charles Batchelor.

THE FIRST COMMERCIAL
TELEPHONE LINE
Apr. 4th 1877

XVIII. Perfecting the Transmitter
The Search for Carbon

IN MY previous articles I have told you how Edison came to embark on his experiments with the telephone, and how he separated the receiver from the transmitter and applied for a patent covering the latter device. We come now to his second great contribution to the telephone.

Edison discovered that the difference in the resistance caused by varying the pressure upon the semiconductor was exceedingly small. In a wire circuit of such large resistance as that connecting two telephones, it was a very small factor. He asked himself if he couldn't get better results by introducing a primary circuit from an induction coil, in which the importance of even a slight change of resistance would be much amplified.

He tried the experiment and it failed. Fortunately, he didn't give up the idea. He investigated to see why, and decided that the great resistance of the semiconductors was the cause. This led him to the conclusion that if he could find some means of reducing their normal resistance to a few ohms, and still effect a difference in its resistance by the pressure due to the vibrating diaphragm, he could use it in the primary circuit of an induction coil.

To accomplish this, he constructed a transmitter in which a button of a semiconducting substance was placed between two platinum discs in a kind of cup-shaped holder. Between the button and the discs was placed a small

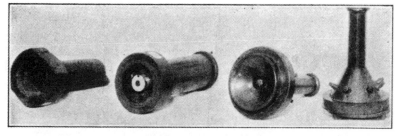

Two on left represent magneto principle; and two on right the dynamic principle used today in dynamic speakers and transmitters. These may be seen in restored laboratory.

piece of rubber tubing, slightly flattened. By it, the vibrations on the diaphragm produced the requisite pressure on the outer disc, thereby varying the resistance of the button which was included now in the primary circuit of an induction coil. He applied for a patent on the use of the induction coil in telephony in December, 1877.([1])

Plumbago was found to give excellent results as a button but the volume of sound was still unsatisfactory. A search was again instituted, and oxides, sulphides and many other partial conductors were tried, one after the other.

Cross section of Edison's transmitter in which small piece of rubber tubing was used between button and platinum discs. Tube is visible just above opening for mouthpiece. This model may be seen on second floor of restored laboratory.

Among them was a small quantity of lampblack which had been taken from a smoking petroleum lamp chimney and preserved because of its intense black color. Out of it a button was made and tested. It was found to possess the remarkable property of changing its resistance with pressure, the ratios of the changes corresponding exactly with the pressure.

⌡ Introduced into the transmitter, it gave excellent results. The articulation was distinct, and the volume of sound sev-

_____

(1) Patent No. 203,013.

Experimental transmitter made by Edison to test use of induction coil, which may be seen inside box below mouthpiece. This model may be seen on the second floor of the restored laboratory.

eral times greater than with the magnetic telephones. It was found that its resistance could be varied from 300 ohms to the fractional part of a single ohm by pressure alone. In February, 1878, he applied for a patent covering the use of lampblack in the transmitter.([2])

The next objective was to find some way to get rid of the rubber tube, which became flattened by the continual vibrations and hence lost its elasticity.

Another startling discovery followed. Edison found that his instrument, unlike all others, did not require any vibration of the diaphragm. The sound waves could be transformed into electrical impulses without the movement of any intervening mechanism.

A metal spiral spring was substituted for the rubber tube but it gave off a musical tone itself, and interfered somewhat with the vocal sounds. He tried thicker springs and each time got better articulation. Finally, he took out the spring altogether and inserted a solid substance and got the best results of all.

Well, he said to himself, the whole question is one of pressure!

(2) Patent No. 203,015.

Transmitter model using graphite instead of lampblack. On shelf in restored laboratory.

It isn't necessary for the diaphragm to vibrate at all!

And so he substituted a heavy diaphragm one-sixteenth of an inch thick and fastened carbon button and plate tightly together. He found that he had discovered the secret; the articulation was perfect and the volume of sound so great that conversation carried on in a whisper three feet from the telephone was clearly heard and understood at the other end of the line.

Some idea of the extent of Edison's researches for materials best adapted to use in his buttons may be obtained from an account of them published in Prescott's work on the speaking telephone about 1879.

'Mr. Edison has endeavored to obtain an approximation as to the number of points of contact on the lampblack button now used. In order to accomplish this purpose, he first placed a Rutherford diffraction grating under the microscope having 17,291 lines ruled on speculum metal within a space of one inch, and by the side of this a button of lampblack; then, by changing from one to the other, he calculated that there were not less than 10,000,000 of points upon the surface of the button, nearly all of which were constantly in use when subjected to the sonorous vibrations. Had the Rutherford grating been ruled both ways there would have been 298,-000,000 of points . . .

'The only defect, if so it may be called, in the button made of lampblack, is that it is somewhat friable; but Mr. Edison's experience goes to prove that if the telephone is made in a proper manner, so that no part of it will, when under the effect of the sonorous waves, vibrate and hammer the button, it will last for months, and, as far as can be seen, will continue to last as long as the instrument that holds it; but if the instrument is ₊so devised that the armatures are allowed to hammer the button, or if the initial pressure is very light and the instrument receives a violent concussion

Sketch of Edison's transmitter from laboratory notebook, February 9, 1877.

(for instance, by being dropped on the floor), the button is liable to crack, but even in this case the volume of sound is not materially lessened. Mr. Edison has attempted to harden these buttons by mixing the lampblack with sugar, tar and other substances previous to moulding, and after moulding subjecting them to a high temperature. This treatment makes them hard but inelastic, and yet far superior to any other substance which he has tried.

'The value of different substances to be used as buttons in the telephone is given below, the first mentioned being the best, and the others in the order given:

Lampblack
Hyperoxide of lead
Iodide of copper
Graphite
Gas carbon
Platinum black

'Finely divided materials which do not oxidize in the air, such as osmium, ruthenium, silicon, boron, iridium and platinum, give results proportionate to this minute division, but many of them are such good conductors that it is necessary to mix some very fine nonconducting material with them before moulding.

'All the conducting oxides, sulphides, iodides, and nearly every metal finely divided has been tried by Mr. Edison, in various states of divisibility and mixed with various substances. Liquids in porous buttons of finely divided nonconducting material render these particles conducting, and they, consequently, act in the same manner but, of course, owing to the formation of gas, polarization, et cetera, they are objectionable.'

I have already mentioned the electrical shops for experiments and the manufacture and repair of telegraphic equipment which were maintained by the Western Union Telegraph Company in New York City. As its general counsel, Mr. Lowrey had been able to arrange to get me a course of training in them, before I came to Menlo Park. The superintendent in charge was a well-known inventor, G. M. Phelps, who had evolved several modifications on the Bell (or magneto) telephone. My first job was on his so-called 'pony' telephone.

It was during that training course that I first came in contact with Edison's carbon transmitter. Mr. Lowrey had

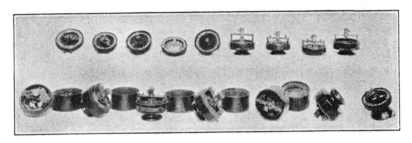

Rows of experimental transmitter models as they appear on one of the shelves on the
second floor of the restored laboratory.

given me a note introducing me to the superintendent, and I
went over to Church Street to look for the Western Union
works.

I had to wait some time before being admitted to Mr.
Phelps' office and was referred by him, after he had read the
note, to an assistant, Mr. Haskins. From the office we went
out into the shop adjoining the office which had all the
features of a mechanical laboratory. Here Mr. Phelps himself
would work when not in his office.

The first job assigned to me was that of drilling holes in a
piece of curved steel, which afterward was to be hard-tem-
pered and magnetized. It was, I soon learned, a part of the
magneto receiving telephone known as the 'Phelps pony
receiver.'

From time to time, my job was changed and within two
weeks or so I had tried my hand on nearly all the separate
parts that were made here for the telephone.

My next assignment was to work on the Phelps 'crown'
receiver which had six permanent magnets, similar to the
single one used in the 'pony' type. It was then that Haskins
told me the Western Union had bought the patent rights to a
carbon transmitting telephone invented by Edison. The
company was planning to set up different kinds of unit telephone stations, using the Phelps pony or crown receiver in
connection with Edison's transmitter.

That was my introduction to the transmitter. Later,
Haskins told me that it had brought out the importance of
the magneto receiver, since, without it, the latter could
have no universal value.

The experiments in progress in this shop at that time were

most interesting to a young student. Among other things, Mr. Phelps was experimenting with a new kind of generator which had revolving contacts instead of brushes. One day, when Haskins was helping his superior, I saw him get such a shock that he went sprawling across the floor.

While here I was given an opportunity to work on telegraph instruments, sounders and relays, as well as resistance boxes and galvanometers like those used by telegraph engineers for testing lines. In November, I went to Menlo Park to join Mr. Edison within the very building where the carbon transmitter had been perfected.

By the time I arrived at the latter place, all of the work, of course, had been completed, and now the carbon buttons used in the transmitter were being manufactured here. Between New York City and Philadelphia, and New York City and Washington, D. C., as well as other points, tests had been made using Western Union wires. In many of them Edison himself took part. Others who participated were President Orton and W. K. Vanderbilt.

The noises were so great, he said, that not a word could be heard when the Bell receiver was used as a transmitter between New York City and Newark.

Mr. Phelps' name figured quite prominently in many of Edison's early telephone experiments as did that of Henry Bentley, president of the Local Telegraph Company, of Philadelphia. In some tests of the carbon transmitter, a line was used between Philadelphia and New York City.

The terminus in the former city was the office of Mr. Bentley's company; that in the latter was the Western Union. Mr. Edison remained at New York City with Orton, G. M. Phelps, Jr., and others; Phelps, Sr., was with Bentley in Philadelphia. (Phelps, Sr., was engaged in trying out his magneto-telephone at the same time as Edison was testing his transmitter.)

'The circuit used was 106 miles in length,' says an old account of the test.([3]) 'The line passed through a maze of wires, crossing five streams in cables, and in New York City passing underground to the Western Union office, which it entered with a mass of other wires.

'The experiments were highly successful, the carbon transmitter working perfectly, every word spoken at one end

(3) *Journal of Telegraph*, August 1, 1878.

of the line being clearly articulated at the other. A number of receivers were attached to the line in Philadelphia, some of them being of the Phelps magneto pattern. The latter received just as clearly and distinctly as the others.'

While working on his telephone transmitter, Edison's fertile brain discovered numerous other ways in which the carbon button could be used. One of these was in his old field, telegraphy. He thought out an idea for a new kind of telegraph relay and had John Kruesi fashion one for him like the sketch below.

This ingenious instrument was styled a 'pressure relay.' It was based upon a principle new to telegraph systems. Edison took advantage of carbon's property of changing resistance under varying pressure. Thin discs of silk or other suitable material were saturated with carbon and placed upon the cupped poles of an electromagnet. The armature, which was provided with a connection to a local battery wire, was laid upon the discs.

Included in a local circuit were the cores of the magnet, the discs and the armature, along with an ordinary sounder and several battery cells. The relay magnet was inserted in the main line in the usual manner.

The main difference between this relay and those hitherto used was that it repeated, or translated, from one circuit into another the relative strengths of the original one. If a weak current circulated upon the line in which this relay had been inserted, the attraction for its armature was slight and the pressure on the discs small; consequently the current circulating within the second circuit was weak. The reverse was also true.

'It is probably the only device yet invented which will allow of the translation of signals of variable strengths from one circuit into another, by the use of batteries,' said the *Journal of the Telegraph*.

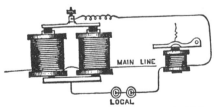

Diagram of Edison's 'pressure relay.' From *Journal of the Telegraph*, June 1, 1877.

this agreement and to permit said Edison at all
proper times to inspect such accounts and
otherwise to take account of the number of articles machines or devices being used by the
Company under this agreement.

Ninth: This agreement shall not be con-
strued to apply to any improvements upon the
system of chemical telegraphy sometimes called
Automatic or fast telegraphy and shall take
effect from March 1st 1877.

In Witness whereof the parties to
these presents have hereunto set their hands and
seals the day and year first above written

The Western Union Telegraph Company
By Wm Orton
A R Brewer   President
Secy
                    Thos. A. Edison

Witness as to
signature of Thos.
A. Edison.
    A. R. Brewer

State of New York,
City & County of New York ss.

On this twenty third day of March
in the year 1877, before me personally
came Thomas A. Edison, to me known to be
one of the individuals described in and who
executed the foregoing instrument, and
acknowledges that he executed the same for
the uses and purposes therein mentioned,

Clarence Cary
Notary Public, in & for
the City & County of New York

Photostatic copy of back page of contract between Edison and Western Union Telegraph Company, dated March 23, 1877, covering inventions made by him applicable to their lines.

XIX. The Carbon Shed
And the Part It Played

THE first interesting event at Menlo Park that I can recall,' writes Mrs. Alice Stillwell Holzer, 'was when Mr. Edison was working on the telephone.'

Mrs. Holzer was then Miss Alice Stillwell, and lived at the Edison residence with Mr. and Mrs. Edison.

'We had a telephone from the house to the laboratory, which seemed very wonderful. One evening the telephone company was giving a concert with the artists in New York and the audience in Philadelphia.

'Mr. Edison had a wire set up to connect with the wire which had been placed between the two cities, and those in the laboratory heard the concert distinctly.'

It is a curious fact that Edison's original patent for the carbon telephone was not granted until May 3, 1892, although he filed its application fifteen years previously, on April 27, 1877.([1])

Two claims were embodied in it:

(1) In a speaking-telegraph transmitter, the combination of a metallic diaphragm and disc of plumbago or equivalent material, the contiguous faces of said disc and diaphragm being in contact, substantially as described.

(2) As a means for effecting a varying surface contact in the circuit of a speaking-telegraph transmitter, the combination of two electrodes, one of plumbago or similar material and both having broad surfaces in vibratory contact with each other, substantially as described.

Edison described the outcome of his efforts as follows:

'The telephone department (of the Western Union) was placed

Alfred Swanson, night watchman, who tended the lamps.

(1) Patent No. 474,230,

The smoking lamps in the carbon house as they appeared when in use. Under the bench are empty boxes for shipping the buttons to New York City.

in the hands of Hamilton McK. Twombly, Vanderbilt's ablest son-in-law, who made a success of it. The Bell company, of Boston, also started an exchange and the fight was on, the Western Union pirating the Bell receiver and the Boston company pirating the Western Union transmitter.

'About this time I wanted to be taken care of. I threw out hints of this desire. Then Mr. Orton sent for me. He had learned that inventors didn't do business by the regular process and concluded he would close it right up.

'He asked me how much I wanted. I had made up my mind it was certainly worth $25,000, if it ever amounted to anything for central station work, so that was the sum I had in mind to stick to and get, obstinately.

'Still, it had been an easy job and only required a few months, and I felt a little shaky and uncertain. So I asked him to make me an offer. He promptly said he would give me one hundred thousand dollars.

' "All right," I said. "It is yours on one condition and that is that you do not pay it all at once, but pay me at the

Carbon house as it has been restored by Henry Ford at Dearborn. It stands near the west fence of the Menlo Park quadrangle.

rate of $6,000 a year for seventeen years"—the life of the patent.

'He seemed only too pleased to do this and it was closed.'(²)

Ere long the battle between the rapidly growing Bell interests and the older Western Union leaders had become a war. During the very year that I went to Menlo Park, the latter concern brought into existence the American Speaking Telephone Company to introduce the Edison apparatus and create telephone exchanges all over the country.

By November, litigation had been initiated by the Bell people, seeking to establish the rights of Doctor Bell as the original and first inventor of the speaking telephone.(³)

It is interesting to note that the most protracted patent litigation in history has revolved around Bell's telephone patent. Five suits have been carried to the United States

(2) *Edison, His Life and Inventions.*—Dyer & Martin, pp. 179-180.

(3) This was compromised on November 10, 1879, when the two litigants came to terms. The Western Union retired voluntarily from the telephone field and, in return, was to receive a royalty of 20 percent of all the telephone earnings of the Bell system while the Bell patents ran. It was also paid several thousand dollars in cash for its apparatus, received 40 percent of the stock of the local systems of New York and Chicago, and exacted from the Bell interests the promise to stay out of the telegraph field. At that time the Western Union had 85 exchanges operating.

An old magazine illustration showing how the lamp chimneys were smoked to produce the soot used in the carbon telephone transmitters.

Supreme Court and all have been won by Bell.

But I must tell you of how Edison made carbon buttons for the Western Union at the time I joined his staff at Menlo Park. They were to be used in manufacturing the Edison transmitter. The carbon shed on the west side of the quadrangle alongside the fence where this was done was one of the first spots that I visited after I started working for him.

Within, I found a battery of kerosene lamps arranged on a bench under a canopy. All were smoking, the yellow flame barely showing through the sooty glass chimneys. The unpleasant smoke was drawn upward by the canopy as a sort of ventilator, and thence carried outside.

If you will stroll over to the west fence and push open the door to the little shed, as it has now been restored, you will see the shelf on which are some of the original lamps that Edison used in making his carbon.

On your right you will see a bench on which are a hand press and pair of scales. In such a press the night watchman, Alfred Swanson, compressed the little buttons of carbon, after he had scraped the soot from the lamp chimneys. On the scales he weighed them carefully to get the exact quantity.

The process of smoking the chimneys was not so simple as it sounds. It was very essential that the soot should be deposited at the lowest possible temperature, and the flame could not be allowed to play upon the deposit, as otherwise it acquired a high resistance and was wholly unsuited to use in the transmitters.

The first step after the chimney had been scraped was to take away the portions that had a brownish tinge. The remainder was then finely ground and placed in the press, or mould. Each button was supposed to weigh three hundred milligrams. Afterward, the buttons were packed in shallow wooden boxes padded with cotton, and shipped thus to New York City.

One of the amusing stories of the laboratory was of a newspaper reporter who happened to visit the shed and found the lamps smoking. He rushed back to Mr. Edison in much distress.

'Oh, Mr. Edison, all those lamps are smoking!' he exclaimed. 'You had better send some one out there right away and turn down the wicks.'

Edison, of course, explained the reason for their smoking, leaving the writer somewhat crestfallen at his excitement.

The smoking lamps were frequently mentioned in the newspapers of that period. The operation seemed to arouse the admiration of the reporters. A writer in the New York *Sun* happened to ask Mr. Edison one day about the telephone.

'Bell's is what is called the magneto-telephone and mine the carbon,' Edison told him. 'Those kerosene lamps that you see smoking yonder are my carbon manufactory. I peel it from the shades and press it into buttons for use i my telephone. '

The Will Rogers of that period was Eli Perkins. He took occasion, of course, to spend a day at Menlo Park with Mr. Edison, and later described the visit as follows:

'When I called on Professor Edison at Menlo Park, he was engaged on a new experiment. He was trying to abstract the heat from the fire, so as to leave the fire perfectly harmless, while the heat could be carried away in flour barrels to be used for cooking.

'Then the professor tried experiments in concentrating water to be used in fire engines, in case of drought. The latter

experiment proved eminently successful. Twelve barrels of
Croton water ([4]) were boiled over the stove, and evaporated
down to a spoonful, and this was sealed in a small phial, to
be diluted and used to put out fires in cases of drought or
where no water can be had.

'In some cases the water was evaporated and concentrated
until it became a fine dry powder. This can be carried around
in the pockets of the firemen.

'I proceeded to elucidate to him my plan for constructing
fireproof flues. I told him that, to make fireproof flues, the
holes of the flues should be constructed of solid cast iron, or
some other noncombustible material, and then cold corru-
gated iron, without any apertures, should be poured around
them.

' "Wonderful!" exclaimed Professor Edison, "but where
will you place those flues, Mr. Perkins?"

' "My idea," I replied, drawing a diagram on the wall-
paper with a piece of charcoal, "is to have these flues in every
instance located in the adjoining house." '

Credit for starting the habit of saying 'Hello' over the
telephone was given to Mr. Edison by F. P. Fish, president of
the American Telephone Company. When the bell rang and
people went to answer the telephone, they used to say 'Are
you there?' or 'Are you ready to talk?' or some other ponder-
ous question. One day when he was called, Edison caught up
the receiver and yelled into the transmitter—'Hello!' Since
then, it has gone clear around the world.([5])

(4) Water from Croton reservoir.
(5) Jones—*Thomas Alva Edison*, p. 99.

Elisha Gray.

XX. The Battle of the Microphones

IF YOU will stop beside the long instrument table at the south end of the second floor of the restored laboratory, you will see there a polished wooden mouthpiece—a concave disc shaped like a telephone transmitter—held upright on a pedestal. Behind its center is a row of charcoal buttons, one behind the other. There are five in all, each supported by a thin metal strip that serves as a kind of spring.

This is the first microphone ever made, and was devised by Edison on April 1, 1877, during his search for a perfect telephone transmitter. In spite of the fact that Edison invented the instrument, a claim to it was set up some time later by Professor Hughes, D. E., in England, and a merry strife was waged between those two noted inventors.

I can recall how bitter it became, for it happened during the spring of 1878. Articles in the newspapers bore such references as:

'We waited a while and chatted about the telephone and the new sound-magnifier of the Englishman Hughes, which Edison declared a "straight steal" from the principle of his carbon telephone.'[1]

Professor Hughes had experimented in the printing telegraph field and his system was almost universally adopted in

(1) New York *Graphic*. June 6, 1878.

Model of transmitter which could be lifted up and carried in hand, like modern European type of telephone. This may be seen on second floor of restored laboratory.

Depot at Smith's Creek, Michigan, as restored by Henry Ford and moved to
Greenfield Village, Dearborn. The youthful Edison was ejected from the Grand
Trunk train at this depot, for setting the baggage car afire. On October 21, 1929,
he arrived at this same depot again in the baggage car of a similar train and
was escorted to the platform by President Hoover.

Europe; it was unfortunate that the controversy between
them grew to such proportions. Naturally, Edison felt keenly
about it, because of the arduous nights and days he had devoted to the study of carbon and sound transmission. While
many of the tricks performed with it by Professor Hughes in
his lectures were new, they all required the use of carbon,
which was clearly Edison's discovery.

The idea of using several pieces of a semiconductor instead of one was tried at an early date, as we have seen, by
Edison. He found that the loudness of the sound was increased by multiplying the number of contact surfaces, but
articulation was impaired. In the form which he invented
April 1, 1877, the piece of charcoal nearest the diaphragm
impinged upon a disc of carbon fastened to the center of the
diaphragm. Thus the current was passed through diaphragm
and buttons.

In May, 1878, more than one year after the Edison invention, Professor Hughes made public a number of interesting experiments in carbon and other materials in connection with a
device to which he gave the name of 'microphone.'

Almost immediately afterward, Edison wrote to the *Scientific American* claiming the origination of the principle of the carbon telephone, and the discovery of the variability of the conducting power of many substances under pressure, which, he said, formed the basis of the construction of Hughes' microphone.

Professor Hughes' answer was that his invention was quite a different instrument from the carbon telephone.

'Save in a very unimportant modification in form, that difference to most people will be imperceptible,' retorted the *Scientific American*, in an editorial on the 'Invention of the Microphone.' 'The principle underlying the inventions is *the same*, although it may have been independently discovered by both inventors.'([2])

Edison himself thus disposed of the matter:

'After I sent one of my men over to London especially to show Preece ([3]) the carbon transmitter, and where Hughes first saw it and heard it, then within a month he came out with the microphone, without any acknowledgment whatever. Published dates will show that Hughes came along after me.'

At the time when the war of words was at its height, people were amazed at the idea of hear-

At the north end of the second floor of the restored Edison laboratory at Dearborn, stands this organ, a faithful replica of the original one which occupied this same spot at Menlo Park.

Model of transmitter invented April 1, 1877, which was progenitor of microphone. Notice the four metal springs behind the mouthpiece, separated from each other by buttons of charcoal. This may be seen on instrument table on second floor of restored laboratory.

ing a fly walk at a distance of many miles, as was claimed for the microphone. They would have been more amazed had someone told them of how the 'mike' was to be used fifty years later with the radio.

One of the objects on the second floor of the laboratory, which was used in the telephone experiments and which always aroused the curiosity of our visitors, was the pipe organ in the north end, at the rear.

It was presented to him by Hilbourne Roosevelt, an inventor and organ builder who had been active in telephone research and who, by the way, was an uncle of Theodore Roosevelt.

Roosevelt invented the telephone receiver circuit with a central station or operator. By this device you are able to complete the circuit automatically by lifting the receiver off the hook. I will refer to him later in discussing the phonograph.

He admired Edison very much and presented the organ to him to aid him in his sound and telephonic experiments. Besides serving as an aid it was used, as one writer of that period remarked, 'whenever, in Mr. Edison's opinion, music's magic strains were needed to sooth the savage breasts of his employes.'

After I began to work here, I took part in many a midnight song fest around this instrument. Lunch usually consisted of soda crackers, ham, cheese and butter, and we gathered in a circle around Mr. Edison and told stories while we ate.

It was then that some one would go back to the organ at the rear end of the room to play some popular tune, such as 'Champagne Charley,' while another would sing the verses and we all would join in the chorus. You may see this organ today, faithfully reproduced by a builder who as a boy worked in the shop where the original organ was made. It is at the north end of the second floor of the restored laboratory. The fact that Mr. Edison's hearing was not so strong as that of a normal man adds interest to the many experiments which he performed in sound. He has said that his deafness was really an asset, since he had to make his instruments so much more perfect in order for him to hear over them.

The incident wherein his hearing was impaired took place near Fraser, Michigan.

'I was delayed in waiting on some of my newspaper customers,' he told Henry Ford, 'and the train started ahead. I ran after it and caught the rear step, nearly out of wind and hardly able to lift myself up, for the steps in those days were high.

'A trainman reached over and grabbed me by the ears, and as he pulled me up I felt something in my ears crack and right after that I began to get deaf. The ear-boxing incident never happened. If it was that man who injured my hearing, he did it while saving my life.'

A cartoon from *Punch*, March, 1878, showing a party talking into the telephone.

This may or may not have started Edison's trouble with his ears; his extreme deafness dates from an operation for mastoiditis some years ago. He has never, contrary to the usual reports, actually been glad that he was deaf. But he is the kind of man to turn a physical ill into an advantage.

Instead of mourning the loss of his hearing, he sought to discover whether there were not some affairs in which a deaf man could be of more use than a man with normal hearing. He once told me that he personally would be glad to have his hearing restored but that he thought he was actually of more use to the country because he was deaf. At another time he said:

'This deafness has been of great advantage to me in various ways. When in a telegraph office, I could only hear the instrument directly on the table at which I sat, and, unlike the other operators, was not bothered by the other instruments.

'Again, in experimenting on the telephone, I had to improve the transmitter so I could hear it. This made the telephone commercial as the magneto-telephone receiver of the time was too weak to be used as a transmitter commercially.'(4)

Old papers and files reveal many amusing stories of the telephone. A reporter who visited Menlo Park about six months prior to my arrival described one of their tests as follows:(5)

'At a table sit two earnest men, each holding alternately to mouth and ear the mouthpiece of a telephone.

' "Well, what are you up to, today?" asks an acquaintance who has sauntered in.

' "We have got the Chicago telephone repeater in the circuit at last. We are now talking through 800 miles of wire, via St. Louis, Cincinnati, Louisville, Washington and Philadelphia—the parabola of the West. It doesn't work well yet.

' "This is the largest circuit ever attempted and it would not be possible without Edison's repeating machine. What's that? Can't hear all the words."

'This last he shouted into the mouthpiece and the words flew to the Mississippi and back in a second, and the man across the table shouted back: "Can you hear me now?" '

(4) *Edison As I Know Him*—Henry Ford, in collaboration with Samuel Crowther. pp. 24 et seq.
(5) *Daily Graphic.* April 2, 1878.

In such manner many tests were conducted at Menlo Park.

Before leaving the microphone, I would like to say that in the battle between Mr. Edison and Professor Hughes, the honors eventually went to the former. An abnormal degree of credulity was required to appreciate its capabilities. The passage of a delicate camel's hair brush was magnified to the roar of a mighty wind. The footfalls of a tiny gnat sounded like the tramp of Rome's cohorts. The ticking of a watch could be heard over 100 miles.

In the development of this mechanism Edison embodied the principle that if carbon varies in electrical resistance with variation in pressure, this variation must be heightened to an indefinite degree if the carbon be permitted to make a loose contact with its partners in the circuit.

The vibrations in the diaphragm are passed successively from carbon No. 1, back of the central button, to carbon No. 2, and so on, with the result of heightening to a marvelous degree the sounds communicated to the telephone receiver.

This principle is applied to this day.

Edison's conception of magnetism in those early days was far in advance of the knowledge prevalent at the time. It embraced all the vital principles that are today employed in constructing the field magnet systems of generators and motors.

To exemplify this statement I shall describe a telephone type made by him in the early part of 1877 while he was experimenting principally with his carbon telephone transmitter, or microphone. The Edison laboratory at Dearborn conserves two of these telephones of 1877 which today would be classified with the 'dynamic' type.

As we know he made many experiments on the magneto principle, such as those fundamentally in-

Edison's dynamic telephone. Notice powerful circular field and diaphragm with tiny coil.

volved in the Bell receiving telephone. He went further, however, and changed the order of things by making the wire coil a movable factor, much as D'Asonval did later in the Dephez galvanometer, or moving coil type.

The Edison dynamic telephone, then, consisted of a diaphragm of mica and attached to it was a coil of fine wire on a tiny cup-shaped bobbin. The magnetic system in this device consists in a strong, circular field of force which was supplied by an efficient electromagnet. This electromagnet is excited by a local battery and is kept constant. The magnet has three coils of wire, each of whose extremities is attached to a binding post on the outside of the telephone; so that, together with those for the coil on the diaphragm, there are eight binding posts. The large number of binding posts served merely for experimental purposes.

The action of this telephone is simple. If the instrument is being used as a transmitter, the coil vibrates in the magnetic field when words are spoken into the mouthpiece; the vibrations induce a current in the tiny wire coil, which today can be amplified to any strength through the improved Edison Effect tubes (radio tubes). When the instrument is being used as a receiving telephone or speaker, the reverse takes place; the tiny wire coil on the diaphragm vibrates as a varying current passes through it, and reception results. The photographs give a clear idea of the Edison dynamic telephone of 1877. It will be noticed that there is no difference in principle or construction between this and the modern dynamic speaker universally used in radio.

When we examine the magnetic phenomenon as known today, we are surprised to see how perfect was Edison's adaptation of it to practical use at that early period. There is small wonder that he was able to make an electric generator of marvelous quality and efficiency, for he knew then the modern principles of magnetism, long before they were formulated into the rules we use today.

When professionals, such as radio or telephone engineers, see the remarkable dynamic Edison telephones at the restored Menlo Park laboratory they are surprised. 'Why, they are the exact counterpart of the modern dynamic loud speakers,' said one such visitor one day ([5]) 'What is more—the modern speaker has its primary effect amplified by the

---

(5)   S. R. Manning, telephone engineer of the Bell Telephone Company.

improved Edison Effect Tube, known as the radio tube.'
From him I obtained the following description of the
modern dynamic speaker, and find it coincides in every
respect with the Edison one of 1877. If you will compare
the illustration on page 140 with the one below, you will
find that to be true.

The most recent type of modern radio loud speaker goes by the name of
Moving Coil, or Dynamic Speaker. Its construction is shown roughly in the
sketch at the bottom of the page.

A shell-shaped magnet having a central cylindrical core *F* is excited by the
winding *G*. The air gap of the magnet is ring-shaped, the end piece *H* of the
shell reaching almost to the core *F*. In the narrow ring-shaped air gap (about
0.05 inch long) is placed a coil of fine wire *E*. The frame on which the coil is
wound is flared for the purpose of cementing to the parchment cone *D*. At
its outer edge the cone is cemented to a thin ring of flexible leather and this in
turn is fastened to a light metal ring *B*. *A* represents the baffle or sounding
board to which, in a radio set, the speaker is fastened.

The voice currents flowing through coil *E* make this move axially, and *E*
in turn pushes the cone *D* back and forth. The winding *G* has many turns of
fine wire to which current may be supplied from a battery or a rectifier. This
coil uses approximately ten watts of power for its excitation.

The voice coil *E* has an alternating current impedance of 10 to 20 ohms at
1000 cycles. The speaker has an efficiency of about 25 percent (in the better
makes). The density of flux in the air gap is about 15,000 lines per square
centimeter.

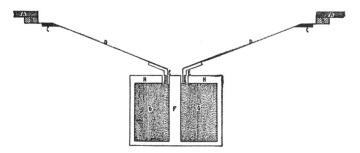

Cross section of the moving coil or 'dynamic speaker.'

:: :: ::

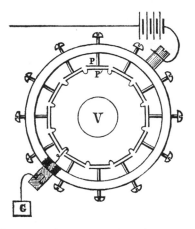

Diagram of Edison's condenser transmitter, forerunner of condenser
type of microphone used in radio today.

XXI. Other Telephone Experiments

DURING his researches into telephony Edison made many interesting variations among his experiments, some of which are recalled now only on the faded pages of musty books. They were chronicled at the time and enjoyed the interest of engineers, but in the years that have lapsed many have been forgotten. Occasionally something is developed which can be traced to one of those early experiments.

I have already told how Edison's carbon transmitter gave the microphone to radio. A kind of microphone based upon the principle of the condenser is now coming into favor, in which we find another Edison development. He made the first condenser transmitters as early as February, 1877.

In his condenser telephone the static charge instead of the strength of the current varied with the voice. There was a circular vocalizing chamber with central mouthpiece, surrounded by plates connected with each other and the ground, these being free to vibrate. Immediately behind each stood a similar plate held at its center by an adjusting screw. The plates in the outside row were electrically connected with each other and with the battery that went to the line. When the inside row of plates vibrated under the influence of the voice or other sound, the distance between the plates varied, changing their static capacity.

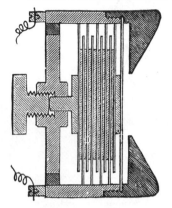

Another type of condenser transmitter devised by Edison.

In December of the same year Edison completed a second condenser differing from the one just described in construction but not in principle. The plates were arranged in the usual way. An initial pressure was put on them by a screw bearing in the solid frame of the instrument. As the diaphragm vibrated, it varied the distance between the plates, altering their static charge and affecting the electric tension of the line.

The effect of the shape of a conductor upon its resistance was demonstrated by Edison during August, 1877, in an interesting series of experiments with a globule of mercury.

The globule rested on a slightly concave metal plate under an ordinary mouthpiece. A needle pointing downward from the diaphragm indented the upper surface of the globule and, as it vibrated, slightly altered the latter's shape. Although very slight, that alteration was sufficient to vary the resistance of the current considerably.

The principle by which a globule of mercury changes its shape during the passage of a current was applied by Edison to a telephone receiver. The receiver consisted of a U-shaped tube in which the globule, together with a conducting solution, was placed. As the currents from the transmitter passed through the tube, they elongated the globule, thus agitating the liquid and vibrating the float fastened under the center of the receiver's diaphragm. (See page 145.)

The other telephones made by Edison during the same month of August, 1877, are very interesting to us as novelties, and as indicative of the scope of his experiments. Seemingly, he overlooked nothing. In the first of the three he used a miniature wet battery or voltaic pile; hence the instrument was called 'a pile telephone.'

A piece of cork was inserted between the diaphragm and a strip of platinum. On the other side of the latter was a plate of

Experiment using globule of mercury and needle.

U-shaped receiver, in which glass tube contained globule of mercury.

copper to which it was fastened and which served as one of the terminal plates of the wet battery. The other terminal plate pressed against the metallic frame of the instrument, so that whenever the pile was included in a closed telephonic circuit, it furnished a continuous current. The strength of the current depended on the internal resistance of the pile and its polarization, controlled or varied by the vibrating of the diaphragm, in other words, by talking. (See bottom of page.)

The second of the three novel telephone instruments had for its diaphragm a strip of thin iron the edges of which had been bent to show that a circular mouthpiece was not essential. (See cut at top of page 146.)

The third was a purely mechanical telephone. In place of a line wire, the illuminating gas circulating in gas pipes was used. The telephone instruments were merely cones fastened by their apex to chandeliers in the place of burners. The larger end of each cone was closed by a thin circular diaphragm. Vibrations were conveyed from one cone to the other through the medium of the gas. (Page 146.)

In November, 1877, Edison's researches led to the perfection of a new kind of transmitter in which carbon was replaced by bibulous paper moistened with water. Being a semiconductor, it changed its resistance as did the carbon when influenced by varying pressure. The paper was kept moist by capillary action, the lower end of the strip resting in a water reservoir. (Top of page 147.)

Another kind of transmitter evolved by him several months earlier was so simple as to require no adjustment whatever. It was formed by a plate of metal resting on the bottom of the hollow instrument and supporting a block of prepared carbon, on top of which a second light metallic plate was laid. (Page 147.)

He varied this construction by replacing the carbon block with a round piece of cloth the pores of which had been filled with pulverized black lead to make

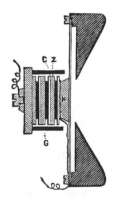

Voltaic pile telephone. K—Cork attached to diaphragm.

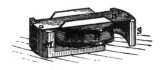

Receiver in which diaphragm
was thin strip of iron.

the cloth slightly conductive. Or fine grains of plumbago were floated on mercury and compressed between the surface and a metallic block that hung down from the center of the diaphragm.

One of the most novel transmitters which Edison devised had the mouthpiece at the side of the vocalizing chamber instead of at the top. The carbon block rested on the diaphragm, which formed the top of the chamber. Three fine cords held the carbon in place so that it would not be dislodged when the diaphragm was vibrating. The resistance of the circuit depended on the connection between carbon and diaphragm, which in turn depended on the pressure of the carbon, constantly changing while the diaphragm was vibrating. As may be imagined, this apparatus was too sensitive to general sounds to which it was exposed to be of value in telephoning. It was evolved during July, 1877. (Bottom of page 148.)

Edison's so-called 'inertia telephone' was made in the early autumn of 1877. When a person talked through this transmitter, the instrument moved instead of the diaphragm. A block of carbon was sandwiched between two metal plates, one of which was fastened to the diaphragm in front, the other to a screw projecting from a framework that was insulated from the diaphragm. (Page 149.)

Edison explained that the degree of pressure with which the carbon rested against the plates was varied during the vibration. 'Thus, after a movement toward the right, the diaphragm suddenly stops, and the carbon presses in virtue of its inertia on the metal plate fastened to the diaphragm.' Prescott says that its action could hardly be attributed solely to inertia.[1]

Before Edison adopted the nonvibrating rigid plate[2] for

---

(1)   Prescott, *The Bell Telephone*, pages 128-129.
(2)   Ibid, pages 121-122.

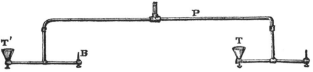

Unique telephone using gas pipes instead of wires and illuminating gas
instead of electricity.

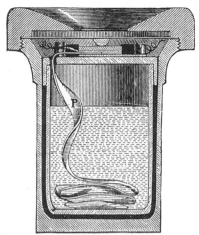

Transmitter in which moistened paper took place of carbon.

his diaphragm, he had to contend with a false vibration caused by the pressure of the diaphragms upon the carbon. This false vibration was not present in the magneto-telephone. Edison had to devise some way of overcoming it. He evolved a type of instrument in June, 1877, which would do that.

The diaphragm carried an armature of soft iron which faced but did not touch a magnet directly behind it. The armature and the magnet were opposite poles of the same magnet (see diagram at bottom of page 149), being connected at the base and polarized by a local circuit. Back of the magnet was a carbon button, against which the magnet pressed. The attraction between B and the armature A varied according to the distance between them. As the diaphragm vibrated and A moved toward B, the attraction increased rapidly and B lessened its pressure against the carbon C.

This arrangement was an improvement over that in an instrument Edison had perfected a few months earlier. In that the diaphragm carried an armature which by its motion changed the potential of two electromagnets. These changes in magnetism compelled a bar situated within their magnetic field to produce the original vibrations. The bar ends were held by the magnetic force against two pieces of carbon (C and C in the diagram at the top of page 150). These pieces and the bar were included in the primary circuit of an induction coil. The resistance of the circuit decreased when the bar was drawn up, and increased as the bar descended.

Another novel transmitter was made by Edison during August of that year, in which the semicon-

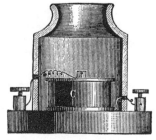

'Fool-proof' transmitter, requiring no adjustment whatever.

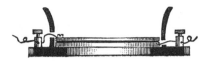

Transmitter in which cloth replaced
carbon.

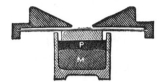

In this transmitter the plumbago (P) floats on mercury (M).

ductor was a collection of
small fragments of cork covered with plumbago.   It
could be used with or without a diaphragm.

In still another type, silk fibers coated with graphite replaced the solid carbon.   (See page 150.)

In his development of the microphone, Edison performed a
large number of experiments apart from those concerned with
the telephone transmitter.   In the preceding chapter I have
described his earliest form of this instrument, devised in
April, 1877, as having four carbon buttons, one behind the
other, each supported by an upright spring.   Another form,
tried but not developed, used two or three large blocks of
carbon, one behind the other.   The carbon blocks were sandwiched between metal plates.   (See top of page 151.)

Other forms of the microphone included one in which ten
plates of silk were used instead of carbon, a mixture of dex-
trine and lampblack having been previously worked into the
pores; another in which fifty discs, whose surface was pro-
toxidized with iron, were held behind the diaphragm in a
glass tube.   (See bottom of page 151.)

In the *Scientific American* of July 6, 1878, as well as in
Prescott's valuable book, Edison described some telephonic
arrangements which are extremely interesting.   There was his
electrophorous telephone, which acted by the approach of
the diaphragm toward, or its recession from, a highly charged
electrophorous (a simple static machine invented by Volta

In the novel transmitter shown above, the mouthpiece
(M) is at the side.

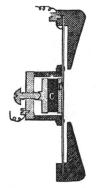

in 1777), consisting of a metal plate and a disc of shellac, ebonite, or the like. The vibrations of the transmitting diaphragm caused a disturbance of the charge at both ends of the line which gave rise to very weak sounds. Either end could be used for transmitting or receiving. To get results perfect insulation was necessary. (See top of page 152.)

In another form of electrostatic telephone, Edison used Deluc piles of twenty thousand discs each contained in horizontal glass tubes mounted on glass, wooden or metal stands.

Edison's 'inertia' telephone, in which the whole chamber moved when the diaphragm vibrated.

The diaphragms, in electrical connection with the earth, were placed opposite one pole of each pile, with the opposite poles joined by the line conductor. Thus any vibration of either diaphragm would disturb the electrical condition of neighboring discs, as in the electrophorous instrument. The vibrations when produced by the voice in one diaphragm gave rise to corresponding electrical changes in the other instrument and reproduced in it what had been spoken in the first. It was said that fair results could be obtained. (See bottom of page 152.)

An electro-mechanical telephone was devised by Edison in still another experiment. Small resistance coils were arranged with connecting springs near a platinum-faced lever behind a diaphragm, so that any movement of the latter caused one or more of the coils to be cut in or out of the primary circuit of an induction coil. The number varied with the amplitude of the vibrating diaphragm. Induced currents corresponding in strength with the variations of resistance were thus sent into the line, where they could be made to act upon an ordinary receiving telephone.

Edison said that by arranging the springs in a sunflower pattern about a circular lever he had succeeded in transmitting articulate sentences over this telephone; the sound, however, was very

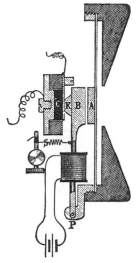

Instrument devised by Edison to overcome 'false vibration.'

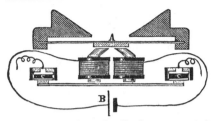

In this transmitter the diaphragm carried an armature.

harsh and disagreeable.

Edison devised a form of water telephone, using a double cell so as to afford considerable variation of resistance for the extremely slight movements of the diaphragm. In the apparatus a wire bent to form the letter "U" was attached to the diaphragm at the center of the arc; its ends were dipped in separate cells. Thus it was made to form part of the circuit when the line was joined to the instrument.

Another series of experiments was conducted by Edison during the year 1877 in what have been called short-circuiting, or cut-out, telephones. In vibrating, the diaphragm cut from the circuit resistances proportionally to the amplitude of the vibrations. In one of the first of these telephones, devised during March of that year, a metal lever vibrating in a vertical plane rested at one end upon a strip of carbonized silk which was part of the primary circuit of an induction coil. In the course of its vibrations, the lever cut from the circuit parts of the silk, the current passing temporarily through the lever. (See page 152.)

Transmitter using small fragments of cork.

In this type, silk fibers were used(F).

In another such instrument, a fine wire of high resistance, wrapped round a cylinder in a spiral groove, formed part of the primary circuit of a coil. A metal spring shaped like an ellipse was fastened at one side of the diaphragm; at the other side it pressed against an uninsulated wire on the cylinder. In moving to the right, the diaphragm flattened the spring, making it impinge upon a greater number of convolutions than if the motion were in the opposite direction. Thus the resistance of the coil depended on the position of the center of the diaphragm. (Page 153.)

A third type used a spring which rested on a narrow strip of metal on the surface

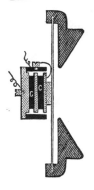

Early types of microphones are shown on left and right, one having two carbon blocks, the other three.

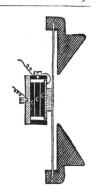

of a glass plate. (Page 153.)

In still a fourth type, a spiral spring was wrapped round a cylinder, the diaphragm pressing against the last turn so that, as it vibrated, the convolutions approached or receded from each other. A very slight motion of the diaphragm was sufficient to cause the first few coils to come together. The number of coils touching each other was dependent upon the amplitude of motion in the diaphragm. The wire was included in the primary circuit of an induction coil, so that the resistance of the circuit fluctuated as the diaphragm vibrated. The same wire was also used as the primary of the induction coil itself, with better results. (Bottom of page 153.)

Many other experiments were made by Edison in this field. Those given here suffice to show the indefatigable energy with which he made his explorations. Research work was his element and his prolific vision and sound reasoning in the work of transmitting sound over wire gave the world a vastly improved telephone. All telephone exchanges today are based on two fundamental instruments, the Bell telephone

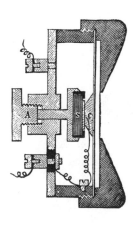

In microphone on left, ten plates of silk were used; in one on right, fifty discs were held in glass tube.

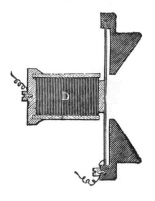

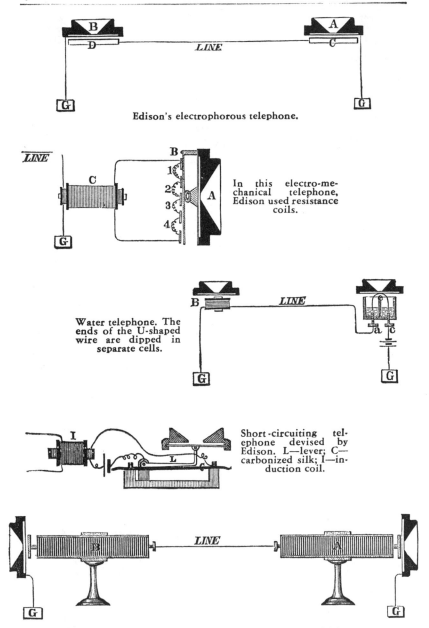

Edison's electrophorous telephone.

In this electro-me-
chanical telephone,
Edison used resistance
coils.

Water telephone. The
ends of the U-shaped
wire are dipped in
separate cells.

Short-circuiting tel-
ephone devised by
Edison. L—lever; C—
carbonized silk; I—in-
duction coil.

Form of electrostatic telephone devised by Edison, in which twenty
thousand discs were used in each instrument.

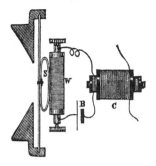

Short-circuiting telephone, using wire (W). S—spring.

receiver and the Edison carbon *transmitter*. Edison's genius solved the pressing needs of mankind by the exercise of original thought, always distinctive, practical and useful.

Before describing Edison's next work, the invention of the phonograph, I should like to summarize briefly his achievements in telephony which we have just been discussing. When the professional as well as the layman examines the various original instruments in the restored laboratory, one surprise follows another. Few, indeed, know that it was Edison who gave the world the telephone transmitter, the perfect complement of Bell's receiver. Few understand that Edison had made a perfect electromagnetic receiver one or two years in advance of Bell, but had failed to grasp its usefulness. His first instrument was designed for an electric buzzer; when used as a telephone receiver it is almost a perfect instrument. His second consisted of two tubes, one sliding over the other, adjustable in telescopic fashion. They were made in 1875 for acoustic telegraph research, but reproduce sounds or the voice as well as any modern receiver.

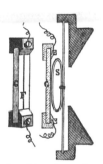

In this short-circuiting telephone of Edison's, the spring (S) rests on a glass plate(G).

When he came to the rescue of the Bell instrument, Edison gave us the carbon transmitter, making the weak instrument a practical, commercial success. Bell's receiver was an exquisite ear, and Edison's transmitter added a healthy lung—a combination needed to give a clear reproduction of the voice. Together, the Bell and the Edison apparatus form an harmonious pair. They have stood the test of time and are used today round the globe. The simple electromag-

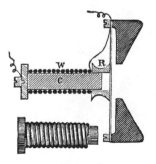

Short-circuiting telephone built by Edison in November, 1877. W—spiral spring wrapped around cylinder (C).

net still serves the one; and the simple element Carbon the other.

Edison's first patent application on the carbon transmitter was made on April 18, 1877. About the same time he developed his first microphone. Telephony owes him another large debt for introducing the induction coil, or transformer. He tried to amplify the small variation by means of the coil, creating a local circuit with its primary, and using the secondary in direct connection with the main line. First results did not promise much, but success came eventually; so that today we may talk over the wires not only for a short distance but for thousands of miles.

There was still another achievement effected by him in this field—namely, the invention of the Edison chalk telephone based on the motograph principle. We shall discuss that instrument at the proper time—the early part of the year 1879.

Francis Jehl using modern telephone. A—Edison transmitter; B—Bell receiver.

A page of illustrations from the New York *Daily Graphic* soon after the invention of the phonograph. At the top on the left is shown the 'under side of the mouthpiece, showing vibrating disc and point.' In the middle at the top are two sheets of tin foil, before and after the impression was made. On the right is the 'funnel for increasing the sound.' The other pictures show: phonograph ready for use; reproducing speech; talking to the phonograph; and placing tin foil on cylinder.

XXII. The Speaking Phonograph

Early Recollections

NOTHING about the laboratory fascinated me so much as the speaking phonograph which stood, as I have already said, on the extreme end of the long table at the south end of the second floor and was the magnet that drew all visitors.

It was truly a wonder machine. Crude as it may seem now, in that early day it was so marvelous that skeptics insisted on trying it out for themselves before they would believe the human voice or even sound could be reproduced.

When I joined the Menlo Park staff the phonograph was still operated by a hand crank, and the use of clockwork for that purpose had not yet been accomplished, although its inventor already had it in mind. Mr. Edison stood there, turning the wheel with one hand, hallooing into the mouthpiece, and watching while the punctures were made on the tin foil.

After a few moments he would set the needle back at the starting point and let it reproduce the sounds while he slowly turned the wheel. Distinguished personages from all parts of the world came to see and listen to the wonderful machine. Some of them filled us with awe. I remember Sarah Bernhardt, the glorious tragedienne, and how her face lighted up with surprise and thrilled with pleasure as she heard her voice coming back to her from the cylinder. Impetuously, she tried to buy the machine and take it away with her, but Mr. Edison persuaded her to wait until he could ship one to her.

And we enjoyed many a chuckle or hearty laugh as our chief permitted his love of humor to contribute to these phonographic exhibitions. Sometimes he would turn the crank very slowly so that the instrument would drawl out the words with great gravity. At other times he would whirl it so fast that the words would fly out of the funnel in a confused babble.

One day I heard something like the following coming from the machine: 'Bmal Elttil a Dah Yram.'

The effect was amazing. It sounded as if an inhabitant of Mars were speaking. I wondered what was wrong and would not be content until I learned what he had done. He had reversed the cylinder and I was hearing the poem of 'Mary's Lamb' backwards.

Some of the other stunts were intended to show 'the range of possibilities of the phonograph, because so many questioned its practicability. He whistled an air from the 'Grande Duchesse' one day into the funnel to show how music could be preserved and reproduced. It came back clear as a fife and in perfect time.

He rang a small bell to show that sounds not made by the human voice could be retained. He would cough, sneeze or laugh into the funnel and let the sounds come back. But the greatest joy of all was when he would pretend to be two men talking, using a deep bass voice for one and a high shrill falsetto for the other. Such a conversation coming back to us over the tin foil

T. ALVA EDISON,
INVENTOR OF THE PHONOGRAPH.

Mr. Edison and his phonograph as they appeared about the time he took it to the White House and demonstrated it to the President and Mrs. Hayes. Note the hand crank, flywheel, cylinder for holding the tin foil and the mouthpiece.

Francis Jehl showing how Mr. Edison used to operate the phonograph for visitors in the Menlo Park
laboratory.   The machine is an original tin foil
phonograph dating back to 1878.

sent us into spasms of laughter.

Mr. Edison himself laughed like a boy while the tears ran down his cheeks. Usually he recited a solemn, sad poem in the deep voice, and interjected sneering or undignified comments with the second voice, thus adding to the amusing effect. I remember one such recitation that was a favorite of his:

'A soldier of the legion lay dying in Algiers,
        (Oh, shut up!)
There was lack of woman's nursing, there was
        (Oh, give us a rest!)
    dearth of woman's tears.
But a comrade stood beside him while his lifeblood ebbed away
        (Oh, what are you giving us!)
And bent with pitying glances to hear what he might say.
        (Oh, you can't recite poetry.)
The dying soldier faltered and he took that comrade's hand
        (Police! Police! Police!)
And he said: "I never more shall see my own, my native land."
        (Oh, put him out!')

Another test which kept us laughing was the use of the same tin foil for two or three different messages, each one being dictated right over the previous one, so that the matrix had to reproduce all three at the same time. The foregoing poem without the interpolations was one of the three, as a rule; the tune 'Yankee Doodle' was a second, whistled, of course; while an automatic counting, such as 'One, two, three, four, five, six,' and so on, comprised the third.

Replica of the first phonograph. This may be viewed today in the restored laboratory at Dearborn, where it rests on the instrument table.

Once I heard him tell of the exhibition of the phonograph that he gave before the assembled scientists and savants of the land in Washington, D. C., during the preceding April on the occasion of the Academy of Sciences meeting. He used the old-style phonograph, with flywheel and crank, cylinder and mouthpiece with diaphragm, and had a 'hollow cone' of paper to reproduce his tones more clearly.

And I heard of the demonstration at the White House before President Rutherford B. Hayes. The hour was one a. m. but that was not too late for the President to be awaiting him. Mrs. Hayes had retired, and as soon as she heard that the wonderful invention was downstairs she arose and quickly joined the party. Every attention was paid to Mr. Edison during the hour he spent there.

Among those present was Roscoe Conkling, an important figure at that time in political circles. He had a habit of dressing his hair so that a wavy curl hung down just above his rather attractive forehead. Mr. Edison saw an opportunity to create a little fun and when he came to talk into the phonograph recited the well-known verse about the little girl who had a little curl in the center of her forehead. Mr. Conkling enjoyed the incident and made a wry face at his tormentor.

The New York *Sun* published a description of our chief operating his speaking machine and it will give you the picture better than can any words of mine.

'The professor was manipulating a machine upon the table before

Prima donna singing into mouthpiece of phonograph. (From a drawing that appeared in *Frank Leslie's Illustrated Weekly* in 1878.)

him. He had something resembling a gutta-percha mouthpiece of a speaking tube shoved against a cylinder wrapped in tin foil, which he turned with a crank.

'The end of a funnel was clapped over the mouthpiece and strange ventriloquial sounds were issuing from it. He shook hands and, pointing to the instrument, said: "This is my speaking phonograph. Did you ever see it and hear it talk?"

First sketch of the phonograph. (From the *Scientific American*, December 22, 1877.)

'The reply was a negative. Thereupon he picked up the gutta-percha mouthpiece, saying: "This mouthpiece is simply an artificial diaphragm. Turn it over," suiting the action to the word, "and you will see this thin disc of metal at the bottom. Whenever you speak in the mouthpiece the vibrations of your voice jar this disc, which, as you see, has in its center a fine steel point.

' "Now for the other part of the machine. Here is a brass cylinder grooved something like the spiral part of a screw, only much finer. I wrap a sheet of tin foil around the cylinder and shove the mouthpiece up to it so that the tiny steel point touches the tin foil above one of the grooves. I then turn the cylinder with a crank and talk into the mouthpiece.

' "The vibrations arouse the disc and the steel point pricks the tin foil, leaving perforations resembling the old Morse telegraphic alphabet. They are really stereoscopic views of the voice, recording all that is said with time and intonations. It is a matrix of the words and voice and can be used until worn out.

' "Now, let us reset the cylinder so that the steel point may run over the holes or alphabet made when we talked into the mouthpiece. The thin metal disc rises and as the steel point trips from perforation to perforation, opening the valves of the diaphragm, the words, intonations and accent are reproduced exactly as spoken.

' "Here, the steel point starts at the same spot as when I talked through the mouthpiece, but its action now is controlled by the perforated alphabet. It repeats what I said. Listen." '

The first phonograph

Sketch in New York *Graphic*, April 2, 1878.

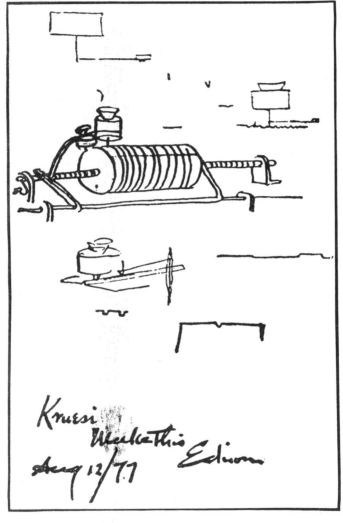

From this rude sketch made for him by Mr. Edison, John Kruesi
constructed the first phonograph.

XXIII. The Speaking Phonograph

How It Was Invented

TO DESCRIBE the circumstances as I understand them whereby Mr. Edison came to invent the phonograph, I must go back to the latter part of 1876, two years before my arrival at Menlo Park, when the automatic telegraphic repeater was first conceived by him. It was an instrument that would record Morse signals and repeat them to one or more stations at the same time. Mr. Edison applied for a patent on February 3, 1877. (See chapter X, page 79.)

As soon as you look at this device you are impressed by the fact that it bears a strange resemblance to the phonograph. It was while he was experimenting with it in the summer of 1877 that he got the idea of the latter machine.

His telegraph lines were connected with the 'repeater' and, through some mistake, additional current was thrown into the motor that drove the discs. The discs fairly flew round, causing the metal point to pass in and out of the indentations so rapidly that the contact spring emitted a sound.

Mr. Edison worked till long past midnight over the machine and when he got home happened to recall the incident of the sound. It haunted him for some time; it would not leave his mind. He resolved to investigate further. One day the idea came of using a point and indentations to make a record of sound and reproduce it.

How to construct a machine capable of doing this was his next problem; and the experiments that followed were varied and interesting. Paper that had been paraffined and waxed was tried with a diaphragm that had a small, blunt pin attached to its center. The results were so encouraging that he continued.

At last, on August 12, he sent for John Kruesi and gave him the rough sketch of a queer-looking instrument, telling him at the same time to make it as soon as possible.

At that time the only machine shop Mr. Edison had was in the rear of the first floor of the laboratory, and its equipment consisted of a few small instrument lathes. There John Kruesi had his office.

The sketch called for a metal cylinder, spirally grooved,

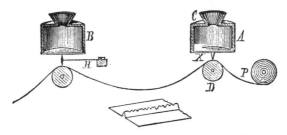

Sketch of first phonograph (From *Scientific American*, November 17, 1877.) **Note** the indented paper edge shown at the bottom.

to be mounted on a long shaft, one end of which was to be tapped with a screw thread of the same pitch as the grooves on the cylinder. The shaft was to run in two upright bearings, one of which was to have an internal thread fitting the thread on one end of the shaft so that the cylinder could be turned and moved laterally by a crank attached to the shaft.

It was also to be mounted on a base. A metal arm was to be attached to the side of the machine, carrying at its upper free end one of the old round wooden telephone transmitter cases. This was to be fitted with a diaphragm having a blunt pin at its center, and was to be constructed to permit slight adjustments.

While Mr. Kruesi was working on the crude machine, he puzzled over what the Chief was trying to make now. The apparatus turned out in the machine shop before that time had been mostly electrical, but here was something that had no coils, magnets, or wires. When it was completed and he had taken it upstairs to Mr. Edison, he could not help inquiring what it was to do.

'The machine must talk, Kruesi,' said Mr. Edison, laconically.

John Kruesi glanced at his boss and smiled in a skeptical manner. He shook his head. The same unbelief was shared by Billy Carman, the bookkeeper, who happened to be standing near and had heard Mr. Edison's reply. He offered to bet a handful of cigars that the machine would not talk. Thus encouraged, Kruesi plunged himself, wagering two dollars.

'All right, boys. Just wait,' Mr. Edison replied.

He took the model Kruesi had made, examined it, tried the cylinder and the metal arm, and then called for some tin foil. He wrapped the sheet round the grooved cylinder and began turning the crank. Suddenly there was a loud scratch; the tin foil had torn across its face.

The bookkeeper winked at the shop foreman, greatly enjoying the fun and thinking of the free cigars he would smoke at Mr. Edison's expense. Mr. Kruesi rapped his forehead in mock seriousness as if to say the poor chief had gone mad.

Their mirth led Batchelor, who was working beside Mr. Edison, to remark, 'Keep your shirts on, boys.'

They fitted the next sheet of tin foil more securely to the cylinder, gluing the ends together carefully; for it had not yet been fitted with the slot that enabled the operator of later machines to clamp the tin foil and hold it taut. When Mr. Edison had finished readjusting the needle, he ran the cylinder back and forth until everything seemed adjusted. At last he was ready to try his invention.

He began to turn the crank once more and, in a loud voice, recited the old favorite about Mary and her little lamb. The mouthpiece was then turned back, as was the cylinder; the former was placed in position again, and Mr. Edison turned the crank. Suddenly the machine began to talk, echoing back the entire story of Mary as it had been spoken.

The good-natured chaffing was hushed; the auditors be-

Mr. Edison gave this phonograph to Francis Jehl on New Year's Day, 1880. It now stands on one of the tables on the second floor of the restored laboratory.

Francis Jehl shows how Edison operated the hand phonograph that stood on the
east end of the long table at the top of the stairs. The same kind of machine may be
seen today in the same position

came spellbound as they listened to the first words from the
machine. It seemed incredible.

That night immortal fame entered the Menlo Park laboratory and the genius of the 'wizard' of Menlo Park was evident
to all. The skeptical public was still to be convinced, and the
practical value of his invention was still to be demonstrated;
the adaptation of the machine to the home was still to come.
But he had now created one of the most simple and yet most
wonderful machines evolved by a human brain.

In his first papers for the patent of the phonograph, Mr.
Edison gave as its object the recording of the human voice
and other sounds in permanent characters, from which the

same sounds could be reproduced at any time. He did not confine himself to reproducing sound by indentations only, apparently seeing from the beginning that sound could also be recorded in a 'hill-and-dale,' or 'lateral cut,' fashion.

The first announcement to the world of the speaking phonograph was made by Edward H. Johnson in a letter to the *Scientific American* published on November 17, 1877, almost exactly one year before I arrived at Menlo Park.([1])

Johnson, you will recall from Chapter IX, was associated with Edison in the development of the automatic telegraph. He wrote:

'Mr. Edison in the course of a series of extended experiments in the production of his speaking telephone, lately perfected, conceived the highly bold and original idea of recording the human voice upon a strip of paper, from which at any subsequent time it might be automatically redelivered with all the vocal characteristics of the original speaker accurately reproduced.'

A sketch accompanied his article as reproduced on page 164.

'Of course Mr. Edison at this stage of the invention,' Johnson concluded, 'finds some difficulty in reproducing the finer articulations, but he is quite justified, by results obtained from his first crude efforts, in his prediction that he will have the apparatus in practical operation within a year.

'He has already applied the principle of his speaking telephone, thereby causing an electromagnet to operate the indenting diaphragm, and will undoubtedly be able to transmit a speech made upon the floor of the Senate, from Washington to New York, record the same in New York automatically, and by means of speaking telephones redeliver it in the editorial ear of every newspaper in New York.

'In view of the practical inventions already contributed by Mr. Edison, is there any one who is prepared to gainsay this prediction? I for one am satisfied it will be fulfilled, and that, too, at an early date.'

Five weeks later Edison appeared at the offices of the *Scientific American* and demonstrated his phonograph to the editors and members of the staff. The report of that thrilling visit was published in the issue of December 22, 1877, and was entitled 'The Talking Phonograph.'

---

(1) Edison's application for patent covering his phonograph was filed December 24, 1877, and granted February 19, 1878. No. 200,521.

'Mr. Thomas A. Edison recently came into this office, placed a little machine on our desk, turned a crank, and the machine inquired as to our health, asked how we liked the phonograph, informed us that *it* was very well, and bade us a cordial good night. These remarks were not only perfectly audible to ourselves, but to a dozen or more persons gathered around; and they were produced by the aid of no other mechanism than the simple little contrivance explained and illustrated below.'

The editor then proceeded to describe the tin foil instrument, and concluded with the following remarkable prophecy:

'We have already pointed out the startling possibility of the voices of the dead being reheard through this device, and there is no doubt but that its capabilities are fully equal to other results just as astonishing. When it becomes possible, as it doubtless will, to magnify the sound, the voices of such singers as Parepa and Titiens will not die with them, but will remain as long as the metal in which they may be embodied will last.

'It is already possible by ingenious optical contrivances to throw stereoscopic photographs of people on screens in full view of an audience. Add the talking phonograph to counterfeit their voices, and it would be difficult to carry the illusion of real presence much further.'

What might be described as the first public exhibition of the phonograph was given in New York City by Mr. Edison before the Polytechnic Association in February, 1878. So much interest was aroused that he looked up his friend Sigmund Bergmann in a small shop in New York City and asked him to tackle the job of manufacturing it. Soon agents were going about the country giving exhibitions of the wonder machine, and others were taking it abroad.

The first important concerts using the phonograph in New York City were aided by Hilbourne Roosevelt, already mentioned as the donor of the organ in the rear of the second floor of the laboratory. To manage them, the services of James Redpath, the founder of the Redpath Lyceum Bureau, a writer whom I shall mention later in discussing the megaphone, were secured. He divided the country into territories, each being leased for exhibition on a percentage basis.

Ear phones enabled more than one person to listen to the same record. (From an early print.)

XXIV. The Speaking Phonograph

Its Development

AS I HAVE said, many distinguished visitors came to Menlo Park to see the machine that would hear, write and speak; and in their wake came reporters and special writers who were eager to give their impressions of this wonderful device. Some of these articles give a picture of the laboratory as it was at that time, and of its master, our chief. Here is one prepared by a young man from the New York *World* not long after the invention was announced:—

The other day a reporter of the New York *World* called upon Professor Edison at his laboratory in Menlo Park, N. J. After greetings had been exchanged the reporter asked, 'How is the phonograph today, Mr. Edison?' 'Oh, about the same as usual,' was the answer; 'but come and ask it. It has an answer for every man, and generally in his own words.'

The reporter followed Mr. Edison to an upper room, where the phonograph was resting on a table. As the cylinder slowly turned he shouted a few words into it and again turned; the phonograph shouted back in the same cheerful

tone that the re-
porter had used:
'How are you?'

Mr. Edison seated
himself before his fa-
vorite invention and
talked, scolded, sang
and whistled to it for
a while, receiving an-
swers according to
his folly or his wis-
dom. After a few
moments the profes-
sor threw himself
back in his chair and
gazed abstractedly
before him. Then he
said, 'It is funny,
after all. You have
to pucker up your
mouth to whistle,
but the phonograph
doesn't pucker one

An artist's drawing made at Menlo Park showing
Mr. Edison and an assistant singing a duet into
the mouthpiece of the phonograph.

bit. Martin,' he continued, calling to one of his workmen,
'come here and sing bass for me.'

A double mouthpiece was placed over the diaphragm of
the instrument, and while Professor Edison sang 'John
Brown's Body' in a loud voice at one side Martin struggled

at the other side
with a bass so
deep that the air
vibrations were
only about three
a minute.

'You didn't
sing loud enough,'
said the professor,
as he shifted the
cylinder.

The clockwork phono-
graph followed the cyl-
inder. A disc turned
much as a record turns
today.

Sketch from New York *Graphic*, April 8, 1878, entitled 'Mr. Edison experimenting with the phonograph in his laboratory.'

'Well, no,' answered Martin; 'I couldn't just get the right chord. But we got it hunky the other day.'

The crank was then turned, and the song was sung by the phonograph with an occasional far-off bass note struggling to be heard. Mr. Edison, thinking he could improve upon this rendering, again sang the song as a solo to the same sheet of foil. When the cylinder was revolved this time the ditty burst forth with vigor, once or twice failing to connect where a note had dragged in the second singing of the tune.

Mr. Edison now rested himself, and the reporter cast his

eyes about the room, at the ceiling and on the floor. Overhead was a net of telegraph wires resembling a huge spider's web, all terminating in a large battery placed in the center of the room.

'Do you use all those wires?' asked the reporter.

'Oh, yes,' was the answer.

'Why do you have that pipe organ which stands in the corner?'

'To record sound.'

'What is that instrument over there?'

'A part of my aerophone.' (See Chapter XXV).

'What is that other one the man is working on?'

'An instrument for reproducing handwriting. I think it will be finished soon.'

'What is this circular plate?'

'Oh, that's for taking messages.'

The reporter now took a turn round the room. There were

Sketch from New York *Graphic* entitled 'Mr. Edison showing the pieces of his improved phonograph.'

thousands of small and large bottles containing chemicals, drugs and oils ranged on shelves along three of the walls. There were hydrofluosilicic acid, chloroform, ether, chloral hydrate, ammoniated tincture of gum guaiac, iodide of potassium, kerosene oil, sulphuric acid and other materials of widely different uses.

'You seem to keep a whole drug store here, Mr. Edison,' remarked the reporter.

'Well,' answered the professor, 'I keep all those things because I don't know how soon I may need them. Whenever I see a new chemical or drug announced I buy it, no matter what it costs. Now here's something I have prepared,' and he handed the reporter a bottle containing a clear, straw-colored liquid. 'That's composed of morphine, chloral hydrate, chloroform, nitrate of amle, cassia and cloves. Those things have no chemical action on each other, and they'll stop any kind of pain immediately.'

'Aren't you a good deal of a wizard, Mr. Edison?' asked the reporter.

'Oh, no,' he answered, with one of his pleasant laughs. 'I don't believe much in that sort of thing. I went to see Heller the other night. His tricks are very good and very clever; and yet I figured them all out but one. The "second sight" is the thinnest of all. Now come downstairs and I'll show you the new model of the phonograph.'

The reporter followed Mr. Edison into the workroom, where about a dozen lathes and machines were in full operation. On one of the tables was the model. The improvement in the phonograph consists in a circular plate's being substituted for the cylinder, and clockwork for the crank. 'This clock movement is a very important improvement,' said Mr. Edison. 'It insures complete regularity and accuracy, and can be thrown out of and into gear instantaneously. We're going to start a publication office in New York when the phonograph is ready.'

'What do you intend to publish?' asked the reporter.

'Music, novels, general literature. Take music to begin with. We shall make phonograph records of orchestral concerts, brass and string bands, instrumental and vocal solos and part songs. The sheets bearing the sound impressions of this music will be removed from the phonograph and multiplied to any extent by electrotyping, and persons can make selections of any compositions they desire. This music may then be reproduced by any phonograph with the original sweetness and expression. And not only that, but the pitch can be raised or lowered by increasing or diminishing the speed of the phonograph.'

'What will such a sheet of music cost?'

'About twenty-five cents.'

'But how can you record an orchestra, since it is necessary in talking to the phonograph to apply your mouth close to the diaphragm?'

'The phonograph will be attached to a hole in one end of a barrel, and from the other end will project a funnel like those used in ventilating steamships. This will receive the music from the entire orchestra, not of course reproducing it with so great a volume. Piano music will be caught by a hood placed over the instrument, the volume of the reproduction being one-fourth that of the piano.'

'What method will be pursued with literary matter?' asked the reporter.

'We estimate that an ordinary fifty cent novel can be contained on this,' said Mr. Edison, tapping the circular plate, which was about six inches in diameter. 'Novels and valuable literature will be read to the phonograph by elocutionists and persons understanding the subjects presented, and the matter will be multiplied by electrotyping in the same manner as music. You see, therefore, that you may have a phonograph in your parlors with an album of selected phonographic matter lying beside it. You may take a sheet from the album, place it on the phonograph, start the clockwork and have a symphony. Then by changing the sheet you may listen to a chapter or two from a favorite novel. This may be followed by a song, a duet or a quartette. At the close the young people may indulge in a waltz without anyone being required to play the dance music. You can easily see,' continued the professor, 'what an advantage the phonograph will be to the blind, and, indeed, I have already received one hundred orders from such persons.'

'What will be the cost of a phonograph?'

'About a hundred dollars. The instrument will be finished in all styles and handsomely decorated.'

This cartoon depicted in humorous vein some of the jokes of 1878 when the new phonograph was coming into use. In the upper left two boys wind the cylinders while a prima donna makes a 'record.' In the upper right, the mischievous wife is starting up a record 'Murder! Police! Fire!' much to her husband's fright. In the left center is an organ grinder carrying a phonograph instead of a music box. The man seated at the desk in the middle cartoon is saying to the salesman: 'Oh, I'm busy. Tell your story to that machine and I'll grind it out tonight.' The small sketch beneath that of the mischievous wife, shows four records operating in unison, with the notation: 'Any church can have a high-toned choir.' The Statue of Liberty in the lower left is 'saluting the world.' At its right is a 'compound double-back-acting duplex shifter, extra gearing, capacity and endurance, without flywheel, large governor. Designed especially for longwinded lightning rod agents.' Above this queer machine is a touching spectacle showing the 'recording of a millionaire's will.' At the lower right, is a suggestion for a safe conference with the Sioux Indians.' Note the phonograph record attached to long rope. Above this cartoon is a 'Fair Shopper' who is ordering 'six yards of Talmadge's last sermon.'

XXV. The Summer of 1878

More Inventions

WE HAVE now come to the summer of 1878 and are rapidly approaching the time when we shall devote all our attention to the search for a successful incandescent lamp. By now Edison was recognized as an outstanding inventor and creative genius, though many so-called scientific men of that day challenged every statement he made, disputed his work and proved to their own satisfaction that his claims could not be true, when judged by the knowledge and reasoning of the time.

He pursued the even tenor of his way, however, undisturbed by either the outbursts of his critics or the extravagancies of his friends. The summer was marked by at least four interesting inventions, the megaphone, the aerophone,

On porch of second floor at Menlo Park Laboratory. (From *Scientific American*, August 24, 1878.)

Megaphone as it appears today on porch of second floor at restored laboratory.

the phonomotor and tasimeter. The first named received its public trial on June 5 from the upper porch of the laboratory. If you will step out on the restored porch, you may inspect the invention as it has been rebuilt in Greenfield Village by Henry Ford.

It was intended to transmit voices over considerable distances. It comprised two ear trumpets, one on either side; with a central mouthpiece through which the voice was sent out. The ear trumpets were much larger than the inner megaphone, being six feet eight inches long and, at the far end, more than two feet in diameter. The central megaphone was distinguished by its bell-shaped mouth.

Those present at the first trial included, besides the inventor, Charles Batchelor, James Redpath, biographer of John Brown, Uriah Painter, noted Washington correspondent, and others.   Batchelor and Painter took one of the devices across the meadow in front of the laboratory a distance of about six hundred yards.   A series of signals had been arranged so that they could communicate to the group on the porch by hand waving to indicate 'I hear' or 'I do not hear.'

Batchelor asked through the megaphone: 'Do you hear me?' and those on the porch signaled they did.   He laughed into the mouthpiece, and then Painter whispered a message, both sounds being audible across the meadow.   Next the two men moved back until they stood approximately one mile distant.

Painter sent a special message to Redpath.

'Do you hear him?' asked some one.

'Perfectly.'

'What does he say?'

'He says: "John Brown's body lies moldering in the

Francis Jehl showing how megaphone was used.

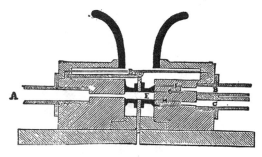

Sketch showing valve of aerophone.

grave," ' replied Redpath, while the others laughed at the sly reference to Redpath's famous book.

'It seemed very uncanny,' said one of the newspaper men present, 'to hold a conversation in an ordinary voice with a man a mile off, without using a wire or electrical contrivance.'(1)

'This is really telegraphing without a telegraph!' Redpath exclaimed.

During the same series of experiments Edison announced that he hoped to complete a small instrument for the use of the partially deaf, which, when connected with the ear, would enable 'any one to hear even the whispers on the stage of the largest theater.'

(1) From New York *Graphic*, June 6, 1878.

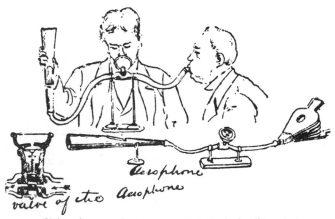

Using the aerophone—from New York *Graphic*, 1878.

Edison's phonomotor (From *Scientific American.*)

Unusual reports about the wide range of the megaphone were spread by visitors at the laboratory during that summer. Persons several miles apart were said to have conversed with perfect ease, and, what appeared even more incredible, the sound of cattle munching grass six miles away was said to have been 'distinctly audible to the denizens of Menlo Park.'(2)

The aerophone was devised to project ordinary tones of speech an indefinite distance and magnify them two hundred times—in other words, a combined amplifier and phonograph. The imitation of the voice was obtained, not by photographing the sound waves on a sheet of tin foil, but by the opening and shutting of delicate valves within a steam whistle or pipe organ. The theory was that the diaphragm's vibrations would be communicated to the valves and cause them to open and close synchronously with the inflections of the voice.

It was not a popular invention; many feared that casual and indiscreet remarks would be roared out to the adjoining neighborhood. The attitude of the public was said to have been one of 'comic wrath,' since it threatened to invade their privacy. In its favor it was said that with it a locomotive could be made to call out the stations; steamships could converse at sea; and lighthouses could thunder out warnings.

(2) *Edison's Life,* by Dickinson, (p. 116).

It was the aerophone that made Edison the subject of an article in the Paris, France, *Figaro*, so wildly exaggerated as to sound almost amusing to readers today. Entitled 'The Astounding Eddison,' it declared among other things:

'Mr. Edison does not belong to himself. He is the property of the telegraph company, which lodges him in New York at a superb hotel; keeps him on a luxurious footing, and pays him a formidable salary so as to be the one to know of and profit by his discoveries.'

A description of his aerophone ended: 'You speak to a jet of vapor. A friend previously advised can answer you by the same method.'

Edison's vocal engine, or phonomotor, was perfected by him during the same summer, and he applied for a patent in August. It was a simple device in which the vibrations of the voice as they acted on a diaphragm were translated into motion through driving a wheel. It was something of a toy.

'Mr. Edison says he will have no difficulty in making the machine bore a hole through a board,' wrote a reporter in the *Scientific American* on July 27, 'but we consider such an application of the machine of very little utility, as we are familiar with voices that can accomplish that feat without the mechanical appliance.'

In the restored laboratory we have one of his models and you are at liberty to observe its operation if you are interested. It has a diaphragm and mouthpiece similar to those of the phonograph, resting on a solid base. Back of the diaphragm is a small section of rubber tubing, against which is a spring. This spring carries a pawl that acts on a ratchet wheel on the flywheel shaft.

When the voice pronounces certain letters, the vibrations of the diaphragm are sufficient to propel the flywheel with considerable velocity.

By now, of course, Edison, though little more than thirty years old, was a world figure. During April he had visited the White House and exhibited his phonograph to President Hayes. He also showed it to the National Academy of Sciences. Special trains were run to Menlo Park by the Pennsylvania Railroad so that excursion crowds could see it demonstrated. Newspapers of that day had columns of reading matter about it. The sobriquet 'Wizard of Menlo Park' was bestowed upon him and fastened itself so that it remained.

He took rank with Franklin, Watts, Morse and New-ton.

The Edison 'myth' grew. When the phonograph arrived in London in the early spring of that year, it was declared: 'Mr. Edison's invention is considered first cousin to the prince of black art. My own impression, after hearing it talk in English, French, German and Hungarian, all at once, was that I had gone mad. The phonograph and the telephone have much increased the kind of dazed wonder with which the Briton looks at an American.'

'The years 1877 and 1878 will live in the record of scientific progress as a period of wonderful discovery in electrical science,' said one enthusiastic American newspaper. 'This period has given birth to the telephone, the chronograph and the still embryonic but undoubtedly successful aerophone. It is perfectly safe to predict that the most wonderful exhibit at the Paris Exposition will be Edison's American phonograph.'

Francis Jehl showing how phonomotor was used. This ingenious invention may be seen on the second floor of the restored laboratory.

The astronomical party at Rawlins, Wyoming, in July 1878. Mr. Edison is second from the right (with his arms folded).

XXVI. The Tasimeter and the Eclipse

THE tasimeter has a special interest for us, since Mr. Edison dedicated it to the public and never sought to patent it. Like so many of his other inventions it grew out of experiments that were being made in an entirely different field. In this case, he was working on the telephone transmitter.

So sensitive was the carbon button to changes of condition, he found, that the expansion of the rubber telephone handle made the transmitter inarticulate and finally inoperative. Iron handles were substituted with a similar result, but with the additional feature of musical and creaky tones which were distinctly audible in the receiver.

Those sounds were attributed by him to the movement of the molecules of iron among themselves during expansion, and he called them *molecular music*. To avoid them, the handle was dispensed with; but, meanwhile, it had done a great service in revealing the extreme sensitiveness of the carbon button.

When Edison found that carbon was more sensitive to the influence of electricity than any other substance within his reach, he sought to apply his discovery to practical use. He devised a heat-measuring instrument which proved so sensitive that it would even register the heat from fixed stars.

He described the machine as a carbon button placed between two metallic plates. The current flowed through one plate into the button and thence through the second plate. Pressing against the plates was a piece or rod of hard rubber. When connected with a battery, external heat changes caused the hard rubber to expand and press the plates more closely against the carbon, or to contract, as the case might be. As the button was affected, so the current varied.

This variation was detected by a galvanometer. It was possible to measure increase or decrease in temperature through the deflection of the needle. By the use of very sensitive galvanometers and the Wheatstone bridge, it was claimed to be possible to measure one-millionth part of a degree Fahrenheit.

Mr. Edison demonstrating the Tasimeter. (From an old print.)

Edison was invited by Professor Langley to adapt the instrument to the measuring of heat of the stellar spectra, and after some experimenting he was able to do so. He focused the heat rays of the distant bodies, concentrating them so as to increase the pressure on the carbon button.

While carrying on these experiments at Menlo Park, Edison was at the same time working on the phonograph and other devices. A total eclipse of the sun was due in July, 1878, and many scientists arranged to watch it at Rawlins, Wyoming, where conditions were expected to be especially good. Edison, feeling the need of some relaxation and thinking that a trip to the remote wilderness of the West would do him good, decided to join the scientists. He prepared to take his tasimeter West and measure the heat of the sun's corona.

The improved instrument was finished just two days before he had expected to start. He was therefore late in getting away and by the time he reached Rawlins every available building in town had been pre-empted by scientists and near scientists already on the scene. The only place left for him was a dilapidated henhouse. A solid base such as his instrument needed to function properly was not to be had.

At length he managed to get a four-inch telescope connected to the tasimeter, which was set in a double tin case, having water at the temperature of the air between the cases. On the night before the eclipse he tried it out on the star Arcturus.

As the image of the distant star was brought on to the vulcanized rubber rod in the tasimeter, the spot of light from the galvanometer moved to the side denoting heat. Five uniform successful deflections were obtained and whenever the star was screened from the rod, the needle returned to zero.

The next day things were less successful. During the morning a strong gale sprang up and disturbed all the 'observatories.' The henhouse rocked to and fro, throwing the tasimeter badly out of adjustment. As the wind increased in violence, Edison ran to a lumber yard, hatless and coatless, to call a dozen men to bring timbers and strengthen the edifice.

The task was completed at 1:30 p. m., and at 2:13 the

Tasimeter as it appears in restored form on second floor of laboratory at Dearborn.

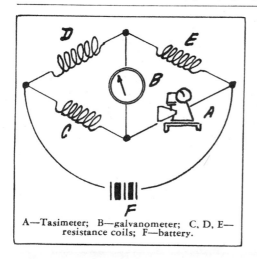

A—Tasimeter; B—galvanometer; C, D, E—resistance coils; F—battery.

shadow of the moon began to steal across the face of the sun. Edison readjusted his instrument only to find that the telescope was swaying so violently in the wind that a satisfactory result was impossible. After a rigging of wire and ropes had been devised, he made another readjustment in frantic haste. As sunlight faded, darkness fell upon the surrounding region. Just before the eclipse the hens which cluttered up the yard he was using went to roost, the darkness convincing them that night had come.

At a quarter past three o'clock the period of total darkness arrived. The tasimeter was still out of adjustment. Though working assiduously, he could not get it into the condition he desired. His difficulties seemed to increase.

When one last moment of totality remained, he succeeded in concentrating the light from the sun's corona on the small opening of his tasimeter. Instantly the ray on the graduated scale swept to the right, clearing its boundaries. Edison was overjoyed. He found that fifteen times more heat had been registered from the sun than from Arcturus. Despite the failure of his instrument to produce satisfactory results, the *Scientific American* declared:

'Seeing that the tasimeter is affected by a wider range of etheric undulations than the eye can take cognizance of, and is withal far more acutely sensitive, the probabilities are that it will open up hitherto inaccessible regions of space, and possibly extend the range of aerial knowledge as far beyond the limit obtained by the telescope as that is beyond the narrow reach of unaided vision.'

It it almost impossible to comprehend the fairylike sensitiveness and delicacy of this instrument. Edison wrote W. F. Barrett, of the Royal College of Science for Ireland:

'By holding a lighted cigar several feet away I have thrown the light right off the scale. With increased delicacy of the galvanometer, the tasimeter may be made so sensitive that the heat from your body—eight feet distant from the instrument—will throw the light off the scale. A gas jet one hundred feet away gives a sensible deflection.'

By using a strip of gelatine instead of hard rubber and utilizing the same principle, Edison

Odoroscope, as it appears today on table on second floor of restored laboratory.

was able to measure moisture. A drop of water on the tip of the finger held five inches distant deflected the needle eleven degrees. An important application of the principle was also used in the detection of icebergs at sea.

When a strip of gelatine was used, the instrument was called an *odoroscope* instead of a tasimeter. In some respects that device proved to be the most novel of all the apparatus. A few drops of perfume thrown on the floor will give a very decided indication on the galvanometer when in circuit with the instrument. Many interesting uses for it can be evolved. One of the odoroscopes may be seen on a table on the second floor of the restored laboratory.

After the eclipse, Edison visited several points in the West, among them Yosemite National Park, Virginia City and San Francisco. Everywhere he was given much attention; for his fame had preceded him. His sojourn in the mountains produced practical results in his next great series of experiments —on the electric light. It was described in a newspaper of the day as follows:

'While visiting the mining regions of the Sierra Nevada and the Rocky Mountains in his late Western tour, Professor Edison was struck with the difficulty which the miners had in drilling and boring, in many cases in the vicinity of rapid mountain streams.

'Except in "placer mining," where the ore is washed out of the bed or the banks of a river, or where expensive steam drills are used, the work of mining is laborious. While he was watching miners drilling by hand, a means of facilitating this work evolved itself from Edison's fertile brain. Turning to his intimate friend, Professor Barker of the University of Pennsylvania, he exclaimed abstractedly:

' "Why cannot the power of yonder river (pointing to a nearby stream) be transmitted to these men by electricity?"

'This thought seemed not to go from Edison's head, and all the way across the plains on their journey home he and his friend discussed various problems for the transmission of power.'

In the New York *Sun* about the middle of September, 1878, Edison made public many of his ideas about the transmission of power and announced his belief that *an electric light would be discovered* which would be easily handled and placed in common use. His predictions led in the beginning to a prolonged argument, but eventually to their fulfillment by Edison himself.

Sketch of Menlo Park laboratory made in 1878.

PART TWO

(CHAPTERS XXVII TO LIII INCLUSIVE)

The Invention of the First Successful Incandescent Electric Light

Evening at Menlo Park

On Christie Street, whenever night,
  Descending, veiled the 'lab' in gloom,
Ofttimes the workmen saw a light
  Shine from that darkened upper room.

A shadow moved across the pane:—
  "The Chief stays late," the workmen said;
Awhile they stood there in the lane
  Watching; and then went home to bed.
          *   *   *   *
Old Christie Street is silent now,
  The workmen one by one have gone,—
A watchman plies his lonely round
  Through the long night till break of dawn.

And who is there to tell him nay
  If sometimes in the lonely dark
Once more he sees a clear white ray
  Shine forth on sleeping Menlo Park?

Wm. A. Simonds

Edison in his workshop—1879. (Drawn by
H. Muhrman, *Harper's Weekly*.)

XXVII. The Problem

MANY men before Edison had experimented with
electricity and shown what happened when a current was passed through a substance. The heating of
metal or other substance to incandescence led some
to try to make a lamp, but their efforts over and over again
merely demonstrated the natural phenomena already known.

Of all the experimenters, only Edison and Lane-Fox had
the remotest idea of the qualities to be sought in an electric
lamp; Edison was the first to vision a system of general distribution of current for domestic purposes, light, heat and
power. His audacious conception of harnessing the mysterious
force—at that time shrouded in mystery—created a furor
throughout the world. Laymen were astounded and scientists
lost much of their dignity. Here was Edison, a graduate,
not of some well-known institution of higher learning, but

of the practical university of life, presuming to solve a problem which they had already pronounced insolvable and which for half a century had eluded the best scientists of both this country and Europe.

That you may have a close-up picture of conditions in the electric-lighting field when Edison began his historic experiments, let me take an excerpt from an outline presented by Frederick P. Fish, eminent technical lawyer, at the forty-second annual meeting of the Association of Edison Illuminating Companies :[1]

What was perhaps the most advanced work, prior to Edison, was done by the Russian Lodyguine who in 1873 developed an incandescent lamp which was exhibited as the best lamp ever made. It had a glass chamber made in two parts, one of which was cemented to the other.[2]

In it was a piece of carbon in an atmosphere of nitrogen. That lamp was burned experimentally. It was exhibited in Paris in 1875 as improved by Kosloff and Konn. Among other improvements made by Konn was the introduction of a series of carbon rods which were so organized that when one burned out the other could be introduced in its place. When they all

_____

(1)   Sept. 27 to Oct. 1, 1926.   (2)   See picture bottom page 239.

Von Guericke's electric machine, 1650. A ball of sulphur was rotated and electricity generated when it rubbed against the hand.

PIONEERS IN ELECTRICITY

Dr. William Gilbert, an Englishman who lived about the year 1600 and held the post of physician to Queen Elizabeth, may be regarded as the first pioneer in the science of electricity. *He was the first to assemble information and facts handed down by the ancients and to conduct experiments in that field.* *Succeeding developments in this science are too numerous to list here.* *It is fitting, however, to recall some of the illustrious names inscribed on its honor roll.* *Each of the workers added something, aiding in some measure to establish facts and principles, and helped succeeding generations to capture the elusive energy and to harness it for practical service to mankind.* *Among the names are those of:*

Aepinus, Ampere, Arago, Armstrong, Abel; Boyle, Boze, Bevis, Beccaria, Brard, Brewster, Brooke, Bennett, Biot, Barlow, Babbage, Balfour, Boltzman, Barclay, Bunsen, Bohnenberger, Bain, Bancalari, Becquerel, Boys; Cuneus (who with Kleist and Muschenbroeck of Leyden invented the Leyden jar, or phial); Canton, Cigna, Cavendish, Coulomb, Cuthbertson, Carlise, Clausius, Cavallo, Cassini, Cazin, Crookes, Cooke, Clark; Dufay, Delaval, Deiman, Sir Humphrey Davy (whom we shall discuss elsewhere), Daniel, Deprez, Draper; Ellicott, Erman, Ewing, Von Ebner, Everett; Benjamin Franklin, the great American; Faraday, the great Englishman; Foucault, Fedderson, Fizeau, Forster, Farmer.

Von Guericke (who made the first friction machine; see page 196); Gray, Gordon, Geoffroy, Galvani (of whom more will be given elsewhere); Grothuss, Green, Gauss, Grove, Gibson, Geissler, Gounelle, Govi; Hawksbee, Haug, Hunter, Humboldt, Henley, Hershél, J. Henry, Harris, Hachette, Holtz, Homes, Helmholtz; Ingenhouz; Jallabert, Jenkin, Joule, Jamin, Jobard; Kinnersley, Knight, Kohlrauch, Kirchoff; Ludolph, Le Monnier, Gay Lussac, Laplace, Lavoisier, Lenz, Lucus, Lippmann; Miles, Menon, Mowbray, Mosotti, Maxwell, Mayer, Muller, Melloni, Mance, Matthiessen, Matteuci, Morse, Mascart, Mitchell, Munro, Muirhead.

Sir Isaac Newton; Nollet, Nicholson, Nairne, Nobili; Oersted, the great Ohm, Oettingen; Paets, Pearson, Poisson, Poggendorf, Pacinotti (whom we shall mention elsewhere); Plicker, Peltier, Page; Quincke, Quet; Reis (whom we mentioned in discussing the telephone); Richman (the Russian who was killed while performing Franklin's experiment with lightning); Robinson, Ritter, Read Morgan, Rosetti, De la Rue, Du Bois Reymond, De la Rive, Roget, Ruhmkorff, Rumford; Smeation, Symmer, Saussure, Seebeck, Savary, Stuart, Smee, Steinheil, Sturgeon, Sprengel (whose name will occur again); Stoletow; Troostwyk, Thomson, Volta (whom we shall mention later); Varley, Van't Hoff, Van Narum; Wall, Sir William Watson, Winkler, Wilson, Wilcka, Walsh, Wollaston, Weber (whose name will occur again); Welther, Wheatstone (another famous name), Wilde, Wimshurst, Widemann; Zollner; and others.

FAMOUS PREDECESSORS OF EDISON.

1, Galvani; 2, Volta; 3, Ampere; 4, Ohm; 5, Davy; 6, Faraday; 7, Weber; 8, Franklin.

burned out, the chamber was taken apart, new carbons put in and the glass sealed up. The arrangement was absolutely useless, even as a single light. It did not even suggest anything practical.

There were people who talked about what was called the 'sub-division of the electric light,' that is, the production of small units of electric light to take the place of gas burners, but it was the unanimous opinion of all competent authorities, an opinion based upon all the laws of physics and all the laws of electricity as then understood, that such a thing as the sub-division of the electric light was utterly impossible. I am going to read to you a word or two from the standard authorities of the day to show how fixed and definite were their views on the subject.

In 1877 Fontaine, an eminent French engineer and scientist, wrote a book on the incandescent light in which he announced his fixed conclusion that the sub-division of the electric light, that is, the development of small illuminating units of electric light analogous to the illuminating units of gas distribution, was impossible. He gave the subject careful study, including in his investigation a series of elaborate experiments with the Lodyguine-Konn lamp, which was far and away the highest development up to that time. In summarizing these tests William H. Preece in a lecture given on February 15, 1879, before the Royal United Service Institution, said:

'It is however easily shown (and that is by the application of perfectly definite and well-known scientific laws) that in a circuit where the electro-motive force is constant, and we insert additional lamps, then, when these lamps are joined up in one circuit, i. e., in series, the light varies inversely as the square of the number of lamps in circuit, and that joined up in multiple arc the light diminishes as the cube of the number inserted. Hence a sub-division of the electric light is an absolute *ignis fatuus.*'

As a result of a most careful series of experiments with the Lodyguine-Konn lamp, he showed that when one lamp in circuit gave a light of nine burners, three in multiple arc gave an aggregate light of one burner; when one lamp in circuit gave a light of fifty-four burners, five lamps in multiple arc gave a light of one-quarter burner (these are various experiments); when one lamp in circuit gave a light of sixty-five burners, five lamps in multiple arc gave a total light of two and one-half burners, and so on indefinitely, thus demonstrating the impossibility of any general system of illumination based upon the incandescent lamp.

All the scientific authorities in the world, including Lord Kelvin, (who however was always conservative and reasonable in his statements), were of the same opinion. The sub-division of the electric light was, said all the scientific men, impossible; and yet at that time Thomas A. Edison had actually solved the problem. He solved it during the development of a lamp in which platinum, in the form cf a filament, was employed. Solving it in connection with platinum did not carry him very far, for the platinum filament lamp was impractical.

None the less, he had worked out experimentally the sound, radically new proposition that the sub-division of the electric light could not be solved by new circuit arrangements or in any way except by the development of a fundamentally new lamp having new and unheard of characteristics, namely, high resistance and small radiating surface. No one before Edison had had the remotest conception of a lamp of that character. He demonstrated the truth of this radically new thought by his experiments with the platinum filament lamp; but the lamp itself was worthless and to realize his idea he had to get a suitable lamp. Without it, his wonderful discovery would have been of no practical value.

At this stage of his work, two things of great interest happened. First, Edison's discovery became known to the world. Incomplete as it was, the prospect of such a competitor was such as to bring about almost a panic in gas stocks throughout the world. In England, a Parliamentary investigation of lighting conditions was made, which seems to have been promoted to a large extent by the threat to the gas industry involved in Edison's alleged accomplishment. In any event, that matter received much attention in the investigation and, as I have said, Thompson and practically all the other scientists who appeared before the Commission scoffed at the suggestion that Edison had accomplished what he was said to have. The eminent engineers all said: 'Don't worry about the sub-division of the electric light. It is impossible.' As before stated Preece, an engineer of high standing and of the most practical type, denominated the suggestion 'an *ignis fatuus*.'

Of course, the fear of a depression in the gas industry because of the competition of the electric light was utterly without foundation. The gas companies throughout the world are still prosperous.

Secondly, Edison had so much faith that even before he had devised the lamp, without which his efforts would have been absolutely fruitless, he went to work to solve the indefinite number of engineering problems that had to be worked out.

From the beginning he had the idea of a carbon burner for his lamp. During 1877 he had spent months in the most careful investigation of carbon in all its aspects, producing carbon sheets and carbon wire, and among other things the carbon telephone transmitter.

When he had solved the sub-division problem, he turned at once to carbon as the ideal substance for the burner of the lamp. His experiments were infinite in number, his thought and effort most profound.

Just prior to his great work the arc system of electric lighting was developed, and was openly declared by scientific men to be the only possible form of electric lighting which could be commercially practical. I remember hearing a man of great intelligence and of some scientific attainment say: 'What a pity it is that Edison is wasting his time and energy and thought on incandescent lighting which is sure to fail; but Brush has an intelligible and reasonable scheme which is well worth pursuing.'

There were any number of arc light companies and some admirable inventions were made by first class men who worked on arc lighting as if there were nothing else in the world. But Mr. Edison paid no attention whatever to it. He realized, as did no one else, that lighting *by incandescence* was of infinite value. He worked entirely on that problem.

That was the way in which his ideas appeared to men who viewed them honestly in the light of laws of physics and electricity *as understood by them.* Edison approached the matter in a different way. He found that, by the sound and intelligent application of those same laws, the stupendous result of the incandescent lamp with its filament of high resistance and small radiating surface could be produced. That was the revolution brought about by Mr. Edison. By the correct application of the inexorable laws of physics, electricity, heat and light, he achieved a result which every one said was impossible.

Leyden jars used by Edison at Menlo Park. Now in
restored laboratory at Dearborn.

XXVIII. Early Seekers After
the Electric Light

THE friction machine and the Leyden jar were the two
principal pieces of electrical apparatus known to people
in the 18th Century. Because of their novelty they
were as popular as radio sets today and almost equally
entertaining.

In Paris, France, Abbe Nollet transmitted the discharge
of a battery of jars through 180 guardsmen, making them all
jump. The Carthusian monks of that city formed a line nine
hundred feet long, and when the hands at the ends met in
contact with 'the electrical phial, the whole company at the
same instant gave a sudden spring.'

About the middle of that century, Franklin performed his
well-known kite experiment to prove that the mysterious
force *electricity* and the natural phenomenon *lightning* were
identical. 'He raised electricity from an interesting novelty
to the dignity of a science.'

Some thirty years later—in 1780, to be exact—a professor at the University of Bologna who enjoyed international repute in the field of comparative anatomy and ob-
stetrics dissected a frog in his laboratory. Near by stood a

friction machine. While the latter was being turned and sparks were being emitted, the professor's assistant touched a nerve of the dead frog. Instantly the carcass was convulsed as if life had been restored.

Professor Luigi Galvani believed he had discovered in electricity the secret of life. He spent years in further experimentation and finally published a book written in Latin, in which he told the news. A sensation followed. Among those whose attention was attracted to the matter was Alessandro Volta, Professor of Experimental Physics at the University of Pavia.

Volta was bold enough to question Galvani's theory. He declared that the frog's legs kicked into the air for the same reason as made the 180 guardsmen jump. Probably Galvani had drawn upon some source of electricity. But what was that source? Was it that the frog's legs hung from the *iron* railing by a *copper* hook?

After eight years of study, Volta became convinced that the contact of two dissimilar metals was enough to generate electricity. He piled silver and zinc discs on each other with moist pieces of cloth between

Spark leaping across gap of four and one-half inches. Made by friction machine shown above.

and connected upper and lower discs by means of a wire. He got—not a shock, but the first steady current in history!

News of his discovery, which took place in the year 1800, caused another sensation. Volta was summoned to Paris to lecture before the French Academy of Sciences, where the presiding officer was the First Consul, Napoleon Bonaparte. Bonaparte was fascinated by the experimenter, who decomposed water and made a thin wire to glow. Many special honors were given Volta. Bonaparte arranged for a special

Sir Humphrey Davy exhibiting his discovery of the first arc light before the Royal Institution in London, 1810. (From a drawing in the *Scientific American* March 29, 1884).

Faraday's dynamo, 1831, in which he demonstrated his discovery of generating a current by means of a permanent magnet. A replica of this is in the Edison Institute collection.

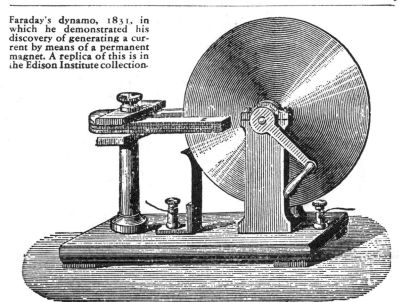

Pixii's Dynamo (1832). A permanent magnet rotated near two coils. Replica in Edison Institute collection.

Below—Dynamo developed abroad by the Alliance Company about 1855 for first commercial installation of electric light.

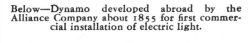

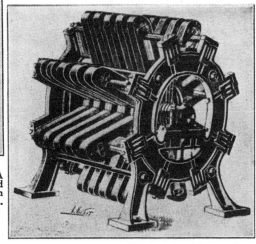

interview, during which he cross-questioned the Italian on the subject of the 'Voltaic pile,' and finally dismissed him with gifts, of both money and honors.

As the new century got under way, it saw the commencement of brilliant researches by Sir Humphrey Davy. He showed that metals and certain other substances could be heated to incandescence, and demonstrated the essentials of an arc lamp, open and inclosed, using two sticks of charcoal. (See picture on Page 202.) During the year 1825, a great law governing electricity was discovered by George Simon Ohm. Then Sturgeon discovered the electromagnet.

From that time on, the problem of transforming mechanical power into electricity occupied the center of the scientific stage. The basic principle was worked out in 1831 by Faraday, the apprentice, assistant and successor of Davy. Little by little, progress was made in developing a generator to make arc lighting possible. One of the magneto variety, known as an Alliance machine, was installed in the Hotel des Invalides in Paris in 1855 for running an arc lamp. As may be noted from the picture on Page 203, it consisted of a large number of stationary permanent magnets in front of which a great many wire bobbins

Von Alteneck's differential arc lamp. Now in Edison Institute collection.

mounted on a shaft were rotated. In 1856 Siemens made his famous shuttle-wound armature.

Three men—Siemens, Wheatstone and Varley—shortly after the close of the Civil War expounded the principles of self-excitation of dynamo machines, and their work, together with that done by Pacinotti, provided all the data needed for the construction of direct-current generators. Zenobe Theophile Gramme, a Belgian who toiled in Paris as a pattern maker, gave the world its first efficient *ring* generator in 1870, eight years before our own great Edison undertook his experiments in search of the incandescent light. (See picture on Page 249.)

Because of the Gramme machine, men were now able to discard batteries. They could tackle the problem of electrical lighting in an hitherto undreamed-of manner. Within two years, Siemens brought out the *drum* generator, designed by his engineer Von Hefner Alteneck. In the following year came Alteneck's differential arc lamp, the first of a truly commercial type and the first to be used extensively (or so they thought at that time). Thus arc lighting obtained a footing.

At the Centennial Exposition in Philadelphia in 1876, only two arc lamps were exhibited. Indeed, the sight of an arc lamp in those days was rare. I recall paying a dime in 1877 to view one that was being exhibited at a circus on Fourteenth Street opposite the Academy of Music in New York City.

The eminent American professor, John Trowbridge, said on January 11, 1879:

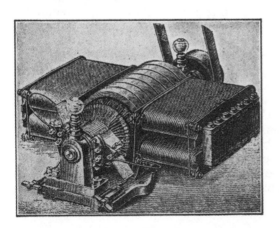

'With regard to the electric light, America is far behind Europe in the progress recently made, and unless some great invention is suddenly made in this country and sanctioned by the Patent Office, we must

View of Alteneck Siemens 'drum' generator.

not look for novelties here . . . In this country there are not more than a dozen establishments lighted by the electric light (arc) while on the old continent they are reckoned by hundreds.'([1])

Less success had attended the efforts to develop an incandescent lamp. Before 1878, all such efforts had failed.

A summary of them was prepared by me not long ago for the New York Edison Company, from which I make bold to repeat certain excerpts here.

The annals of research show that among the men who strove without avail for this discovery were De la Rive in 1820, Grove and Jacobi in 1840, De Moleyns in 1841, Starr in 1845, Staite in 1848, Roberts in 1852, De Changy, Gardner and Blossom in 1858, Farmer in 1859, Adams in 1865, Lodyguine in 1872, Osborn and Kosloff in 1874, Khotinsky and Konn in 1875, and Bouliguine and Woodward in 1876. Draper, Fountain, Sawyer, Lane-Fox, Swan, Van Choate, Childern, Du Moncel, Ruhmkorff, Jablochkoff and Maxim complete the list up to 1879. All of these investigators toiled in the same field and tramped the same treadmill. It remained for Edison to seek new, original methods.

Some employed rods, pencils, or sticks of gas retort carbon, which they filed or worked down to the desired sizes and placed in glass tubes or globes sealed by metal caps. Some tried to evacuate the air with inefficient equipment; others replaced air with nitrogen, while some used their unprotected carbons with the result that these were generally consumed in a few minutes.

Other workers sought to remedy the defect by automatically shifting in new rods. But none could retain a vacuum for the simple reason that their containers were not air tight. All knew that carbon could not fuse, and yet they did not try to learn why the carbons disintegrated so rapidly when subjected to the action of the current.

From De la Rive down to Sawyer, all found that neither rare metals nor carbon could be employed with any chance of success. At length they gave it up and devised, as already mentioned, an automatic means for replacing the burned-out carbons. Even the best lamp of all—one that came out in 1878, received its death warrant from its own inventor, who said in his book that 'to replace a carbon requires a workman's time from two to three hours, and the recharging

(1) *Scientific American.*

of the lamp with absolutely pure nitrogen costs about seventy cents, without taking into consideration the cost of the carbon. It is therefore an impracticable lamp.'

Another fact to remember is that even if any of those early lamps, regardless of cost and bulk, could have been made durable, it would have been impossible to utilize them. Their resistance was so low. Their carbons were thick and short, and the investment for copper conductors to supply current would have been prohibitive.

All these men tried to produce a lamp employing the principle of incandescence. However, light produced by heating a material through an electric current to incandescence is a far cry from a lamp. It merely demonstrates a natural phenomenon. A lamp must incorporate certain requisites to be of practical use. First of all, it must give a steady light and provide a high resistance. To be adapted to domestic use it must be simple, and of light weight. Furthermore it must be flexible and must function under all conditions and in all positions. It must be cheap. Its flame must be noiseless and inoffensive.

None of the men mentioned succeeded in making such a lamp. The most successful was not an incandescent lamp; it was an arc—Jablochkoff's electric candle, which I shall describe in the next chapter.

Siemens (Hefner Von Alteneck) generator (1878).
In Edison Institute collection. First to include drum-
wound armature.

Wallace-Farmer dynamo, 1875. One of these may be seen at restored Menlo Park, Dearborn.

XXIX. Wallace-Farmer and Jablochkoff

EDISON'S first experiments with carbon in the field of incandescent electric lighting were made in September, 1877, at the time he was developing his phonograph and carrying on additional experiments with the telephone transmitter. Some one has spoken of that year as a 'carbon year' for Edison, because 'carbon in some form for use in electric circuits of various kinds occupied the minds of the whole force from morning to night.'

In the beginning a strip of carbonized paper about one inch long, its ends fastened to the poles of a wet battery, was brought to incandescence in the open air to determine how much current was required. As soon as it became incandescent, the paper was destroyed. The experiment was next tried under a glass jar from which the air had been evacuated by means of a hand pump. This burned for about eight minutes before disintegration.

Following his system of 'trial and error,' the inventor

attempted various methods of preventing oxidation but all without success. At least fifty different carbons made of tissue, wood or broom corn were used. Coated with a mixture of lamp black and tar, they were rolled into the fine long form of a knitting needle, and carbonized. He then laid aside the use of carbon for the time, and resumed experiments with almost infusible metals, such as chromium, ruthenium, and so on. Previously, he had tried out platinum, only to discard it temporarily for carbon.

His conclusions in this new effort were that the metal substances were within the bounds of possibility for the purpose, but did not reach the ideal he had in mind. Early in 1878 his experiments were ended, partly through pressure of work on the phonograph and other inventions; partly because he was exhausted and in need of a vacation. I have already described that Western trip and his experiment during the eclipse. Not until September 1, 1878, after his return from the West, did he resume the search.

During that trip the question of generation and transmission of power came frequently to his attention. While visiting mines in the Rockies and the Sierras, he had noticed difficulties encountered by workmen in drilling and boring, in many cases near rapidly flowing mountain streams. Turning to his friend Professor Barker of the University of Pennsylvania, he had remarked:

'Why cannot the power of yonder river be trans-

Wallace-Farmer arc lamp, 1878, consisting of two slabs of carbon between which arc played. Two of these are at restored Menlo Park in Dearborn, Michigan.

mitted to these men by electricity?' (Chapter XXVI, Page 189.)

Professor Barker said that this thought seemed to linger in Edison's mind on their journey home across the plains. As they discussed it again and again, Barker descri d a machine he had recently seen in process of being made. It had been devised by William Wallace, a brass manufacturer of Ansonia, Connecticut, who happened to be a friend of Barker's. His ambition was to build something that would make possible the transmission of power from one point to another by electricity.

Edison, Batchelor, Professor Barker and Dr. Chandler (Professor of Physics at Columbia University) made the trip from New York City to Ansonia in order to learn what progress had been made on this machine. They found it completed. For their benefit Wallace connected it up with eight arc lamps, each having a radiance of about four thousand candles. He called it a *tele machon* and described it as a dynamo-electric machine for transmitting power by electricity.

In a New York newspaper of September 16, 1878, appeared the following explanation of Wallace's invention:[1]

'When power is applied to this machine it will not only reproduce it but turn it into light. It will divide the light of the electricity produced into but ten separate lights. These being equal in power to four thousand candles, their impracticability for general purposes is apparent. Each of these lights is in a substantial metal frame, capable of holding in a horizontal position two carbon plates, each twelve inches long, two and one-half wide and one-half thick. The upper and lower parts of the frame are insulated from each other and one of the conducting wires is connected with each carbon.

'In the center and above the upper carbon, is an electromagnet in the circuit, with an armature, by means of which the upper carbon is separated from the lower as far as desired. Wires from the source

Goblet etched by Edison to commemorate his visit to Ansonia. (From *Electrical Engineering*.)

(1)   New York *Sun*.

of electricity are placed in the binding posts. The carbons being together, the circuit is closed, the electromagnet acts, raising and lowering the upper carbon enough to give a bright light.

'The light moves toward the opposite end from which it starts, then changes and goes back, always moving toward the place where the carbons are nearest together. If from any cause the light goes out, the circuit is broken and the electric magnet ceases to act. Instantly the upper magnet falls, the circuit is closed, it relights, and separates the carbon again.'

An interesting souvenir of Edison's visit at Ansonia was scratched by him with a diamond point on the side of a glass goblet:

'Thomas A. Edison, September 8, 1878. Made under the electric light.'

Before leaving, the inventor told Wallace that he did not believe the latter was following the right path in seeking a practical electric light. 'I believe I can beat you in the search,' he added good-naturedly.

Associated with Wallace in that work was Moses G. Farmer, who lighted the living room of his house in Salem, Massachusetts, during the summer of 1859, using electric lamps made of small pieces of platinum and iridium wire.

Avenue de l'Opera, Paris, illuminated at night by Jablochkoff candles, 1878.

The Jablochkoff candle
bracket for eight candles,
as used in Paris in 1878.

It happened that during the same year of 1878, an exposition was held in Paris, during which an electric candle invented by Paul Jablochkoff aroused the attention of the world to the possibilities of electricity for illumination. Jablochkoff was a former engineer-officer of the Russian army; his 'candle' was used to illuminate some of the streets in Paris during the great exhibition.

This candle was nothing but an arc light operated without mechanism. Instead of two carbons' being placed in a vertical position, one above the other, they were placed parallel, and separated by a layer of plaster of Paris or something similar. To ignite the two carbon sticks, their upper tips were bridged with a plumbago paste which when the current was turned on was rapidly consumed and formed the arc. The candle could operate with alternating current only. Similar machines had been made by Gramme, Lontin, Siemens and others.

Jablochkoff's invention appealed to many; the Societe General d'Electricite financed it. Contained in it was a holder, or bracket, into which four, six or more candles could be inserted. Each burned about one and a half to two hours, at which time another had to be switched in, either by an attendant or automatically. The light fluctuated and changed into different colors, and yet everyone was dazzled.

In public squares, streets, hotels and shops, the Jablochkoff candle lighted the darkness. The thing that awed visitors most, however, was the amazing spectacle seen from the square where the Theatre Francais was situated; for standing there and looking up the Avenue de l'Opera, they saw in one thrilling glance sixty-four electric candles ablaze. For the first time in electric lighting history, a street was illuminated by that means. People were entranced by its possibilities.

First floor of Menlo Park Laboratory, from a sketch published in 1878. Mr. Edison is shown with his latest model phonograph. On left end of table is smaller model built for popular use. This sketch was drawn by an artist during the time of Edison's phonograph experiments.

XXX. The Edison Electric Light Company

Grosvenor P. Lowrey, counsel for the Western Union, who enlisted the aid of New York bankers in financing Edison's electric light experiments.

AS SUBSEQUENT agitation and furor led practical men to attack the electric lighting problem, scientific truths not previously known were uncovered. These accomplishments soon left many of the theorists in the rear, to their dismay. History's first page in the early development of electric lighting will always accord Jablochkoff's name an honorable place, though his system of lighting was short-lived and soon disappeared.

One important result of Jablochkoff's invention was the crystallizing of Grosvenor P. Lowrey's interest in electric lighting. The acute mind of my employer, the eminent jurist and corporation lawyer, grasped the situation; he believed that immediate action was necessary by his friend Edison if the secret was to be found by him, instead of someone else.

Mr. Lowrey had talked with Edison about the benefits that would result from the invention of an electric lighting system, to be used as gas was then being used in the home. The inventor modestly said that he had already experimented in a small way and had been forced to stop because of the heavy expense, but felt confident he could do something.

More equipment was needed in his Menlo Park headquarters before he could proceed in the proper way. At that time the only buildings in his Menlo Park group were the laboratory, the carpenter shop and the carbon shed.

At least two additional structures were required, one of which would serve as a machine shop and another as office

One of the first American commercial dynamos, the Brush. Also made to use for arc lamps.

and library.
These things would cost more money than the inventor could spare.

So much faith did Mr. Lowrey have in his friend that he approached several wealthy clients and asked them to back Edison in the search. When they agreed, he drafted papers for the incorporation of the Edison Electric Light Company, constituted under the laws of New York State. Three hundred thousand dollars were to be raised among the supporters and advanced to Edison, while on his side the latter was to invest his time and ability.

Meanwhile after Edison's return home from his examination of the Wallace-Farmer machine at Ansonia, he resolved first to find out all he could about the production and distribution of illuminating gas, such as was used for lighting New York City and many other places in that period. He bought all the bound volumes he could find and read up on the transactions of gas-engineering societies; he pored over trade journals and read many books.

'His notebooks relating specifically to "electricity vs. gas as general illuminant" covered an astounding range of inquiry and comment. They show that he sought to develop an electric system which in simplicity would imitate gas and in addition would meet all requirements of natural, artificial and commercial conditions. He recognized that "a general system of distribution was the only possible means of economical illumination," and dismissed isolated plant operation as being outside consideration. Luther Stieringer, an expert gas engineer, said that Edison knew more about gas than any other man he ever met.'[1]

The result of all this was his conclusion that the problem of subdividing electric current so as to make electric lighting possible in the home was capable of solution. It only required a stable and high resistance lamp connected in a system of

---

[1] Page 15, Appendix B, Report of Lamp Committee, Association of Edison Illuminating Companies, 1929.

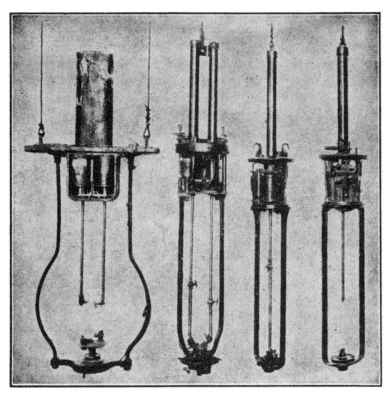

Historic arc lamps in collection of Edison Institute, Dearborn. Left to right—The pioneer Brush arc lamp; the Brush-Adams lamp; the Thompson-Rice lamp; another Thompson-Rice lamp.

parallel mains, and a few other (as he thought) minor adjuncts!

Even at that early date—October, 1878—twelve months before the actual completion of the first practical and successful incandescent lamp, Edison had his plans figured out, as a great general figures out his battle strategy before the first cannon is fired. He knew what he intended to do. Such details as generator, meter, lamp socket, base, switches, fuses, underground conductors, and feeder system were already visioned before the intensive research began.

Small wonder that many spoke of his 'brazen confidence' in himself. His actual accomplishments exceeded even his expectations and the world was amazed that one man could execute so much in so short a time. The secret lay in his early vision, far in advance of realization.

During the month preceding my arrival, a reporter from the New York *Sun* called at Menlo Park and talked with Mr. Edison sufficiently to learn what his plans were. The story of the interview, published on October 10, 1878, enables us to form an accurate picture of what was in the back of the inventor's mind at that early date, *more than a year before the actual invention.*

'Are you positive,' inquired the reporter, 'that you have found a light which will take the place of gas and be much cheaper to consumers?'

'There can be no doubt of it.'

'Is it an electric light?'

'It is. Electricity and nothing else.'

When the inquisitor wanted to know where the electric current was coming from, Mr. Edison peered ahead into the future.

'We simply turn the power of steam into electricity; the greater the steam power we obtain, the more the electricity we get. One object in putting up this new brick machine shop is to ascertain how many electrical jets, each equal to one gas jet, can be obtained from one horsepower.'

The electricity would be made by twenty or more engines stationed in different parts of a city, rather than all at a central point, as was done with gas.

The electric light, he predicted, would be regulated by a screw the same as gas. It could be shut off at any time. No match would be needed to light it. 'There will be,' he said, 'neither blaze nor flame, no singing or flickering; it will be whiter and steadier than any known lamp. It will give no obnoxious fumes nor smoke, will prove one of the healthiest lights possible, and will not blacken ceilings or furniture.'

Shades could be used on it as on gas lamps, he went on. The wind could not blow it out; there would be no explosions or suffocations. One of his most interesting prophecies was that lamps could be made with flexible cords and carried from one point to another and in one direction or another, with the lamps actually upside down if so desired.

When Professor Sylvanus Thompson, the eminent scientist, read all this, he said (*Engineering*, October 25, 1878):

'The reporter of the New York *Sun* in his enthusiasm to repeat the claims of Mr. Edison puts into his mouth state-

ments which exhibit the *most airy ignorance* of the fundamental
principles both of electricity and of dynamics.'

He added:

'Suppose an electric light equal in luminosity to one
housand candles, and we want instead to divide that light
into ten smaller lights. If we introduce ten equal branches,
each will carry one-tenth part of the original current, and the
intensity of light in each will be one-hundredth only of the
original light, or ten candles. We shall get ten lights of ten

Mr. Edison at the dedication of the commemorative tablet at Menlo Park, New
Jersey, May 16, 1925.

candles each instead of one light of one thousand candles.'

Despite this and many similar warnings, the Edison Electric Light Company came into existence October 15, 1878. It may be of interest to quote from the articles of incorporation:

'State of New York, City and County of New York, SS.—We, Tracy R. Edson, James H. Banker, Norvin Green, Robert L. Cutting, Jr., Grosvenor P. Lowrey, Robert M. Galloway, Egisto P. Fabbri, George R. Kent, George W. Soren and Charles F. Stone, all of this City of New York in the County and State of New York, and Nathan G. Miller, of Bridgeport, in the State of Connecticut, and Thomas A. Edison, of Menlo Park, in the State of New Jersey, and George S. Hamlin, of Rutherford Park, in the State of New Jersey, being desirous of forming a corporation pursuant to and in conformity with the act of the Legislature of the State of New York passed February 17, 1848, entitled: "An act to authorize the formation of corporations for manufacturing, mining, mechanical or chemical purposes," and the various acts of said Legislature additional thereto or amendatory thereof, have associated ourselves together for the purposes aforesaid, and in pursuance of the requirements of said acts to make, sign and acknowledge this certificate, and do hereby certify as follows:

'First—The corporate name of the said company is "The Edison Electric Light Company."

'Second—The objects for which the said company is formed are to own, manufacture, operate and license the use of various apparatus used in producing light, heat or power by electricity.

'Third—The amount of the capital stock of the said company is three hundred thousand dollars.'

The Edison Electric Light Company was not the first of that character to be organized. The Brush and the U. S. companies were already in the field, manufacturing arc lamps. Union and Madison squares in New York City were illuminated by that means, as were squares in Cleveland, Ohio, Brush's home town. The arc lamp with its generator had even been applied to the lighting of a building. After exhibiting his apparatus in Boston in 1878, Brush installed it in a clothing store, as an advertising stunt. The arc light was all right for outdoors or for large warehouses and factories, but not flexible enough, too noisy and too cumbersome for the home.

XXXI. Menlo Park in Autumn of 1878

I HAVE told of my first morning at the laboratory and how I became a boarder at Aunt Sally Jordan's. Christie Street, extending from the office building to the Edison home, was the real center of the business and social life of the hamlet. Most of the villagers were connected in some way with work at laboratory or shop, and the houses of most of the families could be seen from the windows of the office.

Besides the Edison home and the Jordan boarding house, the double house occupied by John Kruesi and Charles Batchelor faced on Christie Street, as did the home of Charles Dean, machinist. Later the first electric street-lighting system in the world was installed along this thoroughfare.

A plank walk bordered its edge from the laboratory a distance of 850 feet to the Edison home, along which, from one of the laboratory windows, I could often see Mr. Edison coming or going. He generally wore a skull cap or a farmer's wide-rimmed straw, carried both hands in the front pockets of his trousers according to the style of the time, and strolled along with head bent in thought.

The new brick buildings, the office in the corner and the

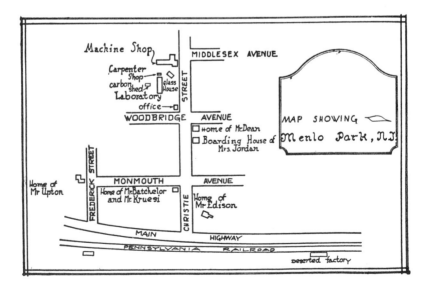

Edison home at Menlo Park (from old photograph).

machine shop in the rear had just been added to the frame structures that previously had comprised the Edison group. On the day of my arrival furniture was being taken from the front of the laboratory to the new office; and machinery was being moved from the back to the new shop.

For the new shop, Edison had ordered an 80-horsepower steam engine from Charles H. Brown, of Fitchburg, Mass., and a steam boiler from Babcock & Wilcox. By November 23 the boiler was set up and the engine was on platform cars down at the depot. The same boiler may be seen today in the restored machine shop at Dearborn, and the engine is an exact duplicate of the original one.

All the buildings were lighted by illuminating gas, which was piped from a distillation plant in the carpenter (or pattern) shop back of the laboratory.([1])   The machine, manufactured by the Combination Gas Machine Company, of Detroit, was installed by James H. Mason, who went down to Menlo Park

(1)   An exact duplicate of this plant now furnishes gas to the restored Edison buildings, and may be seen in the carpenter shop back of the laboratory.

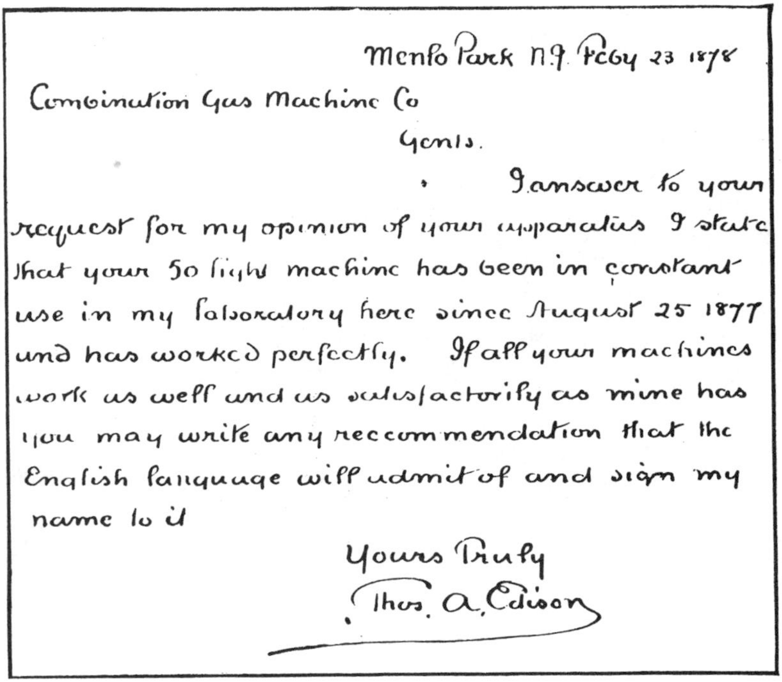

Menlo Park N.J. Feby 23 1878

Combination Gas Machine Co

Gents.

        I answer to your request for my opinion of your apparatus I state that your 50 light machine has been in constant use in my laboratory here since August 25 1877 and has worked perfectly. If all your machines work as well and as satisfactorily as mine has you may write any reccommendation that the English language will admit of and sign my name to it

Yours Truly
Thos. A. Edison

Letter written by Edison recommending gas-making machine. Original is at Dearborn.

from that city for the purpose. It had a capacity of fifty lights, or 'burners.'

At the time of my advent, Milo Andrus was the pattern-maker. H. A. Campbell, another carpenter, started work there about one month before me. When Mr. Edison was visiting the restored laboratory in Dearborn on the fiftieth anniversary of his invention, October 21, 1929, Campbell's name was mentioned. Some one asked where he had lived. 'Over at Metuchen,' replied Mr. Edison, at the same time pointing with his thumb out the window in the relative direction of Metuchen from the old site. On recollecting his whereabouts, he smiled; the restoration had been so faithfully carried out that he forgot for the moment and thought himself back in old Menlo Park.

(²) Campbell's own story of how he became associated

---

(2) P. 14. Technical Bulletin of Dept. of Distributing Stations, N. Y. Edison Co., Nov., 1928.

Advertisement of gas making machine used at Menlo Park.

with the laboratory is as follows:
'I started on the 24th of October, 1878, as a carpenter, which was my trade. Mr. Edison was at that time erecting a two-story brick office building, a brick machine shop, which housed the boiler and the engine, and a little separate house (known as the photographic studio). Upstairs in this house, which sat facing the north so as to get a northern exposure through the roof, there was provided a room for developing negatives . I worked on all of these buildings until they were completed.'([3])

The building last described eventually became the glass house, where the first incandescent electric light bulb was blown. Ludwig Boehm, the glass blower, moved his belongings, his trunk and his zither, to the upstairs room. Here he lived, while working downstairs with his glass-blowing instruments. (See Chapter XLII.)

A description of Menlo Park and the laboratory as it appeared at that time, was published in the *Daily Graphic.*

'We went over to Menlo Park, New Jersey, to see Edison and his wonderful inventions and make some sketches for the *Graphic.* Menlo Park is not a park. It is not a city. It is not a town. Although it is on the Pennsylvania Railroad, it is not even a stopping place, except when the station agent flags the train to take on waiting passengers. It is composed

(3) Subsequently Mr. Campbell worked on the Pearl Street Station, New York City. In 1928 he was superintendent of the Second District, N. Y. Edison Co.

Original induction coil used at Menlo Park. Now in restored laboratory.

wholly of Edison's laboratory and half a dozen houses where his employes live.

'Just north of the track is a long, plain, white wooden building, full of windows and two stories high. This is the laboratory of the Jersey Columbus whose name has suddenly become famous. Many telegraph wires are festooned from it. The first floor is occupied by scribes and bookkeepers in one end, and at the other some ten or twelve skilful workers in iron, who, at anvil and forge, lathe and drill, are noisily engaged in making patterns and models for the genius of the establishment. His iron ideas, in tangled shapes, are scattered and piled everywhere;

Drawing of second floor of laboratory as it was in 1878. (By Francis Jehl.)

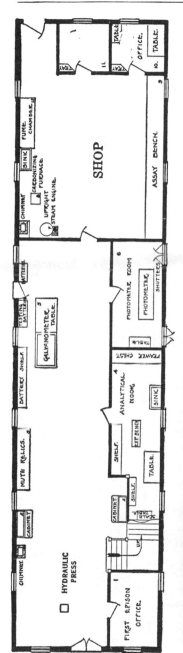

SHOP

ASSAY BENCH.

FUME CHAMBER.

SINK

CHIMNEY

CARBONIZING FURNACE

UPRIGHT STEAM ENGINE

BATTERIES

PRIMARY BATTERY

GALVANOMETER TABLE.

BATTERY SHELF

PHOTOMETER ROOM

PHOTOMETER

SHUTTERS

TABLE

DRAWER CHEST

ANALYTICAL ROOM

SINK

EXP. BENCH

SHELF.

MUTE RELICS.

TABLE.

SHELF.

CABINET

SHELF.

SCALE TABLE

CABINET

CHIMNEY.

□ HYDRAULIC PRESS

UP

FIRST EDISON OFFICE.

TABLE

OFFICE.

10. TABLE.

9

11.

6

4

5

Above—First floor of Menlo Park laboratory as it has been restored at Dearborn. In the center of the left wall is the entrance. In the lower left-hand corner is Edison's old office, from which the furniture was being removed on the day Jehl arrived at Menlo Park to start work. The stairs leading to the second floor adjoin the office. Near the stairs is one of the glass cabinets, on whose shelves are the instruments which have been pictured and described here by Mr. Jehl. Opposite is another cabinet. John Kruesi's old office will be seen on the right. Left—View of floor, showing office at right, steps leading upstairs, and cabinet containing models of early inventions.

Sketch of shop in rear room of laboratory, as it appeared in 1878 before machinery was removed to brick building in rear. (From *Daily Graphic*).   This shop has been accurately reproduced in the restored laboratory at Dearborn.

Gas-distilling machine as it looks today in carpenter shop of restored Menlo Park, Dearborn.

turning lathes are thickly set on the floor and the room is filled with the screech of the tortured metal.

'Upstairs we climb, to a room the size of the building, with twenty windows on sides and ends. It is walled with shelves of bottles like an apothecary shop, thousands of bottles of all sizes and colors. In the corner is a cabinet organ. On benches and tables are batteries of all descriptions, microscopes, magnifying glasses, crucibles, retorts, an ash-covered forge, and all the apparatus of a chemist. At a table sit two earnest men, each holding alternately to mouth and ear the mouthpiece of a telephone.' Thus did the laboratory appear to a visitor in 1878, before the office and the shop were separated from it and moved into the new buildings.(4)

At the time I left New York City, its down town section resembled a forest in which lean poles crowded closely along the streets. On top of the poles were crossarms of wood supporting rows of glass insulators. Lines of wire ran from pole to pole and from insulator to insulator.

In winter these myriad wires, covered with icicles and crusted snow, were a menace to the people of the city. There were telegraph wires, gold and stock ticker wires and private lines; and later high tension arc light circuits were being added. A series of frightful accidents occurred, as a result of which electrocution became recognized as a means of death, and soon as a method of execution.

During that period there was no college or school in which electricity could be studied as a subject; the little then known about its practical side formed a small branch of physics.

(4) *Daily Graphic,* April 2, 1878.

There were but few pieces of electrical apparatus, chief of which were galvanometers, friction machines, Leyden jars, induction coils, batteries, and condensers. Edison's laboratory contained all of these; among them was the Ruhmkorff coil, powerful enough to give a six- to eight-inch spark. Such a coil was called an 'inductorium,' or 'induction coil'; today we know it as a kind of transformer.

The coil consisted of a bundle of soft iron wires wound with two windings of copper wire. One winding of coarse and relatively short length was called the 'primary,' the other of fine wire and greater length the 'secondary.' The primary coil was placed in series with battery and circuit breaker. The induced current in the secondary coil was used to produce physical, chemical or physiological effects much superior to those obtained from the friction machine or the Leyden jar.

Leyden jars could be charged from the Ruhmkorff. The broad principle of the induction coil was first demonstrated by Faraday in 1831. Professor C. G. Page, of Salem, Massachusetts, studied the electrostatic properties of induced, or secondary currents, and in 1836 published the first account of an induction apparatus. He was also the originator of the automatic circuit breaker in that connection. In 1851 Ruhmkorff, of Paris, made the coils that bear his name.

The coil that Edison used at Menlo Park is still in excellent working condition, and may be seen with the other original apparatus in the restored laboratory at Dearborn. He used it, among other experiments all of which I witnessed, in research work on various gases. In trials to which they were subjected, the large induction coil had an important place. It was used with Geissler's tubes to show the great beauty of the stratification of that kind of electric light.

While still with Mr. Lowrey I read an advertisement in *The Operator* (a telegraph paper) regarding Edison's 'inductoriums' of small size for family use and entertainment. Electricity taken from such a coil was deemed beneficial in a number of ways, especially for certain ailments. When we look back and realize how valuable Faraday's discovery has proved, we wonder that it developed so slowly—before it assumed the name of 'transformer.'

Another kind of apparatus that I remember well was the wooden boxed condenser which I found in the laboratory when I first went there. At Menlo Park (as now in the restored laboratory) condensers were strewn about everywhere on both first and second floors. These boxes, which were about nineteen inches long, three inches high, and ten inches wide, contained sheets of tin foil separated by sheets of paper well soaked in paraffin.

These condensers have played an important part in the history of the telegraph; and I don't believe anybody had more to do with them than Edison. We know how vital they are today in radio. The electric condenser has always been an appliance of great importance. Doubtless while working on the duplex, and later on his quadruplex puzzle, Edison began to realize the fact that 'genius is 99% perspiration and 1% inspiration'—as he manipulated condensers and variable resistance boxes in order to obtain a stable method of adjustment!

The condenser was generally called into service in various systems of telegraphy when tantalizing electrical freaks developed; and it became the home remedy in many kinds of practical and experimental work.

Restored carpenter shop in rear of laboratory as it appears today at Dearborn.

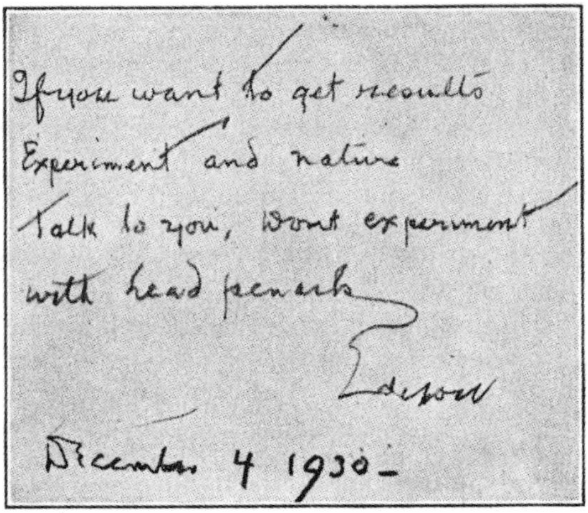

If you want to get results
Experiment and nature
Talk to you, Dont experiment
with head pencils

Edison

December 4 1930—

The above message to the students of the Edison Institute at Dearborn was written by the distinguished inventor on the occasion of a visit during December, 1930. It has been framed and now hangs in one of the buildings in Greenfield Village.

XXXII. The Challenge of the Century

WHEN Edison predicted the coming of the electric light, he sent gas stocks crashing temporarily. The British gas companies were badly worried, and a Parliamentary commission was appointed to make investigation into the possibility of such an invention. After much deliberation, it was pronounced an impossibility, a dictum in which the leading scientists of Europe concurred. This, however, did not dampen Edison's enthusiasm; he paid absolutely no attention to it.

'A young man sat at an acid-spattered pine desk in an obscure New Jersey hamlet, writing in a work-thumbed notebook the most amazing challenge of the century to the scientific world. 'The challenge that was to call forth mockery, derision and ridicule made the bold statement that electricity could be harnessed to produce a new kind of illumination such as never before had been seen, a light as small and cheap as an ordinary gas jet, and much more brilliant, with a further assertion that thousands of such lights could be generated and operated from a central supply, and each capable of separate, independent control.' ([1])

Dr. Paget Higgs, the eminent scientist, wrote: 'Much nonsense has been talked in relation to the incandescent electric light. A certain inventor has even claimed the power to divide the electric current indefinitely, not knowing or else forgetting that such a statement is incompatible with the well-proven laws of the conservation of energy.'

The great savant John Tyndall said: 'I believe I am credited with knowing something of the intricacy of the practical problem involved, and the most that I can say in answer is, that I should certainly prefer having it in his (Edison's) hands to having it in mine.'([2])

Electricity available for home use by the pressing of a button or the pulling of a cord—the idea was so far from the possibilities that it allowed no room even for argument, according to scientific investigators!

Here are a few opinions voiced by leading scientists and electrical experts of that time.

In a lecture before the University College of Bristol, December 20, 1878, Professor Sylvanus Thompson said:
'We have heard a great deal of late of Mr. Edison's dis-

---

(1)   Hugh Weir in *McClure's*, 1922.
(2)   Lecture before the Royal Institute, January 17, 1879.

Grove's incandescent lamp, 1840. A coiled platinum wire burner was covered by a glass tumbler surrounded by water in glass dish to protect the burner from draughts of air.

Edison and Napoleon, showing facial resemblance noted by Sarah Bernhardt. (From an old print.)

covery of a means of indefinitely subdividing the light. I cannot tell you what his method may be, but this I can tell you, that any system depending on incandescence will fail.'

In a lecture at Stevens Institute of Technology on October 17, 1878, a distinguished professor declared: 'There are several very promising directions for experiments on one of which, no doubt, Mr. Edison is at present embarked; but the difference between a promising line of experiments and a successful result all the world's history teaches us is often a distance of many years, to say the least.'

Hippolyte Fontaine, who wrote the well-known book *Electric Lighting*, declared: 'The subdivision of the electric light is impossible of attainment, and the disintegration of carbon when made incandescent rules it out of consideration for small burners.'

John T. Sprague, prominent English electrician, said: 'Neither Mr. Edison nor anyone else can override the well-known laws of Nature, and when he is made to say that the same wire which brings you light will also bring you power and heat, there is no difficulty in seeing that more is promised than can possibly be performed. The talk about cooking food by heat derived from electricity is absurd.'

But the young American inventor down in the New Jersey laboratory was not calculating from their point of view. Before I had been with him very long, I discovered that Edison was using masterly strategy in his experiments. There seemed to be a similarity to the methods of the French conqueror Napoleon I; except that Edison's campaign was for peace, instead of war. Like the French soldier, he knew how to take advantage of each success. Sarah Bernhardt publicly

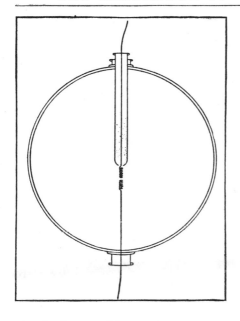

De Moleyn's lamp, first incandescent lamp patented in England (about 1841). Consisted of spherical glass globe in which was open tube containing powdered charcoal. Platinum wire was inserted through tube and another came up from bottom, not quite touching first. The current passed over charcoal dust bridge and heated it to incandescence.

called attention to a facial resemblance between the two.

In telling of a visit at Menlo Park, she said: 'I looked upon this man of medium size, with rather large head and noble-looking profile, and I thought of Napoleon I. There was certainly a great physical resemblance between these two great men, and I am sure that one compartment of their brains would be found to be identical. I do not compare their genius. One was destructive, and the other creative.'

Putting off a thing until tomorrow was a practice unknown to Edison. He kept going forward relentlessly and when an obstacle came in his path either passed round it or turned it to his advantage. That trait was well illustrated during his researches in telephony. In the restored laboratory you will find an endless variety of carbon-transmitting telephones tried by him during that campaign. Electrodes of every shape were mounted in all kinds of positions. Carbon was used in its various forms, both as given by Nature and as produced by man. The swiftness with which this wizard worked amazed his competitors; while others were losing time in discussion or debate, he kept at work.

I also found that he was a new kind of teacher. All his men learned from him, not in the traditional lecture-hall manner, but in a practical way, while solving their problems.

For his preparation of experiments Batchelor was given explicit, terse instructions. After the experiments were under way, every phase was explained. Edison did not do all the talking; he even invited discussion, during which his clear common-sense arguments usually prevailed.

Electricity at that time could not be studied in text-books; such as existed treated it in the most elementary way. Currents were weak, being derived from glass jars; and the electromagnet as found in the telegraph, the telephone, the call bells and the announcers was the only important application of the force to the service of man.

The Menlo Park laboratory was a classroom in advanced electrical engineering, where new precepts and theories were not only advanced but also proved for the first time. In all that, Edison was our leader and teacher. Many of these principles had been learned by him during the years he was a telegraph operator, and later an inventor of telegraphic equipment. He knew the secrets of electro-magnetism as no other man; he observed and studied while he tapped the keys; and the mysterious force so baffling to others was well understood by him in many of its fundamentals.

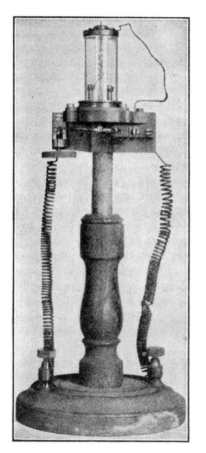

Not having obtained satisfactory results from his trials with carbon as a light-giving element, Edison in the fall of 1878 turned to high fusible metals and began a series of experiments with platinum, iridium, and other rare and costly substances. The melting point of platinum being about 3191 degrees Fahrenheit, it had to be heated close to that temperature, of course, to yield an acceptable light. The first problem to be

Edison's first experimental lamp. Now at Dearborn. Patent No. 214,636.

Edison's second lamp. Now at Dearborn. Patent No. 214,637.

solved was that of preventing the platinum from melting when brought to such a heat. Edison evolved a simple device called a 'thermostatic regulator' and embodied it in his first lamp, for which he signed a patent application on October 5, 1878. This patent was No. 214,636, issued April 22, 1879.

In the restored laboratory may be seen the patent office model of that first experimental lamp. Later models had pedestals made of cast iron for use in subsequent experiments; all of these varied in certain details from the first one, whose pedestal is of wood. A small glass tube mounted on the pedestal contains a double spiral of platinum (as may be noted in the picture on page 234). The spiral is coiled about a straight platinum wire, the regulator.

At its upper end the wire is attached rigidly; at the lower it is connected with a lever. When the current becomes too intense, the straight wire, expanding, short-circuits the spiral. The heat dies and the fusing of the metal is averted. After it has cooled, as it does quite rapidly, the straight wire contracts, of course, and reopens the circuit, permitting the current to pass into the spiral once more and produce light.

Edison's claims to an invention (as set forth in the patent) were: 1. In combination with an electric light having a continuous incandescent conductor, a thermostatic circuit regulator. 2. In combination with an electric light, a thermostatically operated shunt. This lamp failed because the constant expansion of the wire and its pressure on the lever below bent it so that it became unreliable.

His second lamp introduced a more sensitive thermoregulator, which utilized the expansion of the heated air inside the glass tube. He signed this patent application on

November 14, 1878, and the patent was issued to him as No. 214,637. In it he claimed:

'The method specified of regulating the temperature of the incandescent light-giving body, by the expansion of the air or gas in the closed vessel containing the light, acting automatically in the electric circuit.'

A model of this lamp may be seen in the restored laboratory. (See picture on page 235.)

In these experiments, Edison labored patiently and endlessly, sitting for days and nights beside the oblong table on the second floor of the laboratory, where I first found him.

The tricks and antics which these frail contraptions with their tiny levers went through would tax the patience of a Job; only a saintly nature could preserve calm. Often I saw Edison as he reached a crucial point in an experiment dart his fingers through his bushy hair distractedly, or throw away a half-smoked cigar and absent-mindedly take another out of a

Edison's third lamp. Now at Dearborn. Patent No. 218,866.

Edison's electric candle, now at Dearborn. Patent No. 219,628.

vest pocket to tear off the tip with a savage bite.

Whenever anything new developed he usually exclaimed: 'Hulloa! Send for Kruesi.'

Soon John Kruesi, head of the machine shop, would hurry in.

'Here, Kruesi, make this right. It doesn't work as I want it to. You see, it must function like this.'

With that he would explain what he had in mind. The shop foreman would fulfill the order and the inventor would go back to the problem anew. No one can guess how many platinum lamps he

Roller devised by Kruesi for flattening platinum wire used especially for clamps in horseshoe and bamboo filament lamps. Now in restored laboratory.

tested during those experiments, or how many times he sat there till past midnight poring over them.

My task was to keep the Bunsen battery cells in proper condition to be at Mr. Edison's disposal. Batchelor had to make new metal spirals, under the chief's direction, to replace those burned out.

'Aw, bosh!' Edison would exclaim as one expired, 'Got another one, Batch?'

Mr. Edison would place the new spiral in the lamp or, as was often the case, instruct Batchelor to prepare one having different characteristics. It was customary to try many changes and variations during the experiments.

His instructions to me were always brief but explicit.

'Francis, give me another one,' referring to resistance boxes—or perhaps, 'Add another cell or two'—or, 'Do this and see what happens.'

The precious metals were kept in a glass case at the right of the organ in the north end of the second floor of the laboratory. Here were not only platinum, iridium, rhodium, boron, chromium, ruthenium, titanium, but also gold, silver, aluminum, as well as rare oxides and expensive chemicals. Aluminum was not yet known to the housewife as it is today. In the same case were baser metals, such as iron, copper, zinc, cadmium, all in chemically pure state.

Edison's third lamp, using platinum foil instead of a spiral, was fastened to a bracket that could be swung from the side wall, like those used for illuminating gas. It became Patent No. 218,866, signed by him on December 3, 1878.

'My present invention relates to the combination with the light-giving body of a range of levers and contact surfaces arranged in such manner that the current is short-circuited or shunted to a greater or less extent, according to the heat of the incandescent light-giving body.' (See photo on page 236.)

On the same date he made out a patent application for another kind of lamp, an electric candle, and Patent No. 219,628 was issued on this invention. It consisted of a candle formed of finely ground platinum, iridium or other metal, incorporated with nonconducting material like clay.

'The candle can be any desired size or shape, and the metallic particles become incandescent by the passage of the current, and the nonmetallic materials are luminous and increase the brilliancy. This is accomplished by a comparatively small electric current. I mix with such finely divided conductors infusible materials such as oxide of magnesium or zirconium, in different proportions, so as to obtain any degree of conductivity required.'

In other words, as the metallic iridium, which made the composition a sort of conductor, began to heat up the mass, the oxide also became a conductor and gave off light.

Jablochkoff, the Russian engineer, had already tried the same idea, forming incandescent glowers of earthy compositions. When cold, the elements acted as insulators but when heated with a match, changed to conductors of current. The principle was adopted years later both in Germany and in this country; and determined efforts were made to use it in the building of a practical lamp.

A large amount of capital was spent before the attempts were given up. Edison himself experimented with the combination for some time and in various ways before abandoning it. (See picture at top of page 237.)

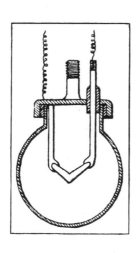
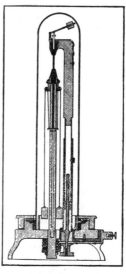

Left—Lodyguine's Lamp, a piece of graphite operating in nitrogen gas. (About 1873.) Its life was 12 hours. Right—Bouliguine's Lamp. (About 1874.) A single long graphite rod of which upper part only was in circuit, in a vacuum. As rod burned, it was automatically drawn up by counterweight, so that a new portion could be burned.

Where John Kruesi and Charles Batchelor lived in Menlo Park

XXXIII. Looking for a Metallic Lamp

EVEN at this early stage in his experiments, Edison was convinced that an incandescent lamp of low resistance would never be practical; nor could he use the only method of distributing current known at that time— the 'series,' which was generally used for arc lights. While such a method was satisfactory for street-lighting, it would never work inside a home. It was impossible to light or extinguish one lamp at a time; the whole system had to be either off or on. And indeed, who wanted an arc lamp in his home, a heavy and cumbersome apparatus that gave off a dazzling but unsteady light, and in which the carbons had to be changed frequently?

The dynamo machines then in use were expensive to

Francis R. Upton.

operate and inefficient; Edison's current had to be derived from a wet battery made up of bichromate cells. One of the things he knew must be accomplished was the devising of a much more efficient dynamo machine. A committee of ten competent scientists had been appointed in 1877 by Franklin Institute to test various makes of dynamos; their report showed that the most efficient thus far was the Gramme, with 38 percent. Edison had one of these machines in the shop. (Chap. XXXIX.)

Estimates of the cost of copper wire made it essential that the voltage used in his lighting system be relatively high; otherwise the cost would be excessive. Professor Barker, Edison's friend at the University of Pennsylvania, estimated that copper conductors for Edison lamps in a given area of New York City would cost $100,000; whereas with the low resistance lamps developed before Edison's the cost was $200,000,-000 for the same area.

The need now was for facts, figures and diagrams. A clear conception of the essentials of the problem was already in Edison's mind; and to make it clear to others, he engaged a mathematician. Francis R. Upton, a Princeton graduate who had studied under the great Helmholtz in Germany, was selected for the job. He arrived in Menlo Park a few days after me and took a room at Mrs. Jordan's next to mine. The old office in the front of the first floor of the laboratory was turned over to him for a workroom for a time.

At first Upton could not understand why Edison wanted

a lamp of high resistance.   Years later in describing his work, he said:([1])

'I cannot imagine why I could not see the elementary facts in 1878 and 1879 more clearly than I did. I came to Mr. Edison a trained man, a postgraduate at Princeton; with a year's experience in Helmholz's laboratory; with a working knowledge of calculus and a mathematical turn of mind. Yet my eyes were blind in comparison with the eyes of today; and as an apology, I want to say that I had company.

'There was the lecturer in London, a good friend of mine (now dead), who said the division of the electrical current was commercially impossible. Another man of high intelligence said that the resistance outside a dynamo should be equal to that in the armature.

'I have recently gone over the article on electricity by George Chrystal, Professor of Mathematics, University of Edinburgh, in the Encyclopedia Britannica of 1878. This article was one of the most useful in the literature of the day to Mr. Edison and his assistants. It helps my apology for ignorance in that there was no mention of a name for any unit of current. Ohm and volt are mentioned in this article, with this qualification, "The determination of the British Association Committee is out by nearly two percent." In the index of the Encyclopedia this title is given: "Unit, electromagnet of current strength." Turning to this in the text, one finds in the margin the words, "Unit of current strength."

'The following definition is given in the text: "It follows, therefore, that the statement of our fundamental principle involves a unit of current strength such that unit length of the unit current, formed into an arc whose radius is the unit of length, exerts a unit of force on a unit pole placed in the center of the arc. From this statement and the definition of a unit negative pole, it follows at once that the dimension of the unit of current is"—(and then follows a formula). It is very evident that in 1878 there were others who shared with me a lack of practically useful thinking regarding electric current.'

All the electrical 'experts' of the day confined their efforts to seeking a light that would be stable. If they could find a substance that, brought to incandescence, could endure,— that is, have life,—they would be satisfied. It never occurred

---

(1) Address before Edison Pioneers in 1918 on the occasion of the first meeting of the association.

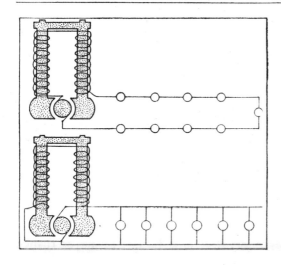

The upper diagram shows lamps connected in series, with constant-current dynamo, only method known before Edison. Below is Edison's plan, the 'multiple' system with constant-voltage dynamo. Current was distributed in quantities needed at constant pressure

to them that if they tried to alter the conditions under which they were working, better results might be obtained. They were obsessed with the idea that success could be found only in the substance used for the light-giving element.

Thus they worked with pencils, or rods, having a large cross section; yet these would have failed even if they could have endured the conditions under which they were operated. A cross section always means a large amount of current, and a strong current means a large cross section of copper mains to lead the current to the lamp. None of Edison's predecessors gave this matter a thought, for none had dreamed of a new system. They only tried to make something that could be called a lamp.

Edison's fertile brain conceived the new system and the conditions under which it should be operated, and put that system into tangible form step by step. First he required a lamp that would fulfil the conditions of the system. Then he had to have an efficient generator, an electric meter for registering the current, a mode of regulating the system, sockets, switches, fuse wires, underground conductors and all the other equipment. It was an herculean job for one man.

The lamp, he reasoned, must have high resistance and small radiating surface. He had to speculate on all the conditions that the lamp must meet to be commercial and practical. In those days men were not able to calculate with such units as volts, webers (later rechristened 'amperes') or ohms. In their experiments they did not question the qualitative proportions

Patent No. 224,329, dated January 23, 1879, in which a carbon rod was pressed against the platinum point.

of results obtained. They were satisfied if they got some wee sign of a result; they did not dare to assert what the results should be.

Edison was of another sort. Like a Napoleon, he first planned his strategical campaign and then fought the battle; he never rushed forward without knowing what to do. Thus he reasoned with his lamp. It must have high resistance—which meant a small current. This idea alone was the theoretical salvation of commercial distribution of electrical energy; it was the foundation of all systems of conductors.

He found that one of his spiral platinum lamps consumed about ten webers (amperes) of current at ten volts. This indicated a resistance of one ohm. He calculated what cross section of copper would be necessary for conveying that current a certain distance from the source with a stipulated percentage of drop in voltage lost in the line.

Next he obtained a cross section of copper and calculated that if he could make a lamp that consumed only one weber (ampere) of current, with voltage raised to a hundred, the lamp would have a resistance of one hundred ohms. In determining the cross section of copper necessary for sending one weber of current the same distance with the same percentage

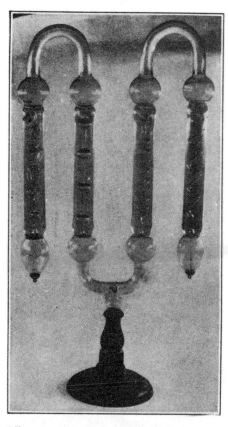

Edison experimented with Geissler tubes, trying to increase their light intensity. Forerunner of Neon lights of today.

of drop of tension in the line, Edison found that only one-hundredth of the weight of copper was necessary.

Thus he saw that the solution of a commercial system of parallel distribution of electric energy lay in the fact that all receivers of current, whether lamps, motors, or what not, must have high resistance, or its equivalent. His reasoning—that is, common sense—was at that period far in advance of the time; which was one reason so many challenged or criticized him. No savant reasoned in like manner or had the capacity to understand the drift of his logic.

He progressed step by step, going slowly and with infinite pains and ransacking every corner of the field, beating the bushes, looking under logs and stones, and conducting what was probably the most thorough search known to history.

He tried everything. He used a reflector to concentrate heat rays on a piece of zircon, making it luminous. He caused a slender rod of carbon to rest upon one of platinum, producing a resistance through the inferior contact and causing the carbon to burn brightly. An arrangement of weights kept the carbon rod pressing against the platinum. (See picture on preceding page.)

He investigated the notion of having each householder become his own light-manufacturer. He used an induction coil with two batteries and sent a current through Geissler tubes of special make. (See picture on page 245.)

After he had become convinced that a low resistance lamp was impractical, he invited his financial supporters to come down to Menlo Park one evening and demonstrated to them that a different lamp and different system were necessary.

The weather was cold and raw; a high wind blew across the fields surrounding our rectangle. We had made ready several platinum lamps and, after the coils had been coated with oxide of zirconium, had mounted them on little brackets along the north side of the machine shop, above the benches where the mechanics worked.

The train pulled in at the depot and the bankers—Mr. Morgan, Mr. Lowrey and the others—walked up. They stopped at the library for half an hour or so while our chief reported to them verbally on the results of his experiments thus far. Soon the little group crossed the yard and I heard Mr. Edison call 'Francis!'

That was my cue. I fell into step at the rear of the procession.

Kruesi had already placed a Gramme generator on a belt in the machine

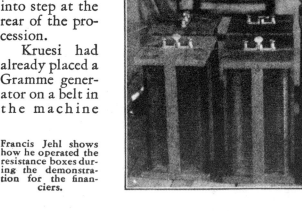

Francis Jehl shows how he operated the resistance boxes during the demonstration for the financiers.

shop. After we had taken our places, Edison gave a brief outline of the evening's program. As he mentioned the platinum coils, he asked Batchelor to hand him one (already coated) from the supply in the latter's pocket.

At length Edison concluded his remarks and the time came for the experiment to proceed. At his signal the little shop was darkened and we all sat in shadow. It was a gloomy moonless night. The chief spoke up.

'Let 'er go, Kruesi,' he called. Then, after a moment:

'Francis! Get down there by the resistance boxes and put them all in.'

I hurried down the line and checked my boxes to make sure that all were in series and connected with the lamps.

'Got 'er connected, Francis?'

'Yes, sir.'

'Cut out one box.'

I obeyed. No results appeared. The shop was still as dark as ever. Slowly the vague outlines of faces or figures could be discerned.

'Cut out another.'

As I did so, the lamps blinked to life, showing a dull red barely visible. Edison knew then where he was.

'Cut out another, Francis.'

The commands followed rapidly as I removed one box after another until the lamps burned a bright cherry red. At that point he explained to his audience what was necessary to change the light from red to white.

'Cut out another,' he went on.

The lamps glowed a soft white, which became stronger as I plugged out still another resistance box. The coils were almost melted by the terrific heat. Each of the lamps gave off six or seven candlepower. In that early day, this was deemed sufficient.

Suddenly one of the lamps gave way like a shooting star. The line of lights died out. The shop was plunged in darkness.

'There you go,' said Edison. 'You see, the system is not practical. When one burns out, it is as bad as if the whole circuit had broken. The lamps are not practical, either. Low resistance lamps will never work.'

Batchelor took out one of his small coils, jumped to the table and inserted it in a lamp, while I broke the current at Edison's command. 'Batch' repeated this operation three or four times, as lights burned out. When everyone was at last convinced, Edison shouted: 'All right,' indicating that the show was over.

Afterward the bankers and Mr. Lowrey returned to the office building and talked with Mr. Edison until train time. Meanwhile, I returned to the second floor of the laboratory to complete some work. As it was not yet ten o'clock, I decided to read the book on *Electrical Testing* which Mr. Lowrey had presented to me and which I was studying with much absorption.

In the midst of my self-imposed lesson, footsteps sounded on the stairs and soon the chief came up alone. He seated himself near the table that ran along the east wall. Soon he seemed to fall into a deep abstraction, in which I did not attempt to disturb him. His hands were thrust into his side pockets. The mental picture of him as he sat wrapped in thought, pondering his experiments, wondering what steps should be taken next, gazing into space, was burned indelibly on my memory.

He took off his skull cap and tossed it onto the table among some Bunsen cells that had been placed there to furnish current for experiments. In the pale flickering light of the gas jets, he reminded me of a painting I had once seen of Napoleon staring moodily into the future and striving to discern it.

Half an hour passed before he moved. At last, picking up the ends of two wires that led down from the battery, he toyed idly with them. Some charred paper lay on the table beside a Bun-

One of brackets used to support lights during demonstration described in this chapter. (Now in restored laboratory at Dearborn.)

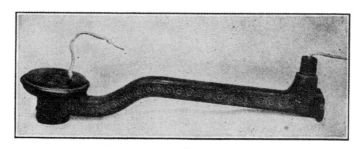

Another of the brackets used at demonstration. (Now in restored laboratory at Dearborn.)

sen burner. He touched it with the two ends, as if curious to see what might happen.

The result was startling. For an instant a bright light illuminated the laboratory, and then died away.

Some months later he arrived at the point in his experiments where he took up carbonized material as a possible substance from which to make filaments. Some of his first successful filaments were of paper. Perhaps the incident just related remained in his mind and suggested the value of paper.

Gramme generator of 1877. Now in restored laboratory. Furnished current for Edison early in 1879 when he demonstrated the impracticability of series platinum lamps.

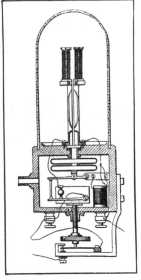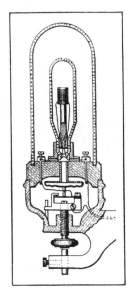

Left—Edison's first high resistance lamp, from Patent No. 227,227. Spools of clay stood in the glass globe surrounded by coils of platinum wire. Thermostat regulator below. Right—Edison's first high resistance lamp to use a vacuum. From Patent 227,229, signed April 12, 1879.

XXXIV. Occluded Gases—Another New Discovery

WE NOW come to the series of experiments in which Edison, searching for a high resistance lamp, decided to try a vacuum. At the outset he worked with a mechanical pump that stood on a table at the west side of the laboratory. With it he exhausted most of the air inside a large glass bell in order to study the effects of the vacuum on platinum spirals or foil as an electric current was passed through them.

My part in the experiments was to prepare the bell and then work the pump. To begin with, I greased the rim of the bell, turning it round and round on its seat to be sure that a proper seal had been made against the entrance of air. I then operated the pump, using both hands, one on each handle.

When the gauge was within one or two millimeters of a perfect vacuum, the experiment usually commenced. Incidentally, forcing out the air to the extent mentioned took a strenuous application of muscle.

I recall vividly the day on which Edison while engaged in one of these experiments made the discovery that had much to do with forwarding his search for the incandescent electric light. A platinum curl had been placed between the two binding posts inside the bell. After the air had been exhausted, the 'chief' sent a current through it, at the same time watching the gauge.

After an instant he turned abruptly to me and declared: 'Francis, this pump is leaking.'

Now I had prepared it with the utmost care and could not understand the reason for his criticism.

'Are you certain,' he went on, 'that you greased it properly?'

I was certain, but as Edison always wanted to be 'dead certain,' he had me take off the bell and regrease its rim while he oversaw the operation. As may be imagined, I rubbed on the grease with considerable vigor, and saw to it that the contact was as nearly perfect as possible. It satisfied him.

'That ought to do,' he said. 'Let's start again.'

I worked the pump, drawing out the air, and although it was cold weather beads of perspiration trickled down my forehead. The current was turned on again. Once more, as before, the gauge lost ground, indicating that the pump was leaking or else that

Francis Jehl operates mechanical pump to exhaust air from glass bell on right, showing how he did it at Menlo Park in 1879.

some strange phenomenon was taking place.

'Keep on pumping,' I was told. Batchelor was summoned. 'Batch, keep your eyes on this gauge,' said the chief.

Soon the assistant had noticed the defect.

'By George,' exclaimed Batch, 'the gauge is going up. The pump must be leaking.'

'But it's not,' returned Edison. 'I'm sure of that.'

Out of this experiment came a most important discovery— namely, that occluded gases are released by metals when heated in a vacuum, and that after they have been finally expelled, the continued heating of the metals no longer affects the vacuum. It remains unchanged.

Edison further learned that the residuum was a hard and homogeneous metal of altered properties, capable of being forced with current to give a light of twenty or twenty-five candle power instead of five or six as was the case before the gases had been expelled.

When he completed his researches on occluded gases, Edison knew he had found the key that would later open the door of success.

The only evacuator at his disposal was the mechanical pump. He was now convinced that to take full advantage of his discovery, he must obtain a pump designed by Sprengel, the German scientist, which was operated by mercury.

Another problem was the devising of a globe of glass from which the air could be exhausted to produce the highest obtainable vacuum.

Where to obtain a Sprengel air pump was the question. A telegram from the laboratory to New York City started a wide inquiry, but none could be found anywhere.

One day the matter happened to be mentioned to Upton, our mathematician, who recalled that Professor C. F. Brackett, of Princeton University, had recently received one from Germany for use in that institution.

'Do you think the college will lend it to us?' asked the chief. 'Why don't you go down and find out?'

Princeton was only a short distance south of Menlo Park on the way to Philadelphia. Upton went over on the following day as suggested. He soon returned, bringing the pump with him. He had carried it on his back from Metuchen, where his train had stopped.

Mercury was immediately ordered by telegraph from Eimer Amend, our New York City supply house. Upton himself

John A. Yunck.

mounted the pump on its stand, placing it beside the table on the east side of the laboratory near the stairway, where it was soon in use.

To Batchelor was assigned the task of making tools and draw plates through which the wire could be made fine. When asked how fine, Edison had replied dryly, 'five-thousandths of an inch in diameter'; which made Batchelor look up sharply to see whether his chief was joking.

Kruesi had the job of building forms through which the little spools of infusible substance could be pressed into shape. As a guide for size he was to use the press in the carbon shed which made carbon buttons for telephone transmitters.

Another necessary adjunct was a more satisfactory container of glass, so that the vacuum could be increased. As there was no glass blower at Menlo Park, Edison took a suitcase full of spools of pipe clay wound in platinum wire to John A. Yunck in Philadelphia. Yunck was an expert glass blower with a shop at 1126 Market Street. He had blown many scientific glass instruments for Professor Barker, and when Edison commenced his experiments with the high resistance platinum lamp in the early part of 1879, was recommended to him by Barker. Edison arranged with Yunck to enclose them completely in glass bulbs.

Later Edison wanted to buy out Yunck's business and bring him to Menlo Park, but could not persuade him to accept the offer. Yunck suggested the name of William Holzer, also a Philadelphian. When the latter came to Menlo Park and joined Edison early in 1880, Yunck bought out the Holzer business.

During the brief interim when the glass bulbs were being blown, I was assigned the duty of cleaning the mercury with acids. I also had to wash it with water and dry it. Today, when I recall those lamps, I wonder why they have not received more attention in the history of electric lighting. They were exactly like the successful ones which came later, except in the material composing the light-emitting conductor.

When the first lamp of this April series was placed on the Sprengel pump, I had the honor of operating the latter

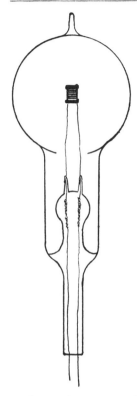

Sketch by Upton of Edison's first high resistance lamp in vacuum without thermostat regulator. Note how it resembled later successful lamp except in filament. From *Scribner's Monthly*, February, 1880.

while Edison stood by and expelled the occluded gases. When he was satisfied, he sealed it off from the pump with an alcohol lamp and blow pipe. The new light was then inserted in a stand and inclosed in a second chamber connected to a hot-air regulator.

If Edison could at that time have obtained one of the high-fusion metals we have since discovered, such as osmium, tantalum or tungsten, the commercial incandescent lamp would have been born then, I am convinced, instead of six months later.

Edison applied for the patent covering this lamp in April, 1879. It was Patent No. 227, 229. A drawing of the lamp, taken from the patent application, appears at the beginning of this article. He said:

'I am enabled to obtain a nearly perfect vacuum which is permanent; and at the same time give the platinum wire a new and unknown property of great value in electric lighting. This is, that a platinum wire which melts in the open air at a point where it emits a light equal to four candles, will, when operated upon as described, emit a light equal to twenty-five candles without fusion.'

He also said:

'By the use of such high resistance lamps I am enabled to place a great number in multiple arc without bringing the total resistance of all the lamps to such a low point as to require a large main conductor; but, on the contrary, I am enabled to use a main conductor of very moderate dimensions.'

Following these came other experiments in which the thermostatic regulators were discarded. The last-named lamps resembled the one which was finally successful, except that instead of a carbonized filament we used a small compressed spool of zircon wound with a thin platinum wire and insulated with pyro-solution. Edison was still searching persistently for an ideal and efficient solution.

In February of the next year, Upton published an article in *Scribner's Magazine* in which he spoke of this problem as follows:

'One of Mr. Edison's greatest difficulties was to get an insulating substance that would not melt nor become a conductor in the intense heat generated by the current, in which case the electrical flow instead of traversing the whole length of the wire would flow across from layer to layer or otherwise from wire to wire. This difficulty diverted his attention from platinum to carbon, which is infusible.'

* * *

Following the line of reasoning described in some of the preceding chapters, Edison laid down the supreme law for transmission of electrical energy. His law holds good for all systems, whether for 10, 110, 220, 500, 100,000 volts or more. To make possible the transmission of electrical energy commercially, the receiver (that is, the lamp, motor or transformer) must have such a resistance that, in consideration of the length of the transmission line, the energy lost will be within limits of economical practice.

Men could not understand such an arrangement at that period, for this problem had never before arisen. It was Edison who first brought up the question. And I remember that Sawyer, who was considered a good electrician, told Edison openly that resistance was a detriment in anything electrical and that he (Sawyer) was striving to make the carbon rod for his lamp have as low resistance as possible.

The whole trouble was that most of us at that time did not know that webers x volts = energy. They believed that the stronger the webers, the greater the energy; and in a certain sense they were right. Edison, however, employed tension to overcome the effect of resistance, and thereby made electricity a salable commercial commodity. Thus when he found that a lamp of 10 webers at 10 volts required 100 times more copper than a lamp of 1 weber and 100 volts, most men could not understand it.

The light given out by both lamps was practically the same, for the energy consumed was equal; yet few understood how to 'juggle' with webers and volts to produce the same effect with the least quantity of current.

Edison's ideas were far in advance, and his able mathematician, Francis R. Upton, translated them into figures. As I have told you, Upton at first did not understand, either, but Edison in his own way, using matches to illustrate his points, soon convinced him.

Upton put it in algebraic figures as follows:

Denoting the current by 'W,' volts by 'V,' resistance by 'R,' we have $W = \dfrac{V}{R}$, which is Ohm's law. Denoting length of transmission line by 'L,' and cross section of wire used for transmission by 'S,' we have $R = \dfrac{L}{S}$. Substituting this value for 'R' in Ohm's law, we have W = V divided by $\dfrac{L}{S}$ = $\dfrac{WL}{S} = V$, or $\dfrac{WL}{V} = S$.

Here is the fundamental law for the transmission of electrical energy as it was first expounded by Edison. Let me give you an example. Take a lamp with 10 webers and 10 volts, and find the cross section required to transmit energy 1,000 feet at a 2 percent loss. Substituting these figures in our equation we have $S = \dfrac{10 \times 1000}{0.2} = 50{,}000$.

Or take a lamp with 1 weber and 100 volts and a 2 percent loss in the line. We have $S = \dfrac{1 \times 1000}{2} = 500$, which is 100 times less cross section of metal needed for the lamp working on 100 volts and 1 weber than for the one consuming 10 webers at 10 volts.

Upton simplified the above equation by Ohm's law. The resistance of the one lamp was one ohm, and that of the other 100 ohms. Thus the one-ohm lamp would require 100 times more cross section of metal in its line than the other at the same percentage of loss in transmission.

Restored group of Edison buildings at Dearborn.

XXXV. Menlo Park Activities: Spring-1879

AS THE search for the metallic high-resistance lamp continued through the Spring of 1879, many other rare metals besides platinum were tried. As I have already said, experiments were made with boron, rhodium, iridium, ruthenium, chromium, titanium and zirconium, their fine hairlike wires being coated with oxides called 'pyro-insulators.'

After Edison began to build the glass lamp, he made the leading-in wires of platinum, because the coefficient of platinum in expansion or contraction, he discovered, was the same as that of glass. Previously he had tried many less costly materials—copper, iron, and so on—only to find the stems of the bulbs cracked as the wires became heated. Since platinum had to be used, he visioned a demand for enormous quantities once the lamp was perfected and wanted to be prepared in advance with knowledge of where the metal could be obtained.

One of his associates who was actively connected with the search was 'Major' Frank McLaughlin. I first came to know him in the early part of 1879. He seemed to be an old friend

1—'Doc' Haid, the chemist; 2—Francis Jehl in 1879; 3—Stockton L. Griffin, Edison's secretary; 4—Martin Force; 5—John W. Lawson; 6—'Major' Frank L. McLaughlin.

of Edison's. One day, while we were in a long confidential chat, he told me something of his history. He had tried many adventurous means of livelihood, among them prospecting in Australia, where he had 'gone broke.' After managing to return to the United States, he drove a coal cart for a time in Newark, where he struck up an acquaintance with Edison, then at the shop on Ward Street.

When Edison, now at Menlo Park, took up the work on rare metal filaments, he recalled McLaughlin and sent for him. After several conferences McLaughlin was hired to go West to prospect for platinum. Some weeks later the first bags of ores arrived, and thereafter samples came with unfailing regularity.

A few months after his first visit, McLaughlin returned. It was rumored that he had struck it rich, not in platinum but another metal. He was dressed according to the Western fashion and wore a wide slouch hat; on his shirt bosom and fingers sparkled glittering stones. He now wore the title of major which he had acquired somewhere west of Omaha. To me he seemed to have stepped out of a Bret Harte romance.

Later he brought an unusually fine walking stick as a present for Edison. The knob was inlaid with varicolored quartz rich in gold, including samples from the Major's mines. When last I heard of this precious cane, it was still in the Edisons' possession.

Three years after the events of '79 I was sent to Europe by Edison on the steamship *Arizona.* Much to my pleasure I found that one of my fellow passengers was to be 'the Major.' When we met at dinner the first night at sea, he seemed equally glad to find me. He told me he was en route to London in search of capital for his mining ventures. Before the ship had been long out of port I discovered that he spent all his time playing cards, not pinochle, but the good old American game of poker, which he had learned in the mining camps. At Liverpool I left him and our paths did not again cross. A tragic end in a Western mining camp closed his adventures.

The following item, which appeared in the *Scientific American* on July 26, 1879, gives an interesting account of the method used by Edison in his search for metals:

'As an evidence of the faith of Mr. Edison and his colleagues in the system of lighting by incandescence, we mention the fact that they have prospectors searching for platinum in all the mining regions of the country. Mr. Edison is confident that the metal exists in large quantities in this country, and he has sent out circulars which read as follows:

"From the Laboratory of T. A. Edison
Menlo Park, N. J., U. S. A.

"Dear Sir: Would you be so kind as to inform me if the metal platinum occurs in your neighborhood? This metal, as a rule, is found in scales associated with free gold, generally in placers.

"If there is any in your vicinity, or if you can gain information from experienced miners as to the localities where it can be found, and will forward such information to my address, I will consider it a special favor, as I shall require large quantities in my new system of electric lighting.

"An early reply to this circular will be greatly appreciated.
Very truly,
Thomas A. Edison."

'Specimens of platinum and iridosmine sprinkled upon a

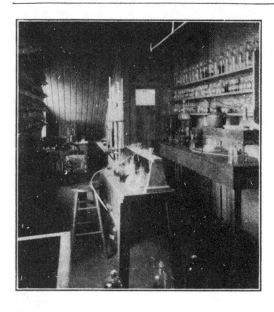

Where 'Doc' Haid as-
sayed the mineral ores.
Nook on ground floor
of laboratory as restored
at Dearborn.

card were sent
with these circu-
lars. The differ-
ence in the metals
is easily detected
with a microscope
or a magnifying
glass.

'Many replies
inclosing samples
of platinum have
already been re-
ceived at Menlo
Park, and the
metal has been
found *in situ* in two places. Mr. Edison has a stamp mill and
all the apparatus required for reducing ores of various kinds.
His facilities for reducing refractory ores and metals are
particularly good.'

On September 20, this sequel appeared in the same paper:
'Notice was taken some time since of Mr. Edison's circular
letter of inquiry with regard to the possible occurrence of
platinum in various parts of the country. Mr. Edison informs
us that, so far, he has received some three thousand replies.
Instead of being an extremely rare metal, as hitherto supposed,
platinum proves to be widely distributed, and to occur in
considerable abundance.

'Before Mr. Edison took the matter in hand platinum had
been found in the United States in but two or three places—
in California and in North Carolina—and in these places it
occurred but sparingly. It is now found in Idaho, Dakota,
Washington Territory, Oregon, California, Colorado, Arizona, New Mexico, and also British Columbia.

'It is found where gold occurs, and is a frequent residual
of gold mining, especially placer mining. Mr. Edison thinks
he can get three thousand pounds a year from Chinese miners
in one locality. One gravel heap is mentioned from which a
million ounces of platinum are expected. Hitherto the product

of the entire world would not suffice to supply electric lamps for New York City. Now Mr. Edison believes that our gold mines will supply more than will be required. The possible uses of this metal in the arts, however, are so numerous that there is no danger of an over-supply.

'In addition to platinum, Mr. Edison finds, among the large number of samples received daily, many other valuable metals and minerals, so that his researches in this direction are likely to result in increasing greatly the resources of our country in respect to the rarer and more costly minerals and metals.'

A good story is told relating to Edison's search. When his attention had been drawn to thorium as a metal with a high fusing temperature, he immediately applied by letter to an eminent mineralogist requesting him to send a small quantity of this exceedingly rare metal to Menlo Park. The *savant* replied with some Yankee sarcasm that it would afford him

Edison in the 'Assay Nook.' (From an old drawing in *Leslie's Weekly.*)

infinite pleasure to put a few hundredweights at the inventor's disposal but that this would be attended with great difficulty, since it would be impossible to obtain even half an ounce in the whole United States.

Edison, the story goes, sent for McLaughlin to come East, and informed him that in a gold mine in a northern state, beneath a mass of valueless flint, some monarite crystals from which thorium is obtained had been unexpectedly discovered. Giving him a letter of credit the inventor said: 'Start at once, and bring me in as short a time as possible a hundred pounds of monarite.' Three days later twenty miners were at work in the mine under McLaughlin's direction. He paid his workmen liberally and allowed them all the gold brought up, seeking only the monarite for himself.

A few weeks later he returned to Menlo Park with the hundred pounds of monarite. Edison began at once to reduce the ore, keeping at it till he was able to send the cynical *savant* several pounds of thorium.

Edison kept his secretary, Stockton L. Griffin, busy writing letters to all parts of the country and to many points abroad, asking for information about platinum. One such letter was even sent to the United States Minister at St. Petersburg, Russia, in July, 1879, inquiring the amount of platinum mined and produced in Russia, its price, and to what ports it was exported.

Among the ores and tailings received at the laboratory, gold and other metals were continually intermingled. Another line of research consequently presented itself, that of discovering processes through which these valuable metals might be extracted economically.([1])

The back room on the ground floor of the laboratory was set apart for this purpose; here the ores were subjected to preliminary tests. A young fellow, John W. Lawson, was in charge. Lawson was born at Spuyten Duyvil, in New York State, and came to Edison in January, 1879. As he had some practical knowledge of assaying, when the hunt for platinum began he was assigned the first assays of the ores reaching us. If any ore was found to contain traces of platinum or any

(1)   The first of a number of patents applied for by Edison in the metallurgical field came in April, 1880, for a magnetic ore separator. It was No. 228,329. It used magnets or electromagnets to separate magnetic substances from nonmagnetic, after both had been fed through a hopper.

George Simon Ohm

other rare metal, it was taken to 'Doc' Haid.

Lawson was a tall loose-limbed fellow with rugged features. His nickname, 'Basic,' given by Edison, seemed to fit him admirably. One day some visitors had become involved in an argument over a certain oxide. Lawson told them bluntly that it couldn't be heated in the way they suggested, because it was a *basic* oxide. Edison was told of the remark and exclaimed: 'Lawson is right!' Thereafter he called Lawson 'Basic.' Lawson had a dry wit and made an agreeable companion. He smoked a corncob pipe with a short stem.

Doctor A. Haid, an experienced assayist and chemist of German descent, who occupied the little nook under the stairs on the ground floor, was affectionately known to us all as 'Doc.'

While nicknames are our subject, you may be interested in Upton's. Edison called him 'Culture,' another most appropriate epithet; for the youthful-appearing mathematician was nothing if not cultured.

Another workman who toiled in the laboratory during this period was Patrick Kenny, mentioned in the account of the autographic telegraph. Like 'Doc' Haid he lived outside the village, and came and went morning and night. Kenny worked in the front part of the second floor of the laboratory, where he sought to perfect a system of facsimile telegraph. In this he utilized two heavy brass balls, one in each of the machines, actuated by a small motor.

When Kenny came to work in the morning

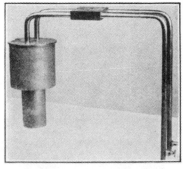

The standard 'ohm,' used in checking resistance of electrical apparatus at Menlo Park.

Wheatstone bridge. This apparatus was continually in use at Menlo Park

and was toiling assiduously to regulate the balls, the joking inquiry was often made: 'Well, Kenny, how are they today? Behaving themselves?' Old Patrick would sigh and wave a hand back and forth as much as to say: 'They're as bad as ever.'

The search for platinum and the hundreds of experiments with metallic lamps, extensive as they were, comprised only a part of the activities at Menlo Park during the winter, spring and summer of 1879. It is hard to understand how a single individual could have been directing operations in so many fields at the same time; for Edison directed and controlled all our efforts. His was the master mind.

During that period he succeeded in developing a dynamo of revolutionary design and unbelievable efficiency to generate the current to be used for his future system. He built the first one of this new type and gave it to Commander G. W. DeLong for his ill-fated expedition to the Arctic on the *Jeannette*.[2]

During the same time he succeeded in devising an entirely new kind of telephone receiver—the motograph or electrochemical telephone—made without the electromagnet as used by Bell. As the transmitter had already been invented by Edison, the addition of a receiver made him the originator of a complete telephone system.

He introduced it successfully in England, establishing

---

(2) Within a year (1880) he was erecting a huge dynamo and connecting it directly with a steam engine, setting the first milestone in electrical engineering.

Sliding Wheatstone bridge, used in measuring low resistance.

Above, left—Thomson high resistance reflecting galvanometer, and right—Thomson low resistance reflecting galvanometer, which were used so much in Menlo Park in testing apparatus or measuring current.

the first central exchange in London; in fact, the first telephone exchange in Europe.

Meanwhile he continued to improve the carbon telephone transmitter, which contributed a much-needed efficiency to the magneto-type receiver.

Demonstration and improvement of his phonograph occupied another portion of his time. The instrument was ex-

Left—the galvanometer scale was used at Menlo Park with the reflecting galvanometers. A kerosene lamp provided the light that was thrown on the galvanometer mirror and reflected back on the scale.

hibited abroad, notably in England, France, Germany, and Austria Hungary, and orders were received from every part of the globe for the machine that could talk.

Some of his time was taken up in designing new electrical apparatus to aid in his experiments, in devising methods of measurements so that he could test his results and in making practical the use of electricity. In this direction, Upton was a great help.

The present generation has not the faintest idea of the obstacles with which Edison had to contend. Electrical testing of a practical sort was still in an embryonic stage. Of course, the need was not insistent until after the practical incandescent lamp and the commercial 90-percent-efficient generator were born; there had been no call for proficient methods of testing such things. They simply did not exist until Edison astonished a gaping, incredulous world.

Try to picture a time when there were no instruments for measuring volts or webers directly; it was like a carpenter or a mechanic without his foot rule, or the butcher or the grocer without his pound scale. (The 'weber' was the unit of current in those days; it was later renamed the 'ampere.')

We had to ascertain tension and current in roundabout ways requiring a good deal of patience; for in exploring uncharted territories we had to use pioneer implements and methods.

No one had ever thought of an arc lamp or generator requiring or giving a certain number of volts or webers, and watts were not yet dreamed of. Electric arc light equipment was not tested or described in electrical units, and the power it absorbed was stated in mechanical units—horsepower or foot pounds computed either from a steam engine by means of a steam indicator, or by a mechanical dynamometer under various names. A practical system of measuring electrical units was lacking. Edison created the need for it. In fact, he once said he would leave the measuring instruments to be made by the 'infinitesimals,' those men who had so much time they were able to devote a month to a hair's difference.

An electrical foot rule existed, but only on paper; and for a long time it was criticized by scientists. Little notice was taken of it. I refer to the fundamental law of electricity enunciated by George Simon Ohm in 1827, $C = E/R$ establishing the relation between electromotive force, current and re-

sistance. Without it electrical science would still be like a ship at sea without a rudder.

Ohm was eventually re-established after many years of effort. His law was recognized in 1841 by the Royal Society in London, and years later by the British Association, whose attention had been called to the matter. The verification of Ohm's law was intrusted to Prof. G. Chrystal of the Cavendish Laboratory. The results of his tests cleared away once and for all any doubt of the accuracy of Ohm's law. More than that, they proved that it was strictly a physical law. Many other laws have since been established as sequences or corollaries.

That was in 1876, the year in which Edison moved to Menlo Park. The ohm was designated as so many feet of iron telegraph wire of a certain diameter. If Ohm's great law was not accepted definitely until 1876, you must not wonder that three years later, in 1879, we knew little about its practical application.

Electrical science was still in its infancy. Should you desire to trace it further, or look into the old books and journals of science, you will not find Ohm's name. You will not find it even in Faraday's *Experimental Researches in Electricity* published in 1839, 1844, and 1855, volumes 1, 2 and 3. Though that great experimenter recorded many discus-

Helmholtz-Gaugain tangent galvanometer.

sions and controversies, and also expounded many laws, it is astonishing that he never included Ohm's law among them! The ohm was the only unit of electricity we at Menlo Park could utilize with facility or to the highest degree of accuracy. We had a standard ohm and two Wheatstone bridges, one of them of the sliding type. A bridge as a means of measuring electrical resistance was first introduced by Hunter Christie of the Royal Military Academy at Woolwich, England, in 1833 and, like Ohm's law, remained unnoticed until 1843, when Wheatstone developed it and made it into a standard apparatus. (Let us not forget Christie.)

The Wheatstone bridge was valuable in many kinds of test work. Upton coached me thoroughly in its manipulation, until in a few months I became a sort of official tester at the laboratory. The book that G. P. Lowrey gave me also proved valuable in my work.([3]) In the bridge method of testing, it was necessary to use good galvanometers, of which we had an assortment. When fine measurements were required, we employed Thomson's high or low resistance reflecting galvanometers.

Galvanometer action was discovered by Oersted in 1820. Its practical application was the work of Schweigger and Poggendorf. The main use of the reflecting galvanometer is that of an index, or pointer, consisting of a beam of light which, of course, has no weight. A beam of light from a kerosene lamp falls upon a tiny mirror suspended with the movable magnetic needle system of the galvanometer. From the mirror the light is reflected to a graduated scale. The Thomson mirror galvanometer, being very sensitive, was in those days one of the most practical instruments on the market. It was used extensively by telegraph and cable companies, as well as in laboratories of scientists.

We had two other kinds of astatic galvanometers which came into use before measurements became exact. The astatic system of magnetic needles in a galvanometer was introduced by Nobili in 1825. In the early eighties came D'Arsonval and reversed the order of action in the galvanometer; he had the coil movable in a powerful magnetic field, making it aperiodic or 'dead beat.' This principle is used in all practical galvanometers in volt, ampere or watt meters of today. An old Helmholz-Gaugain tangent galvanometer which also lay about the laboratory was never used.

---

(3)   Kempe on *Electrical Testing*.   (See page 17.)

The spectroscope, which Bunsen and Kirchhoff discovered in 1859, has furnished man with a wonderful method of analyzing substances through their spectra. Bunsen and Kirchhoff did great work in that field. Edison often used the instrument and became adept in reading it. He investigated substances used in his experiments when he wanted to be sure of their purity. He examined them with the spectroscope as well as the microscope.

I recall many occasions when he and Upton discussed the subject and argued about the Fraunhofer, or dark, lines in the spectrum; when the matter would not be quite settled, 'Doc' Haid, the German chemist, would be called in to give his opinion. As Edison was a sharp reasoner and had a wonderful sense of observation, such amiable disputes generally resulted in his favor.

Upton worked many months translating into figures Edison's ideas about networks of conductors, losses, drops of voltage and all the intricate problems involved. Edison supplied him continuously with new conditions as each subject was finished. It is difficult today to realize how much patience and clear-headed thinking was required.

In these early calculations, the Kirchhoff laws and those of other German physicists were employed—and what terrors they were! Upton had to solve literally hundreds upon hundreds of equations. After he had gone over them twice, I had the task of verifying them with my Vega logarithmic tables, the work consisting of addition, subtraction, multiplication and division. This kept me busy during the time when experiments were delayed for some reason or other and I was free.

At that time, few saw any connection between potential and ordinary electric phenomena. Many thought that only current (quantity) was the magnitude register of work, without taking potential into consideration. Upton ransacked the *Philosophical Magazine*, the *Comptes Rendus*, the *Poggendorf Annals, Dingler's Polytechnical Journal* and other musty volumes of scientific societies in search of data, trying to put Edison's ideas into practical form. Edison had uncovered problems that were never before dreamed of in the realm of theory. He was about to revolutionize all existing theories in such a way as to take both theorist and practitioner unawares. To both he opened vast fields. Our knowledge of the science and our use of it today are founded on his conceptions.

After Upton finished his tables and charts Edison would study and analyze every part. His logic amazed us. He drew such convincing inferences that often Upton was forced to check back over the tables and reconstruct his work, only to find Edison in the right.

The most astonishing element in Edison's reasoning was his disregard of some of the long-established rules deemed fundamental facts, especially those relating to magnetism. He relied on common sense to point the way. His motto was 'Seeing is believing.'

Home of Francis Upton in Menlo Park, to which he moved after his marriage.

Early type of the Edison electromotograph telephones without separate transmitter. May be seen today on shelf in restored laboratory at Dearborn.

XXXVI. 'Loud-Speaking' Telephone The Electromotograph

RETRACING our steps briefly, let us go back to the late months of 1878 to consider Edison's operations outside the United States, and in so doing lead up to his telephone activities in England, and his invention of a new kind of telephone in the Spring of 1879.

The story of Edison's researches—entirely apart from those on the electric light—form a chapter of extraordinary interest. The scope of his experiments would have challenged any man. It became necessary for him to stop suddenly and find an entirely new type of telephone receiver to supplant that of Bell without infringing the Bell patents or making use of the electromagnet principle.

The very thought of such a task would have bewildered not only the average individual but even a scientist. To have to undertake it while engaged in the search for a practical electric light seemed like asking too much. Yet Edison not

Repair kit carried by 'trouble shooters' for electromotograph telephone. Note spare cylinders of chalk. Now at restored laboratory at Dearborn.

only assumed the new burden, but was able to devise a new type of dynamo—the incandescent lamp generator for parallel working, and to perfect other jobs of similar importance. And he was successful in all.

Before we discuss the telephone invention, a review must be made of the Paris International Exhibition of 1878, at which among other things Edison showed his phonograph. Here a storm brewed that gave forewarning of one which was later to arise in England. As to the Paris happenings, I quote from the *Scientific American*:[1]

'It is but a few weeks ago that the world gazed in astonishment at the amazing exhibition which two juries of the French Exhibition made of themselves over the phonograph. The jury of the class of instruments of precision declared that this instrument could not be considered at all as one of precision, but merely a toy; consequently they sent it to the class of telegraphy to be rewarded.

'But the telegraphers replied that it was of no use whatever in telegraphy, and refused to examine it. The consequence was that the most wonderful invention in the whole Exhibition came near being unmentioned and unrewarded. Fortunately, and to their credit, the French people cried, ''For shame!'' through their journals, and the phonograph received its reward.'

Edison was made a Chevalier of the Legion of Honor, one of the four or five Americans so honored on this occasion. The humiliating treatment of the phonograph formed only

---

(1)   Supplement, December, 1878.

part of the difficulties in Paris. The *Scientific American* continues:

'The most astonishing example of stupidity yet remains to be mentioned, in connection with the recent action of some of the members of the Academie des Sciences. It may be remarked here that a large number of the great savants that compose this institution show themselves bitterly opposed to the reception of all communications which are of a nature to in any way modify their ancient convictions. They seem to be particularly touchy on the subject of electricity.

'A good specimen of this was given at the session of September 9th (1878) when M. Du Moncel, after having captured the attention of the intelligent audience, stepped up to the desk of M. Bertrand, the secretary, and handed him some documents relating to the latest discoveries of Mr. Edison, "that astonishing inventor (says *Electricite*) who has more genius in himself alone than a whole scientific senate."

'Seizing with ill-concealed impatience the papers that his fellow member presented, and without taking time to examine them, the secretary declared formally that the *Comptes Rendus* could not accept them. "That precious collection," said he, "receives nothing but original documents. Those which, presented in the name of Edison, have been deflowered by publication in an American scientific journal, are not worthy of finding the least place in it."

'M. Du Moncel was replying sharply, when he was interrupted by M. Bouillaud, who said he could not understand why M. Du Moncel was forever returning to the charge with new phenomena more marvelous than the preceding. He did not wish M. Du Moncel prevented from speaking, but he did wish that he might be restrained from repeating experiments to the Academy before he had tested them.

'It is proper to say that the illustrious Doctor Bouillaud was one of those clear-sighted academicians who chimed in with M. Sainte Claire Deville when the latter a few months ago, exclaimed at a full meeting of the academy that phenomena of the phonograph were produced by a clever ventriloquist.

'The French papers do not state whether the Edison documents were subsequently accepted for the *Comptes Rendus*.'

As scientific achievements are neither of a national nor a political character, the incidents just mentioned might have taken place in any other country as well as in France. Pro-

Two types of motograph telephones perfected by Edison. That on left is equipped with a spring which was wound by hand and when released, served to revolve the cylinder of chalk. That on the right had a tiny electric motor like the electric pen, the motor serving to turn the cylinder of chalk when the phone was in use. Both of these forms were designed to eliminate the inconvenient crank with which the earlier types were equipped. They may be seen on one of the shelves of the restored laboratory at Dearborn.

fessional jealousies exist in all lands. Here in America similar incidents took place as our chief produced his great inventions. In fact, the controversies that raged here were frequently more bitter even than those just narrated. France herself later showered honors upon Edison. In 1889 he was made a Commander of the Legion of Honor.

Now for the telephone story. Five years previously, when Edward H. Johnson was assisting Edison on the automatic telegraph([2]), Edison had become acquainted with Colonel George E. Gouraud, who subsequently became his London representative, with offices at 16 E. Lombard Street, London E. C. 2. Called to England to demonstrate his automatic telegraph before the British postal telegraph authorities in 1873, Edison had met Gouraud personally. The acquaintance continued after Edison's return to America, and now, in 1878, Edison asked Gouraud again to represent his interests, this time in the introduction of the carbon transmitting telephone. The Edison Telephone Company was formed; telephone station equipment and a large number of instruments were made up by Bergmann and sent to London. Prospects seemed bright. Johnson, who had been directing the introduction of the

_____
(2) Chapter IX.

Interior of telephone box, showing cylinder of chalk, connected with round diaphragm. As it appears to-day in the restored laboratory.

phonograph, was sent across as Edison's personal representative.

Unfortunately the Bell interests were just as eager to promote the use of their system in England and suddenly threatened to sue the Edison people, as they had already done in the United States(³). The Edison interests had been pirating the Bell receiver, while the Bell people were infringing the Edison transmitter. (This was before the Bell interests obtained the rights of the Edison carbon transmitter from the Western Union).

Edison learned of the tribulations of his representatives in England when they cabled him news of the threatened suit by the Bell people. Colonel Gouraud's secretary was a young man named Samuel Insull.

'I remember writing the cable,' said Insull recently in a letter to me, 'and receiving a reply to it the next day from Edison, stating that if we would wait sixty or ninety days he would supply a new form of receiver.'

So the English people 'held the fort' while Edison, in the midst of his metallic lamp and other experiments, took on the task of finding a telephone receiver entirely different from Bell's. The riddle was solved during February and March by application of the motograph principle which he had already used in constructing a telegraph relay that could replace the Morse one, if necessary(⁴). This was the principle that had been hailed as a brilliant discovery back in 1874.

In his application for the patent, signed March 24,(⁵)

(3) Page 130.   (4) Chapter X.   (5) Patent No. 221,957.

Edison outlined his invention as follows:

'The combination, with the acoustic telegraph and diaphragm, of a roller that receives a revolving motion and contains an electrolytic material, and a spring or presser connected with the diaphragm and resting upon the roller.

'The combination, in an acoustic telegraph, of a moving surface containing electrolytic material, a diaphragm, a presser or spring extending from the diaphragm and resting upon such surface, a screw through a fixed support acting upon the presser to vary or adjust the friction between the moving surface and the presser.'

It was described as 'a diaphragm and a cylinder of compressed chalk about the size of a thimble. A thin spring connected with the center of the diaphragm extended outwardly and rested on the chalk cylinder, and was pressed against it with a pressure equal to that which would be due to a weight of about six pounds. The chalk was rotated by hand.'[6]

In other words, he made chalk talk. It transmitted sound much more clearly and

(6) Dyer & Martin, *Edison, His Life and Inventions.* Vol. I p. 184.

Exterior of electromotograph telephone as it appears on wall of restored laboratory at **Dearborn.**

loudly than the Bell instruments. When a person called Menlo Park from New York City, his voice could be heard coming over the 'loud-speaking telephone' from a distance of a thousand feet.

Six of these receivers were made by Bergmann and shipped posthaste to England in charge of Charles Edison, Edison's nephew, son of William Pitt Edison, manager of the street railway system at Port Huron, Michigan. The nephew had been with his uncle at Menlo Park for several months, and despite his youth (he was not yet nineteen years old) seemed destined to have a brilliant future.

As yet, the invention had not been shown in the United States, outside the laboratory. The English journals praised it highly. Professor Barrett was quoted in *Nature* (March 20):

'Mere ingenuity in contriving machines does not add to the sum of human knowledge and if Mr. Edison were merely a clever inventor and nothing more, I should feel less interest in the man. It is, however, a noticeable feature of Mr. Edison's inventions that they, in general, contain some new principle, some original observation in experimental science, which entitles him to the rank of a discoverer.'

Engineering, the English technical journal, in its issue of March 21 declared that Edison had produced, through the invention of the electromotograph telephone in conjunction with the carbon transmitter, 'what must be acknowledged to be the most perfect telephonic system that has yet been brought forward, and which alone would be sufficient to give to its inventor a high place among scientific discoverers.'

It added that 'no one who has heard Mr. Edison's new telephone can fail to have been astonished at its clear, articulate and loud tones; it might appropriately be called "The Shouting Telephone," for its voice is louder than that of any ordinary speaker. Where it is in use it is of course unnecessary to go at all near the instrument, for it may be fixed against the wall of an office and its messages heard at any part of the room.' (Like the radio set of the present day.)

While the first models were being demonstrated and introduced in London, back at Menlo Park we were busily engaged in familiarizing men with the instrument so that they could go abroad to help in its installation. Edison had been asked to send twenty men; he brought about three times that number from New York City in order to sift them out.

His method was a simple but effective one. A miniature

Edison's 'loud-speaking' telephone in its finished form. On right is extension arm with receiver to fit against ear.

telephone exchange was set up in the laboratory, with wires from wall to wall, upstairs and down, and ten 'loud-speaking' telephones arranged at intervals. Edison went from one to another, putting each out of order in different ways, while the students followed in his footsteps to discover and repair the damage. 'I would cut the wires of one,' said Edison, 'short-circuit another, destroy the adjustment of a third, put dirt between the electrodes of a fourth, and so on.' A student was allowed five minutes to find the trouble, and had to succeed in locating it ten consecutive times before being qualified for the London assignment.

The shouting and hullabaloo inside the laboratory can only be imagined. Being hard of hearing, Edison went about his work unperturbed, while the rest of us were nearly deafened as 'Hello-Hello-Hello' re-echoed from corner to corner.

Martin Force, a good-natured, willing worker, looked after the wires or explained their hook-up to the raw recruits. He has already been mentioned in the account of the phonograph demonstration.([7]) He came to Menlo Park from the near-by village of Dover and had been trained by Edison for

(7)   Page 170

general handy man round the laboratory. He was especially handy at constructing wooden apparatus needed in experiments.

Insull had the honor of acting for the first half hour as the first amateur telephone operator in the first London exchange. In his capacity of secretary to Colonel Gouraud he witnessed and took part in the telephone's introduction.

'I remember a celebration of one of the Royal Societies at the Burlington House on Piccadilly,' says he. 'We had a telephone line running across the roofs to the basement of the building, I think it was to Tyndall's laboratory in Burlington Street. Mr. and Mrs. Gladstone came through while I was handling the telephone at the Burlington House end. Mrs. Gladstone, speaking over the line, asked the man at the other end whether it was a woman or a man at our end, and the reply came in loud tones that it was a man!'

Another who helped in introducing the telephone in England was James Adams, associated with Edison from Newark days. He died shortly afterward while still abroad. The document pictured on page 81 bears his signature.

The instrument was exhibited to the Prince of Wales and many other distinguished personages in London. Among the young chaps who applied for a job was George Bernard Shaw, then a stripling still ignorant of the laurels that his fame as a dramatist was to bring.

Shaw's description of the men sent from America was amusing:

'Whilst the Edison Telephone Company lasted, it crowded the basement of a high pile of offices in Queen Victoria Street with American artificers. These deluded and romantic men gave me a glimpse of the skilled proletariat of the United States. They sang obsolete sentimental songs with genuine emotion; and their language was frightful even to an Irishman. They worked with a ferocious energy which was out of all proportion to the actual result achieved. Indomitably resolved to assert their republican manhood by taking no order from a tall-hatted Englishman whose stiff politeness covered his conviction that they were relatively to himself inferior and common persons, they insisted on being slave-driven with genuine American oaths by a genuine free and equal American foreman. They utterly despised the artfully slow British workman, who did as little for his wages as he possibly could; never hurried himself; and had a deep reverence for one whose pocket could be tapped by respectful behavior. Need I add that they were contemptuously wondered at by this same British workman as a parcel of outlandish adult boys who sweated themselves for their employer's benefit instead of looking after their own interest?

'They adored Mr. Edison as the greatest man of all time in every possible department of science, art and philosophy, and execrated Mr. Graham Bell, the inventor of the rival telephone, as his Satanic adversary; but each of them had (or intended to have) on the brink of completion an improvement on the telephone, usually a new transmitter.'

Announcement of the invention was made in this country during April. *The Journal of the Telegraph* published a brief description in its issue of April 16 with the added information that it 'was attracting much attention abroad.' The *Scientific American* followed two weeks later ([8]) with almost an entire page devoted to it. Several illustrations were given, along with the following statement:

'Mr. Edison has recently improved his carbon telephone so much that in conjunction with a magnetic receiver it far surpasses for power and clearness of articulation every other system of telephone that has been introduced.

'As long, however, as there was in connection with the instrument no more powerful receiver than the Bell telephone, or instruments of similar principle, the carbon telephone, though possessing many points of superiority over other systems, was limited in its power to the capabilities of the receiver with which it was connected, and until quite recently no receiving telephone had been introduced which would develop or do justice to the power of the carbon transmitter.

'Mr. Edison has now applied, with remarkable success, the principle of the electromotograph to the construction of a telephone receiver, which on account of its extraordinary power and perfection, must before long supersede the feeble instruments of other systems and secure to itself a great commercial future.'

What was said to be the first public exhibition of the new telephone in this country was made on the evening of June 9 before the closing session of the Franklin Institute in Philadelphia. Henry Bentley, president of the Philadelphia local Telegraph Company, conducted it with a rude box that he

(8) April 26, 1879,

had obtained from his friend Edison the previous evening at Menlo Park.

'Mr. Bentley slipped a wheel of chalk upon an axle inside the little box, and as the transmissions were received from the office of the telephone company, he continually turned a small crank projecting from the box. This caused the transmissions, which under other circumstances could not be heard at a distance of more than two or three feet from the receiver, to be audible in all parts of the hall . . . Whistling of such airs as "Yankee Doodle," "Sweet Bye and Bye" and "Poor Little Buttercup" was particularly distinct and accurately transmitted.'[9]

Edison continued to make changes of a practical nature, and model after model was sent to London. In the fall the Edison chalk receiving telephone appeared in definite form. In it, both Edison's carbon transmitter and his chalk receiver were combined in a single unit. The model may be seen today in actual operation in the restored laboratory at Dearborn.

Among the cleverest telephone men sent by Edison to London was James A. Lighthipe, who was intrusted with taking this latest model to Johnson. Lighthipe had an active part in the installation of the new apparatus and in the replacing of the older types.[10]

It is hard to appreciate how intensely Edison worked on the electromotograph telephone during 1879. Lengthy letters were written weekly in longhand by him and his assistant Batchelor and sent to Johnson, explaining the changes in the models and the new chemical solutions with which the chalk cylinder was to be moistened.

Bergmann worked night and day in his Wooster Street shop, coming frequently to the laboratory to consult our chief. The historic models on display in the restored laboratory tell more convincingly than words how much toil was expended on this telephone in Menlo Park during 1879.

A word in closing about the nephew, Charles Edison. From London he went to Paris, where he worked both with the new telephone and in the introduction of the quadruplex telegraph between that city and Brussels. While thus engaged he suddenly died in the late fall of 1879, not yet 20

(9) *Journal of the Telegraph*, July 1, 1879.
(10) Lighthipe later went to Belgium in the interests of the Edison telephone. Subsequently be became identified with the incandescent light development. He was an esteemed member of the General Electric Company's staff in California, where he also became electrical engineer for the Southern California Edison Company.

years of age. His body was shipped home and buried in Port Huron amid deep sorrow at the untimely termination of a promising career.

Another young man who was actively employed on the chalk telephone was James M. Seymour. He was among those designated by Edison to go across to London to help in its introduction, and would have gone had a cable not been received requesting that no more young men be sent. Later, however, he went abroad in the Bell company service and played an active part in the introduction of that system in several countries, including Russia.

It may be of interest to add that his father owned an iron works in Newark, New Jersey, and delivered to Edison the iron for use in the earliest dynamo machines. Seymour signed the parchment for the DeLong dynamo. (Page 296.)

EDISON AS HE APPEARED IN 1880.

(From an old photograph.)

XXXVII. Work and Play at Menlo Park-1879

SO SATISFACTORY did the motograph telephone prove to Colonel Gouraud and his associates that they cabled Edison, asking for a price on it. Edison urged them to make an offer, and when they replied: 'Offer thirty thousand,' he accepted immediately, assuming, of course, that they meant thirty thousand dollars.

You can imagine his unbounded surprise when the draft proved to be for pounds instead of dollars. He received approximately five times as much for the invention as he had expected.

Visitors coming to the laboratory at Menlo Park were always delighted to hear the 'loud-speaking Edison telephone'; for not everyone in 1879 had as yet listened over a telephone. And those who had heard the common magneto Bell receiver got a surprise when they listened over the motograph. The latter belched out conversation like a modern loud speaker.

In the telephone squad at the laboratory was a practical joker who rigged up a mock telephone box the front of which fell down like a trapdoor whenever a catch was released. A cord ran along the wall, apparently the out-going wire of the telephone. Inside the box was a mechanical contrivance filled with water or perfume which, when the door fell open, would spray on anyone in front.

George Carman, brother of our bookkeeper, joined Martin Force in showing the Edison loud speakers to some young ladies one day. From their talk I gathered that they were intimately acquainted. Carman explained the device to a stout maiden from Metuchen: 'You just holler "Hello, Hello" into this tube,' pointing to the transmitter. 'I'll go to the other end and talk with you.'

The damsel began as directed and when there was no response called louder and louder. Carman was near by holding the cord. When she grew hoarse, he jerked the cord and the trapdoor flew open. The young lady was both frightened and sprinkled, while the others laughed gayly. What she told Carman need not be repeated here.

Yes, now and then the fun cropped out in those high-pressure days. It helped relieve the tension. The spinster telephone' was only one of the jokes. Our midnight lunch was a time of revelry; and when it was ordered, we knew that Edison was going to plow through the night without respite. Swanson, the night watchman, carried it up. The fare generally consisted of soda crackers, cheese, butter and ham supplied by the little store. During the repast we boys would circle round Edison, spinning yarn after yarn to entertain the group.

Sometimes a member of the party would go to the organ at the rear of the room and play a popular 'tin pan' alley tune. A song would start, in which the lot of us would join. This midnight pause was always welcome, and no one enjoyed it more than Edison. His boyish fun-loving spirit came to the surface in its warmth of companionship.

More 'boys' attended these midnight lunches than were supposed to; for when those not engaged in the lamp experiment heard of a lunch in prospect they sneaked in, and when the fun was over, disappeared. No fault was found; for these 'deadheads' helped increase our jollity.

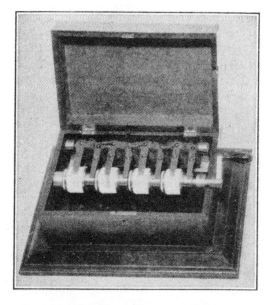

'Motograph battery' devised by Edison. Current was generated when one turned the crank, rotating the four chalk cylinders. Now on shelf in restored laboratory.

The use of chalk cylinders in the motograph telephone gave Edison a new idea, which he developed during the early summer. He found that it was possible by turning the cylinder to generate a weak electric current. (See picture on Page 285.)

Forthwith he arranged four such cylinders on a nonconducting shaft and connected each of the platinum springs to the metallic boss of the adjoining cylinder. When the cylinders were turned, a current equivalent to that of two Daniell cells was derived.

'Mr. Edison is investigating the action of this peculiar battery,' said a writer in the *Scientific American.* 'Whether the current is due to decomposition of the solution with which the chalk is moistened, or to capillarity or some other cause has not been definitely determined.'(¹)

I must tell you about the famous 'sonorous voltameter.' Newspaper reporters from New York had a habit of dropping in at Menlo Park to quiz our chief, hoping to get something new to write about. Sometimes they became a nuisance. To one such young man was unfolded a tale that brought headlines announcing a great discovery.

The joke was that the discovery had been known for years; persons versed in electrical knowledge grinned broadly when they read the story in the *Herald.*

'What have you invented that's new?' asked the reporter. 'Something that's not older than a few days?'

'Have you seen the sonorous voltameter yet?' asked Edison.

The reporter admitted that the sonorous voltameter was outside the pale of his scientific education and asked for light on the subject. Following is his account of the explanation:

'Edison doffed his hat and by a dexterous throw landed it on a table several feet away. He then took paper and pencil and drew a "sonorous voltameter."

' "There she is," he exclaimed joyfully, as he put the final touches to a complex arrangement of wires, batteries, tubes and funnels.

' "What is she good for?" inquired the reporter, adopting the inventor's metaphor and gazing on the unintelligible combination.

' "First class arrangement. Tells the strength of telegraph batteries to a dot. It makes you hear their strength. This end of the wire, you see, makes oxygen and this end hydrogen.

---

(1) July 26, 1879.

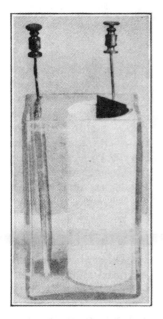

One of standard Daniell cells used at Menlo Park for voltage determination. May be seen in restored laboratory.

The bubbles rise and make a noise, which is magnified by the funnel. These glass tubes indicate the intensity of the current by degrees and the funnel indicates the same by sound. You take your watch and count the number of ticks caused by the bubbles per second. Just try it some time."

'The reporter promised that the first time he found a battery lying round without an owner he would clap on a sonorous voltameter and find out all about it.'

Back in 1878, before anyone else had dreamed of the feasibility of distributing electricity for domestic purposes, Edison was planning his electric central station. Among other essentials, some method of measuring current sold to customers would be of first importance, he realized. So he planned a meter.

The first Edison meter was made during 1879. Long before its completion, he had had his plans all in mind, as was shown in December, 1878, when he described them to a reporter of the *Herald:*

' "Is it true that you have perfected a machine for measuring current?" asked the reporter.

' "Yes," replied the inventor.

' "How is it to be used?"

' "One will be placed in every house where the light is used. It registers infallibly the quantity of electricity consumed, using for the purpose a thousandth part of the quantity consumed in the house." '

Edison's meter was the first to register faithfully the amount of current a consumer used, thus furnishing an equitable and satisfactory means of charging for service.

It was designed on the principle of electroplating. Faraday had found that the transfer of metal from one plate to another in an electrolytic bath was exactly proportional to the current. Edison's first meter held a glass jar in which two copper

Edison's first meter. Now in restored laboratory at Dearborn.

plates were suspended in a solution of sulphate of copper. The cover of the cell was so arranged that one of the plates was easily removable by means of an insulated clamp with a thumb screw; the other plate, which was thick and cylindrical in form, was intended to remain in the cell to allow the copper to be transferred electrolytically from it to the other plate.

In circuit with the cell Edison inserted a high resistance, and the whole with the cell was shunted to the extremities of the coils of an electromagnet, so that when the main current passed through the electromagnet only about one-hundredth part passed through the cell. The object of the electromagnet was to interrupt the main line in case of a short circuit. It had a pivoted armature through which the main current passed; this was pressed against contacts by means of an adjustable spring. It was not affected by ordinary current; when a short circuit occurred, however, the power of the electromagnet would overcome its tension and pull it down, interrupting the current. A spring latch then held the circuit open. In order to avoid arcing between the contacts, Edison shunted the points with a short thin wire that would take the whole current for an instant and then melt so that the electromagnet and the wire acted as a double safeguard.

The meter was so connected with the main line that the current deposited the metal from the cylindrical plate on the removable one. Its gain in weight formed the basis for calculating the amount of current consumed.

The meter registered perfectly and was in strict accordance with the number of lamps used at any time; however, as it was shunted and consequently acted in a closed circuit, a minute counter current prevailed that redeposited some of the metal when the meter was idle. To obviate this, experiments were conducted with all kinds of metals and solutions, which were intrusted to me to carry out under Edison's direction. All that development came after the incandescent lamp was perfected.

Edison's 'electro-meter' was described in the famous article in the New York *Herald*, December 21, 1879, as follows:

'The apparatus for measuring the amount of electricity used by each householder is a simple contrivance consisting of an electrolytic cell and a small coil of wire, appropriately arranged in a box, the latter being of about half the size of an ordinary gas meter, and like a gas meter it can be placed in any part of the house.

'The measurement is obtained by the deposit of copper particles on a little plate in the electrolytic cell, such deposit being caused by the electric current passing through the cell. At the end of any period, say one month, the plate is taken by the inspector to the central office, where the copper deposit is weighed and the amount of electricity consumed determined by a simple calculation.

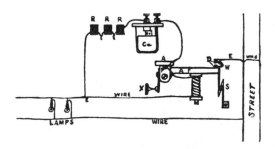

Diagram of Edison's meter and system. (From *Scribner's Monthly*, February, 1880.)

James Gordon Bennett's steam yacht the *Jeannette*—From a print in the *Scientific American*.

XXXVIII. Building First Dynamo

The *Jeannette*

YOU have heard how during the early part of 1879, when Edison was toiling night and day on the metallic lamps, he evolved and introduced a brand-new telephone system. That was only part of his labors in that period.

One of the most difficult and far-reaching of these efforts was that dealing with the dynamo, which as I have already said, our chief studied and produced at this time.

Among the visitors who came to see us in the early part of 1879 was Lieutenant Commander George Washington DeLong, of the United States Navy. He came to consult Edison about the Arctic expedition which James Gordon Bennett, proprietor of the *New York Herald*, was then fitting out, and which DeLong was to head. Bennett had acquired an old steam gunboat of the Royal Navy, the *Pandora*, and had rechristened it the *Jeannette*.

Bennett stipulated that this bark-rigged steam yacht should be officered and manned by Navy men. DeLong, a dashing, brilliant officer, was chosen to command it; asso-

Edison and some of his assistants on the steps of the laboratory. Upton sits on Edison's right, and 'Batch' on his left. Johnny Randolph's head is visible just behind Edison's. 'Doc' Haid is on Upton's right. In lower row (left to right) are Francis Jehl, Martin Force, 'Alf' Swanson and 'Griff'. The tall man in the back row wearing the hat is 'Basic' Lawson. On his right is James Seymour. On the left of Johnny Randolph are George E. Carman, 'Major' McLaughlin and John F. Ott. Picture taken in 1879.

ciated with him were Lieutenant Chipp, executive officer; Lieutenant Danenhower, navigator; Dr. Amber, surgeon; Melville, chief engineer; Dunbar, ice pilot; Mr. Newcomb, taxidermist; Mr. Collins, meteorologist and scientific observer; and a picked crew of regulars. In all, thirty-two persons were in the party.

DeLong was a jolly fellow, and often brought laughter with him. Edison volunteered to provide an electric-light plant composed of an arc lamp together with some of his platiniridium and oxide of zirconium coated incandescent lamps of the series type, for the expedition. A way of generating current was needed so that the lamps could be used in the Arctic night. Edison set about devising it. The bipolar type of generator was selected by him, with plenty of iron in the field magnets, and plenty of soft iron wire as the core of the armature. For a winding on the armature, Edison chose the drum type. Upton and Kruesi were called in, the former to make a drawing of the armature coils and windings, the latter to draft out working drawings of the machine for the shop.

Upton's job of drawing the drum armature winding was a most difficult one, though today it seems simple. He had practically no information to guide him. Firms engaged in that business did not give out their shop methods or secrets.

Upton pored over the table, making experimental sheets on which the lines simply would not come out correctly. One day as Edison stopped in to look over the work, he offered a suggestion.

'Why don't you have Kruesi make up a few small wooden models of the drum?' he asked. 'Then you can take string and actually wind it round the block, instead of drawing imaginary lines.'

'But,' Upton protested, 'that wouldn't be scientific.

'What do you care,' countered Edison, 'if it does the work?'

So Upton agreed to try it out. As soon as he saw how practical it was, and how much it helped him, he grew enthusiastic. Meanwhile, Edison suggested that we hold a winding bee in the laboratory, with a cigar as prize for the contestant who could beat the others winding one of the wooden models correctly. I asked Upton to give me a few pointers, which he did as follows:

Drawing a circle, he divided it into ten equal parts and numbered each from one to ten, representing the beginning or

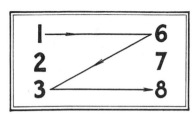

'Begin at 1 and connect its other end, 6, to 3. The other end of 3 is 8.'

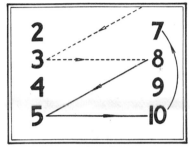

'Connect 8 to 5. Its other end 10, goes to 7.'

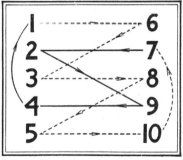

'The other end of 7 is 2. From 2 it goes to 9, then to 4, and to 1.'

the end of five coils. One and 6 were ends of the first coil, 2 and 7 the second, 3 and 8 the third, and so on.

'Now,' said he, 'begin at 1 and connect its other end 6 with 3. The other end of 3 is 8, which is to be connected with five. Its other end 10 goes to 7. The other end of 7 is 2. From 2 it goes to 9, then to 4 and then to the beginning at one.' Thus the circuit is closed and the direction of the current is correct.

'When you understand the diagram, try to make one with seven coils.'

Whenever I found time, I used up sheet upon sheet of paper trying to design that seven-coil diagram. At last I showed one to Upton, who found it correct. It was worse than a charade.

Meanwhile Kruesi got Andrus to make small wooden drums, and John Ott put in nails representing the positions round which the coils were to be wound.

Six of us competed, Edison, Batch, Kruesi, Force, Upton and I. The 'Bee' commenced about half past eight, after all had been refreshed at supper. Upton explained what was required, how to wind the twine round the block so that the end led to the last nail. The end, however, must meet the beginning from the opposite side of the wooden core. In other words, if one commenced at the beginning, one always went down one side and up the other, as the drum was turned.

Mart looked at Kruesi, and Kruesi at Batch, and all three no doubt thought of the farmer giving directions to the city

Front page of *Scientific American* telling of loss of *Jeannette* expedition.

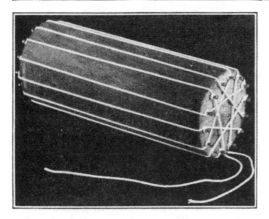

Replica of wooden model of drum as used at Menlo Park for 'winding bee.' May be seen in restored laboratory at Dearborn.

man: 'You turn to the right and then left, left to the right, etc., and you will get there in a half an hour.'

After the match had started, 'Griff' came upstairs to speak to Edison, who departed with him as if something important were in need of attention. Kruesi was the first to give up. It seemed to me that Upton was taking it easy like a cat with a mouse; he wanted to give the others a chance. My end came out wrong; so I had to unwind it again, as some of the others had already done. At the end of the first stipulated ten minutes, Upton finished his, and so won the Edison cigar. As he did not smoke, he passed the prize on to Kruesi, who gladly accepted it.

Upton showed 'Batch' and the others step by step how he had wound his drum. In this way the night soon passed. Drum winding was a puzzle in those days. Later, the textbooks explained it using colored diagrams to make it clear.

After the theoretical and mechanical details had been finished, Kruesi set his men to work and we soon had the armature shaft and core. Edison instructed us how to insulate the core, and told Upton how to wind the wire. Then Martin Force and I commenced our part of the job. We wound the core with calico tape and soaked it in an insulating solution which had been prepared downstairs in the chemical nook by the chief himself.

Someone suggested that we place a sheet of parchment paper over the calico, and have each write his name on it, with Edison heading the list. After the chief had signed, Upton, Batchelor, Kruesi, I, and Force followed.

Another who signed was James Seymour, of the shop. While visiting in Orange a few years ago I met Seymour and learned from him that he had worked on the *Jeannette* commutator and signed the parchment.

When the dynamo armature was finished it was taken to the shop and placed in position with its field magnets, which meanwhile had been wound from a lathe. Its first test, which was off a pulley, gave good results.

The *Jeannette* dynamo was about the size of the smallest type made by Edison later in his New York machine shop, having a fifteen lamp capacity. The arc lamp made for De Long was constructed so that the upper carbon revolved, keeping the arc in the center. We copper-plated the carbons, and had to make an extra rigout to do so.

'I'll tell you what,' said Edison to DeLong one day, 'I'll make a frame with a large wooden wheel and crank for you, so you can belt the dynamo on it when you have no steam, and your crew can take a hand driving the machine. It will keep them warm.'

The frame resembled the mechanical outfit used in small machine shops in the old days for driving a lathe, the power being supplied by apprentice boys. When this was finished, it was carried into the yard and the dynamo belted on; and then the workmen in the laboratory, the machine shop and the office took turns in driving it. Bets were made as to who could drive it longest. With timepiece in hand, Edison acted as referee.

It was great fun; yet when I recall how much exertion was required and think of those poor devils who worked in dingy shops turning lathes by hand power, I realize how great a blessing was given us by Edison when he found the means of supplying even the smallest of shops with power. After the DeLong outfit had been thoroughly tested and approved, Edison had it cased up securely and shipped to the West Coast. On July 8, 1879, after a rousing farewell DeLong left San Francisco for the Arctic.

He found Wrangell Land a rather insignificant island. After leaving it, his ship ran into ice packs, and on September 20, was frozen in. And there for twenty-one months it drifted about. On June 11, 1881, it was crushed by the ice near New Siberia Island, five-hundred miles from the delta of the Lena. The heroic band attempted to reach the Siberian Coast in three small boats, one of which went down in a terrific storm. Shore was reached by the others. One found a settlement, the other, with De Long, came ashore in an uninhabited region. Unable to find succor, he and his group perished.

Among the survivors of the other boat were Melville, Danenhower, Noros and Ninderman. Noros lived at Fall River, Massachusetts, until April 4, 1927, rounding out a peaceful career as a letter carrier. He was decorated by Congress.

Finis was written on the tragedy on February 23, 1884, when the *Scientific American* told the story of its sad fortune, as follows:

'The curtain is about to fall upon the sad tragedy of the *Jeannette* expedition. This enterprise, begun five years ago under such very auspicious circumstances with everything to aid it that human intelligence and worldly wealth could furnish, will soon celebrate its mournful failure in the funeral of the gallant leader who sacrificed his life, his all, to the cause of discovery and science. The bodies of Capt. De Long and his companions are now on the ocean, and in a few days will be received with civic and military pomp, and laid away to rest amid the tears of a sympathetic and appreciative country.'

It is interesting to observe that the master of the submarine *Nautilus*, in which Sir Hubert Wilkins sought the Arctic Ocean in 1931, was Commander Sloan Danenhower, son of the Lieutenant Danenhower who was navigator of the *Jeannette*.

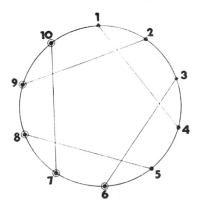

Diagram of five coil armature connection viewed from front end. Drawn by Francis Jehl.

TABLE OF THE AMERICAN EXPERIMENTS.

NAMES OF THE MACHINES.	Weight in Pounds.	COPPER WIRES. Of the Armature. Size.	COPPER WIRES. Of the Armature. Weight	COPPER WIRES. Of the Magnetic System. Size.	COPPER WIRES. Of the Magnetic System. Weight	Revolutions of the Armature in one Minute.	Foot-Pounds of Power expended for each Candle of Light.	Horse-Power.	Light in Candles. Total.	Light in Candles. Per Horse-Power	Foot-Pounds of Power expended for each Candle of Light.	Sizes of Carbons.	Length of Carbon consumed per Hour. +	Length of Carbon consumed per Hour. −
		in.	lbs.	in.	lbs.							in.	in.	in.
Large Brush ...	475	·81	32	134	100	1,340	107·606	3·26	1,230	377	87·4	$\frac{3}{8} \times \frac{3}{8}$	1·78	0·34
Small Brush ...	390	·63	24	96	80	1,400	124·248	3·76	900	239	137	$\frac{5}{8} \times \frac{5}{8}$	1·91	0·58
Large Wallace.	600	·42	50	114	125	800	—	—	823	—	—	—	—	—
Small Wallace.	350	·43	$18\frac{3}{4}$	98	41	1,000	128·544	3·89	440	113	292	$\frac{1}{4} \times \frac{1}{4}$	2·45	0·075
Gramme........	366	·59	$9\frac{1}{2}$	108	$57\frac{1}{2}$	800	60·992	1·84	705	383	85	$\frac{1}{4} \times \frac{1}{4}$	3·15	0·55

Chart showing results of tests of some generators prior to Edison's.

XXXIX. Dynamos of 1877-78; Studies in Magnetism

BEFORE continuing, I should like to quote an old theorem in which many scientists of that day placed confidence, rather than in common sense or reason. Three tables of dynamo tests made in 1877 and presented here will give the reader an idea of the state in which the art was at that period.(1) Those were the days when an ohm was designated as equal to 396 feet of Number 9 iron telegraph wire. In the old volume before me I find the following:

'Further, there is a general principle which is found in nearly all electrical effects capable of a maximum, and which ought always to be present in our minds. It is this: in order to be under the best conditions, the electrical generators must be arranged in such a manner that *their internal resistance shall be equal to that of the external circuit.*'

Scientists and dynamo builders were obsessed with this idea, which had been propagated sometime before the quotation was published. I well remember how Edison in 1879 pooh-poohed the idea.

'It is ridiculous,' he said. 'Do you think I want to lose 50 percent of the power I apply? Why, electric lighting could

(1) *Electric Lighting,* by LeComte Th. du Moncel, published at Paris by Hachette, 1880, and translated into English by Routledge, F. C. S., in 1882.

never be worked out commercially on that basis. They simply don't know what they are talking about. They must do a little more thinking on the consumption side. I am going to try to make my internal resistance as *low* as I possibly can.'

In 1877, a commission was appointed in England to examine the various electric generators then available. It was composed of Tyndall, Douglass, Sabine, Edwards, Drew-Atkings, and Minster, all well known in science. This commission stirred things up in America; for the Franklin Institute then appointed a commission consisting of Briggs, Rogers, Chase, Houston, Thomson, Rand, Jones, Sartain and Knight. The work of these commissions and the results attained are tabulated in the three accompanying tables.

After glancing at these tables we are apt to think that the data given is limited and incomplete. We must not forget that they were made at a period when men knew but little about the fine points needed in electric generators.

An engineer can dig out things from these tables that a layman cannot. Needless to say, all the generators tested were arc light machines; for the practical incandescent lamp had not yet been born. It is apparent also that the results of electrical machinery were given only in mechanical nomenclature, showing again the backward state of electrical science at that period.

The tables are historically interesting in many respects, and show why Edison's hopes were enhanced when he resolutely commenced to construct a dynamo-electric generator of his own design for his system of *parallel electric energy distribution.* In fact, DuMoncel in his book remarks satirically that 'Edison has also to invent a generator of unheard-of power and in this he says he is sure of succeeding. But in the meantime he has to try those which are at present in use, in order, no doubt, to find which comes nearest to his ideal, that it may supply the most advantageous data for constructing his own.'

Michael Pupin, eminent professor of Columbia University, scientist and electrical engineer, said in 1929:[2]

'Light's Golden Jubilee is a fitting occasion to say a few words about Thomas Alva Edison's great achievement in the perfection of the incandescent lamp.

'A noted wit once described Mr. Edison's greatest achievement in the following three words—"Filament in *vacuo.*"

---

(2) N. E. L. A. Bulletin, Sept. 1929, Vol. XVI, No. 9.

Comparative Table of English Experiments

KIND OF MACHINE	Classification of the Machines in order of Merit	Luminous Intensities per H.P. — Diffused — Carcel Lamps	Luminous Intensities per H.P. — Diffused — Candles	Luminous Intensities per H.P. — Condensed — Carcel Lamps	Luminous Intensities per H.P. — Condensed — Candles	Total Luminous — Diffused — Carcel Lamps	Total Luminous — Diffused — Candles	Total Luminous — Condensed — Carcel Lamps	Total Luminous — Condensed — Candles	No. of Revolutions per Minute	Motive Force absorbed in Horse-power	Weight (lbs.)	Dimensions Height (feet)	Dimensions Width (feet)	Dimensions Length (feet)	Price (£)
HOLMES	6	68·00	476	68·00	476	217·57	1,523	217·57	1,523	400	3·2	5,740	5·24	4·32	4·92	550
ALLIANCE	5	77·57	543	77·57	543	279·00	1,953	279·00	1,953	400	3·6	4,075	4·82	4·49	4·32	494
GRAMME, No. 1	4	108·29	758	179·57	1,257	573·71	4,016	951·86	6,663	420	5·3	2,853	4·06	2·58	2·58	320
GRAMME, No. 2	4	108·29	758	179·57	1,257	573·71	4,016	915·86	6,663	420	5·74	2,853	4·06	2·58	2·58	320
SIEMENS, large size	3	130·14	911	216·00	1,512	1276·00	8,932	2116·86	14,818	480	9·8	1,305	1·17	2·32	3·62	265
SIEMENS, medium size, No. 58	2	136·29	954	226·00	1,582	477·00	3,339	791·29	5,539	850	3·5	420	0·83	2·32	2·16	100
SIEMENS, medium size, No. 68	1	179·14	1,254	297·14	2,080	591·14	4,138	980·57	6,864	850	3·3	420	0·83	2·32	2·16	100
2 HOLMES, coupled	—	61·71	433	61·71	432	401·57	2,811	401·57	2,811	400	6·5	11,480	5·24	4·32	9·84	1,100
2 GRAMMES, coupled	—	93·29	654	155·00	1,085	981·29	6,869	1628·00	11,396	420	10·5	5,706	4·06	2·58	5·16	640
2 SIEMENS, medium size, Nos. 58 & 63 coupled	—	184·43	1,291	395·86	2,141	1217·14	8,520	2019·14	14,134	850	6·6	840	0·83	2·32	4·32	200

This chart and that facing it show the results of tests made by the English commission.

NOTE—*Condensed* light is the arc formed by direct current and *diffused* light is the arc formed by alternating current.

'But a whole book could be written about the vast amount of work which Mr. Edison and his assistants had to perform in order to get the right kind of filament and the right kind of vacuum.

'The noted wit, who succeeded in formulating the shortest

	Number of Candles for each Light measured horizontally — Total	Per Horse-power Absorbed	Revolutions per Minute	Lamps used	Nature of the Motor	Revolutions per Minute	Cylinder Diameter in Inches	Cylinder Strokes in Inches	Engines Horse-power per Light — Nominal	Effective Total	Absorbed	Localities	Observers	Observations
Holmes	1,533	476	400	Holmes	Steam	—	13	18	10	—	3·2	South Foreland	Douglass	Alternating Magneto-Electric Currents.
Alliance	1,953	543	400	"	"	—	—	—	10	—	3·6	"	"	
"	3,000	667	400	Serrin	"	—	1,	—	—	—	4·5	Paris	Allard	
Méritens, large	8,600	1,228	650	Holmes	Gas	156	9	16	8	10·9	7·0	Royal Institution	Douglass	
" small	1,860	1,240	880	Duboscq	"	156	9	16	8	4·2	1·5	"	"	
Siemens, medium	4,100	1,254	850	Siemens	Steam	—	13	18	10	—	3·3	South Foreland	"	
" " small	—	—	—	"	Gas	158	9	16	8	8·9	5·4	London Stereoscopic Co.	Amos.	
" " small	—	—	—	"	"	155	9	16	8	8·2	4·7	"		
Gramme, for a single light, (A)	960	330	—	Serrin	Steam	115	—	—	12	3	2·7	La Chapelle, Paris	Chemin de fer du Nord	Dynamo-Electric Machines with Continuous Currents.
"	1,824	730	920	"	"	—	—	—	—	—	2·5	Rouen	Powell	
"	2,850	1,018	892	"	Gas	143	6¼	12	3⅓	—	2·8	Paris	Tresca	
"	2,520	740	830	Brush	Steam	—	6	8	—	5·1	3·4	Edmundson, West-minster	Shoolbred	
"	705	383	800	"	"	—	6	8	—	—	1·84	Philadelphia	Committee of the Franklin Institute	
Large Brush	1,230	377	1,340	"	"	—	6	18	—	—	3·26	"	"	
Small "	900	239	1,400	"	"	—	9	8	—	—	3·76	"	"	
Large Wallace	823	113	800	"	"	—	6	8	—	—	—	"	"	
Small "	440		1,000	"	"	—					—	"	"	
Gramme Division Machine, 16 lights	350	—	640	Jablochkoff	"	142	10	13	20	—	3·89	Avenue de l'Opéra Paris	Allard	Dynamo-Electric Machines with Alternating Currents.
Gramme Division chine, 20 lights	—	—	650	"	"	110	9¾	13	20	—	1·25	Thames Embankment	"	
Lontin Division chine, 6 lights	570	—	350	Serrin-Lontin	"	—	9½	13½	9	—	—	St. Lazare Station, Paris	Chemin de fer de l'Ouest	

New chart showing later tests of generators. These tables and that on Page 298 are reproduced from Du Moncel's book *Electric Lighting*, published in 1880.

description, omitted to mention a very essential element in Mr. Edison's electrical lighting system. This element represents another epoch-making achievement. *It is the invention and development of the low-resistance dynamo-electric machine* which fed the incandescent lamps, all connected in parallel.

This invention, added to the perfected incandescent lamp, gave us the incandescent lighting of today.

'The incandescent lamp, therefore, together with Mr. Edison's power distribution system between circuits connected in parallel, is Mr. Edison's great achievement which we are celebrating in Light's Golden Jubilee.'

The ill-fated *Jeannette* and Commander DeLong with his brave crew will always be remembered tenderly and occupy an important niche in the first chapter of the story of Edison's search for the electric light. Because of that expedition, Edison was led to seek at an earlier date a dynamo-electric generator different from those in use at that period. The *Jeannette* dynamo was his first; the study he gave it introduced him to scientific premises upon which his future 90 percent efficient dynamo was to be predicated.

Not long after DeLong sailed away, Edison set Upton at work on experiments seeking data to be used in building his second generator. It was side work for 'Culture'; he divided his time between network calculation and magnetism experiments.

In the chapter 'A Lesson in Magnetism,' some of Edison's ideas on that subject have already been described. I have prepared a summary of them from that review.(³) In reading them, you must not forget that most of these ideas were not to be found in the textbooks of the period, until Edison put them there. In conversation with Upton, Edison said:

'Magnetism follows a law just like that controlling electric current. When you put too much current into a wire, you make it hot. And when these other fellows use too many windings of wire in their magnet field and too much current for a small cross section of iron, they throttle the lines of force out of the right path.

'I believe you can saturate a piece of iron so that you can't force another line into it. I want you to make some experiments with that idea and see whether I'm not right. I don't agree with these electricians who say the wire coils are everything.

'The best and cheapest form of magnet is the old horseshoe style a boy can buy at any hardware store. That's the kind of model I want you to follow.'

'But no one is using that kind, Mr. Edison,' said Upton.

'So much the better. Don't look at any of the dynamos

that have been produced so far, Upton. Ours has got to be entirely different. We intend to use it for incandescent lamps, while those now in use are for arc lamps. Our job is to avoid their bad points.

'Can you tell me some bad points, Mr. Edison?'

'I've already mentioned one. Too little iron. Bad iron contacts is another. Just like a bad contact between wires carrying current. It's a big drawback.'

'Nobody has ever thought that contacts made any great difference with magnetism.'

'I'm sure they do. A bad contact which interrupts the flow of the force will put resistance in its path. We must make our contacts for magnetism equally as good as those for a current of electricity.'

'Too much air space should not be allowed in the field. I think the poles of the magnet should fit against the armature rather than be separated so far from it.'

'Do you think that separation increases the resistance to the flow of the magnetic force?'

'I do. You're catching on, Upton. Did you ever play with a horseshoe magnet when you were a boy? Do you recall the bar that lay across the two ends of the horseshoe? When you removed it to a distance it wouldn't respond to the pull of the magnet, but as you shoved it nearer and nearer, suddenly it felt the drag of the force and snapped over against the poles. Now, think that over and apply it to our job.'

'I think I see your point. When distance or air intervenes, it forms a resistance.'

'Another point we want to change is the kind of material used in moving parts. Some present day dynamo armature cores are made of *solid iron*, and yet people wonder why they get hot when running. Back at Newark while making my telegraph instruments, I always found soft iron the best to use in my coils. I made it red-hot and annealed it before using. I long ago found that an electromagnet containing bad iron would often stick.

'We want an iron that won't retain magnetism as steel does. We want it to let the magnetism fly out as soon as we stop the current. It must be able to change its force whenever we change the current, up or down. You've studied under Helmholtz and you've been to college; so you ought to be able to work these things out.

'Why don't you have Kruesi rig up a shaft for you that

can be driven by a belt and pulley? Then you can make armature cores having various qualities or put together in various
ways and try them out while running. Get the running parts
of the core well divided. Remember what I said about the
heat. Try discs made of thin sheets of iron; try thick sheets;
try soft iron wire.'

Upton asked: 'When you were making your telegraph
instruments did it make any difference whether you wound
the magnet with thin wire or with thick?'

'No difference. The magnetic action was about the
same.'

'But I don't understand. If the wire is thick, isn't the current much stronger? When the wire is thin, there is more
resistance. The current is weaker.'

'That's right,' replied Mr. Edison. 'I won't dispute that.
When you use thick wire in winding a coil, you make fewer
turns than when you use thin wire. In the former case, the
current goes through fewer turns and so is stronger. In the
latter, it goes round the magnet many more times, even though
it is weaker. The resulting magnetism is about the same,
either way.

'Let me explain it to you by an example. Suppose you took
a single battery and connected with it a spool of thick wire
in which the wire went round the spool—say, ten times.
Let the resistance equal ten ohms and the current have the
strength of one weber. We'll turn on the juice and send that
one weber into the coil. It will go round the spool ten times
and produce a certain magnetic effect.

'Now we'll slice that thick wire up lengthwise into ten
equal lengths and connect them together. What do you get?
Ten times the resistance, don't you?' 'Yes, sir.'

'On the other hand, you can now wind the spool with
about one hundred turns instead of ten, can't you?' 'Yes, sir.'

'But—since the resistance is ten times greater, the current
has only one-tenth the strength, hasn't it?' 'Yes, sir.'

'That one-tenth of a weber goes round the spool a hundred
times. Every ten turns which it makes will give you the same
magnetic effect as a single turn of the thick wire; and the hundred turns will produce just as much effect as ten turns of the
thick wire did. That's my idea.'

'By Jove!' exclaimed Upton eagerly. 'Nobody—not even
the scientists have ever thought that out before! It's something new. It's just what we need in making a dynamo.'

Prof. G. F. Barker, University of Pennsylvania, inspecting Edison's new dynamo. (From print in *Scientific American* October 18, 1879.) Note dynamometer in rear, and beyond, steam engine and boiler as restored in Menlo Park machine shop today in Dearborn.

XL. The Dynamo Is Finished—
'Long-Legged Mary Ann'

BY MIDSUMMER Edison had completed much of the detail of his system. A writer in the *Scientific American* declared:(1)

'It would seem from what is at present being done in the Menlo Park laboratory that there are hundreds of points in the problem of electric lighting that have not been considered by experimenters; among these are the proper treatment of the metal or mineral to be subjected to the intense heat required to bring it to incandescence; the insulation and protection of the electrical conductors; the meter for the

(1) July 26, 1879.

measurement of the current; and the generator of electricity, which is, after all, the most vital point in the system.

'The machine which is to supply the current has been completed and is now undergoing a series of tests to determine its efficiency. Ninety-six percent of the power applied to the machine is realized in the electric current, and 82 percent of the power is made available outside of the machine. This is about double the effective exterior current realized by other machines.

'In order to measure the power required to drive the generator, Mr. Edison has tried every dynamometer within reach and condemned them all. At last, after considerable experiment, he hit upon a simple contrivance. He claims that with this apparatus he can measure the one hundredth part of a horsepower.

'A weighted box rests on a platform scale, and is provided with a pulley for receiving the driving belt, which passes over the driving pulley, under a tightener, and over a driven pulley. The number of foot pounds of power used will be indicated by the lifting of the box and the consequent lightening of the load on the scale. Five percent is deducted for the angle of the belt and for friction.'

The responsibility for this end of the work fell upon Upton, under Edison's direction. Trials were made with the field magnet coils wound in shunt fashion, in series, and in a compound way, that is, shunt and series coils together.

I assisted Upton in the last-named trials and recall how the armature current that passed through the series coils was dissipated in a variable copper resistance made for the purpose hurriedly, since we had as yet no incandescent lamps to perform that function.

It was part of Upton's work to observe the tension of the dynamo. We set up the Thomson reflecting galvanometer in a corner of the machine shop and standardized it roughly with a few common Daniell cells.

Measuring the current was a difficult task with engine, dynamo and shop machinery all running at the same time. Upton used the dampening effect of the magnet of the galvanometer to get his readings.

While the shunt magnet coils were in action and the dynamo was loaded, Upton added or removed series coils, in time proving that a constant potential with a varying load

Dynamometer in restored Menlo Park machine shop, at Dearborn. Compare this picture with that at head of chapter and note faithfulness of restoration.

could be maintained when the series coils were properly apportioned. I think it is safe to say that no dynamo builder anywhere at that time possessed the knowledge of shunt, series and compound wiring that Edison had. He studied them in all their phases.

One of his first series of experiments after the field magnet and the armature shaft were built was to wind the cores with three layers of number 10 copper insulated wire. The magnet was excited by the current from the Gramme machine, having in its circuit some wooden resistance boxes. These consisted of copper wire wound in the notches of an upright wooden frame made of two boards joined in the middle at right angles. Each box formed a unit, and could be inserted or cut out by means of a metal plug. Armature cores were made of various kinds and qualities of wrought and cast iron, varying from solid cores to thin plates. In each iron core was drilled a hole where a thermometer could be inserted. An iron core was attached to the shaft. Upton then connected it with the belt and ran it for an hour or two, during which the field was excited.

This method of pioneer testing was purely comparative. From time to time tests were made on the speeds of the core and of the Gramme machine. They were supposed to be the

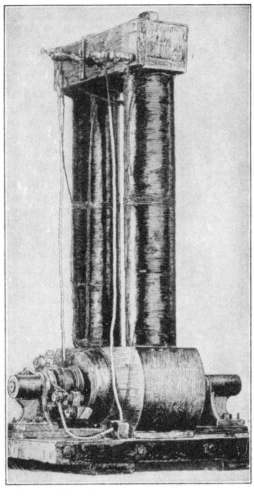

same. He ascertained the temperature of the core when it was started, and again when it was stopped after a certain time. Then he found to what degrees of heat it had been subjected by the action of the Foncault currents (as we called eddy currents in those days).

Generally, one test was checked by a second test, and in that manner the whole series of cores were examined for heating. Results were surprising; cores made of soft iron, divided, showed the least rise in temperature. Edison had already noticed, after running the Wallace machine for some time, that its solid iron cores became unusually hot. Others had passed this complexity over as being inevitable. Edison regarded heat as energy; and since energy is costly, he believed the overheating to be pure waste. He attributed the low efficiency of the Wallace machine partly to that cause.

The core with the least rise in temperature was wound with Number 20 iron wire, which had been previously well annealed in a charcoal fire and covered with a skin of oxide. That core was selected for further experiments; the field magnet

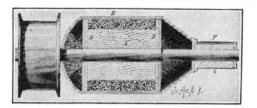

Armature of Edison's first
successful dynamo. (From
Scientific American, October
18, 1879.)

with shaft and core was transported from the machine shop to the upper story of the laboratory. There Upton wound one coil—two or three turns of fine copper insulated wire upon the iron wire core, while the ends were attached to the shaft. He had a sort of wooden lever fastened to the pulley in such a way that it could only move through a certain angle. The lever was weighted at one end. When the lever was raised to the upper stop and then released, it fell to the lower stop, causing the coil to move a part of a revolution in a certain time. The ends of the coil on the armature core were connected with an astatic galvanometer dampened by means of a permanent magnet, resistance and shunt. When the coil moved through the known angle at a certain speed, the induced current produced a 'kick' in the needle of the galvanometer. This was read and noted.

Of course after many observations had been made, the mean of them all was taken. And as the angles of the coil were successively changed by a turn of the wooden lever to the next angle, Upton obtained a comparative picture of the electromotive force generated in his coil at successive angles during one complete revolution. By adjusting the standard cells to produce the same 'kicks,' he obtained some idea of actual values. With the aid of the exploring coil on the iron wire core, Upton went through many other experiments, varying the current that flowed through the field magnet. Each time he ascertained the strength of the current in webers by means of electrodeposition. These experiments were most tedious; for we had to be careful about securing the proper deposition by regulating the current passing through the cell, shunted for the purpose. As we knew the resistance of the deposition cell and that of the shunt, the strength of the current could be calculated. Later we calculated it with the Edison chemical meter in the same way.

Current strength was determined by means of a deposition cell having a shunt—a method of calculating that we understood; and yet it never once entered our heads to take the drop of potential on that shunt—an easy thing to do—and thus by Ohm's law obtain the strength of the current direct. We were so near that method, and yet so far from it!

As he kept increasing the current in the field magnet, Upton arrived at length at a saturation point, after which he did not gain any special advantage through increase in voltage of the exploring coil. The electromagnetic effect produced by a coil of wire was proportional to the number of turns in the coil, and to the strength of the current flowing through it. The product of those two factors was constant, and gave the same effect whether the turns on the coil were numerous or few, and the current weak or strong. This law was abused in many of the earlier machines where insufficient iron cross section was provided to direct the magnetism thus created. When conducting his investigations, Upton always noted the weber turns and with his other data had all that was necessary to put the results of his work in proper form.

He discovered that a weber turn (that is, an ampere turn) was a constant factor, a given number of which always produced the same effect magnetically. This point was practically new to the scientific world at that time.

In those days the makers of dynamos simply oversoaked their magnet circuit with current, knowing nothing about magnetic saturation. They thought the more the current they sent through the coils, the greater the effect they would obtain. It never occurred to them that the increased current effect would be scattered in every direction but the right one.

It must be said to Upton's credit that the work, as well as the calculation involved in it, required the expert abilities both of a mathematician, and of a physicist. Like Maxwell with Faraday, Upton was the one who interpreted Edison's ideas and translated them into mathematical form. What he did was a classical piece of pioneer investigation conducted under extreme difficulties. His work paved the way for the more elaborate work of Hopkinson and Kapp.

After having the privilege of assisting him in those experiments, today I can only repeat what Edison himself said in an article written for the *Electrical World and Engineer:*

'As I now look back, I sometimes wonder at how much was done in so short a time.'([2])

Besides introducing the field magnet with very long core but of sufficient cross section, which design was characteristic

(2)   March 5, 1904.

of all early Edison dynamos, Edison was the first to wind a drum armature with an uneven number of coils. He was also the first to use a large number of coils having few turns, instead of few coils having a great number of turns like the Siemens machine, which possessed a commutator having an even but small number of bars. The Edison commutator had an uneven but large number of bars.

All the characteristic features that were so distinctly Edisonian in later dynamos were to be found in that small bipolar one made for the ill-fated *Jeannette*. It should be remembered that we did not call the machine a 'dynamo' at that time. To us, it was a 'Faradic' machine, named by Edison after the great Faraday.

The first Edison dynamo had a flat wooden base without wooden cross pieces to reinforce it, as did later ones until they were given all-iron bases. The cross-shaped metal piece upon which the poles of the magnets stood was of brass, later changed to zinc when iron bases were used. The *Jeannette* armature core contained layers of soft iron wire, instead of the thin sheet-iron disc lamination that made up the armatures of the three machines used during the demonstration in December, 1879.

The first published description of the dynamo appeared in the *Scientific American* on October 18, 1879, and evoked a storm of controversy and bickerings among those who did not believe such a dynamo could be built.

'I can scarcely conceive it as possible,' wrote a great electrical manufacturer,([3]) 'that the article could have been written from statements derived from Mr. Edison himself, inasmuch as so many of the advantages claimed for the machine and statements of the results obtained are so manifestly absurd as to indicate a positive want of knowledge of the electric circuit, and the principles governing the construction and operation of electrical machines.'

As if that were not enough, he declared: 'How anyone acquainted with the laws of the electric circuit can make such statements is what I cannot understand. The statement is mathematically absurd.'

Other statements followed in similar tone, some waxing highly sarcastic, others pretending to lament the spectacle newspapers were making of our chief. It was even hinted that he had a mischief-maker among his workmen.

(3) *Scientific American*, Nov. 1, 1879.

Dr. Charles A. Seeley thus indicted us: 'His (Edison's) reputation as a scientist is smirched by the newspaper exaggerations and no doubt he will be more careful in the future. But there is a danger nearer home, among his own friends, and in his very household . . .

'Why does he say such things as: "Mr. Edison claims that he realizes 90 percent of the power applied to this machine in external work." Perhaps the writer is a humorist, but such jests are not good.'(4)

That claim of Edison's many experts and scientists were unable to swallow.

'It implies,' said the manufacturer, 'either that the machine *is capable of increasing its own electromotive force nine times without an increased expenditure of power*, or that external resistance is *not* resistance to the current induced in the Edison machine.'

Edison's new generator, described in the *Scientific American*, was the largest that had ever been made up to that time. The field magnets were said to be 'immense.' They were about fifty-four inches high and weighed 1,100 pounds. We nicknamed it 'the Long-Legged Mary Ann.'

The magnet cores were made of wrought iron wound with a coarse cotton-covered wire. They were six inches in diameter and three feet long, and the pole pieces were more than ten inches high and nine wide. The magnetic circuit was completed by a yoke six inches high and seven wide. When one considers the smooth and carefully scraped contact surfaces with which the members of the magnet were connected, one cannot but admire the versatility displayed by Edison in arriving at his solution of the dynamo problem.

Already Edison was planning his first central station. We find in the published article this statement: 'Although the current from the armature may be used to excite the field magnet, Mr. Edison finds it more economical to charge the field magnet by means of a separate machine. *In fact, he intends to charge a battery of such generators with a single faradic machine of this sort.*'

(4) *Scientific American*, Nov. 15, 1879.

This picture, taken in 1880, shows many of the early workmen, as well as some who came later. Top row (left to right): 'Basic' Lawson, ——, ——, Ludwig Boehm, 'Batch,' Jehl, Upton, 'Doc' Haid. Second row:——, David Cunningham, Edison, 'Major' McLaughlin, Tom Logan. Third row: Johnny Randolph, Charles Flammer, George Dean, George Carman, John Ott, James Seymour, John Kelly. Bottom: Alfred Swanson, Martin Force, 'Griff,' Milo Andrus.

Edison's electric motor. (From a print in the *Scientific American*, *October 18, 1879.*)

XLI. A New Electric Motor
The Machine Shop

D URING the period in which Edison was perfecting his dynamo, still another line of experimenting had been absorbing part of his attention. I refer to the electric motor. Little was known of the practical workings of this important device and many mistaken ideas concerning it were held.

When Edison stated, back in the fall of 1878, that the same current which furnished light could also be used to provide heat and power, his critics got out their cudgels and came after him. Such a rash prediction, they asserted in no uncertain terms, was absurd.

Earlier experimenters studying the motor had been puzzled by an effect that was later recognized as a counter-electromotive force. They regarded it as something to be overcome, an injurious drawback. Edison became convinced that it was quite otherwise; he compared it to a safety valve. When the motor was put to work, it permitted only as much current to pass as was required; as the load was increased, the 'valve' released more current.

The flexibility of the direct-current motor impressed him greatly. Indeed, he had been interested in it ever since the days of the electric pen. You will recall that the pen used a tiny motor at its upper end to drive the shaft. That was the first electric motor in history to be manufactured commercially and sold in quantities.

One of his important discoveries about the motor was that, when connected with a line, it was a current-receiving unit

Sewing machine in restored laboratory at Dearborn, connected to replica of Edison's first electric motor, visible on floor back of machine.

like the lamp; and its consumption was equivalent to that of a certain number of lamps.

Aside from the electric pen motor, not more than half a dozen types of electric motors were to be found in the country at that time, and these were crude and chiefly experimental. When connected up, they admitted so much current that investigators were discouraged. The characteristics of the device had not been studied, the main thing seeming to be to get it to revolve. I doubt whether any one had glimpsed the great future awaiting it.

Edison's motor, because of its ample iron cross section, small air gap, and low magnetic resistance, yielded a counter-electromotive force that surprised even him. It required but little current to run when not carrying a load, increasing its requirements proportionately as the load was added.

The first description of the new electric motor was published in the article in the *Scientific American* that announced his dynamo. To quote:

'Figure 3 shows Mr. Edison's new electric motor intended for running sewing machines, small elevators, lathes and other light machinery, by connecting it with the same wires that furnish the current for the electric lamps. Its construction differs but slightly from the electric generator. The armature is arranged parallel with the magnet instead of transversely, and the magnet is formed of a single casting.([1]) In other respects it is like the generator, having the same form of armature, also commutator, cylinder and brushes.'

One of the earliest demonstrations of the motor in the laboratory was its running of a sewing machine. We hooked the motor to the same wires that brought current for the lamps, thus proving that what the scientists had declared was impossible could be done. You may see a replica of machine and motor today on the second floor of the restored building. You will observe that one wire is green to indicate incoming current, and the other red to indicate outgoing. In those days, we thought it necessary to distinguish wires in that manner. This sewing machine motor was the first domestic shunt motor to run on a high tension multiple arc circuit.

When the New York *Herald* published its famous edition of December 21, 1879, announcing the invention of the in-

---

(1) The reporter was in error. The core and the yoke were of wrought iron, only the pole pieces being of cast iron.

Restored machine shop at Dearborn, viewed from northeast corner.

Original Menlo Park boiler as it now appears in restored boiler room, Dearborn.   Its fire was lighted by Edison.

candescent light, it included the motor as a part of the Edison electric lighting system. That description of the first practical application of electricity to household use signaled the beginning of the end of woman's drudgery. Entitled 'A Domestic Motor,' it reads:

'By constructing a machine in the form shown, there is obtained an electric motor capable of performing light work, such as running sewing machines and pumping water. It forms part of the inventor's system and may be used either with or without the electric light. To run an ordinary sewing machine it requires only as much electricity as is necessary to give out one electric light of the strength of a common gas jet.

'To put in operation on a sewing machine, the housewife

has merely to attach it by a little belt with the wheel of the sewing machine, and turn on the electricity by touching a little knob conveniently attached. The cost is the same as if she was burning one electric light.'

A few men were added to the Menlo Park crew during summer and fall of 1879. To the staff in the office where 'Griff,' Johnny Randolph and William Carman, the book-keeper, toiled, was added Samuel D. Mott to serve as patent draughtsman. George Carman, Will's brother, did odd jobs in both the office and the laboratory.

Under Kruesi in the machine shop was a hard-working crew, to which others were joined when the new dynamos were started. I have mentioned some of the old-timers, John F. Ott, Charles Dean, Jim Bradley, Tom Logan, David Cunningham, John Hood and others. To these were added William S. Andrews, Alexander Mungle and Jim Holloway.

Of these, John Ott continued to serve until the day of

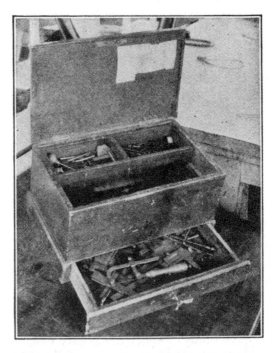

John Kruesi's original tool chest. Now in office of restored machine shop.

Looking into restored engine room from main part of machine shop at Menlo Park, Dearborn.

Edison's death on October 19, 1931. The splendid old mechanician, now for some years an invalid, was so stunned by the news of his master's passing that he did not survive the shock by a day. His invalid chair and crutches were placed at the foot of his master's bier.

Dean, whose house stood next to the boarding house, had been with Edison in Newark, as had Ott and Bradley. When we started to manufacture lamps commercially in Menlo Park in 1880, Bradley was made master mechanic of the new works. Dean went to New York City with Edison in 1881, where he became foreman of the Edison Machine Works.

William S. Andrews came to Menlo Park in the beginning of November, 1879, and served under Kruesi in the shop. He was a bright, educated man, a mechanician with scientific training. He succeeded me as chief of the testing room at the Edison Machine Works when I was sent to Europe and later took an active part in the introduction of the Edison system —he and Frank J. Sprague erecting the first three-wire plant at Sunbury, Pennsylvania, in 1883.

The tiny drills and taps made by Andrews for the platinum clamps of the paper and the bamboo lamps are now a part of the Edison Institute collection.

John Hood had the important job of steam engineer, and as such bossed the 80-horsepower Brown steam engine that furnished power in the shop. An exact duplicate of that engine, obtained from a New England silk mill, may be seen today in the restored shop at Dearborn. John Hood provided power for the first experimental dynamos, and later for the first experimental station at Menlo Park in 1879 as well as the second and larger station in 1880-1881. He was steam engineer for the experimental Jumbo of 1881, which was connected directly with a high-speed Porter Allen engine. Edison shortly thereafter sent him to London to assist Edward Johnson in the erection of the exhibition central station at 57 Holborn Viaduct, which was put in operation on January 12, 1882.

Hood proved his ability there, for the new steam plant worked without a hitch. A year later he was called back to New York to manage the Pearl Street Station, which he started on September 4, 1882. So he had the distinction of starting the three important central stations of early lighting history, those in Menlo Park, London and New York City. Hood recalls one incident that took place at Menlo Park when Edison was showing some visitors through the machine shop. One of them, while looking at the engine, asked: 'Where is the governor?' Edison answered, with a twinkle: 'Oh, he's up at Trenton.'

Jim Holloway was sent to England to assist Hood; and when the latter was called back to America, he remained behind and took charge. He assisted later in erecting the plant at the Crystal Palace Exhibition.

David Cunningham went from our shop to France, where he helped Batchelor erect the French plant at Ivry-sur-Seine near Paris. Like the others, he was an able, efficient mechanic and a faithful servant of the French Edison company.

In the office of the restored shop, on the left as you enter, you may see the old chest containing the working tools of that master mechanic, John Kruesi. A gift to Henry Ford from a son of Kruesi's, they now occupy an honored place among the relics of Menlo Park.

At the far end of the restored shop stands the boiler house, containing the original Babcock and Wilcox boiler used in the first shop and later moved to Orange for use in the new plant. Edison subsequently presented it to Mr. Ford. The fire now burning in it, as well as that in the boiler and carbonizing furnace in the laboratory, was started by Edison when he was in Dearborn during Light's Golden Jubilee, and it has burned night and day ever since. If you happen to be in the village in the morning, at noon or at quitting time, you may hear the shop's steam whistle blow its shrill signal as it did in the old days.

Another interesting exhibit in the restored shop is the safety vertical steam engine near the center of the hall, connected with the line shaft by belt. An engine like this supplied power to run the machines; the Brown engine was largely used to operate the dynamos.

The shop is equipped with machinery of the period, all the lathes from the original shop having been previously moved to Orange and thence brought here when the shop was restored.

A word of tribute to the memory of our workers in the machine shop, who did their share, also, in contributing to our success. Their patient skill at the bench, lathe, and elsewhere shaped the apparatus that our great chief wanted for his experiments. His success often depended on their ability in moulding the materials to suit. Their ideas had to be blended with those of our chief's, and in their efforts an honest conscientiousness meant much. The world is indebted to those silent workers of the shop, as it is to all such workers everywhere.

William S. Andrews.

Alexander Mungle.

XLII. Search for Lamp Resumes
The Little Glass House

BEFORE I narrate the stirring events that led up to
October 21, 1879, when they were crowned with the
invention of a successful incandescent lamp, it might
be well briefly to summarize the search as already
related in these pages.

In the fall of 1877—two years previously—Edison made
his first experiments with strips of carbonized paper, trying
them in open air and under the glass bell of a mechanical air
pump. The strips were oxidized so rapidly that no satisfactory results were obtained.

Next he experimented in a small way with chromium,
boron, ruthenium, and such other fusible metals as were on
hand. Already the need of a lamp of high resistance was im-
pressing itself on his mind.

Then came the invention of the phonograph, causing a
cessation of the lighting experiments for several months. So
long and arduously did the inventor work on his new discovery that he was forced during the summer of 1878 to take
a vacation, with some months of travel in the West.

Presentation of glass house by General Electric Company to Henry Ford for removal to Dearborn.

In the early fall he resumed his studies in electric lighting with renewed vigor. Experiments with metallic lamps using spirals of platinum and other rare metals formed the first part of these investigations. About this time he expressed his belief that he had solved the problem. The excitement that ensued caused a panic in gas stock and aroused parliament to appoint a commission in England to inquire into the possibility of such a solution. After taking the testimony of the leading scientists of the period, the commission declared that the light was unlikely if not impossible of success. An editorial in *Engineer* declared: 'If the current can be successfully divided among dozens of such lamps, then may gas makers quake, but nothing of the kind may be done.' (Feb. 14, 1879.)

In that period there were but few who understood Edison and the trend of his reasoning. There was, however, an Englishman, St. George Lane-Fox, who had the same objective as our chief. He was an able investigator with clear vision, who, like Edison, appreciated the value of high resistance and small radiating surface in the successful electric lamp. As yet his efforts had been unsuccessful. He deserves mention as ranking next to Edison among the many investigators who were striving at that time to bring forth a light.

As I have said, Edison was not working on a lamp alone.

He had in mind a complete system of current distribution embracing many other articles of apparatus besides the lamp; among these was the generator, in itself a remarkable achievement in electrical progress.

In August, 1879, scientists of the country gathered at Saratoga Springs, New York, for the annual meeting of the American Association for the Advancement of Science. Edison and Upton attended. The former read a paper on his discovery of occluded gases and the method of expelling them. At the same time he demonstrated his motograph, or 'loud-speaking telephone,' in the presence of that other great inventor, Dr. Alexander Graham Bell. Upton told of Edison's efforts in the building of a practical and efficient current generator.[1]

Satisfied that he had a practical generator, Edison in this same month took up the search for a stable filament once more. He was convinced that it was impossible to produce a practical metallic filament from the metals then known; so he turned his attention again to carbon. He decided that it would speed matters if he engaged a glass blower to obviate the necessity of carrying the precious, flimsy filaments to and fro between Menlo Park and Philadelphia, as had been done in earlier trials.

Thus it happened that on a day in August, 1879, a dapper, rosy-cheeked young man with foreign accent entered the laboratory and announced that he was Ludwig Boehm, and that 'Meestair Ettison' had hired him to be our glass blower. Boehm came from Germany where he had worked as an apprentice under the great German *meister*, Dr. Heinrich Geissler. As America seemed to offer more opportunities

Ludwig Boehm

than the Fatherland he had migrated here and obtained a job, which he quit to accept one with Edison.

A place was set aside for him on the ground floor of the main laboratory, and here he arranged his apparatus. According to the journeymen's custom of carrying their tools with them, Boehm brought a bellows and a glass-blowing table like the one now in the little Glass House at Dearborn.

Edison obtained a stock of glass tubes for him as well as glass enamels, in all varieties. Boehm now began the construction of a number of Sprengel pumps. Edison also experimented with pumps, testing them with different calibers of tubes, studying vacuum pumps and seeking a more practical way of exhausting air from the glass bulbs intended for use in later experiments.

As a result the Sprengel pump was found to be best suited and was retained until after the invention of the lamp, when Edison again turned his attention to air pumps to find a way of producing lamps in quantities. The idea of combining the Sprengel pump with that of Geissler occurred to him. Upton was requested to make up the necessary drawings. A McLeod gauge was added as well as a spark gap and two extra chambers for absorbing moisture and mercurial vapors. We made three such combination Sprengel-Geissler pumps, which may be seen today in the restored laboratory. They represent the first experimental lamp factory run on a production basis. I suppose you will smile when I tell you that this lamp factory produced about twenty-four lamps in twenty-four hours, which in those days was a considerable number.

These pumps had many ground and greased cocks and connection pieces that caused a great deal of annoyance. Often the pumps were 'frozen'—that is, the grease became dry and hard enough to stick; and whenever we manipulated them frequently, something broke. One of Boehm's chief tasks was to repair them.

We had to study not only the pumps but also the type of lamp bulbs, another development originated at Menlo Park. We studied methods of sealing and of passing platinum wire through the glass stem. We had to decide the kind of glass best suited for the work.

All this experimentation presented an additional problem for Edison to master, which he dug into purposefully. Later I shall tell you in detail about the air pumps and the glass, and how we simplified the work to a surprising degree. First let me recall something of the little glass house and its tenant, Boehm.

When he came to work with us that August, Boehm took a room in Mrs. Jordan's boarding house. After two others were placed in with him, he obtained Edison's permission to

Glass-blower's equipment as restored in glass house, Menlo Park.

Actual relics of glass blower recovered from dump at Menlo Park by Henry Ford.   Now in glass house at Dearborn.

move into the attic of the glass house, where he henceforth made his home.

As Boehm was able to provide the laboratory with sufficient experimental glass objects without working after hours, he usually had his evenings to himself. He had brought his zither to Menlo Park. Nights when the rest of us were working he often played German songs in his attic, yodeling in accompaniment. The act amused the 'boys,' who would sometimes sneak out of the laboratory, gather outside the glass house, and suddenly join in. The caterwaul they set up was anything but sweet-sounding and usually drew from Boehm a German-American scolding that caused more mirth.

Sometimes after he had gone to sleep they would pile up stones and at a signal throw them on the slanting roof of the house. The first time this trick was played, he came rushing out as if a cyclone had struck the town. On dark, quiet nights a 'ticker' would suddenly be applied to his window. This was a thread pendulum consisting of a string about twenty yards long with a bit of iron at one end; it produced 'a rapping and a tapping' that would have put Poe's raven to shame. Boehm, of course, complained about these pranks to Edison,

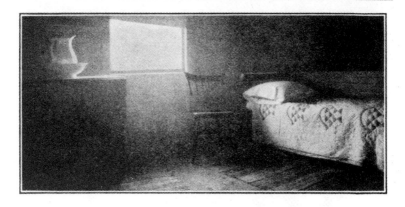

Boehm's attic in glass house as restored today at Dearborn.

who though he had solved many difficult problems, never *could* discover the perpetrators of the jokes.

After Edison moved from Menlo Park to West Orange, a chicken farmer rented this famous quadrangle, remodeled the glass house into a family dwelling, and wired a yard round the old machine shop for a chicken run. The building was salvaged in time by the General Electric Company and transported to the Edison Lamp Works at Harrison, New Jersey, as a treasured relic. It was later removed to the recreation farm of the lamp works, Mazdabrook, as a more appropriate setting.

In 1929 it was presented by the General Electric Company to Henry Ford for addition to the Edison group at Menlo Park in Dearborn. The ceremony of presentation took place at Parippany, New Jersey, in the presence of the distinguished inventor himself. Mr. Ford gave Edison the original key as an assurance that he 'was always welcome to come back to the old shop.' Removal of a board from the building by each of the two men symbolized its demolition prior to being transferred to the spot where you see it today.

As you enter the glass house door, note on the right of the entrance the old-fashioned developing rack used in that early period to hold photographic plates which had been placed in the sun to develop.

Inside on the wall opposite the door is a rack of shelves displaying relics of glass blown in this house back in 1879, and recovered from the 'dump.' Among them will be found half-formed globes, test tubes and other chemical apparatus.

Leftward of the doorway are two blast blowers used in blowing the glass. The operators sat on stools and worked the bellows with their feet, leaving the hands free to care for the glass. The apparatus is similiar to that used by Boehm and later by others.

The racks with tube material for use in blowing may be seen in the northeast corner. Note the skylight overhead, part of the photographic studio equipment; and ascend the ladder to the attic, to see Boehm's living quarters and his famous zither.

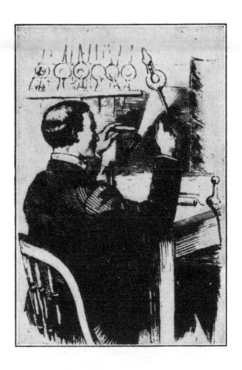

Boehm at his glass-blowing. (From *Frank Leslie's*, Jan. 10, 1880.)

Edison 'carbonizing' filaments at Menlo Park. (From a picture in *Scribner's*, 1880.)
A replica of the furnace now stands in the rear room of the restored laboratory.

XLIII. The 'Tar Putty' Lamp Carbonizing

I HAVE often been asked what prompted Edison to start his carbon experiments that August with the 'tar putty' lamp. The answer to the question is found in *The Herald* article previously quoted, in which we find the following:
'There occurred, however, at this juncture a discovery that materially changed the system and gave a rapid stride towards the perfect lamp. Sitting one night in his laboratory

reflecting on some of the unfinished details, Edison began abstractedly rolling between his fingers a piece of compressed lamp black mixed with tar for use in his telephone. For several minutes his thoughts continued far away, his fingers in the meantime mechanically rolling the little piece of tarred lampblack until it had become a slender filament. Happening to glance at it, he conceived the idea that it might give good results as a burner if made incandescent. A few minutes later the experiment was tried, and, to the inventor's gratification, satisfactory although not surprising results were obtained. Further experiments were made, with altered forms and composition of the substance, each experiment demonstrating that at last the inventor was on the right track.'

In conducting his experiments with the 'tar putty' lamp, Edison tried many kinds of carbon, such as lamp black, graphite, carbon from bone, blood and so on. The same wide search was made among binders—tar, sugar syrup and other hydrocarbons. He would pass along the shelves of the laboratory to see what could be used in the experiments.

One may say carbon is carbon; yet it is not true that all carbon substances are interchangeable for a specific use. While coal and diamonds are carbon, no one would think of using either for making a filament. 'If that putty works,' he said, 'it would be easy to press it through a die and get it perfectly even.'

The carbon substances and the binders were worked up for hours and hours in a mortar and then kneaded hours more in order to obtain an even, homogeneous mass. That work Edison generally assigned to me. He always kept an eye on me and often came over and tested the material, taking up a sample and rubbing it between his fingers. On finding it sufficiently pliable, he rolled it between two slabs of hard polished wood into a filament. If the compound was sticky, it was set aside to dry or mellow.

The next step was to roll the filament into spirals, using a small tubelike cylinder of some raw substance that would also be carbonized with the putty spiral. Cylinders of cardboard or the like were used.

Carbonizing followed, and it was then that most of our troubles began. Perhaps the spiral filament, shrinking more than the form on which it was wound, would consequently be broken when it came from the furnace; sometimes the

Putty, or carbo-
hydro, filament.

spirals would stick together, or something would seem wrong in the process of carbonization. Putty filaments were next wound with iron wire to prevent the windings of the putty from touching one another.

Those were hard days for Edison, and yet he worked tirelessly; his perseverance was amazing. Others would have abandoned the task as impossible; he kept right on. No experimenter before him had visioned a filament of carbon, nor had any believed that such a filament could be made to serve as the light-giving element of a lamp.

As I have said, the process of proper carbonization was most difficult. If a spiral happened to come from the furnace intact, we had then to find a way of forming a connection between its tips and the wires leading into the bulb from the outside. Previous seekers for the incandescent lamp had used pencils or rods of carbon in their early experiments and, of course, found no difficulty in connecting these with metallic conductors by clamps or by pressure against carbon blocks. In our case, things were vastly different, the fragile spirals being extremely difficult to handle.

After the filaments came from the furnace, their legs were encased in tiny cylinders of hard carbon. One end of the cylinder had a hole drilled in, and the other was shaped somewhat like a cup. The leading-in wires were forced into the holes, whereupon the legs of the spirals were inserted in the cup openings.

With the aid of a magnifying glass such as watchmakers use, we began to fill up the little space remaining in the cup, using powdered carbon or carbon paste, during which operation many filaments were ruined. Batchelor was the only one of us who had the deftness and the patience to carry on this work; and yet with all his adeptness, more than 50 percent of those first carbon filaments were broken before they left his hands. Another 10 percent or more were shattered before Boehm finished trying to seal them inside glass bulbs.

Even then they were not out of danger. Frequently the vacuum pump 'out of pure cussedness' would agitate the

Muffle furnace of the type used in carbonizing filaments. May be seen in small shop at rear of restored laboratory.

mercury, making it shoot upwards into the bulb and break the filament into bits.

Still other filaments were spoiled when we subjected them to the current to drive out the occluded gases. A bad connection would cause arcing.

In view of all these difficulties and breakages, two or three experimental lamps a week was a goodly average for us at the beginning.

Realizing that he must have a better means of carbonizing, Edison ordered a good muffle furnace. Iron and later graphite moulds were made. He studied carbonizing thoroughly, seeking to find the best process, and eventually learning how to give the carbonized filaments a bright steellike appearance and a springy hardness. Using the methods he had discovered in the elimination of occluded gases, he improved the process greatly. Slowly—no, rapidly—he approached his goal.

One of the experiments was to carbonize or calcine the material before using it in the preparation of the putty from which the filaments were made. This process made the carbon more dense and even. He changed the method of connecting the legs of the filament with the platinum leading-in wires. The new way was to attach to each leg a small piece of platinum wire by moulding a bond of plastic carbon material round the connection. When the filament was carbonized, the bond held securely and the contacts were good. The other ends of the platinum wire were then inserted into tiny connection pieces attached to the leading-in wires in the glass stem.

In brief, he now possessed a way of obtaining an almost perfect vacuum; and he was able to make a good electrical

The Edison shop of 1877 as it has been restored at Dearborn. Here the phonograph, carbon transmitter, and many other inventions were made.

contact between the legs of the filament and the leading-in
wires. The next step was to find the best material of which to
make filaments; for he had decided that the 'putty' lamp
would never be a practical success. Like the metallic lamp,
it had to give way to something else, in this case, to the
vegetable fiber. In the next chapter I shall tell how all kinds
and grades of silk, cotton and linen threads were experimented with in turn. Edison found that he could make them
of any desired resistance by simply rubbing them with a
plastic compound of tar and lamp black or other hydrocarbon mixture.

Other experiments consisted in filling a bulb with gases
that do not support combustion. 'Doc' Haid helped in this
work; it was his job to make the gases in his chemical nook.
We tried hydrocarbon gases and found that the hot filament
became coated with a skin of carbon. The best results, Edison
decided, were obtained from a high vacuum.

Still the search continued. As the days passed, results

Another view of restored shop in rear of laboratory. Some of shop lathes were presented to Henry Ford by Edison.

grew noticeably better. Our filaments were now generally carbonized in the shape of a hairpin or a horseshoe, a form that gave less trouble when being prepared for the carbonizing chamber.

Meanwhile, Edison tried many different metals and alloys in search of a material less costly than platinum that could be used for the sealing-in wires. The net result was his decision to continue with platinum, because its coefficient of expansion under heat is about that of glass.

:: :: ::

XLIV. The Chest of Drawers
Quest of a Filament

NOT far from the head of the stairs on the second floor of the old laboratory stood a bulky square cabinet, or chest of drawers. On one side were five rows of drawers, seven in each, providing thirty-five drawers altogether in a compact unit. On the opposite side was a sort of workbench with room for two chairs and with a flat top on which to spread the work. This chest has been restored at Dearborn.

Edison spent much of his time in this spot during the filament days, sitting with his back to the sink and facing the laboratory room. Over the top of the chest was spread a miscellaneous collection of test tubes containing carbon in various forms, and apparatus seemingly disarranged but actually each having its special purpose.[1]

The drawers were used for storing such supplies as corks, little scoops, rubber corks, perforated corks, filtering paper, rubber tubing, test tubes, files, rolls of litmus and other paper for making ordinary tests, zinc plates for wet batteries, and tools of all descriptions.

A raised platform between the rear of the chest and the sink served to lift the chairs to a comfortable height for experimenting. Edison and Batchelor sat there side by side, deeply engrossed in some study, 'Batch' carrying out the directions of his chief while the latter watched results or corrected things that were not according to his ideas.

While they were working on the platinum lamp, coating the spirals with certain high-fusible oxides, either in powder form or in solution, it was one of Batchelor's jobs to dry the spiral in the flame of an alcohol lamp. I recall him putting on the powdered oxides of high fusion and holding them fast by means of the heating.

When they were not using the workbench, I was privileged to do so and found it handy in cleaning and putting up the wet battery, one of my regular tasks. Usually one of the

---

(1)   One of the chairs behind the restored chest of drawers was actually used by Edison.

Chest of drawers as restored at Dearborn. On right is tray containing fibers. Glass slabs hold carbon paste as it was left by Edison after his visit here in October, 1929.

other men helped me, returning the jars to place as fast as they were refilled.

Edison was the first to use the word 'filament' in electric light terminology. This fact helped him later in maintaining his patent rights before the law courts. Everyone else used the word 'rod,' or pencil, and, as one judge expressed it, the difference between a 'rod' and a 'filament' was the difference between failure and success.

The hunt was a long, tedious one. Many materials which at first seemed promising fell down under later tests and had to be laid aside. Every experiment was recorded methodically in the notebooks. In many there was simply the name of the fiber and after it the initials 'T. A.,' meaning 'Try Again.'

Literally hundreds of experiments were made on different sorts of fiber; for the master seemed determined to exhaust them all. Threads of cotton, flax, jute silks, cords, manila hemp and even hard woods were tried.

Some of the fibers being worked at the moment were piled conveniently on top of the chest; and today you may see them still in the same spot. Others were stored in jars along the shelves. An examination of the labels on the jars as they stand today on the shelves along the east wall of the restored laboratory will give an idea of what an infinite variety were examined.

Chinese and Italian raw silk both boiled out and otherwise treated were among those used. Others included horsehair, fish line, teak, spruce, boxwood, vulcanized rubber, cork, celluloid, grass fibers from everywhere, linen twine, tar paper, wrapping paper, cardboard, tissue paper, parchment, holly wood, absorbent cotton, rattan, California redwood, raw jute fiber, corn silk, and New Zealand flax.

The most interesting material of all that we used in our researches after a successful filament was the hair from the luxurious beards of some of the men about the laboratory. There was the great 'derby,' in which we had a contest between filaments made from the beards of Kruesi and J. U. Mackenzie, to see which would last the longer in a lamp. Bets were placed with much gusto by the supporters of the two men, and many arguments held over the rival merits of their beards.

Kruesi, you know, was a cool mountaineer from Switzerland possessed of a bushy black beard. Mackenzie, as I have explained, was the station master at Mt. Clemens, Michigan, who had taught telegraphy to the chief in the early days after the young Edison had saved the life of Mackenzie's small son Jimmy. His beard, or rather, his burnsides, were stiff and bristling.

As I now recall, he won the contest, though some claimed that an unfair advantage was given him; that less current was used on the filament made from his beard than on that from Kruesi's. Be that as it may, both burned out with considerable rapidity.

As you stand on the second floor of the restored Menlo Park laboratory and examine the bench side of the chest of

East wall of restored laboratory. On shelves may be seen tall glass jars containing samples of wood and other materials used by Edison in his search for a practical filament.

drawers where Mr. Edison used to sit while seeking suitable materials for filament, you will observe certain materials placed in certain positions on the top, as if some definite reason existed for their station there.

That surmise is not unfounded. These materials remain today exactly as they were left by Edison on the occasion of his visit here on October 21, 1929, when he sat at this bench once more and with his own hands produced half a dozen filaments of sewing thread, just as he had made them fifty years before. Come with me and watch closely while I explain to you the significance of each of these objects.

On the southwest corner is a flat glass tray holding specimens of vegetable fiber, woods, weeds, and grasses, and beside them are twines awaiting the disposal of the experimenter. In the tall glass jar others may be seen softening in water, and in the glass funnel on the stand are still others. Sometimes Edison steamed them to make them pliable.

When he had finished with the specimens on the tray, those that remained were taken away and a fresh supply was placed there so that he could go on with his experiments.

Adjoining the collection of fibers is a glass plate, the surface of which is black and oily. On this are two narrow black wormlike rolls of carbon paste separated from a batch of paste which fills the far corner of the plate.

These rolls, or parts of them, are actually filaments in the first process of making. They go back to the so-called 'putty' stage, being made from lamp black that has been calcinated, ground and pulverized in a mortar for hours and hours.

Pulverizing was one of my jobs. Often I sat before a table, grinding carbon for ten, twelve and even fifteen hours at a time before the chief would consider it fit for working into a filament. It was with such materials, ground finer than the finest flour, that Edison made his pastes.

On the day of Edison's visit here, he sat at this bench with some of the carbon paste before him. He took up pieces of sewing thread to impregnate them; he stroked and rolled them, kneading in the carbon paste all the way. When that was done, he placed the filament in a mould of crude fire clay or iron which had been filled with carbon powder to crowd out all the air and thus prevent oxidation.

The filaments were now ready to be carbonized. In the old days, Edison took them downstairs to the room in the rear where the carbonizing furnace stands, and there continued the process of carbonization. After long hours in the furnace and more long hours of cooling, the filaments were taken out. They resembled nothing so much as long black hairs.

While at Dearborn in October, 1929, Edison showed Messrs. Ford and Jehl how he impregnated the filament material with carbon paste.

A few raw fibers made by Edison when he was here in October, 1929, were given by him to Henry Ford, who twined one on a stick and inserted it in a long glass tube. It may now be seen beside the glass plate which bears the carbon putty, and rests there as a completed sample of raw filament made by the hands of the 'wizard of Menlo Park' himself.

On the glass plate nearest the north edge of the top is another batch of black carbon paste, and lying upon it a spatula, just as Edison slapped it down after completing the filaments.

You will find on this chest various receptacles containing carbon paste just as it was once mixed together by Edison. There in that test tube rack you will find tubes with various carbon ingredients that he made, changing the qualities from time to time according to the nature of the work on which he was engaged. You will find a test tube containing a supply for warming over an alcohol lamp or a Bunsen

Another view of top of chest of drawers as Edison left it after his visit to restored laboratory in October, 1929. Note the carbon paste, spatula, old mortar.

burner. Here is a test tube filled with syrup of rock candy—almost pure carbon.

Under the glass bell is a solution just as he used to have it in the early days, to keep it from evaporating too rapidly.

When Edison had finished making the sewing thread filaments on his last visit here, he turned to me and said:

'Francis, give me the kerosene.'

In the old days he used it to cleanse his hands and scour them free of the sooty carbon. Fifty years ago we kept a jar of it on the northeast corner of the table top; and now, just as then, he naturally seemed to expect some to be on hand.

And it was. If you will look on the corner mentioned, you will see it there today.

I reached over and handed it to him. He washed his hands, afterward accepting a towel from me with which to wipe them dry. The sink served an especially useful purpose for him in that way; he could have either hot or cold water for cleansing.

On top of the chest is a pair of scales. Its purpose will be readily seen when I explain that in the early days we worked a great deal with the metrical system, using the gram and kilogram, millimeter and centimeter, and in thermometer work the centigrade.

One other object on this chest of drawers will perhaps attract your attention, apart from the old reconstructed mortar which I have already described in a preceding article. It is the notebook with cardboard covers and its label from the Laboratory of Thomas A. Edison, resting near the front edge of the table top. This laboratory notebook and others scattered about the room performed a most important service in the routine at Menlo Park. Thousands of pages were filled with notations, setting down meticulously every detail and observation so that a permanent record might remain. The original ones are all safely secured today in a vault at West Orange, New Jersey.

In this particular notebook are several pages on which I scrawled certain messages that might sound meaningless were it not for the explanation that they were answers to remarks made by Mr. Edison during his visit here. Because of his extreme deafness, I wrote my answers to communicate them to him, using the notebook for that purpose.

Second shunt motor built by Edison. Operated a windmill at the Menlo Park residence for pumping water when wind was not blowing. Now in restored laboratory at Dearborn.

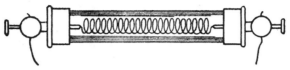

De la Rive's lamp (1820), said to be first incandescent lamp. A platinum
wire operated in a vacuum.

XLV. Perfecting Our Methods
The Goal in Sight

WHENEVER we made an incandescent lamp for our
experiments, we had to go through the following
processes:
First, the raw material for the filament had to be
chosen. I have already told you that Edison tried everything
he could lay his hands on, and when some material exhibited
good qualities, he noted in his book 'T.A.'—*Try Again.*
Among the other materials, he once tried common cotton
thread from a spool. It was not satisfactory; yet he per-
ceived something that prompted him to mark it for later
trial. The second test was made with a special thread from
the Clark Thread Mills in Newark, where Charles Batchelor
and Will Carman had at one time worked.

The second step was the preparation of the raw filament.
This work Edison always did himself, just as when he demonstrated it before Henry Ford at Light's Golden Jubilee.

Third, each filament had to be carbonized, a process he
attended to personally on the experimental lamps. Only
after he had mastered the art thoroughly and desired carbons
in quantity did he instruct 'Basic' Lawson ([1]) and some of the
new men in the art and assign them to the job.

Fourth, Kruesi supplied the copper wires, on the end of
which short pieces of platinum had been twisted.

Fifth, Boehm blew the glass stem, inserting in it the
copper-platinum wires.

Sixth, after being carbonized the filament was placed on
the glass stem of the bulb. This delicate task was always
performed by 'Batch' in Edison's presence.

Seventh, Boehm inclosed the stem with its filament
within the fragile shell of a glass bulb.

---

(1)   Lawson became chief carbonizer at the first commercial lamp factory.

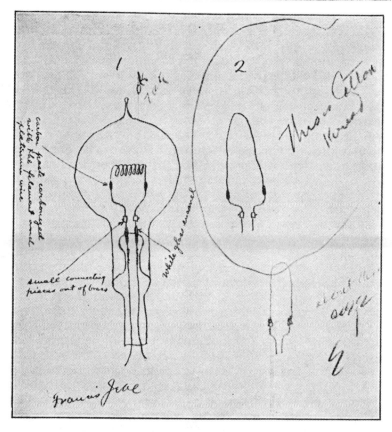

Sketches of early filaments. Nos. 1 and 2 were made by Jehl and the third was added by Edison himself. The inventor's notations may also be discerned: 'OK T.A.E.'—'This is cotton thread'—'about this size. E' Sketch No. 1 shows lamp as it appeared in the patent drawing. No. 2 filament preceded No. 1.

Eighth, I placed the bulb on the vacuum pump and began evacuating the air. Martin Force relieved me on rare occasions.

Ninth, after the vacuum was obtained, it was always Edison who drove out the occluded gases and manipulated the lamp. When the difficult research period was past and the development period came, Edison often intrusted this whole process to me.

Tenth, when the lamp was finished, it was given a life test, the process consisting in sending a current through the filament at an approximate candle power and noting the number of hours it lived. The life test before November, 1879, was generally conducted in conjunction with other work. Experimental lamps would last from a few minutes to many hours, their value not becoming known until they had finished the test. A lamp was born when it died.

This outline does not convey a fair idea of the tedious, back-breaking and heart-breaking delays experienced as we went through the various processes. 'Batch' sometimes spent two or three days getting a filament on the stem, only to have it break; whereupon the work had to be done over. And an accident was no wonder; for a carbon filament thin as a hair had to be connected with a length of wire equally thin! The hours spent in waiting while the carbonized filaments were in the furnace can hardly be estimated.

So with the process of driving out occluded gases. It had to be performed precisely, step by step, with at first but little current for short periods and then a gradual increase during six or eight hours, when finally the filament could stand the whole heat of the electricity without disintegrating.

I have but to close my eyes to see once more the picture of our patient, painstaking, keenly observing chief carrying on his endless experiments, and at the same time educating and directing us. We never thought him wrong, whatever leading scientists said. Our quest never seemed vain or foolish.

I see him tap carefully on the bulb with sensitive fingers as he watches for spots or irregularities in the carbon. If its condition appears good he proceeds even more carefully. If it does not, he is not greatly worried. I have never seen a man so cool when great stakes were at odds.

After the lamp, good or bad, has finished its test he breaks it open and takes it to the microscope to study the filaments, seeking the reason for the failure of the slender black thread-like substance.

I have said he added the term *filament* (as applied to the electric light) to our language. A note in the London technical journal *The Electrician*, of December 14, 1888, page 156, declared:

'If Edison had no other claim to immortality—and some people believe he is astonishingly well provided in this respect—he still, we think, deserves all the credit which has ever been awarded him for his invention of the definition-defying term "*filament*." The highest available forensic,

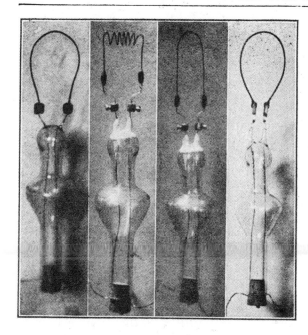

Early mountings of experimental filaments.

judicial and scientific skill of this age and country has been brought to bear upon the question, and that not once only, but over and over again, and still, as Judge Cotton plaintively remarked this week, we seem to be no nearer knowing what a filament really is.

'His Lordship inclines to think that it must be something which "is formed before carbonization"; but this only serves to show how far a reconciliation of legal subtleties and technical obscurities may remove the final issue from the category in which he who runs may read. For if this be indeed the definition of a filament, then our admiration for the inventor of the term will be more than ever profound!'

Accompanying this chapter is a set of four illustrations that show more clearly than I can describe a few of the different methods of mounting the first experimental filaments upon the stem. They also depict some of the principal stages in the evolution of the lamp itself. It is interesting to note that there are no radical differences between the stages.

The stages reveal our attempts to make a better and more stable filament and to improve the mode of attaching that filament to the leading-in wires of the stem. In each example may be seen the glass stem, the outgoing copper wires that were twisted to the platinum sealed ones, and the method of attaching the filament.

The first of the four filaments shown is for use in the putty, or hydrocarbon lamp. It is mounted on the glass stem in an experimental manner, more for the purpose of testing the filament than for securing a permanent way of bonding the filament to the leading-in wires. The latter operation was effected by means of small cuplike blocks of carbon containing holes into which the platinum leading-in wires were forced. The filaments were placed in the cavities, and the space plugged with graphite or carbon paste.

The second and third filaments represent the putty thread or vegetable fiber in spiral and hairpin form. Regarding this stage Edison said: 'I have discovered that if platinum wire is used and the plastic lampblack and tar material is moulded around it in the act of carbonization, there is an intimate union by combination and by pressure between the carbon and the platinum, whereby a nearly perfect contact is obtained without the necessity of clamps. Hence the burner and the leading-in wires are connected with the carbon ready to be placed in the vacuum bulb.'

The third illustration shows the same bonding, except that the filament has the hairpin shape. Let me explain this method of binding more fully, so that you may perceive how difficult it was of execution. After the raw filament had been prepared, its ends were bonded to a piece of platinum by a putty made of tar and lamp black; it was then placed in the carbonizing furnace. After carbonization we were lucky if we found two or three filaments fit for use. With his delicate touch, Batchelor engineered the platinum ends into the binding posts to connect them with the leads of the stem.

The carbon filament, being fragile, would not stand much manipulation; it was no wonder the process entailed hours of toil. When the filament was ready to be placed in a bulb, Boehm sometimes broke it. And how our hearts would sink! Edison would throw away his cigar, ejaculate something, shake his head, and then: 'Well, let's start again.'

The fourth illustration is ahead of our story, though the experiment followed immediately after October 21. It depicts how the historic paper horseshoe filament with the end shanks was mounted on the glass stem. In this method small platinum clamps were attached to the leading-in wires, pinching the filament at its shanks, the pressure being regulated by tiny screws.

If you will examine the earlier methods, you will notice that the copper outgoing leadings of the lamp were simply twisted together with the platinum wire and then soldered. In the first stage, the platinum wires were sealed in the upper part of the glass stem with the additional small globule of glass round them. In the second, Edison coated the wires with glass or glass enamel for some distance above and below the glass partition of the stem. His object was not only to secure an air-tight union, but also to prevent arcing. In the fourth, the 'trousers' were used only on the top of the stem that extended inside the lamp.

The final stage of mounting was not accomplished until toward the end of 1880 when we were using filaments made of bamboo. A new and simpler glass stem appeared, as we shall see, in which the leading-in wires were solidly incased in the upper part of the tube. This, when heated in the blow-pipe, was simply pressed together with the wires in one stroke, which formed a better and more efficient way of sealing.

Comparing the present-day lamp with that of 1880, we see that it still clings to all the vital elements and characteristics of the lamp discovered by Edison more than half a century ago.

)

:: :: ::

The Old Mortar

NOTE—*One day when Henry Ford was visiting the site of the Edison laboratory at Menlo Park, New Jersey, he found the pieces of the old mortar that had been used there in experiments half a century before. He took them home, matched them together, and on the occasion of Mr. Edison's visit to the restored Menlo Park at Dearborn, handed the bowl to him.*

I

Here on this chest of drawers I sit and wait
For the return of him who placed me here.
He said, as in his hands they laid my form
And on this ledge he set me down himself,—
As many a time he did in those old days:—
'Here's where it always stood. Here it belongs!'

II

The crowds in passing stare; but what of them?
I dream of other crowds in years gone by.
Ghostlike they tread the stairs and fill the room.
They come to hear a voice repeat its song,
To see a new light burning in the dusk,
And mark the dawning of a larger day.

III

There is no tale to write of what I did,—
I only served my master as he chose.
Within my bowl he ground his mixtures fine,
Pounded his powders, pulverized his paste.
One day a workman dropped me. Out I went,
Cast to the dump among the broken shards.

IV

Neglected in the dust of passing years,
I lay forgotten till another came;
Within my scattered parts he saw the clew
To all those yesterdays at Menlo Park.
With his own hands he matched my sides again,
Restored my fragments each one to its place.

V

One day my master climbed those steps once more,
With his own hands he set me on this ledge.
'Here's where it always stood. Here it belongs!'
Said he. And now I wait for his return,—
A humble mortar dreaming of the past,
While shadowy figures linger on the stairs.

Wm. A. Simonds

Where the invention of the successful lamp took place, and where its fiftieth anniversary was marked by its re-enactment, October 21, 1929.

XLVI. October 21, 1879

IN THOSE halcyon days of youth and enthusiasm, when sentiments were magnified almost to the verge of hallucination, the laboratory appeared to the writer—especially when the mellow red rays of the October setting sun lighted it with a bewitching glimmer—like an alchemist's den of 'yore, the place where nature's elements were transmuted. With our spirit of devotion to the great master, it does not astonish me that, because of the work he was doing and the surroundings in which he always stood, strangers and friends alike called him 'the Wizard of Menlo Park.' With electricity and related physical forces in their infancy Edison, without erroneous dogmatism or speculative opinion, sought and found their hidden truths and developed them for man's good in present and future generations.

We now come to October 19, 1879, a Sunday morning when another sewing-thread carbonized filament lamp, finished the day before, was placed on the pump for extraction of the air. Edison, sitting in a chair directly opposite the pump, watched as it worked, noting the large cylinders of air being pressed down by the likewise large cylinders of

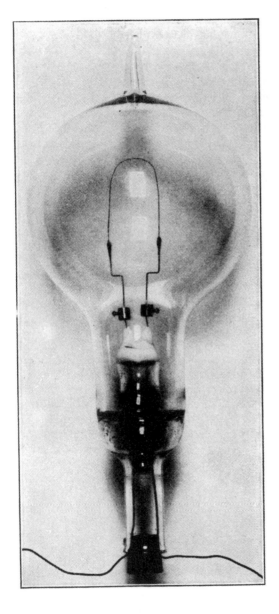

Replica of first successful incandescent lamp made by Edison, using filament of carbonized cotton sewing thread.

mercury, which as time passed became smaller and smaller. When the stage of metallic clicking arrived, he took a small alcohol flame and began to heat the bulb of the lamp—as in past experiments—in order to heat, expand, and dry the air remaining in it. This operation was continued from time to time until the clicking increased in violence. He then attached one of the wires from the battery of the bichromate cells to one of the lamp's terminals and with the other end of the battery wire touched for an instant the other lamp wire. As a result the vacuum in the lamp became suddenly depressed, large bubbles of air appearing again in the pump tube.

During the whole operation I was kept busy transferring the

Monument erected by Edison Pioneers at Menlo Park, N. J., to commemorate achievements of Thomas Alva Edison in that locality.

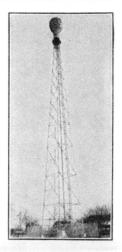

Beacon light made in replica of Edison's successful lamp and erected at Menlo Park, N. J.

jar. To do this I substituted an empty jar and, mounting a small stepladder, poured the full one into the reservoir on the top of the pump stand, from which the mercury was fed and regulated in the pump by a rubber hose and adjusting clamp. Edison continued to apply the battery current to the carbon lamp filament from time to time, increasing its intensity as well as the time of its application until the occluded gases were driven out and the air pump exhibited the highest attainable vacuum. After the full current had been left on for some time with the pump still working, Edison requested Boehm to seal off the bulb. Boehm, though it was Sunday, always kept himself in readiness for such work. The lamp was ready for its life test about eight o'clock in the evening.

Sunday was always the best time for work: the men engaged in the office or the machine shop were at home on that day, leaving Edison undisturbed by noise, interruptions, or inquiries. On this particular Sunday the only work to go on was that of evacuating and treating the lamp, which, as already mentioned, required about ten hours; and the only

—*Drawn by Harry K. Flemming*

Preparing the first successful incandescent lamp for its life test. This lamp was lighted in the evening of October 19, 1879, and burned continuously for more than forty hours. Edison is seen driving the last of the occluded gases from the filament with current from a battery. Francis Jehl is replenishing the supply of mercury in the reservoir of the Sprengel pump. Upton stands behind Edison with Charles Batchelor. The bearded man at left is Kruesi, and in background are Martin Force and Ludwig Boehm.

other man present was Batchelor who, with Edison, prepared new filaments for further tests during intermissions in their attendance on the pump.

Upton, Kruesi, Boehm, Force, and Lawson came in occasionally to see how things progressed—though in the routine of experiments it was nothing new to see a pump working and a lamp with its filament under treatment; nor was there any reason to suppose that the great electrical miracle was at last to happen on that particular Sunday. To Edison the day's work seemed satisfactory, for he said little and appeared pleased.

As the life test alone would decide the question of success or failure, Sunday passed without unusual excitement. We had tested many lamps before, none of which had attained the success expected by Edison; hence the lamp now under test might yet exhibit some of the antics of its predecessors. Lamps that had appeared fairly healthy as they came from the pump had developed deficiencies when put to the test; some had arced at the points where the filament legs were attached to the leads; some had shown bright spots, which were, in reality, weaknesses in the filament; some had broken down after a few minutes, because of bad sealing-off or deficient workmanship. In all cases, Edison had diligently sought the cause of failure.

Without much comment Edison now requested the writer to put the new lamp on the stand and to connect it for the life test. That Sunday night, long after the other men had gone, Edison and I kept a death-watch to note any convulsions or other last symptoms the lamp might give when expiring.

The lamp, however, did not expire! In the morning we were relieved by Batchelor, Upton, and Force. The lamp continued to burn brilliantly all that day, passing the twenty-four hour mark. We were stirred with hope as each hour passed, more and more convinced of progress. Bets were made and general good humor existed all round. All sorts of discussions of problems yet to be solved were the order of the day. The night of the 20th of October again brought quiet to the laboratory as the watch continued, this time composed of Edison, Batchelor and me. During the night between the 20th and the 21st, Edison, judging from the appearance of the lamp still burning without flaw, seemed satisfied that the first solid foundation of the future of electric

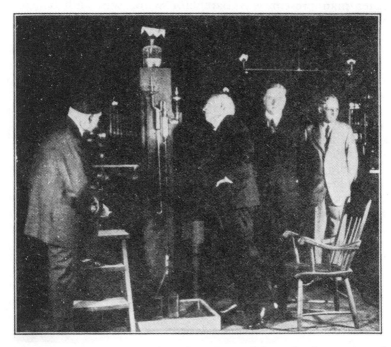

Re-enactment of invention of Edison's incandescent light on October 21, 1929, in
restored laboratory.

lighting had now been laid.   The lamp held out heroically
that night and the following day until, between one and two
o'clock in the afternoon of Tuesday, October 21, 1879, it
had attained more than forty hours of life—the longest
existence yet achieved by an incandescent lamp.   The 'boys'
from all departments came to take a squint at the little
wonder and to express their joy.

Edison now yielded to the temptation, as often before in
his experimental work, to force the lamp with successively
higher voltages, until in a dazzle of brightness it gave out.
It was then examined in all its details, the globe broken
open and the filament subjected to the microscope in accordance with Edison's custom.   This method of testing lost the
original lamp as a relic for the future.   Its death on that fair
afternoon nevertheless marked in history the birth of incandescent light and the attainment of a stable commercial
filament that could with certainty be duplicated and developed

further. October 21, 1879, has ever since been celebrated the world over as Edison Lamp Day.

That day often recalls to my mind a fable recounted to me by a venerable white-bearded Turk when I was at Philippopolis on business for Edison in 1884. He said that when a man fails in his struggle to create a beneficence for the human race he incurs the displeasure of Nature, or Allah, who thereupon denies his spirit rest after death. He said that there is an urge in Nature which helps man unravel its benign secrets in the measure of his ability to probe in the dark. When some future genius has the sublime sagacity to probe successfully, he concluded, the tormented spirits of those who had failed find eternal rest.

I have often thought of this fable when reviewing the past, especially that night when Edison and I kept vigil alone. I seem to vision, perhaps under stress of exalted fancy, the specters of disappointed men who, before Edison, had tried to find a practical commercial lamp. I see them gathered in the shadows of the laboratory eagerly keeping watch with us over the lamp. The *danse macabre* is on! The lamp lives! The specters all vanish, and only we mortals remain to hail a new advent.

* * *

In Edison's own words: 'We sat and watched it with anxiety growing into elation. It lasted about forty-five hours, and then I said, "If it will burn that number of hours now, I know I can make it burn a hundred!'

The great German historian Emil Ludwig has said: 'When Edison, the father of the American Nation, the greatest living benefactor of mankind, snatched up the spark of Prometheus in his little pear-shaped glass bulb, it meant that fire had been discovered for the second time, that mankind had been delivered again from the curse of night.'

October 21

1879 --- 1932

Through the long night, so still and dark,
  While all the world in silence slept,
  A man and boy their vigil kept,
By a new light in Menlo Park.

Glass formed its globe, and cotton thread
  By his own fingers shaped and bent,
  Served as an inner filament,
While wires from jars the current led.

Strongly it burned. So clear and bright
  It shed its rays, and on and on—
  Could it but last until the dawn,
And mark the conquest of the night?

Thus watched they on that upper floor,
  Silent, its fate as yet unknown,
  Nor did they spend those hours alone—
A waiting world stood at the door.

A world whose day had just begun,
  Fifty and three long years ago,
  Nor guessed the blessings soon to **flow**
From that lamp made by Edison.

Nor was the glow on that dim stage
  Revealed alone by his new light,
  A brighter radiance glowed that night,
The dawning of a nobler age.

Wm. A. Simonds

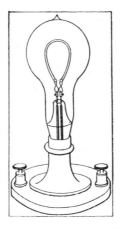

First perfected lamp with tonglike clamp
for paper filament.

XLVII. A New Filament
A Cardboard Horseshoe

WHEN Edison had finished examining the thread carbon filament under his microscope on October 21, 1879, he was not satisfied; the carbon presented a structure that was far from being homogeneous. He remembered having made many other filaments from various materials which, when carbonized, presented a denser, much better form of carbon than this one of thread. Thus it happened that on the afternoon of October 21, when 'Batch' asked whether to send Boehm the other two thread filaments to be incased in bulbs, Edison answered: 'No.'

He later concluded that it might be well to let Boehm have one of them for a special test of the air pump with a McLeod gauge attachment to ascertain in figures the degree of vacuum we had obtained.

Turning to me he said: 'Francis, where is "Culture"?' He usually referred to Upton as 'Culture' when he was in an exuberant humor. I found Upton in the machine shop explaining to Kruesi some points about the new generator. I told him he was wanted 'upstairs,' which meant in the laboratory. When he shortly appeared, Edison explained his plan and asked him to make a sketch of the McLeod gauge, an account of which he had read in *Nature*, an English scientific periodical.

'Have Boehm make one and connect it with the Sprengel air pump,' he said.

Upton was soon at work drawing a plan for the glass blower. Boehm worked that night until eleven and finished the gauge while Upton waited. We then mounted it. Upton, who stayed with us that night, made tests to calibrate it, and then from the data calculated a table whereby we knew exactly the degree of evacuation obtained. We now inserted the second thread filament lamp and evacuated all the air from the bulb. As I have already indicated, the object was simply to get a vacuum and not to manipulate the thread filament. Edison wanted to obtain exactly the degree of vacuum it was possible to obtain, and an approximation of that obtained when the successful lamp was sealed off. When that was done the testing with the McLeod gauge commenced. The result was Edison's famous promulgation: '*I have discovered that even a cotton thread, properly carbonized and placed in sealed glass bulbs exhausted to one millionth of an atmosphere, offers from one hundred to five hundred ohms' resistance to the passage of the current and that it is absolutely stable at very high temperature.*'

Another fact Edison wanted to know was how much power, or energy, in definite and exact figures, the lamp consumed. Crude tests had shown the approximate amount, but now he desired exact data. In 1879, yes, up to a year or so later, there did not exist even in the minds of great physicists any plan for measuring electrical energy directly. Indirect methods were all we had. Upton himself, mathematician and physicist, student for a year under the great Helmholz at Berlin, was at a loss when Edison put the question to him.

To quote from his remarks in 1918: 'In 1879 the question was asked of me how much power an incandescent lamp consumed. The answer could only be conclusively given after finding out how long it took the lamp to heat a known weight of water a certain number of degrees. This method was not criticized when put before such competent men as Professors Rowland and Brackett. In this year (1918) if a small boy were asked how much power an incandescent lamp used he would do an elementary sum of watts and candles and give the answer.

'In 1879 the results obtained by heating water were used to check up calculations reached by employing Clark cells, standard ohms and an electric dynamometer which Edison had made for me.'

So little was known of electricity that such calculation could only be reached by means of James Prescott Joule's law, formulated in 1840, concerning the heat produced by the passage of electricity through a conductor of known resistance. That law gave us the foot pounds, which were then converted by a roundabout method: a lamp used or consumed so many foot pounds, and so many foot pounds made a horsepower. The watt was unknown; it was first suggested by Sir William Siemens in his presidential address before the British association in London in 1882. He was also the first to construct a watt meter by substituting a volt coil for a current coil in his dynamometer.

We acknowledge our debt in electricity to the labors of Davy, Ohm and Faraday; Joseph Henry had a hand in the work too. Among these great men I place George Simon Ohm upon the most

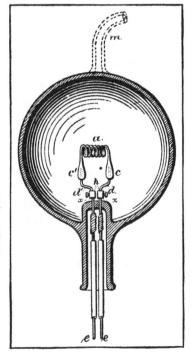

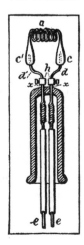

Below—Spiral after carbonization, ready to have bulb blown over it. (From Patent No. 223,898.)

Drawings from Edison's application for electric light patent. Above—Plastic filament material before being wound into spiral. Right—Lamp complete.

Thomson reflecting high resistance galvanometer used for testing current at Menlo Park. Now at Dearborn.

elevated pedestal; for his equation of $C = \dfrac{E}{R}$ governs every fundamental in the electrical workshops of the world. Ohm's law is the most valuable asset that modern electrotechnics possesses; it is the very essence of electrical economics.

Ohm, an insignificant schoolmaster, was derided when he expounded his law in 1827; it seemed too simple. The high-hatted mathematicians were outraged that a plain schoolmaster should offer a simple equation to bring out a law governing the antics of the mysterious fluid. Scientists had later to accept his law; for it was truth. It took a long time to recognize and substantiate the correctness of his conclusions, as also to know how to apply the law and to be satisfied that all vagueness concerning the relation between current, tension and resistance had vanished. Though we possessed standard ohm resistances and Wheatstone bridges, could measure infinitely low or high resistances, and could make a shunt of a known resistance, yet we did not know a single simple method of determining current. We possessed standard batteries with which, using Thomson's high resistance reflecting galvanometer, we could likewise determine tension (or voltage). Thus we had in an easy and practical way the units of resistance and tension. Yet no one had the common sense to tell us how to get the current. No budding thinker appeared on the horizon to tell us to measure the resistance of a part of the wire through which the current flowed, and then take the drop of potential on that known resistance, all of which could have been most easily done. With E and R given, the other unit, C, would have appeared. In other words it simply amounted to taking a known shunt and the drop of voltage on it.

Even in 1880 theorists were behind as regards the value of Ohm's law. I well remember the case of a noted professor who in testing one of Edison's carbonized cardboard lamps, used the deposition cell to obtain the quantity of current the lamp consumed. Had he understood $C = \dfrac{E}{R}$, it would not have been necessary to go to such trouble to obtain it, nor to get at the various resistances of the carbon as the current was varied. With a shunt method all could have been elegantly done.

The general way of obtaining the amount of current in those days, and the

Quadrant electrometer used at Menlo Park to measure tension.

Electrodynamometer made at Menlo Park in 1879 for measuring current. A replica is now in restored laboratory.   (From sketch in *Scientific American*.)

method employed by most professors, was by the deposition cell, the weight of the metal deposited in a certain time being the basis for calculation of the current.   It required two or three hours' time.   There was another method seldom used. It consisted in the use of a scientific instrument called an 'electrical dynamometer'; much time was needed to determine the constants of the instrument and additional time to make the calculations therefrom.   It was necessary to repeat the process three or four times; for never were the same results obtained.   The mean of all was taken.   In the end, recourse was had to the deposition cell, which checked the whole. These instruments, being most unreliable, served a splendid purpose in the demonstration of amperian effects to a class. Our dynamometer at the laboratory was used (or rather tried) by Upton two or three times.   It taxed his patience so much, however, that he gave it up in disgust.   And, I must say, I had never before seen Upton's patience jarred!   Edison said: 'It's a mighty fine scientific looking instrument but it doesn't work.'

As already mentioned, the best method thus far of deter-

The water calorimeter used at Menlo Park in testing the first lamps. Note thermometer and lamp attached to cover.

mining the energy consumed by a lamp was with the water calorimeter, in accordance with the method employed by Lenz, who, with Bacqueral, confirmed Joule's law. It was a method which promoted congeniality: after it was set going we had merely to keep the tension constant on the lamp that heated the water—and while waiting, we swapped stories.

Edison felt the situation keenly. He once remarked to Upton that in the matter of weights and measures in electricity we were far behind the times.

Edison, satisfied regarding the amount of vacuum that the Sprengel air pump could produce, resolved to make some experiments immediately with cardboard carbon filaments.

He requested 'Batch' to hunt up some fine Bristol cardboard. As we had several grades at the laboratory, some samples were brought for Edison's selection. After one of these had been chosen, 'Batch' was requested to cut out raw filaments in horseshoe shape. Two flat iron forms

Another view of calorimeter showing thermometer in position.

were hurriedly made as crude patterns from which to fashion the first carbon filaments of the Bristol cardboard type. They were cut without 'shanks.'

Edison took the completed filaments downstairs and was soon engaged in packing them into an iron mould for carbonization. Again he spent the night tending the furnace; in the morning the carbon filaments were ready for Batchelor to mount. While the carbonization was going on, 'Batch,' under the chief's instructions, made a few tiny clamps of springy wire in the shape of an '8'—somewhat resembling the old-fashioned fireplace scissor tongs with which a hot piece of wood or coal was lifted. These tiny tongs would grasp the flat ends of the carbon filament and hold them fast. At the lower end were placed small brass pieces to connect with the leads on the stem. After Batchelor had made one for approval, he turned the job over to Kruesi, who in turn trusted John Ott to make a few. Thus Edison went over to a new method of connecting filament legs to the leads, a very simple one, as compared with that by which the thread

Combined Geissler-Sprengel pump used for extracting air from two lamps at one time. On second floor of restored laboratory.

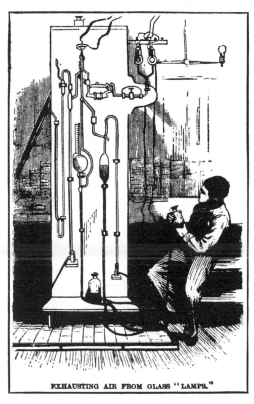

EXHAUSTING AIR FROM GLASS "LAMPS."

Sketch of combined pump from *Frank Leslie's,* January 10, 1880. Francis Jehl is boy shown in picture.

filament had been held.

Late in the afternoon of October 22, 1879, the first of these paper filament lamps was on the pump undergoing the same processing as that accorded the thread one. Of those early experimental incandescent lamps not one was kept as a relic for posterity; for when it had ceased to function it was broken up so that we could examine all its details and at the same time retrieve the platinum that it held. When horseshoe paper carbon lamps were made in large quantities for the demonstration of the Edison system in December, 1879, some were preserved and remain to this day. They are the relics of the period after Edison had won his first success and had entered the development stage.

These lamps with the tong clamps Edison had intended to use in his first public demonstration, a picture of which is to be found in the famous New York *Herald* issue of December 21, 1879. The lamps on the whole were not quite satisfactory, however, for we discovered that vibration had a bad effect on them. A large percentage of the carbons shifted from side to side; in other words, they were not held firmly by those springy tong-shaped clamps. Many would arc because of this weakness. The lamps were therefore taken down and a new die was hurriedly made in which the cardboard material was firmly clamped between the two parts; the raw filaments were then pared out with a sharp knife on both the inside and the outside of the die. We show a picture of these original forms on page 379. These filaments had shanks. And a different kind of clamp was evolved, known in Edison history as one that held the carbon fast by means of a tiny screw bringing both ends of the clamp tightly together.

The above incident explains for the first time why Edison did not wish to have the famous New York *Herald* article appear on December 21, 1879. He was not ready for the demonstration on account of the change that had to be made in the clamps. Article and illustrations were all in type, however, and I well remember how disappointed Edison was when the article appeared notwithstanding his express order! Why it happened is another story; and the occurrence had its consequences. It was well, historically, that the publication was made; for it forced that significant exhibition to take place two or three weeks earlier than it would otherwise have done. We worked day and night to get the lamps with the new platinum clamp ready—and everything turned out well, after all.

The first paper lamps, born in the latter part of October, were manufactured in the same manner as the thread lamp. Their life test much surpassed that of the earlier one. They passed the hundred-hour mark and some reached as high as the 170th. They behaved so well that we put them on a wooden rack which Force had made and tagged each with a number, noting the time when it was put into action. If one went out at night while we were away, we took the mean of the time during which we were not observing and added it to the number of known hours of life; a few hours more or less made no difference.

Never in all my Menlo Park days did we have such a rush as in the latter part of October and in November. 'Batch' was cutting the new paper filaments and Edison carbonizing them. John Ott and William S. Andrews were making the new kind of clamps, Boehm was blowing his glass part, and I was at the pumps. Those days and the succeeding ones gave the old laboratory an altogether different aspect; the quiet atmosphere of the creative period, which practically ended in October, gradually disappeared, and the new was in

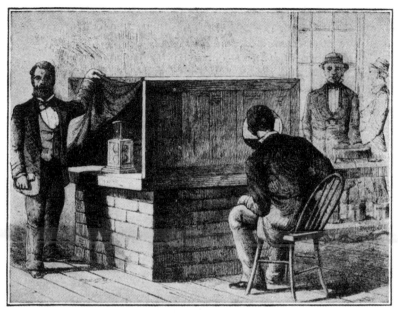

Upton's testing table in use on ground floor at Menlo Park. (From sketch in *Scientific American.*)   Upton is holding curtain and Jehl is reading instruments.

marked contrast. We were in a sort of preliminary manufacturing period.

I was now given a helper, a young man named George Hill, whom I instructed in the operation of the pump. In December many new faces appeared, not only in the laboratory but also in the machine shop. New hands were hired in October to help get ready the Edison dynamos. 'Basic' Lawson was taken away from ore assaying and taught to handle the carbonizing process; he was to participate for the first time in the electric light work, now that the creation period was passed.

Edison remarked toward the end of October that every element in the process of constructing a practical and commercial high resistance lamp was now assured, the difficulties were flattened out and development must commence. As a preliminary step he explained to Upton his idea of making a combination vacuum pump, in place of the Sprengel one used heretofore.

'You see,' Edison continued, 'the Geissler pump can be

operated while the Sprengel works. With it the first large quantities of air can be removed, and then the Sprengel will continue to take out the remaining air. With the McLeod gauge we can measure our vacuum. By the way, we could also have a spark-gap tester on, together with the drying chamber that we have been using.'

With Edison's rough sketch of his idea before him, Upton set about drafting a plan for Boehm. While he was at work Edison came in and, indicating with a pencil, asked: 'How would it be to add another chamber here where we can place some gold leaf to keep the mercury vapors from getting into the lamps while on the pump?'

Now, that was a hard proposition, not for Upton but for the glass blower. Boehm sought Edison out and told him so. Edison knew how to handle his men, from Batchelor the master craftsman to Swanson the night watchman. When any one seemed perplexed over a new job, he knew how to appeal to them, encouraging them to use their brains and their inventive faculties as well as their dexterity. He would flatter their self-esteem and arouse a determination that would draw them out of their lethargy.

When Boehm came to him, he said: 'Now look here, Boehm, you aren't a common glass blower. You are a scientific one. I can get a common glass blower at half what I am paying you; but I want a man like you that can use his brains!' Boehm flushed with appreciation.

'You worked for the great Geissler himself at the University of Bonn in Germany and while there wore a little red cap, did you not? Is there anything too difficult for a man who has helped the master glass blower of the world and who was given a degree, a doctorship, as Geissler was for his beautiful hand work and tubes?'

Boehm always had a good opinion of his own work, for which the boys often teased him. His story of 'the little red cap' gave us plenty of opportunity for banter. One night while we were engaged on some lamp experiments, he came into the laboratory and took a seat. It was early evening and a few others were about the place telling stories and cracking jokes. At last Boehm broke in: 'You know, at the University in Bonn where I was, all the students wore little caps—those that had just entered wore green ones while those that had been there for some time, high-toned students among whom was also a prince, all wore little red caps.' Extending his

Testing table as it has been restored on ground floor of laboratory at Dearborn.

chest importantly, he concluded, 'I, too, wore one of those little red caps.' He had hardly finished the last word when the boys set up a roar of laughter that shook the old laboratory; they stamped their feet and held their sides!

The University at Bonn had given Geissler a large room for his glass-blowing establishment, making it convenient for him to work out glass apparatus without going outside. Now, Boehm was a poor boy whose parents had put him in apprenticeship to the professor to learn the glass-blowing trade. He had no doubt found the little red cap somewhere and used it. His intimation to us, however, was that he was a 'high-toned student.'

When Edison mentioned the red cap, Boehm promised that he would succeed without a doubt in making a Sprengel -Geissler combination pump.

'I knew you could do it,' said Edison, and Boehm went away filled with determination.

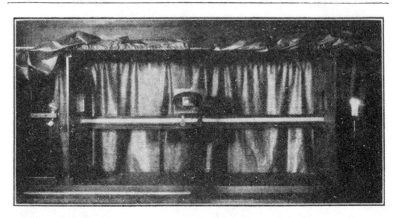

Bunsen photometer as restored in laboratory at Dearborn. Lamp is in compartment at left and two candles in one at right.

The blowing of that combination pump was no easy matter; only a most dexterous craftsman could execute it. When we look at the array of glass tubes, ground cocks and other parts, we are convinced that Boehm did a fine job and we wonder the combination was not broken more than once. The first pump of the kind took him several days to make, for he was doing other things at the same time. This pump could evacuate air from two and sometimes three lamps at a time.

That November we were finding it difficult to conduct electrical measurements on the table upstairs in the laboratory; for when any one walked across the floor, the mirror of the Thomson galvanometer bobbed and danced like a seismograph during an earthquake. Previously such tests had been infrequent but as the development period advanced many were needed. Edison wanted a ready method for determining voltage, since we now had a generator for producing current and could use it when the machine shop engine ran.

'What are we going to do about this?' Edison asked Upton. Upton proposed a sort of testing table such as Helmholz had in his laboratory in Berlin.

'Good!' said Edison. 'Get it going and let us place it just outside the room where Lawson is.'

Upton consulted Kruesi and asked for a bricklayer and a carpenter. Thus on the ground floor near the partition that separated the general chemical and the carbonizing room from the front of the building, the Helmholz testing table was marked out. Two large squares were sawed in the floor planks; the earth was removed to a depth of ten feet and brick piers were built to a convenient table height. Upon them was placed the table, consisting of three sections of wood to prevent warp.

The task of making this table was given to H. A. Campbell, one of the carpenters whom I have already mentioned. He was also identified with the carpenter work required for the exhibition of 1879.

The last time I saw Campbell he related a reminiscence I had almost forgotten. Now and then in the early days when work was slack in the shop, Edison would discharge or lay off some of the hands. They would never accept the dismissal, however, and when Monday morning came would be back at the bench.

'You know I told you not to come!' said Edison, and they would laugh and say he was joking. Edison would smile at their bravado and tell Kruesi to try to find them some work.

When the testing table was finished, Upton gathered the instruments together and laid out a system for testing voltage, resistance, and so on. He also had a Bunsen photometer made, which was placed near the testing table in a dark room opening off the main floor. As I was always coached by Upton in any new methods of testing, I now received charge of the testing table as well as the photometer.

In the restored laboratory at Dearborn you may see the testing table today, resting on the original piers recovered from old Menlo Park by Henry Ford. You may enter the photometer room nearby and see for yourself how we tested the candle power of early lamps.

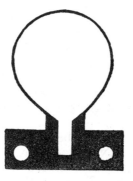

Exact size of cardboard
filament before carboniz-
ing. For eight candle-
power lamp.

XLVIII. Data On the Lamp
Cardboard Filament

THE cardboard lamp with the 'horseshoe' form was the
first commercial one. It was the type of lamp used
on the SS *Columbia*, in the first commercial order received by Edison. I have recorded the data concerning
this lamp because of its great historical value.

I remember how, after the first paper filament lamp was
made, Edison wanted to know the amount of energy it consumed. Upton tested it with the calorimeter and found, as
I recall, that an energy of 2,500 to 2,800 foot pounds was
consumed. I refer to a sixteen candle power lamp. Edison was
satisfied; optimistically he calculated that better economy
would be attained as the art of manufacturing advanced.

In general, the only electric units with which we worked
were volts and ohms. Every Bristol cardboard lamp was tested
in those respects—voltage at sixteen candles, resistance when
cold. The carbons from the mould or from the furnace did
not all have the same resistance. When inserted in a lamp
they showed a variation in voltage at sixteen candles.

The voltage used at the first public demonstration of
Edison's system was between 75 and 80, the same being a mean
voltage between the nearest and the farthest point of supply.
That was also one reason Edison did not want the New

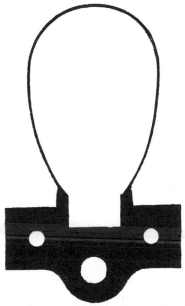

Exact size of cardboard 'horseshoe' filament for sixteen candle power lamp, before carbonizing.

York *Herald* article to appear as soon as it did. He wanted the first exhibition of his system to use 100-volt lamps but did not have time to develop them.

Few know that Edison was pressed by his financial backers to hurry his exhibition. Newspapers and journals were impatiently clamoring for something tangible in the lamp Edison had promised the world. Finally he yielded and gave the long-awaited demonstration, in which the carbonized Bristol cardboard lamp was used. As he was meanwhile diligently at work trying to produce the 100-volt lamp, little additional testing was done with the cardboard lamp. Here at Dearborn we have made filaments from Bristol cardboard and other kinds of paper.

In July, 1880, he obtained the desired result with bamboo filament and discontinued the use of cardboard. Improvements in the bamboo filament lamp from time to time made it more and more stable. The second practical lamp, it was used for a decade. The birth of the Bristol cardboard lamp, however, and the exhibition of the system during December, 1879, and for some months thereafter, proved to the world that Edison had laid down the tenets of a commercial system of electrical distribution.

I will now relate some of the facts concerning the Menlo Park 'horseshoe' cardboard lamp. The glass used was known as 'lead' glass; it was furnished by Eimer and Amend, of New York City.

The mean dimensions of the Bristol cardboard glass bulb, which was round in shape, were as follows:

Its diameter was about $2\frac{13}{32}$ inches. The neck was about $1\frac{1}{16}$ inches in diameter and $1\frac{1}{2}$ inches in length. The stem, made from a ⅟₁₆ inch tube, had a length of about 3 inches; it was blown differently at various points, as will be seen from the illustration. The tip of the lamp was extended somewhat conically to a length of ⅕₁₆ inch. The platinum wire that passed through the glass stem had a diameter of about .014 inch and was twisted about a copper wire (telegraph fashion) with a diameter of .020 inch.

The first lamp base was formed by simply soldering the copper wires each to a piece of copper foil, as shown in the picture. It was held in position by thread wound about it, as will also be seen from the illustration. The two copper wires were held apart inside the stem by a cork at its end. The mean measurements of the form (²) from which the raw horseshoe filaments were cut were about the following for the sixteen candle power lamp, commonly known as the "A" type at that time:

The width was .0275 inch, and the length from shank to shank about 4⅜ inches.

For the eight candle power lamp, designated at the time as the "B" type, which had filaments that were circular in shape, the width and length were .025 inch and 2⅞ inches, respectively.

At the request of Henry Ford, we have been conducting experiments at the restored laboratory in carbonizing and reproducing the horseshoe filament. The 'lost art' is being revised. And it must be solemnly confessed that we realize more than ever the difficulties with which Edison had to contend, what patience he possessed, and with what faith he continued his work in carbonization until he succeeded in making his filament. These remarks apply also, of course, to his carbonizing experiments with other materials. Many scientists will concede that when more than fifty years ago a few were trying to make incandescent lamps having a pencil, or carbon rod, the resistance of which varied from one to four ohms, it must have been a stupendous undertaking for Edison to make a carbon in the shape of a filament that was to have a resistance of a hundred or more ohms. As my friend Dr. John W. Lieb, former senior president of the New

---

(2) **Both the sixteen and the eight candle power raw filament forms are at the Dearborn Edison laboratory. See pictures on page 379.·**

An original cardboard filament lamp now at restored laboratory. Note the improvised contact plates taped on at base. Sixteen candle power.

York Edison Company and eminent Edison pioneer, once remarked:

'Because Edison did not always choose to follow the paths beaten by his predecessors, because he often sought out lines of investigation and experiment which were original and untried, because he looked for the solution of the problems before him in the unobvious, the unexpected, he has been taken by many as a purely empirical worker, a lucky experimenter, the embodiment of the cut-and-try, haphazard method of research and investigation. Nothing could be further from the truth, as witness the stern logic with which he pursued relentlessly and industriously his fundamental idea of finding the complete electrical analogue of the gas-lighting system.'

We at the Dearborn laboratory went to work with the knowledge that the horseshoe filament had been produced by Edison and could, no doubt, be produced again without much difficulty. In Edison's case, the task was undertaken with the consciousness that it had never been accomplished before. A carbon filament, unlike a metal wire, is fragile and lacking in elasticity. In our present work at the laboratory we have found the difference between *then* and *now*. Between those two words is a gap of more than fifty years during which rapid progress has been made and experience gained.

With all the wisdom acquired, the problem of reproducing the paper filaments through proper carbonization having right resistance, small radiating surface and stability was not an easy one. I remember well how Edison manipulated them; I might say I passed through the experience with him; yet, when the task was started at the Dearborn laboratory, we had again to battle with forgotten obstacles. Again we realized that success would not have been possible had not Edison in those early days 'taken the bull by the horns' and himself performed the various manipulations that come under the heading of carbonization. There was no one at the laboratory with his vision, foresight and persistence. I am sure that if he had left the solving of the problem of carbonization to any one of his assistants they would, at the end of two or three weeks, have given up the job as impossible.

In Edison's dictionary there was no such word. His patience, common sense and indomitable persistence won the great battle and gave the world the utilities for sending civilization spinning forward.

Another original cardboard filament lamp now in restored laboratory. Eight candle power.

I have already told you that the raw filament of the paper horseshoe lamp prepared from the old form has a length of about 4.38 inches and a width of .0275 inch. When the filament comes out of the furnace, its length has shrunk to about 3.13 inches and its width to about .018 inch. The shrinkage through carbonization thus gives the ratio of 35 to 24 for its length, and .0275 to .018 for its width.   If our raw filaments were made from cardboard .010 inch thick, the thickness would shrink during carbonization to .006 inch. The electrical potentiality of the carbon depends upon the material used. If you carbonize two filaments both having the same dimensions but made from different qualities of paper, their resistances will be different though carbonization take place in the same mould and under the same conditions.

The results obtained at the Dearborn laboratory closely correspond with the results that Charles L Clarke obtained while he was at Menlo Park, New Jersey. It was in March, 1880, that Edison intrusted to him the determination of certain characteristics pertaining to the paper horseshoe lamp. Clarke found that the shrinkage had the ratio of 15 to 11.

Form in which sheet of cardboard was placed for trimming to horseshoe shape. In restored laboratory. For 8-candle power lamp filament.

His treatise on 'Edison's First Commercial Lamp,' which appeared in the *General Electric Review* in May, 1929, is a valuable historic contribution to the *bona fide* literature of the art. The approximate difference of about 3 percent between the results obtained by us at the Dearborn Edison laboratory and those of Clarke in old Menlo Park can be easily accounted for in many ways.

The forms pictured on this page were presented to the Edison Historical Collection by John W. Howell, lifelong lamp expert, who was engaged at the Edison Lamp Works in 1881. Howell was educated at Stevens Institute of Technology in Hoboken, N. J. His first job was at the Edison Lamp Works at Menlo Park.

Another form for larger size filaments of cardboard. Now in restored laboratory. This form was for 16-candle power filament.

Cardboard filament lamp and 'figure 8' clamps, as shown in *Herald* article. This replica was made by Francis Jehl in the restored laboratory at Dearborn.

XLIX. The New York *Herald* Article of December 21, 1879

THERE was hustle and bustle during those last days of November and the first part of December, 1879, for we were all much excited. Test trials were made from time to time, and whenever a fault was revealed in the apparatus, it was swiftly corrected.

Among our visitors was Marshall Fox, a reporter of the New York *Herald* who enjoyed Edison's confidence. He and the illustrator who accompanied him spent two weeks gathering material and pictures for a story about the light. The article was revised by Upton, after which Edison was promised it would not appear before a specified date.

Imagine our surprise when we woke up on Sunday morning, December 21, and found the article spread over a whole page of the news columns. Edison was much displeased, and told Upton he considered it a breach of confidence. It developed that the newspaper had not actually been guilty of such a breach, for permission had been given to publish the story, although not by Edison.

As I have said, the article came out before he was ready, and compelled him to go ahead with the first public exhibition, using cardboard filaments and old-style clamps.

An interesting tale has been told concerning what happened in the *Herald* office when the edition produced its 'scoop.' Thomas B. Connery, the managing editor, rushed with one of the first copies into the office of the city editor, Albert E. Orr.

'How did that stuff get into the paper?' he demanded, spreading it out. 'Lights strung on wires! You've made a laughing stock of the *Herald*. What will Mr. Bennett say?'

'Probably that this is the biggest newspaper beat in a long time.'

'But,' continued Connery, 'don't you know it has been absolutely demonstrated that such a light is against the laws of nature? Who wrote that article?'

'Marshall Fox.'

'How could he have allowed himself and his paper to be imposed on so? Where is he? Send for him. We must do something to save ourselves from ridicule.'

Connery is said to have demanded the discharge of Fox, though the reporter was the 'star' man who had accompanied the scientific expedition to Wyoming in the midsummer of 1878 to watch the eclipse. The matter ended happily however. Fox was not discharged nor did the *Herald* have to retract its story. *Later Edison declared that it was the most accurate story of the time concerning his invention*(¹).

EDISON'S LIGHT

---◆---

The Great Inventor's Triumph In Electric Illumination

---◆---

A SCRAP OF PAPER

---

(1)   *Electrical World and Engineer*, March 5, 1904.

It Makes a Light, Without Gas or Flame, Cheaper Than Oil

◆

SUCCESS IN A COTTON THREAD

◆

The near approach of the first public exhibition of Edison's long looked for electric light, announced to take place on New Year's Eve at Menlo Park, on which occasion that place will be illuminated with the new light, has revived public interest in the great inventor's work, and throughout the civilized world scientists and people generally are anxiously awaiting the result. From the beginning of his experiments in electric lighting to the present time, Mr. Edison has kept his laboratory guardedly closed, and no authoritative account (except that published in the *Herald* some months ago relating to his first patent) of any of the important steps of his progress has been made public —a course of procedure the inventor found absolutely necessary for his own protection. The *Herald* is now, however, enabled to present to its readers a full and accurate account of his work from its inception to its completion.

Edison's electric light, incredible as it may appear, is produced from a little piece of paper—a tiny strip of paper that a breath would blow away. Through this little strip of paper is passed an electric current, and the result is a bright, beautiful light, like the mellow sunset of an Italian autumn.

'But paper instantly burns, even under the trifling heat of a tallow candle!' exclaims the sceptic, 'and how, then, can it withstand the fierce heat of an electric current.' Very true, but Edison makes the little piece of paper more infusible than platinum, more durable than granite. And this involves no complicated process. The paper is merely baked in an oven until all its elements have passed away except its carbon framework. The latter is then placed in a glass globe connected with the wires leading to the electricity producing machine, and the air exhausted from the globe. Then the apparatus is ready to give out a light that produces no deleterious gases, no smoke, no offensive odors—a light without flame, without danger, requiring no matches to ignite, giving out but little heat, vitiating no air, and free from all flickering; a light that is a little globe of sunshine, a veritable Aladdin's lamp. And this light, the inventor claims, can be produced cheaper than that from the cheapest oil.

Were it not for the phonograph, the quadruplex telegraph, the telephone and the various other remarkable productions of the great inventor, the world might well hesitate to accept his assurance that such a beneficent result had been obtained, but, as it is, his past achievements in science are sufficient guarantee that his claims are not without foundation, even though for months past the press of Europe and America has teemed with dissertations and expositions from learned scientists ridiculing Edison and showing that it was impossible for him to achieve that which he has undertaken.

When Edison began his experiments in September, 1878, he had just returned from the inspiring scenery of the Rocky Mountains, where he had been enjoying a little recreation after several months of hard labor. He was ripe for fields and enterprises new. A visit to a Connecticut factory where an electric light was used concentrated his thoughts on the subject of lighting by electricity, and he determined to attack the problem. Previous to this time, although he had roamed broadcast over the domain of electricity, wresting from it, as is well known, many of its hidden secrets, Edison had scarcely thought of the subtle fluid in connection with practical illumination. Now, however, he bent all his energies on the subject, and was soon deep in the bewildering intricacies of subdivision, magneto currents, resistance laws and the various other branches going to make up a system of lighting by electricity. The task before the young inventor was divisible into two parts.

First—The producing of a pure, steady and reliable light from electricity; and

Second—Producing it so cheaply that it could compete with gas for general illumination.

Of the two systems before him—viz., voltaic arc and the incandescence system, Edison chose the latter as his field of operations. Prominent among the difficulties incident to incandescent lighting, it will be remembered, was the liability of the platinum (when that metal was used) to melt under the intense heat of the electric current, and the liability of the carbon, when that was employed, to gradually become dissipated under the combined action of gases and the electric current.

As between platinum and carbon as the substance to be made incandescent, Edison took up platinum and devoted first his attention to the obtaining of some device to prevent the platinum from melting under the intense heat of the electric current. An ingenious and simple contrivance met the requirement. He arranged a small lever, about three inches long, so that the expansion of the platinum (caused by the heat) beyond a certain degree would close it, such closing making a new passage for the electric current and cutting it off from the incandescent platinum. When the latter contracted, as it did the moment the heat was lessened, the lever returned to its normal position and allowed the electric current to again pass through the platinum. By this device the inventor hoped to be able to keep the incandescent platinum always below its melting point. The contrivance is described in his first patent as follows:

'Electric lights have been produced by a coil or strip of platinum or other metal that requires a high temperature to melt, the electric current rendering the same incandescent. In all such lights there is danger of the metal melting. My improvement is made for regulating the electric current automatically passing through such incandescent conductor, and preventing its temperature rising to the melting point, thus producing a reliable electric light.'

'Figure 1 shows one form of the device. The incandescent metal is in the form of a double spiral A, the two ends terminating upon the posts b, c, to which the con-

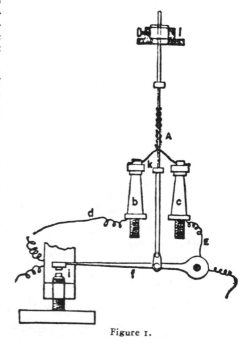

Figure 1.

ductors d, E, are connected. A circuit closing lever, f, is introduced in the electric circuit, the points of contact being at i, and there is a platina, or similar wire, k, connected with the lever, f, to the headpiece or other support, l. The current from a magneto machine is connected with the wires E and d. The current then flows from E to the post, c, thence around the platinum spiral to b, and is carried off by the wire, d. Now, when the rod, k, of platinum becomes heated to too great intensity its expansion closes the lever, f, and the current then passes from E, through f, and not through the spiral at all. In this way the lever cuts off the current every time the heat becomes too intense.'

Numerous other devices of a similar character were tried and for a while they all worked satisfactorily, but the inventor finally discovered that the constant expansion of the platinum rod k and its pressure upon the lever f bent it so that it became unreliable and it was, therefore, abandoned.

The next regulator was in the form of a diaphragm, which cut off the electric current from the platinum every time the diaphragm was pressed outward beyond a fixed limit by the heated air. The regulation thus produced was so rapid that the eye could not perceive any diminution in the strength of the current. But this also was inadequate in many respects. The next important modification in the light was the substitution for the platinum spiral of finely divided platinum incorporated with non-conducting material. When the electric current was passed through the combination the platinum particles became incandescent and the non-conducting material incorporated with them became luminous and increased the brilliancy. One advantage by this form not previously attained was that a very weak electric current produced a good light.

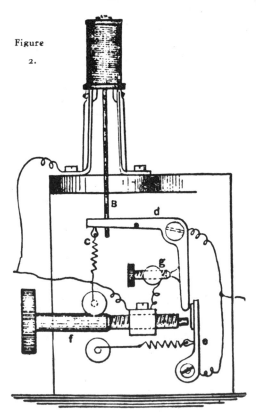

Figure 2.

After this followed a device for obtaining more light-giving surface, the platinum being wound in the form of a small bobbin, first having been coated with a non-conducting coating that was not injured by the heat. With this arrangement a new form of regulator was used. The lamp at this stage is shown in Figure 2.

A is the incandescent bobbin, between the coils of which is a coating of magnesia. The top of the bobbin has a metallic cap

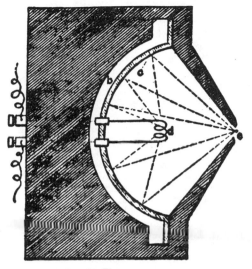

Figure 3.

connected to the lever, d. A spring, C, draws the rod, B, downward with considerable pressure, and this, of course, places pressure on the top of the bobbin, thus keeping the wire in contact with the upper end of the coil. The bobbin, A, expands as a whole by the heat and draws the rod, B, upward. This brings the lever attached upward and allows the lever, E, to come in contact with the screw, f, permitting the current to find a passage other than that afforded by the incandescent material.

The inventor next followed with a new regulator and a meter for measuring the amount of electricity used; also an automatic switch connecting the regulator with the line leading to the machine for generating the electric current.

The next was a unique idea, making the platinum give the light as it were by proxy. By means of a reflector he concentrated the heat rays of the platinum upon a piece of zircon, causing the latter to become luminous. Figure 3 shows the apparatus.

A is a mass of non-conducting material, b is an air space, c is a polished reflector of copper coated with gold, d is a platinum-iridium spiral, which becomes heated by the passage of the electric current through it, E is a thin piece of zircon that receives the heat rays thrown off by the reflector, C, which heat rays bring up the zircon, E, to vivid incandescence, making it give out a light much more brilliant than the light of the platinum spiral, C. With this form Mr. Edison tried numerous experiments, and from time to time made many alterations and improvements, but eventually the apparatus was placed in the category of non-successes.

Realizing from the first the necessity of the light giving substance offering much resistance to the passage of the electric current—a necessity in extensive subdivision of the light—the inventor throughout his experiments kept a close watch for substances and forms that gave suitable resistances. In Figure 4 is shown a form of lamp disconnected from the regulating apparatus, which largely embodied the above requirement and for a time gave good results.

A is a spiral of carbon with two large ends, B, e, connecting with the wires leading to the machine for generating the cur-

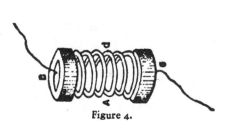

Figure 4.

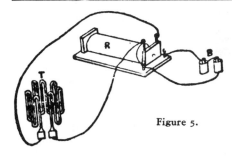

Figure 5.

rent. This device was tried for several weeks, but did not, as a whole, give satisfaction.

Branching off from the line of investigation he had been previously following, Mr. Edison at this time began experimenting with a view to having the light produced locally—i. e., arranging for each householder to become his own manufacturer of light, thus dispensing with mains and central stations. The apparatus which he used for this purpose is shown in Figure 5.

R is an induction coil such as are used by peripatetic showmen at fairs and other places when they give electric shocks to inquiring sightseers at so much per shock. It is operated by two cells of battery, B, and wires lead from it to the glass tubing, T, from which the air has previously been extracted, and the passage of the electric current through the tubing gives out a light. This plan is analogous to what is known as the Geisler tube arrangement, the difference being in the form of the tube and the extreme smallness of the bore and also in the degree of vacuum produced. Mr. Edison succeeded by this arrangement in obtaining a light of several candle power with a moderately powerful induction coil. The light, however, was not the one sought after so persistently by the inventor, and so it took its place in that part of his laboratory occupied by inventions not in use.

Once more Mr. Edison made a departure. He moulded powdered metallic oxides in the form of sticks and subjected them to a very high temperature. In this connection he obtained very fine results from the native alloy of osmium-iridium called tridosmine, which alloy he used in the form of a powder enclosed in a tube of zircon. The electric current passing through the same brought it to a beautiful incandescence.

The inventor's next important move was the adoption of carbon in connection with the platinum as the substances to be made incandescent. He caused a slender rod of carbon to rest upon another of platinum, the inferiority of contact between the two at their point of meeting producing a resistance to the passage of the electric current and causing the carbon to become highly incandescent, while the platinum attained only a dull red heat. The carbon rod was kept pressing upon the platinum by a weight ingeniously arranged. A dozen or more forms of this lamp were made; but, after all, the inventor was obliged to return to platinum as the substance most suitable, all things considered, for being made incandescent. For two months he worked at platinum day and night, only to find that platinum, as he had been using it, was entirely worthless for incandescent lighting. To many experimenters this would have proved a discouragement perhaps fatal, but it had the effect only of increasing Edison's determination.

After scores of new experiments he arrived at the true causes of the defects and hastened to apply the remedy. 'I have found,' he writes, 'that when wires or sheets of platinum, iridium or other metallic conductors of electricity that fuse at a high temperature are exposed to a high temperature near their melting point in air for several hours by passing a current of electricity through them and then are allowed to cool, the metal is found to be ruptured, and under the microscope there are revealed myriads of cracks in various directions, many of which reach nearly to the center of the wire. I have also discovered that, contrary to the received notion, platinum or platinum and iridium alloy loses weight when exposed to the heat of a candle; that even heated air causes it to lose weight; that the loss is so great a hydrogen flame is tinged green. After a time the metal falls to pieces; hence wire or sheets of platinum or platinum and iridium alloy as now known in commerce are useless for giving light by incandescence—

First—Because the loss of weight makes it expensive and unreliable and causes the burner to be rapidly destroyed.

Second—Because its electrical resistance changes by loss in weight, and its light-giving power for the total surface is greatly reduced by the cracks.

'The melting point also is determined by the weakest spot of the metal.

'By my invention or discovery I am able to prevent the deterioration of the platinum or its alloys by cutting off or intercepting the atmospheric action. A spiral wire or other forms of platinum is placed in a glass tube or bulb, with the wire near its ends passing through and sealed in the glass, and the air is exhausted from the glass. The platinum wires of the spiral are then connected to a magneto-electric machine or battery, the current of which can be controlled by the addition of resistance. Sufficient current is allowed to pass through the wire to bring it to about 150 degrees Fahrenheit. It is then allowed to remain at this temperature for ten or fifteen minutes. While thus heated both the air and gases confined in the metal are expelled by the heat or withdrawn by the vacuum action.

'While this air or the gases are passing out of the metal the mercury pump is kept continually working.

'After the expiration of about fifteen minutes the current passing through the metal is augmented so that its temperature will be about 300 degrees Fahrenheit, and it is allowed to remain at this temperature for another ten or fifteen minutes.

'The mercury pump is to be worked continuously and the temperature of the spiral raised at intervals of ten or fifteen minutes until it attains vivid incandescence and the glass is contracted where it has passed to the pump and melted together.

'The wire is now in a perfect vacuum and in a state heretofore unknown, for it may have its temperature raised to a most dazzling incandescence, emitting a light of twenty-five standard candles, whereas before treatment the same radiating surface gave a light of only about three standard candles. The wires after being thus free from gases are found to have a polish exceeding that of silver and obtainable by no other means. No cracks can be seen even after the spiral has been raised suddenly to incandescence many times by the current, and the most delicate balance fails to show any loss of weight in the wire even after it is burning for many hours continuously. I have further discovered that if an alloy of platinum and iridium is coated with the oxide of magnesia and subjected to the vacuum process described, a combination takes place between the metal and the oxide, giving the former remarkable properties. With a spiral having a radiating surface of 3-16 of an inch light equal to that given by forty standard candles may be obtained, whereas the same spiral, not coated by my process, would melt before giving a light of four candles. The effect of the oxide of magnesia is to harden the wire to a surprising extent and render it more refractory. A spiral made of this wire is elastic and springy when at high incandescence. I have found that chemically pure iron and nickel drawn in wires and subjected to the vacuum process may be made to give a light equalling that of platinum in the open air. Carbon sticks also may be freed from air in this manner and be brought to a temperature where the carbon becomes pasty and on cooling it is homogeneous and hard.'

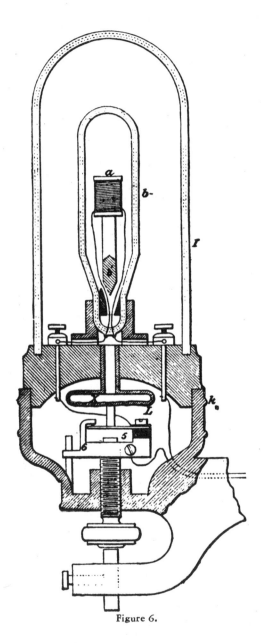

Figure 6.

About this time another truth dawned upon the inventor—namely, that economy in the production of light from incandescence demanded that the incandescent substance should offer a very great resistance to the passage of the electric current. Concerning this the inventor writes:—'It is essential to reverse the present practice of having lamps of but one or two ohms (electrical units) resistance and construct lamps which, when giving their proper light, shall have at least two hundred ohms resistance.'

The lamp, as it stood at this stage of the inventor's progress, is shown in Figure 6.

In this figure, a is the burner or incandescent platinum in the shape of a bobbin supported within the vacuum tube, b, by a rod, b, of the same material as the bobbin. The vacuum tube, b, is sustained by the case, k, and around said tube, b, is a glass globe, l. Within the case, k, is a flexible metallic aneroid chamber, L, that opens into the glass case, l, so that the air, when expanded by heat, can pass into the aneroid chamber and give motion to the flexible diaphragm, x, and parts connected therewith. When the current circulating around the bobbin, a, becomes too intense and heats the latter too highly, the air within the glass case, l, is expanded and bulges downward by the diaphragm, x, and the pin thereon pressing upon the spring, 5, and separating said spring from the block, 6, breaks the circuit to the burner. The temperature within the globe, l, lowers immediately and the parts return to their normal position, closing the circuit through the burner to 5 and 6. This opening and closing of the circuit is but momentary, and, therefore, the uniform brilliancy of the light is not affected and there is no danger of the burner becoming too highly heated.

The lamp, after these latter improvements, was in quite a satisfactory condition, and the inventor contemplated with much gratification the near conclusion of his labors. One by one he had overcome the many difficulties that lay in his path. He had brought up platinum as a substance for illumination from a state of comparative worthlessness to one well nigh perfection. He had succeeded, by a curious combination and improvement in air pumps, in obtaining a vacuum of nearly one millionth of an atmosphere, and he had perfected a generator or electricity producing machine (for all the time he had been working at lamps he was also experimenting in magneto-electric machines) that gave out some ninety percent in electricity of the energy it received from the driving engine. In a word, all the serious obstacles toward the success of incandescent electric lighting, he believed, had melted away, and there remained but a comparative few minor details to be arranged before his laboratory was to be thrown open for public inspection and the light given to the world for better or for worse.

There occurred, however, at this juncture a discovery that materially changed the system and gave a rapid stride toward the perfect electric lamp. Sitting one night in his laboratory reflecting on some of the unfinished details, Edison began abstractedly rolling between his fingers a piece of compressed lampblack mixed with tar for use in his telephone. For several minutes his thoughts continued far away, his fingers in the meantime mechanically rolling out the little piece of tarred lampblack until it had become a slender filament. Happening to glance at it the idea occurred to him that it might give good results as a burner if made incandescent. A few minutes later the experiment was tried, and, to the inventor's gratification, satisfactory, although not surprising, results were obtained. Further experiments were made, with altered forms and composition of the substance, each experiment demonstrating that at last the inventor was upon the right track.

A spool of cotton thread lay on the table in the laboratory. The inventor cut off a small piece, put it in a groove between two clamps of iron and placed the latter in the furnace. The satisfactory light obtained from the tarred lampblack had convinced him that filaments of carbon of a texture not previously used in electric lighting were the hidden agents to make a thorough success of incandescent lighting, and it was with this view that he sought to test the carbon remains of a cotton thread. At the expiration of an hour he removed the iron mould containing the thread from the furnace and took out the delicate carbon framework of the thread—all that was left of it after its fiery ordeal. This slender filament he placed in a globe and connected it with the wires leading to the machine generating the electric current. Then he extracted the air from the globe and turned on the electricity.

Presto! a beautiful light greeted his eyes. He turns on more current expecting the fragile filament instantly to fuse; but no, the only change is a more brilliant light. He turns on more current, and still more, but the delicate thread remains entire. Then, with characteristic impetuosity and wondering and marvelling at the strength of the little filament, he turns on the full power of his machine and eagerly watches the consequence. For a minute or more the tender thread seems to struggle with the intense heat passing through it— heat that would melt the diamond itself—then at last it succumbs and all is

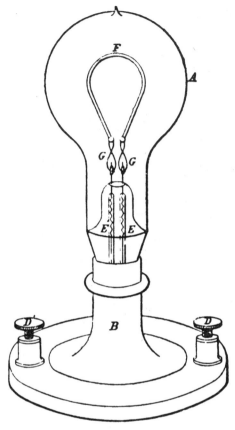

Figure 7.

darkness. The powerful current had broken it in twain, but not before it had emitted a light of several gas jets. Eagerly the inventor hastened to examine under the microscope this curious filament, apparently so delicate, but in reality much more infusible than platinum, so long considered one of the most infusible of all metals. The microscope showed the surface of the filament to be highly polished and its parts interwoven with each other.

It was also noticed that the filament had obtained a remarkable degree of hardness compared with its fragile character before it was subjected to the action of the current. Night and day, with scarcely rest enough to eat a hearty meal or catch a brief repose, the inventor kept up his experiments, and from carbonizing pieces of thread he went to splinters of wood, straw, paper and many other substances never before used for that purpose. The results of his experiments showed that the substance best adapted for carbonization and the giving out of incandescent light, was paper preferably thick like cardboard, but giving good results even when very thin. The beautiful character of the illumination and the steadiness, reliability and non-fusibility of the carbon filament were not the only elements incident to the new discovery that brought joy to the heart of Edison. There was a further element—not the less necessary because of its being hidden—the element of the electric current.

The inventor's efforts to obtain this element had been by far the most laborious of any in the history of his work from the time he undertook the task, and without it, absolute success to electric incandescent illumination could not be predicted, even though all the other necessary properties were present in the fullest degree.

Passing over the scores of experiments made since the discovery that the carbon framework of a little piece of paper or thread was the best substance possible for incandescent lighting, we come to consider the way in which the same is prepared at the present time in the laboratory.

With a suitable punch there is cut from a piece of 'Bristol' cardboard a strip of the same in the form of a miniature horseshoe, about two inches in length and one-eighth of an inch in width. A number of these strips are laid flatwise in a wrought iron mould about the size of the hand and separated from each other by tissue paper. The mould is then covered and placed in an oven, where it is gradually raised to a temperature of about six hundred degrees Fahrenheit. This allows the volatile portions of the paper to pass away. The mould is then placed in a furnace and heated almost to a white heat, and then removed and allowed to cool gradually. On opening the mould the charred remains of the little horseshoe cardboard are found. It must be taken out with the greatest care, else it will fall to pieces. After being removed from the mould it is placed in a little globe and attached to the wires leading to the generating machine. The globe is then connected with an air pump, and the latter is at once set to work extracting the air. After the air has been extracted the globe is sealed, and the lamp is ready for use. Figure 7 shows the lamp.

A is a glass globe, from which the air has been abstracted, resting on a stand, B. F is the little carbon filament connected by fine platinum wires, G G', to the wires, E E', leading to the screw posts, D D', and thence to the generating machine. The current, entering at D, passes up the wire E to the platinum clamp, G; thence through the carbon filament F to G', down the wire E' to the screw post D'; thence to the generating machine. It will be noticed, by reference to the complete lamp in Figure 7, that it has no complex regulating apparatus, such as characterized the inventor's earlier labors. All the work he did in regulators was practically wasted, for he has lately realized that they were not at all necessary—no more so than a fifth wheel is to a coach.

He finds that the electricity can be regulated with entire reliability at the central station, just as the pressure of gas is now regulated. By his system of connecting the wires the extinguishment of certain of the burners affects the others no more than the extinguishment of the same number of gas burners affects those drawing the supply from the same mains. The simplicity of the completed lamp seems certainly to have arrived at the highest point, and Edison asserts that it is scarcely possible to simplify it more. The entire cost of constructing them is not more than twenty-five cents.

The lamp shown in Figure 7 is a table lamp. For chandeliers it would consist of only the vacuum globe and the carbon filament attached to the chandelier and connected to the wires leading to the generating machine in a central station, perhaps a half mile away, the wires being run through the gas pipes, so that in reality the only change necessary to turn a gas jet into an electric lamp is to run the wires through the gas pipe, take off the jet and screw the electric lamp in the latter's place. Although the plans have been fully consummated for general illumination the outline of the probable system to be adopted is the locating of a central station in large cities in such a manner that each station will supply an area of about one-third of a mile. In each station there will be, it is contemplated, one or two engines of immense power, which will drive several generating machines, each supplying about fifty lamps.

Mr. Edison's first experiments in machines for generating the electric current did not meet with success. His primal apparatus was in the form of a large tuning fork, constructed in such a way that its ends vibrated with great rapidity before the poles of a large magnet. These vibrations could be produced with comparatively little power. Several weeks of practice proved, however, that the machine was not practical, and it was laid aside. Then followed a number of other forms, leading up gradually to the one at present used. Bearing in mind the principle common to all magneto-electric machines —viz., that the current is produced by the rotation of magnets near each other

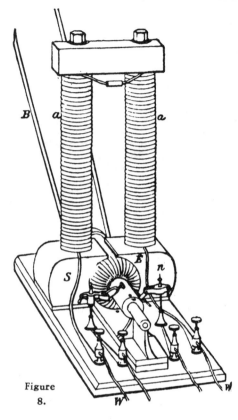

Figure
8.

—it will not be difficult to understand, in a general way, how his machine operates. Figure 8 shows the generating or Faradic machine as Edison terms it, in honor of Faraday, complete.

In this figure, a a are two upright iron columns, three feet high and eight inches in diameter, wound with coarse wire and resting upon the base, n and s, which form its magnetic poles. This part of the apparatus is called the field of force magnet. Fixed on an axle, so as to freely revolve between the poles n and s, is a cylindrical armature of wood, e, wound parallel to its axes with fine iron wire. When the cylinder or armature is made to revolve rapidly between the magnetic poles n and s, by means of the belt B, driven by an engine (not shown in the cut), there is generated in the wire surrounding the armature e strong currents of electricity, which are carried off by the wires, W W, to the electric lamps.

By constructing the machine in the form shown in Figure 9 there is obtained an electric motor capable of performing light work, such as running sewing machines and pumping water. It forms part of the inventor's system and may be used either with or without the electric light. To run an ordinary sewing machine it requires only as much electricity as is necessary to give out one electric light of the strength of a common gas jet. To put it in operation on a sewing machine the housewife has merely to attach it by a little belt at A with the wheel of the sewing machine, and turn on the electricity by touching a little knob conveniently attached. The cost is the same as if she were burning one electric light.

The apparatus for measuring the amount of electricity used by each householder is a simple contrivance consisting of an electrolytic cell and a small coil of wire, appropriately arranged in a box, the latter being of about half the size of an ordinary gas meter, and like a gas meter it can be placed in any part of the house. The measurement is obtained by the deposit of copper particles on a little plate in the electrolytic cell, such deposit being caused by the electric current passing through the cell. At the end of any period, say one month, the plate is taken by the inspector to the central office, where the copper deposit is weighed and the amount of electricity consumed determined by a simple calculation.

In addition to the various parts of the system above described, there are a number of other details, not so important to be sure as those of which sketches have been given, but nevertheless essential to make up the complete plan of economical electrical illumination. A description of these latter will not be attempted, as a proper understanding of them involves a technical knowledge of the laws of electricity. The entire system embraces an amount of work so extensive that one naturally wonders how a single man in such a brief space of time as fifteen months could possibly have planned and perfected it all. And surprise becomes greater when it is considered that during this period Edison found time to make other inventions. A sextuplex telegraph, or apparatus for sending six messages on one telegraph wire in opposite directions simultaneously, saw life during the progress of the electric light, patents for the same having only just been issued. Several new and important improvements in his chalk telephone, by which the efficiency of that invention is greatly increased, also attest his industry and versatility of genius.

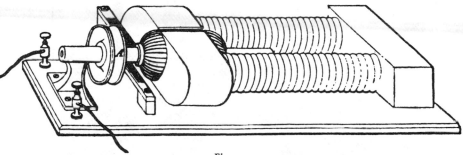

Figure 9.

The remainder of the article included a brief review of the experiments others had made to solve electric lighting. It closed with an important paragraph, entitled 'Edison's Assistants':

Before concluding this article it is only proper that due credit should be given to those whose untiring energy and skilled handicraft made possible the perfection of the great inventor's system—viz., his chief laboratory assistants: for, although Edison's was the mind that originated all, theirs were the hands that deftly carried out his wishes. Principal among his assistants, and so intimately associated with him in his work that his absence from the laboratory is invariably a signal for Mr. Edison to suspend labor, is Mr. Charles Batchelor. For the past eight years Mr. Batchelor has worked side by side with the inventor, carrying out his plans with rare ability, and to his energy and skill is due not a little. Next come Messrs. Upton and Kruza (Kruesi), both heads of departments, the one attending to the fine electrical work and the other to the mechanical details of the machine department. Among the others whose ability has helped to contribute to the inventor's great success, each in his particular sphere, are Mr. Griffin, Mr. Carman, Mr. Jehl, Mr. Force and Mr. Baum (Boehm).

'THE MAN WHO MOVES THE WORLD'

The drawings in the two top corners are entitled: 'The Darkness of the Past' and 'The Light of the Future.' In the lower right corner is 'Ye Necromancer of Old.' The large figure in the center is Edison. Note the telephone receivers on the shelf beyond his head; the electric signal bell; the tin foil phonograph on the table behind his chair; the wet batteries and so on. In the lower left corner, a panic in gas stocks is depicted. This cartoon appeared in the *Graphic*.

Christie Street in restored Menlo Park, Dearborn, showing
lamp posts with cardboard filament lamps.

L. Sawyer's Challenge
What the Critics Said

THE issue of the New York *Herald* that announced the
completion of the electric light also contained an
editorial of more than ordinary interest, entitled
'Edison's Eureka—The Electric Light at Last.' After
relating how the world had been disappointed at the failure
to bring it out as early as promised, the writer went on to say:

By this story it will be seen that Mr. Edison has finally elaborated a lamp
for the use of electricity that is simpler than any lamp in common use in the
houses of the people; as simple as the gas burner itself and more manageable;
a lamp that cannot leak and fill the house with vile odors or combustible
vapors, that cannot explode and that does not need to be filled or trimmed.
Once more, therefore, the public may reasonably anticipate a time when they
will be free from nearly all the annoyances and grievances of ordinary lighting
apparatuses and in the full enjoyment, besides, of a light compared to which
every other, save daylight itself, is a mere glimmering and gloaming; compared
to which, indeed, even the daylight of about one-third the year is a deteriorated
and adulterated article. People generally knew the soft glory of the light
electricity would make, but they never dreamed of the possibility that it could
be applied without an apparatus so complicated that it would need a special
education to enable them to take care of it.

Perhaps, therefore, this may be regarded as the supreme point of Mr. Edison's achievement in this field—that his last invented lamp is one of such unexpected and remarkable simplicity. His lamp may be screwed on at the end of any ordinary gas burner and the wires from the electric battery may be conveyed to it in the tube that served to convey the gas to the same burner. Whether the wires thus connected come from a battery in another part of the house, or from some larger common reservoir of electricity outside the house, is a point as to which householders will be able to choose for themselves, since both sources are contemplated by the inventor. Mr. Edison, it will be seen in the narrative, has contrived a battery for household use which can be adapted to any different number of lamps and to other uses also—can light the house at night and run the sewing machine or rock the cradle all day. For country houses, or for the houses in the city of people who want to keep themselves out of the clutches of corporations that may succeed the gas companies, that will be the chosen source of electricity. But in every city this subtle fluid will be made on a large scale and served to houses at a fixed price as gas is now served, and of course the street lamps must be served from such great public laboratories.

Edison's discovery of a substance upon which electricity could produce the light of incandescence with comparative inexpensiveness and perfect effect is one of those little romances of science with which the pathway to every great invention is strewed. Platinum was a great obstacle for a while in this hunt; and, not altogether satisfactory in operation while of extremely high value, it seemed at the moment as if it might make the search altogether vain. But the happy discovery of the uses of a bit of cotton thread has turned in a moment the whole current of this story into a fortunate channel, and we are rejoiced to congratulate not merely Edison, but the people of all civilized nations, upon Edison's success.

The ink on the *Herald* pages was hardly dry when the first of the challenges to Edison's claims was being written. The author was William E. Sawyer, a rival inventor and electrician, who had been struggling for at least two years to perfect an electric lamp. Furious at the announcement, he sat down and penned a letter to the New York City newspapers:

If a party possesses an interest in something that he considers valuable, he is not very likely to part with it, especially if it be something in the line of electric lighting, where what may nominally be $1 may really be $1,000. Therefore when Mr. Edison sells out all his interest in his electric light there is a reasonable chance for a suspicion that he considers his invention worth very little.

Mr. Edison's reputation before the public is founded upon the newspaper publications about: (1) The quadruplex telegraph; (2) the telephone; and (3) the phonograph.

As to the quadruplex telegraph, I may say that it was an adaptation of the French and German systems. When Edison took hold of the 4-plex there were already known five systems of 2-plex, three of 4-plex, and three of 6-plex and 8-plex.

The 4-plex of Edison was a failure. A modest young gentleman, assistant electrician of the Western Union, Mr. Garritt Smith, made it a success, and some day he will get the credit for this invention, for he, and not Edison, is the genius in this case.

As to the telephone, Mr. Edison is not the inventor. Andrew Graham Bell is the inventor of the telephone.

As to the phonograph, which really made Mr. Edison's reputation, it is of no earthly value, and the manufacture by Bergmann has practically been dropped. The real inventor of the phonograph will never be known, for I understand that Mr. Edison anticipates a Western man but three days in priority of invention.

Now, all that remains for Mr. Edison is electric light. He is going over the same ground that Bouliguine, Lodyguine, Kosloff, Konn, Starr King, myself and others have traversed—first, iron; second, platinum; third, carbon in different shapes. And Edison has failed, in my opinion. To show that I mean what I say, I deny every one of his allegations made at the Saratoga convention of the American Society for the Advancement of Science, and specifically, I challenge him:

First—To maintain a vacuum in his lamps.

Second—To run his carbonized paper lamp three hours. (In practice, in a perfect vacuum, it will last twenty minutes.)

Third—To consolidate platinum by heating electrically in the Sprengel vacuum, as he claims.

Fourth—To prove that his dynamo electric machine develops not ninety but even forty-five percent of the foot pounds applied to it.

Fifth—To show that he can obtain a light of twenty-five candles from platinum with less than three horsepower.

Sixth—To show that platinum or iridium will not disintegrate in twenty hours' actual running.

Seventh—To prove that, with his carbonized paper lamp, he can obtain two lights of ten candles each per horsepower.

Eighth—To show that the effect of the oxide of magnesium is to harden his wire, and make it more refractory.

And I further allege that all Mr. Edison's statements are erroneous, and I offer $100 as a prize for him to prove each of the above eight allegations. Let him run one of his lamps three hours, and the public will be satisfied that I am correct.

Intense interest in the light was aroused both in New York City and throughout the country. Gas manufacturers had been resting easily, convinced that Edison's efforts would come to naught. The new bombshell did not frighten them nearly so much as the article of the previous year. Nevertheless, on Christmas Eve a delegation of gas officials called at the laboratory and obtained a demonstration of the new lighting system. Edison did not hesitate to show them everything he had. Said the *Herald.*

The inventor devoted two hours and a half to an exhaustive exhibit and explanation of the marvelous electric apparatus which was brought into play during the evening. Wires leading from the generator in the laboratory connected with and illuminated a number of the adjacent residences, and two street lamps in front of the inventor's office threw out a bright light. Mr. Edison first proved that the electric current is capable of subdivision. He then showed his visitors the two main electric conductors which furnished light for the entire laboratory. Afterward he hung a number of lamps side by side, each

Replica of the cardboard lamp as reconstructed by Francis Jehl and presented to Henry Ford on the latter's birthday, July 30, 1932.

one giving out an equal light, and not the slightest variation in the light of the other lamps was noticed. Light after light was attached until the illuminating power of the conductors seemed unlimited, and then the gentlemen declared themselves more than satisfied that subdivision of the electric current had been accomplished.

Mr. Edison next gave an elaborate illustration of the manufacture of the various parts of the lamp and the manner in which the vacuum in the glass bulb is attained. The generator, in full operation, was also viewed, and the inventor explained its intricate workings.

A device for weighing on an actual platform scale the power employed in the process of generating was examined, after which the visitors were treated to a view of Mr. Edison's electric motor, designed for running sewing machines and other light machinery in private dwellings. The uses of a number of other scientific apparatus were explained. The inventor took particular pains to answer all questions by a practical demonstration on the spot. At a late hour the party returned to New York.

A few days later an eminent scientist appeared in the columns of the New York *Times* with an interview cautioning the public against too ready acceptance of the 'discovery.'

Professor Henry Morton, the President of the Stevens Institute of Technology, who is well known for his researches in physics, and whose experiments were a source of unfeigned pleasure and astonishment to Professor Tyndall, recently sent a communication to the *Sanitary Engineer* protesting against the trumpeting of the result of Edison's experiments in electric lighting as 'a wonderful success,' when 'every one acquainted with the subject' will recognize it as a 'conspicuous failure.' To this was added the statement that Edison 'has done and is doing too much really good work to have his record defaced and his name discredited in the interests of any stock company or individual financiers.' Edison, to whose attention this letter was called, was reported in a newspaper yesterday morning as inviting Professor Morton or any other electrician to visit the Menlo Park laboratory and see the light in practical operation. In conversation with a *Times* reporter yesterday, Professor Morton said that, for several reasons, he did not think he would accept Mr. Edison's kind invitation. 'What is needed to be learned,' said the Professor, 'is the durability of these new lamps of Mr. Edison's and the actual economy in the conversion of power into light by his arrangement. For example, according to the statement in the *Sun*, Mr. Edison places his present lamps and machines as yielding him what is equivalent to 10 gas burners for every horsepower. Now, my own experiments with the best dynamo-electric machines—such as those of Siemens, Weston, Brush and Maxim—using the ordinary carbon poles, show that we may obtain a light of from 1,200 to 1,600 candles per horsepower. Assuming a gas burner to be equal to from 12 to 16 candles, this would be about 100 burners per horsepower. As compared, therefore, with the electric light obtained between carbon poles, Mr. Edison gets only 10 percent, showing, therefore, precisely that enormous loss in the division of the light which has been alluded to before as one of the standing difficulties in the way of the practical application of such a system as Mr. Edison is working upon. This is taking simply his apparently rough estimate. For any definite and certain conclusions, prolonged and careful experiments, entirely under the control of the investigator, are absolutely necessary.'

As regards the durability of Professor Edison's new lamps, Professor Morton was not at all sanguine. 'Lamps,' said he, 'in all essential respects identical with those described by Mr. Edison have been in constant experimental use for several years past, with one invariable result, namely, that, while the carbon would operate successfully for periods varying from a few hours to several days, it has been found utterly impossible to render them reliably permanent. It is, therefore, in my estimation, here also necessary that experiments of some length, likewise under the entire control of the investigator, should be made in order that a decisive conclusion may be reached. With reference to the confident assertions of success which reach me from various quarters, I must fall back upon my experience of a little over a year ago. Every one remembers how, at that time, Mr. Edison read some remarks of mine by the light of his then brilliantly glowing electric light, and pointed to it as a shining refutation. In turning over some old letters a few days since, I came across one from a friend of mine, who is a scientific man of high standing, and was at that time on very intimate terms with Mr. Edison. This letter is dated October, 1878, and in it I am assured that Mr. Edison's lamp is a perfect success, capable of replacing a gas burner with perfect ease, and that when I see it I shall, no doubt, be charmed with its simplicity and efficiency. When I reflect that this previous complete success has been since abandoned by Mr. Edison, I feel that a little caution is needed in accepting the enthusiastic conclusions of his friends, even when they are illuminated by the shining electric lamps which occasion them.'

'Can you tell me, Professor,' asked the reporter, 'what are some of the chief difficulties in the way of the success of Mr. Edison's light?'

' Well,' Professor Morton replied, 'the first difficulty of all is the production of a lamp which shall be thoroughly reliable, and neither complicated nor expensive. All attempts up to the present lamp in this direction are acknowledged to be failures, and, as I have pointed out, there does not seem to be any novelty such as would authorize us to hope for a better success in the present one. The next difficulty is in the economical production of small lights by electricity. This is what is commonly meant by the phrase "dividing the electric light." Up to the present time, and including Mr. Edison's latest experiments, it appears that this involves an immense loss of efficiency. Next comes the difficulty of distributing on any large scale the immense electric currents which would be needed and to provide for their equal action at different points under varying conditions of the number of lights used. In reference to this, as far as I judge from the reports, Mr. Edison has been running not over fifty lights in all, while his 80 horsepower engine ought to supply 800 lights. The small number actually in use does not, therefore, develop this problem in any practical way.'

'The question of measuring the current,' added the Professor, as the reporter turned to leave, 'the loss involved from the necessity of running the machinery without a moment's intermission during the entire time that any light is needed—in other words, the absence of any storing capacity in electricity—and various other matters of detail, while less important than the three principal difficulties which I have given you, are, nevertheless, very serious difficulties in the direction of a successful practical application of electricity for general illumination.'

On this the *Herald* commented drily, under the caption: 'Farthing Science and the Electric Light':

Mr. Morton, of the Stevens Institute of Technology, is the last 'great' man who has favored the world with his opinion on the electric light. He is satisfied that it is a failure. He has always been satisfied to that effect since he examined the subject. In fact, he will not have it on any terms, and when a man of his eminence actually refuses to consent to the electric light it is but little short of impertinence for Mr. Edison to invent it, and apologies are due from him to the Professor. Instead of apologizing, however, he simply denies what the Professor says. Both gentlemen's words are given in today's *Herald* as we find them printed in the columns of the *Sun*. Mr. Morton pities Edison and protests against the harm the *Herald's* account of his invention must do his reputation, assuming as he does that the account is grossly false; but Mr. Edison says 'every word that was printed in the *Herald* article was literally true'; and he seems to intimate that he does not regard Professor Morton's knowledge on topics related to the electric light as superior to that of all other men—a point on which apparently he and Professor Morton are at odds. Professor Morton is apparently one of those average men of science who are amply endowed to fill one little circle and are pretty thin outside of that circle. He believes that the world is finished and that there is no room for new inventions. As Lord Russell was willing to consent that the progress of the British people might be admitted to go so far as he approved, but held that the point so gained must be a finality, so this professor will not admit that there may be any movement in the progress of invention beyond his finality; which is gas.

Edison at close of 1879.

LI. New Arrivals in December 1879

AS I have already related, the cotton thread lamp of October 21, 1879, possessed all the elements of practical success. It had high resistance and small radiating surface; it was stable and durable.

This first practical incandescent lamp was immediately followed by the first commercial lamp, the carbonized paper horseshoe lamp. The latter was more homogeneous in filament structure than its predecessor. Edison chose it for the public demonstrations, with the intention, however, of incorporating certain improvements. One was to increase the resistance of the filament which, as I have said, ranged from 130 ohms cold to about 70-80 ohms heated.

The unexpected appearance of the article in the New York *Herald* on December 21, 1879, interfered with his plans. However, as the news had already leaked out, exhibitions had to be given nearly every day even before that publication. By giving the demonstrations before the year's close he was able to enter them on record in 1879. On the other hand, the same demonstrations gave the buccaneers who play on other men's ideas more time to infringe the essentials of his lamp even while he was developing it.

With my helper George Hill, I had already furnished about eighty lamps, not counting those that had already been made with the peculiar 8-shaped tong clamps. 'We will get more men now,' said Edison, 'and rush the development while giving our demonstrations.'

Perhaps it would be well to introduce here the names of the men engaged during this development period.

One was Charles L. Clarke([1]). Clarke visited his Bowdoin College classmate, Francis R. Upton, at Menlo Park in December, 1879. Like Upton, he had finished his education in Germany. He had studied civil engineering, acquired experience in railroad construction and in mechanical designing for steel-making and rolling-mill machinery. He was a fine mathematician. When Upton explained Edison's system to him, he was filled with enthusiasm. He was introduced to Edison and, before he knew it, was engaged to join the crew. Closing his employment as teacher in a military school near Philadelphia, he came to Menlo Park February 1, 1880.

Clarke began, so to speak, as Edison's second mathematician, and gradually supplanted Upton, who was glad to be relieved for more congenial work of a semiscientific nature. Clark's first job was computing a table of 'gauge, weight, ohms, and other measurements for copper wire to be used in the new system. He then began the computation (I believe the first in history) of the spherical candle power of the horseshoe filament lamp. Edison set him to making a chart of the degree of illumination along the side and end walls of a room, using first one lamp, and then two. Here we again see Edison's vision and thinking capacity in the minute problems involving his lamp. Clarke also figured out other questions for Edison,

Charles L. Clarke in 1879.

(1) Marking the climax of 50 years of service, Mr. Clarke in April, 1934, was presented with the medal of the American Institute of Electrical Engineers at Schenectady.

Sketch of testing table, from an old print.

one being whether it was more advantageous to connect
distribution mains with the central station than to supply
them at distant points from the station through feeders.
Clarke determined the size of the underground conductors
that Wilson S. Howell laid down for the second Edison
demonstration late in 1880. Clarke also gave more or less
attention to the electric locomotive work at Menlo Park.

Assisting Edison and Upton, Clarke made the calculations
and drew the plans for the first Edison steam dynamo, and
later arranged nearly all the particulars for the 'big economy
test' on January 29-30, 1881, the last of its kind at Menlo Park.

Sandwiched in with other work were his motor experiments using the Edison dynamo as a motor. Clarke knew little
about electricity when he came to Menlo Park. On Upton's
advice he brushed up with vigor, taking advantage of every
opportunity to make himself familiar with the new art. As
he had a good mathematical mind, he was able to juggle
differential and integral calculus to determine the most economical relation between interest on conductor investment

Wilson S. Howell.

and cost of energy lost—later worked into a law by Sir William Thomson. Edison put the problem to Clarke in such simple, common-sense language that Clarke saw at once it was a matter of maximum and minimum calculus.

One day when Clarke was beginning to familiarize himself with purely electrical matters, he sauntered up to my testing table (at the suggestion of his good friend Upton) and expressed a wish to use it for measuring the resistance of some wire he had brought with him. I hesitated to let him have the standard Wheatstone bridge because Edison had instructed me to let no one 'fool' with it.

I gave him the sliding bridge we had made; but that didn't suit him. He had studied about the other one, and wanted some practice with it. As Clarke was always a congenial fellow, I risked letting him have the standard, telling him to be very careful to use only battery current in measuring. Taking his own way, however, he used instead eighty to ninety volts from the line I also was using. When he proposed to use only high resistance coils, I warned him not to because they would burn out.

Well, sometimes you can't tell even mathematicians what to do. No sooner had Clarke handled the first plug of the bridge than there was a hissing noise, as if a safety plug had blown out. The standard Wheatstone bridge had ceased to be a standard! Several coils were ruined. When Edison heard of it, he shook his head sadly and bade me fix it as best I could.

With a letter to Professor Brackett provided by Upton, I called at Princeton College the next day. Using German silver wire, I was able to measure out new coils according to the standard there.

Clarke now knew why Edison had made a lamp of high resistance with small radiating surface. That coil was one —only it had no life. Thus one learns through experience.

Friend Clarke soon knew as much of electricity as the others. And when Edison went to New York in 1881, Clarke was made chief engineer of The Edison Electric Light Company at a salary so much higher than the weekly wages he had received at Menlo Park that he nearly fainted from surprise.

Wilson S. Howell came in December, 1879. He had studied at Blair Academy in Blairstown, New Jersey. He has told me since, however, that he went to the college on the hill at Menlo Park. In a letter to me he writes:

'In December, 1879, Francis R. Upton invited a party of young people to visit Mr. Edison's laboratory at Menlo Park, I being one of the party. We saw there the first public lighting of a few of the streets of Menlo Park by the old paper horseshoe carbon filaments. I was so impressed by what I saw that on the following morning I again visited the Edison laboratory, sought out Mr. Upton and requested that I be permitted to work in the laboratory in order to gain information which would enable me to be the first to benefit from the commercial application of Mr. Edison's invention of a system of incandescent lighting.

'Mr. Upton referred me to Mr. Edison, who discouraged my application by saying that the world was full of young fellows who knew little or nothing of electricity. Upon my agreement to work without compensation for the privilege of standing at the feet of the master, I was told to take off my coat and get to work.

'Immediately on my arrival at Edison's laboratory,' Howell relates further, 'I was put to work under your orders exhausting lamps, working with a young man named Hill. I stuck at this job for several months.'

Howell's character, his devotion to Edison, were exemplified a few years later when he was approached by some one who tried to induce him to leave Edison, with his brother John W. Howell, and join an opposition camp. Howell's answer to this ' suggestion was: 'Mr.

William J. Hammer.

Blank, our loyalty to Edison is sincere and our detestation of
infringers of Edison's patents is beyond expression.'

Howell's services to Edison were manifold and valuable.
He was intrusted with the laying of the underground conductors that served for the second demonstration of 1880-
1881, which we shall describe in its proper place. A stanch
pioneer, he took part in the erection of many plants and stations. He was chief of the 'lamp testing bureau' organized
by the Association of Edison Illuminating Companies. This
'lamp testing bureau' eventually became the Electrical Testing
Laboratories at 80th Street and East End Avenue in New
York City, now under the able management of its president,
Preston S. Millar. We shall hear more of Howell as our story
proceeds.

About the same time, another young man by the name
of William J. Hammer came from Newark, New Jersey. He
started under conditions similar to those laid upon Howell;
for Edison had made it a rule to take on recruits at first as
volunteers, until he should learn whether they were worth
their hire. Hammer had attended school in Newark and had
afterward found a position with the Western Malleable
Nickel Company. In the middle of December, he came to the
laboratory and, like Howell, was placed in the exhausting
department. When the bamboo lamps came, he had charge
of tabulating results during the life tests.

Hammer once wrote me as follows:

'You had charge of pumps for a considerable time with
Hill, Herrick and others under you, and for some time, while
you ran the pumps in the daytime, I ran them at night.'
Each of the boys worked his shift at the pumps, and as other
work came up was transferred.

Hammer continues in his letter.

'As you will remember, this vacuum apparatus consisted
of a combination of a Sprengel drop pump and a Geissler lift
pump, together with a McLeod gauge and tubes containing
phosphoric anhydride and a gold leaf with a spark gap at the
top connected with an induction coil and battery. You will
remember that Mr. Edison decided that this type of pump was
too large, unwieldy and expensive for the new lamp works and
he offered a prize for the best design of a simple and inexpensive
pump. I remember that you won the prize, which I believe
was one hundred dollars, for your simple form of the Sprengel
drop pump.'

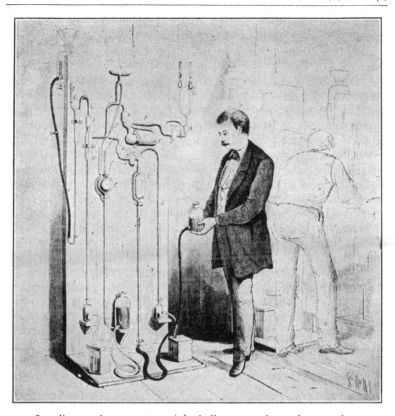

Speeding up the evacuation of the bulbs—two exhausted at one time.

I may state here that the prize was not a hundred dollars. I received 1.6 shares of the stock of the Edison Electric Light Company with the remark: 'Keep it under your cap, Francis.'

It was Edison's custom in those days to reward such of the boys as did their work well and followed his instructions. For he was particular, when he gave an order, about having it executed in every detail; he did not want any deviation from his instructions. Other methods or one's own ideas could be tried later.

Hammer took an active part with some of the others in installing the new lamp works in the old factory down by the Pennsylvania Railroad tracks. In his letter to me he says:

'I remember that I installed with my own hands the first ﹥

two hundred of these pumps at the lamp works . . . We turned out fifty thousand lamps the first year, and for years your pumps were used entirely for exhausting the Edison lamps.'

Hammer also took part in the erection of the line that connected the lamp works with the laboratory machine shop, the first commercial transmission line in practice: it carried current generated at the machine shop to the lamp works to be used for light as well as for power in driving the electric motor to raise the mercury for the lamp pumps through an Archimedes screw. Hammer was later sent to England to assist Johnson in the erection of the exhibition central station at Holborn Viaduct and the Crystal Palace Exposition of 1882. After spending some time with the German Edison Company at Berlin, he returned to the United States in 1883 or 1884 and proceeded actively with Edison work in this country.([2])

Albert B. Herrick has also been mentioned. He writes: 'My chance came to me through Edison having sent an article for publication in *Scribner's Monthly*. That was early in 1880. The article was written by Upton. Before publishing it the editors, to convince themselves, sent one of their scientific staff to Menlo Park. Young Herrick went along. While Edison was explaining his system and the paper horseshoe lamp to the representative, he noticed Herrick.

'And what is this boy going to do?'

'I do not know,' Herrick stammered.

'Well, then come here and work.'

And so he was hired. The invention of the carbonized paper lamp lured not only these boys but many others, who all took their part in the work of development. A little later I shall introduce the others employed during this period and the year 1880.

---

(2) Mr. Hammer passed away in April, 1934.

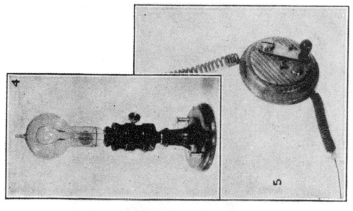

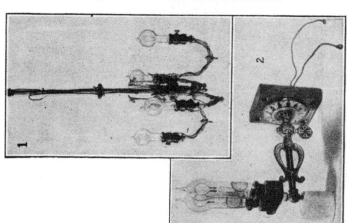

1. First chandelier fitted with electric lamps. It was a gas fixture equipped with earliest type sockets and thumb screw switches. 2. Bracket fitted with two small 8 candle power cardboard filament lamps. 3. Bracket fitted with single 16 candle power lamp. 4. Pioneer type of table lamp. 5. Earliest switch, modeled after telegraph. All these are now in Edison collection at Dearborn.

Francis Jehl at the 'regulator' wheel, where the line pressure was kept constant. On ground floor of restored laboratory.

LII. Getting Ready for the Demonstration

AS THE first public demonstration, to be given on New Year's Eve, drew nearer, the New York City newspapers published daily dispatches from the Edison laboratory. Interest in the work became widespread. As no better picture of our activities could be painted than that given by the reporters themselves as they actually saw things, we shall continue to reprint here extracts from their stories:

The first is from the *Herald* of December 28:

The laboratory of Mr. Edison at Menlo Park was brilliantly illuminated last night with the new electric light, the occasion being a visit of a number of the inventor's personal friends. Forty lamps in all were burning from six o'clock until after ten. The various parts of the system were explained by the inventor at length. As a practical illustration of his method of subdividing the electric current he had two copper wires of about an eighth of an inch in thickness leading to the generating machines placed side by side on cleats along tables nearly the entire length of the laboratory. To these he connected lamp after lamp by merely fastening little wires to each of the parallel supply wires and then attaching them to the lamps. The illumination or extinguishment made not the slightest perceptible difference in the strength of the current.

Twenty electric lamps burned with exactly the same brilliancy as did one when the other nineteen were disconnected. The light given was of the brilliancy of the best gas jet, perhaps a trifle more brilliant. The effect of the light on the eyes was much superior to gas in softness and excited the admiration of all who saw it.

A new feature, shown by the inventor for the first time, was the method of regulating the strength of the current to be used at the central stations. By moving a little wheel the assistant in charge of this branch of the system was enabled to readily vary the strength of the electric lights from the merest glimmer to a dazzling incandescence. When the latter point was reached the little horseshoe paper presented the appearance of a beautiful globe of fire. The method of obtaining the vacuum in the little glass bulbs of the lamps was also explained and proved highly interesting.

(The manipulation of the new feature, called a 'regulator,' was my job during those demonstrations.)
The next story is from the issue of December 29:

'Wonderful!' When you hear this word rolled out once in a while with the proper intensity of accent, as in the grand chorus of the *Messiah*, it has a lifting effect upon the emotions. When you hear it three or four hundred times in a day it begins to lose force and you search about for synonyms. Out here at the home of the wizard in these times you listen to it from the lips of battalions of visitors, and you sympathize with the men of Athens who grew weary of hearing a great citizen called 'Aristides the Just.' All this while you are under the influence of the wonderful yourself. It is not only the little glowing globes hung here and there, but a thousand and one things appeal to your sense of admiration besides, above all of which towers, as the creator does above his creature, the man himself.

'It is not much of a place,' said a Philadelphia millionaire to a New York capitalist, yesterday, as they looked around at the dozen or so of houses that dot the otherwise bare hillside that is called Menlo Park. But few thought about such things, though the view across the pleasant, undulating country, now wrapped in a light garment of snow, with the brown skeletons of the woods breaking the sky line, is soothing and charming. All came with one passion—the electric light and its maker. They are of all classes, these visitors, of different degrees of wealth and importance in the community and varying degrees of scientific ignorance. Few, indeed, are they who can approximately measure what has been done in this matter, and still fewer those who, knowing its worth, admit it. But the homage of the mass to genius which they cannot comprehend makes up in quantity at any rate for any shortcomings in quality. It is a time of rapid conversions. The little horseshoe holds its own.

Outside the building called the office, on two ordinary lamp-posts, gleamed, last evening, two little electric lamps. Afar off they seemed two large globes

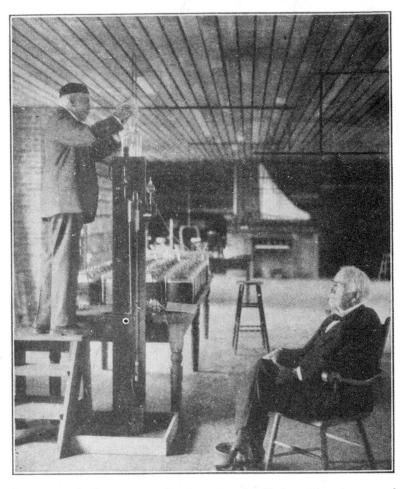

During one of Edison's visits to Dearborn, Francis Jehl showed how he operated the Sprengel vacuum pump, pouring mercury into tube at top.

of fire. It was not till you came close by that you saw the little incandescent hoop of carbon held up by its delicate platinum clamps inside the small globe exhausted of air. In the office the lights were all electric. In the library upstairs it was the same. Over in the laboratory, upstairs and downstairs, it was the same. Such volleys of questions as were pouring out! Every assistant and even every boy was examined. All who came were satisfied. The visitors learned—for it was easy as Hamlet said lying was—to set the little carbon hoops alight by laying them down between the two wires on the main table. And Edison was there—a study to all, but divined by none. By and by the visitors moved off, now stopping to look at the chalk telephone that speaks aloud. You hear of ohms and circuits, generators and so forth. They have been round the strange, complicated looking vacuum pumps, made out of glass tubing twisted up and twisted down.

They have been down where the beardless boy with all the enthusiasm of an artist blows the lamps, seals in the thin wires and inserts the carbon hoop and leaves it all ready to be exhausted of air. There is a fascination about glass blowing, and this young Mr. Boehm, while a man in his business, is a child in his fancy, and he becomes as joyous over the delight of the onlookers as ever was a boy in a baseball field. He is a blue blood glass blower, and tells you his titles to skill with the conscious pride of a university graduate—for is he not a pupil of the late Dr. Geissler, whose fame is world-wide, but whose blowpipe is now laid away forever. The visitors have been around to see the engine, the generators, the regulators, the dynamometer. Satisfied about the electric light, they have asked about the tasimeter, the microphone, the phonograph and a dozen other things, as though they wanted to improve every instant before the train starts. At last they go in twos and threes down the hill to the railroad track, and it is all 'wonderful!' 'marvellous!' 'wonderful, wonderful!' among them till the train takes them away and Menlo Park is left to itself.

The third extract, which is from the *Herald* of December 30, referred to me and my duties at the regulator wheel:

It was quiet out here this morning and through the day as far as visitors were concerned. The machine shops were running full blast, and the laboratory was endued with its mysterious activity to the full. You would get the idea at first that in this place work was only taken up spasmodically, because you might see a man in broad daylight asleep on a bench, but shortly you discover that they only leave off work for short spells. Hence a peculiar Bohemian air about the place and all who are in it that might be a sign of demoralization in any other establishment in the world.

The afternoon trains brought some visitors, but in the evening every train set down a couple of score at least. All immediately started for the scene of the laboratory, and a good many of those simple people who hold that Rome was built in a day and those modest people who believe that the hinges of the universe should turn upon the pivot of their desires expressed disappointment that they did not step out of the train upon a scene from fairyland. The moon was obscured by clouds, the way was dark up the little plank road, and the new white lamp-posts seemed to be stretching up their long fingers to clutch a little light from the heavens since Edison would not give them any of his little horseshoes. In fact, as the inventor said to me today, he is only waiting for another electric generator to be finished to light up all these long white fellows in what is out of courtesy called a street. It will, he expects, be ready today, and tonight he hopes to have fifteen street lamps and several of the houses lighted up.

'It is a mistake to suppose,' said Edison, 'that a few lamps here or there over Menlo Park is all I want. I intend to make an actual test of my eighty horsepower engine and to put on every lamp it will run. I hope to have 800 of them. I shall put a dozen of them over there a mile away and turn them on and off from this window. I don't know where I'll put them all, unless along the fence. So everybody will have plenty of time to see them. It will take weeks to get them all out, though we are working night and day.'

The stream of visitors passed through the shops, admired and wondered at the steady electric lights and called things by all sorts of laudatory epithets. Now and again a well-informed visitor would catch Mr. Batchelor or Mr. Upton and ply him with questions upon candle power, gas-jet power and kindred intricate matters that are 'caviare to the general.' A particular object of interest was the register for regulating the strength of the current. Young Francis Jehl stood by it with all the solemnity of a patriarch, and explained it lucidly to all who desired. A current passing through a galvanometer deflects a small mirror at the back of which is a tiny magnet. Opposite this mirror, at a couple of feet distance, is a board along which, horizontally laid, is a scale. Through a slit in this board a ray of light passes from a lamp. The ray falls upon the small mirror, which, as the current is stronger or weaker, casts the reflection to the right or left upon the scale opposite. As more lights are put on more electricity is needed, and Francis turns an indicator, near which is an electric light, just as they do in a gas house when more or less pressure is called for by the consumption.

'It may be done automatically,' said Mr. Batchelor, in answer to a gentleman's inquiry; 'but it hasn't been thought out yet.'

The visitors seemed never tired of lighting the lamps upon the main table by simply laying one between the two long wires. Most were content to ejaculate 'Wonderful!'

There is no particle of doubt in any one's mind that the electric light is a success and a permanent one. I spoke yesterday of the enthusiasm of a young glassblower; but it is a curious instance of Edison's brain force that this enthusiasm is common to all about the place. It is not unusual in such establishments for the inquirer to find here and there a captious understrapper who with very little encouragement will proceed to belittle their master. I have found nothing of the kind here. Edison animates the men and boys—there is scarcely a gray head in the establishment—with his own indomitable, persistent spirit. It is not merely in talking to a stranger, but in working, that this is seen.

Edison's chief assistant, Mr. Batchelor, will glow like a carbon lamp when he is asked a question. Secretary Griffin, who sits up in the office, generates enthusiasm with eighty horsepower if you hint at a desire for information, and it is all done with *bonhomie* and has nothing of 'shop talk' about it. Mr. Upton is genial and answers questions with textbook exactitude, although the object or process may be only a week old. The truth is Edison attracts the right kind of people for his work, and his 'go' keeps them going. It is not mere day's work that he exacts from them or himself.

Following is the final story before the demonstration, printed on December 31:

All day long and until late this evening Menlo Park has been thronged with visitors coming from all directions to see the wonderful 'electric light.' Nearly every train that stopped brought delegations of sightseers until the depot was overrun and the narrow plank road leading to the laboratory became alive with people. In the laboratory the throngs practically took possession of everything in their eager curiosity to learn all about the great invention. In vain Mr. Edison sought to get away and do some work, but no sooner had he struggled from one crowd than he became the center of another equally as inquisitive. The assistants likewise were plied with questions until they were obliged to suspend labor and give themselves over to answering questions. Not a little trouble was experienced in keeping the crowds from damaging the

'Doping' the filament beside the Sprengel pump in the restored laboratory.

various apparatus in the laboratory. Requests and notices not to touch or handle were unavailing. One of the best of the vacuum pumps was broken by some over-meddlesome strangers, who, during the temporary absence of the attendants, began experimenting on their own account.

Four new street lamps were last night added making six in all which now give out the horseshoe light in the open air. Their superiority to gas is so apparent, both in steadiness and beauty of illumination, that every one is struck with admiration. The laboratory office and machine shop and the houses of Mr. Batchelor and Mrs. Jordan, were all illuminated, the total number of lights being sixty. The house of Mrs. Jordan, situated near the laboratory, has been thrown open for the accommodation of guests, and having several of the electric lamps in operation affords, perhaps, the best view of the light in actual household use.

Among the visitors were a number of scientific gentlemen who minutely examined the light in all its parts. Their opinion as well as the opinion unanimously expressed by the non-scientific was that Edison had in reality produced the light of the future. Although the inventor has fixed no day for a general inspection by the public at large, desiring not to be completely overrun with visitors to the impediment of his work, the public exhibition may be said to be actually going on now, as many hundreds have already come and hundreds more are coming, and no impediments are thrown in the way of those who desire to satisfy their curiosity.

The story continued with a description of 'a night with Edison' containing a first-hand report of one of our midnight suppers beside the organ.

Now let me tell the story of a night with Edison. The last visitors had departed and Menlo Park was in its normal solitude. The two gray-bearded old men who had stood conversing—it seemed to me all day and all evening —at the head of the steps leading down the bank to the railroad track were gone away. Great clouds swept across the sky and the light from the hotel and grocery of Deacon Davis was the dim glare of the random kerosene lamp. All the electricity seemed to have died out of the place, and I looked about for possible occupation. Edison had gone to his house below an hour before; the boys up at the laboratory had told me that he would scarcely come back before morning, but still as I walked in the direction of the shops there was assurance of life there in the lights at the windows. Some people are at work I thought; for as I drew nearer I could see shadows flitting upon the panes. Then I heard the notes of an organ, and who would believe it in these days of progress, and above all at Menlo Park? the notes that came were those of *Pinafore*. The little outer office where they test the telphones was tenantless. In the distance a solitary, aproned figure stood before the small furnace where they bake the little carbon horseshoes, so I ascended the stairs. At the far end of the long apartment which had exchanged its electric brilliance for the light of an occasional gas jet were scattered about eight or nine of the assistants, lounging on stools and benches, and at the extreme end, seated before the organ, was one of them rolling out the too familiar melody. Then this is what came to my ears:

MacGregor—
    I am the Wizard of electric light,
Chorus—
    And a wide-awake Wizard, too.
MacGregor—
    I see you're rather bright and appreciate the might
      Of what I daily do
    Quadruplex telegraph or funny phonograph,
      It's all the same to me;
    With ideas I evolve and problems that I solve
      I am never, never stumped, you see.
Chorus—
    What, never?
MacGregor—
    No, never!
Chorus—
    What, never?
MacGregor—
    Well, hard - - -.

A groan escaped from my bosom, and the line was left uncompleted. It is evident, I thought, that Edison is not coming back tonight. They called out to me, and I came forward shocked, positively shocked. And there was no trace of apology for this desecration of the fame of science in the tones of Mr. Batchelor when he said:

'We're having a little music. Sit down and join us.'

MacGregor at the organ was still rolling off *Pinafore*, then 'switching off' into Strauss and 'letting her have a full current' of Offenbach.

'We're going to have a grand piano here for the boys shortly. That organ's frightfully out of tune.'

So it was, and the sturdy Mac was like the organ, but the boys listened to him as intently as Joseffy's audiences. Van Cleef came down the shop holding a black piece of iron in a tongs. He laid it on a bench to cool, for it was not long out of the furnace. Then he took one like it and began unscrewing it to place the cardboard horseshoes in it that were to be carbonized. Boehm, the glassblower, came up in his best attire.

'Say, Boehm, bring up your zither,' said George Crosby, who all day long had been working the delicate vacuum pumps and now rested for a space.

'Up here?' said Boehm, blushing; 'play here, now?' looking over doubtfully at me.

'Go ahead!' said Batchelor; 'that organ's in a terrible state.'

Boehm brought up the zither from the glass house and laid it on the bench before him. Crosby forced MacGregor away from the organ. The German lad sat down and tuned the strings.

'I had a good teacher at Bonn,' he said, slowly, 'but I forget much.'

He began to play, and all the grimy faces bent forward to listen. It was a quaint German serenade, that sounded as though far away from the focal point of materialism we occupied. There was something of dreamy moonlight on the Rhine in the tinkling treble and moaning bass strings.

'That's lovely music,' said MacGregor.

'Boehm,' said Batchelor, 'play something else with those shake notes in it; they go right down my back.'

'Shake notes? What is that?'

'Tremolo,' I suggested. He played again an exquisite melody, and Batchelor bent forward, as he put it in his material way, that would reduce every emotion to the stimulation of a particular ganglion, so he might feel the music going 'right down his back.'

But during the playing a man with a crumpled felt hat, a white silk handkerchief at his throat, his coat hanging carelessly and his vest half buttoned, came silently in, and, with his hand to his ear, sat close by the glassblower, who, wrapped up in his music, was back perhaps in his native Thuringia again.

'That's nice,' said he, looking round. It was Edison.

The glassblower played on, and the scene was curious. Standing by a blazing gas furnace he had lighted, Van Cleef with bare folded arms, listened or else shifted the hot irons with his pincers, but he did it gently. Edison sat bent forward. The others who had taken up one tool or another moved them slowly. Far back through the half-darkened shop young Jehl might be seen lifting the heavy bottles of gleaming quicksilver at the vacuum pumps, and the soft music was delicately thrilling through it all. It was the wedding of spirit and matter, and impressed me strangely.

'Can you play "The Heart Bowed Down?" ' said Edison, suddenly.

'No, I cannot.'

'Here, whistle it some of you.' Five or six whistled, and Boehm shook his head.

'Can't play it? Well, Crosby what's that other tune?'
'My poor heart is sad with its dreaming,' said Crosby.
'Yes, play that?'
'I cannot.'
'Play anything,' said Crosby, 'it's all the same to him and us.' Boehm played. Edison seemed to be fidgeting about 'The Heart Bowed Down.' He took a writing pad from his pocket and scratched rapidly with a pencil on it for some minutes. He beckoned to Boehm.
'Can you blow that?' He handed him a rough drawing.
'Yes,' said the boy, 'you mean that for a circle? Yes; that will be better.'
In a minute, zither and glassblower were gone, and they took all the dreamy spirit of fatherland with them. The concert was over. It was about half past ten. Conversation turned on scientific topics, roaming over wide fields, the boyish assistants breaking in here and there like young colts, Batchelor turning round now and again from his minute study of finished carbons to declaim with more than ordinary emphasis on particular points. Owing to Edison's slight defect of hearing we naturally spoke rather loud, and that conversation would have sounded oddly in any stranger's ears. The acuteness of Edison's perceptions was what struck me most, and often desultory as our talk seemed, he struck off keen observations that surprised me. I felt rather in doubt whether I ought to go down to my sleeping place or remain, and about eleven o'clock I asked Edison if he was going to work or going home.
'That's just as it strikes him,' said one near me in an ordinary voice.
'Are you in a hurry?' said Edison. 'I'm not.'
'I'd like to see some of your platinum lamps,' I said, 'if it's not troublesome.'
'Come over here,' and he led the way to a glass case in the corner, where a medley of contorted glass globes and tubing lay upon cotton wool. He took some of them out and explained them—how low the resistance of platinum was compared with carbon, and so on; how he coated the fine wire with almost infusible oxides to insulate it, so that in nine feet of it reeled around a bobbin the electric fluid would have to run along the entire length of it.
'I ransacked the world,' said he, 'for scarce metals and spent lots of money in reducing ores. I have little bottles here that cost me a couple of hundred dollars.'
'Didn't you find the text books and authorities save you a great deal of time in these matters?'
'They're mostly misleading,' said he sturdily. 'I get mad with myself when I think I have believed what was so learnedly set out in them.'
'What,' I said, aghast, 'are the books wrong?'
'I'll tell you what I mean; there are more frauds in science than anywhere else. There are two classes of them—first, the pure scientists without practical knowledge, and next the practical men without any science. You take the pure scientist—mind you, I don't speak of such men as Faraday, Regnault or Bunsen, nor such men as Maxwell, or Sir William Thompson; what they say is so is so, because they proved it before they said so; but take a whole pile of them that I can name and you will find uncertainty if not imposition in half of what they state as scientific truth. These men did not work for money, and they had only reputation to work for. They have time and again set down experiments as done by them, curious out-of-the-way experiments that they never did and upon which they founded so-called scientific truths. I have been thrown off the track often by them, and for months at a time. You see a great

name and you believe in it. Try the experiment yourself and you find the result altogether different.'

'Can you name some of these so-called truths?'

'Yes, plenty. I tell you, to an earnest inquirer books are a detriment. Say, Van Cleef,' said the bold young man raising his voice, 'bring me the *Dictionary of Solubilities*.

It was brought up from some recesses downstairs.

'Look here,' he continued; 'with common things that nobody wants to test they'll serve you well enough. Ah! here,' he pointed to an oxide of baryta; 'Look: one says, "insoluble in water," another, "sparingly soluble in water." So it goes. You will find here sometimes fifty authorities, all giving different statements about one thing. Do you see that name, there, given as an authority? That man wrote a book on the art of scientific discovery, and he never made but two or three little bits of discovery in his life. Now, you'd think platinum was pretty well known, but the books say it is infusible except in an oxyhydrogen flame. Why,' and he laughed, 'I can melt it in the flame of a candle. Come here; I'll melt some in that gas jet.'

At this point I appear in the chronicle:

We crossed the laboratory and he took up a spool of very fine platinum wire, broke off about nine inches of it and held it in the gas jet. It shriveled up, but held together. I looked at him incredulously.

'Hey, Francis, bring me that microscope.'

Francis in due time appeared with a large instrument, green with verdigris. Edison laughed as I looked at it.

'Oh,' said he, 'we keep things here for use. That cost $300, but I've had ten times its value out of it. Haeckel, Evolutionist Haeckel, you know, never uttered a truer thing than when talking about laboratories with costly instruments kept shut up in glass cases, he said the quantity of work done was in inverse proportion to the quantity of apparatus.' Adjusting the microscope, he continued, 'Look in here now. You see along the magnified wire a number of little globules, that is where the platinum has fused, and I can do it in a candle. They talk without much thinking. They found a thick wire wouldn't melt in a gas flame, so they said platinum couldn't be melted there. If they were the first to discover water they'd say you couldn't boil it, because they tried burning a tallow candle under a cask of it.'

'Are you an evolutionist?'

'Oh, yes: I believe in that. This is magnesium; of course you've seen it burn,' and he tore off a piece of the ribbon and lighted it. It flamed out. 'The peculiar moonlight color in the voltaic arc light is due to the impurities in the carbon, magnesium among the rest. What's the matter with you, Francis?' he said, turning to young Jehl, who was sitting moodily by.

'I'm hungry,' blurted out Francis.

'Where's the lunch?' said Edison.

'There was none ordered,' said Francis, more despondently; 'we didn't think you were coming back to work all night, and now we're here and there's nothing.'

'Get us something to eat,' said Edison. 'You see, the carbon used is made out of powder, held together by various substances. If they were to use chemically pure carbon, they would place the light away out of reach, it would cost so much; and pure or not, they must use a foreign substance to make it hold together. George, bring me a stick of carbon and a filament.'

He put the little filament under the microscope and it looked like a cake of coal. Then he broke off a piece of the carbon stick and heated it with a blow-pipe to show the impurities under the microscope.

'You said a while ago that books and authorities were a detriment; that seems very strong to me.'

'Remember how I qualified it. But I tell you I'd rather know nothing about a thing in science nine times out of ten than what the books could tell me—for practical purposes, for applied science, the best science, the only science. I'd rather take the thing up and go through with it myself. I'd find out more about it than any one could tell me, and I'd be sure of what I knew. That's the thing. Professor this or that will controvert you out of the books, and prove out of the books that it can't be so, though you have it right in the hollow of your hand all the time and could break his spectacles with it. I never take anybody's word that anything can't be done, if I as much as suspect it can. I showed you in that book over there how they trip each other up.'

We had to make phosphoric anhydride for the vacuum pumps, and that's a job. We light the phosphorus and run. The vapor of it is terrible, but it's nothing to osmic acid. You remember a great Parisian scientist once held up a vial of it and said there was enough to suffocate the entire population of Paris if they were passed through in a file. I thought that was too strong. I took just a little sniff of it once, and I tell you it was terrible—the worst I ever came near. It stung my nose and caught me in the throat.

'The book was right that time. That was the right kind of scientist.'

It was well after midnight now, and I heard some of the boys tramping upstairs, while Edison now with the peculiar nocturnal brightening of the human owl, talked in an unbroken string about the strange metals with unfamiliar names he had had such apparent fun in reducing.

'I think the Almighty made carbon especially for the electric light. What's this for?' George held something in a brown paper out before him.

'Herrings,' said George; 'smoked herrings.'

Edison looked around glumly. 'Is this the best you can do?' Francis was seated on a stool, a herring in one hand, a cracker in the other, his mouth full of cracker and herring and his whole face beaming.

'He's happy,' said Edison. 'Help yourself; we don't entertain in this way.'

'Pot luck,' said the *Herald* correspondent, cheerfully.

'Everything agrees with me,' said Edison. So the repast went on. We were a merry crowd of seven there at one in the morning. The inventor's face beamed with good humor, and he joked with the boys who are on such a pleasant footing with him, intimate in expression, but it was always a pleasure to see the respectful alacrity with which they looked after him at all times; just now they were looking for tender herrings for him. Francis, from smiles and laughing gradually assumed a more settled expression indicating that the process of digestion was rapidly taking place, and in a very short time he was asleep on the edge of one of the benches, with the *Dictionary of Solubilities* for a pillow. One by one they dropped off. George actually went to have a look at his vacuum pump before curling up on a bench, and Edison and the *Herald* man, with just one other who, however, took three sleeps meantime sat talking till four o'clock. What did he talk of? Well, who could tell. Like a fresh-hearted city boy out in the fields for a holiday, he ran through the gardens of science in a way at once fascinating and surprising. Reminiscences of old times when he was a telegraph operator jogged elbows with dissertations on chemistry, electricity, light, heat, dynamics, statics.

As I was leaving the laboratory I saw the inventor with his coat over his arm, looking for a soft spot upon the benches.

WHEN THE WORLD CAME TO MENLO PARK

Artist's portrayal of New Year's Eve demonstration December 31, 1879,
when Edison's lamp was shown to the public.

'The lamp that blazed the way to modern illumination.'

LIII. The New Year's Eve Demonstration

NEW Year's Eve arrived at last. Special trains from east and west pulled in at the little depot and disgorged their eager passengers, who came all agog with interest and curiosity. Old-fashioned wagons brought farmers and their families, carriages wheeled up and unloaded private parties.

They saw four houses illuminated, streets lighted, and many lamps burning in and around the Edison buildings. Again we turn to the newspapers of the period for a first-hand description of that historic occasion. The first article is from the *Herald* (New York):

Edison's laboratory was tonight thrown open to the general public for the inspection of his electric light. Extra trains were run from east and west, and notwithstanding the stormy weather, hundreds of persons availed themselves of the privilege. The laboratory was brilliantly illuminated with twenty-five electric lamps, the office and counting room with eight, and twenty others were distributed in the street leading to the depot and in some of the adjoining houses. The entire system was explained in detail by Edison and his assistants, and the light was subjected to a variety of tests. Among others the inventor placed one of the electric lamps in a large glass jar filled with water and turned on the current, the little horseshoe filament when thus submerged burned with the same bright steady illumination as it did in the air, the water not having the slightest effect upon it. The lamp was kept thus under water for four hours. Another test was turning the electric current on and off on one of the lamps with great rapidity and as many times as it was calculated the light would be turned on and off in actual household illuminations in a period of thirty years, and no perceptible variation either in the brilliancy, steadiness or durability of the lamp occurred. The method of regulating the supply of electricity at the central station was explained in detail, as was also the electric motor; the latter was made to pump water and run a sewing machine with only as much electricity as was necessary to give out an illumination of the brilliancy of an ordinary gas jet.

' To illustrate, Mr. Edison simply attached the wires of the motor to an electric lamp, disconnecting the latter. The rapid changes from light to power and from power back again to light attracted much attention and elicited not a little admiration. The method of producing the current, the mode of measurement of the electricity consumed, the manner of connecting the wires and the other incidental details were practically illustrated. The simple method of preparing the horseshoe filament attracted much attention. At one of the tables in the laboratory an assistant sat with a small punch in his hand punching from pieces of cardboard the little horseshoes. Another assistant then

placed several at a time in an iron mould five inches square and placed the latter in the furnace. At the expiration of a little more than an hour the mould was taken out and the carbonized papers shown. At this stage they are quite fragile, and it is only after being subjected to the action of the electric current that they become reasonably strong. The vacuum pumps were kept working, and hundreds witnessed the method of

Regulator wheel on second floor of restored laboratory, connected with one on ground floor and used to demonstrate control of current from distance.

Front page of New York *Daily Graphic* showing scenes at the first public
demonstration in Menlo Park, December 31, 1879.

obtaining the vacuum in the bulbs of the lamp. The wires leading from the generators to the various lamps were followed in all their connections. They were ordinary copper wires of about one-eighth of an inch in diameter.

The regulation of the current was carried on in the lower part of the laboratory, a young man by the aid of a small wheel turning off the current to any degree desired. Attached to all the chandeliers, which are of the pattern frequently used, were screws, by the turning of which the light could be turned on or off as readily as gas. The center of attraction during the exhibition was Edison himself, who was attired in a rough suit of working clothes. For hours he was surrounded, first by one throng and then by another, and he found it almost impossible to get away. Many had come in the expectation of seeing a dignified, elegantly dressed person, and were much surprised to find him a simple young man attired in the homeliest manner, using for his explanations not high sounding, technical terms, but the plainest and simplest language. The sceptics were severe in their cross-questioning, but to all their interrogatories as to expense, amount of horsepower consumed, proposed method of working and all other details he gave prompt, simple and direct answers, which were readily understood and always convincing. When argued with that the gas companies could reduce the price of gas much lower than it was at present and still make a profit, thus successfully competing with the electric light, he referred to the electric motor to be used in connection with his system, pointing out that even if gas and electricity cost exactly the same to produce the electric motor could make a vast difference in favor of electricity, insomuch as the plant of the latter would be kept in use nearly all day and night—in the daytime furnishing power, in the night time furnishing illumination—while the gas was serviceable for only four or five hours every night, being idle throughout the day, but he insisted that without the electric motor gas could not be produced nearly as cheap as electricity under any circumstances.

Among the visitors present were several gas company officials and electricians, who subjected the system to a close examination, Edison ordering every facility to be given them for making all the tests they required. Among the prominent persons present were W. E. Chandler, of New Hampshire, ex-Secretary Robeson, and Senator Plumb, of Kansas. All the visitors seemed satisfied that Edison had actually solved the problem of practical household illumination by electricity. The street lamps will probably be kept burning nightly for several nights to come, but the inventor will be compelled if he would make any headway toward getting ready for the general introduction of the light, to close the laboratory to the multitude, leaving them to see and examine the light in the street lamps and dwellings in Menlo Park. No scientist or expert, however, he states, will be denied the privilege of thorough examination of the system until all are satisfied. It is contemplated by Mr. Edison before long to light up a square either in Metuchen or Rahway, adjacent towns, the current being transmitted from Menlo Park.

The second tells how the interest and excitement continued the following day (*Herald*, January 2, 1880):

If ever the patience of scientist was tried by the surging in upon his privacy of the curious multitude, Mr. Edison's patience has certainly been tried during the past six days. To satisfy the curiosity of the earnest inquirers on science, and to practically answer the critics and sceptics, Mr. Edison ordered the doors of his laboratory thrown wide open, that all might see and judge of his electric light. Anxious on the one hand to avoid the appearance of anything

Fig. 1—Cardboard horseshoe filament; Fig. 2—Cardboard before carbonization; Fig. 3—Lamp itself; Fig. 4—Edison's first socket. Note above hand the lamp in socket on bracket. (From *Scientific American,* January 10, 1880.)

like a show or fair, and on the other hand to give every opportunity to those who were honestly sceptical as to the practicability of the light, he set no particular night for a public exhibition of the same, but directed a week ago that no person who should come to Menlo Park to see the electric light be excluded from the laboratory. Availing themselves of the privilege hundreds of persons came from all quarters. During the first few days the crowds were not too large to interfere with the business of the inventor's assistants, and all went well. Every courtesy was shown and every detail of the new system of lighting explained. The crowds, however, kept increasing. The railroad company ordered extra trains to be run and carriages came streaming from near and far. Surging crowds filed into the laboratory, machine shop and private office of the scientist, and all work had to be practically suspended. Yesterday the people came by hundreds in every train. They went pellmell through the places previously kept sacredly private. Notices not to touch or handle apparatus were disregarded. The assistants were kept on the jump from early till late guarding the scores of delicate instruments with which the laboratory abounds.

Up to nearly midnight the rush continued and this morning an inspection revealed, as the result of the visitation, a broken vacuum pump and the loss of eight electric lamps, which had been stolen by vulgar curiosity searchers. Tonight the rush was still greater, and from dark until ten o'clock trains, wagons and carriages deposited loads upon loads of visitors in this ordinarily quiet hamlet. Of course hundreds of those who came were well-bred people, who meant not to take, and did not take, advantage of Mr. Edison's good nature, but it is to be regretted there were others, and they were numbered by the score, who cared nothing for science, who regarded the laboratory as they would a circus. By eight o'clock the laboratory was so crowded that it was almost impossible for the assistants to pass through. The exclamation, 'There is Edison,' invariably caused a rush that more than once threatened to break down the timbers of the building. The assistants, however, stood firm at their posts watching keenly for depredators. Messrs. Batchelor and Upton stood guard over the main wires leading to the generators. Van Cleef and Bogadore remained at the vacuum pumps and Force and Poiner watched the dynamic machines. The various other assistants were doing duty in other parts of the laboratory. Their vigilance was more than once rewarded by detecting persons rudely handling the apparatus.

One maliciously disposed person was caught trying to short-circuit the wires by placing across them a small piece of copper. His opportune detection prevented the extinguishment of all the lights. Mr. Edison early in the evening sought seclusion in his private office, but the occasional arrival of distinguished visitors, who were satisfied with no one else for explanations, made it necessary for him at times to emerge from retirement and go through for the thousandth time the ordeal of shaking hands and answering questions. When it is remembered that Edison is one of the most retiring of men, detesting all pomp and show, resembling the Indian in his desire to get away into the forests of solitude, whence he cannot be followed, a desire aptly illustrated in his living in the secluded hamlet of Menlo Park, with only a dozen houses and meager railroad accommodations, the unpleasant character of his new position can readily be appreciated. Tonight he gave orders that work be again resumed in the laboratory, and the latter closed to the general public, directing, however, that the private dwelling in Menlo Park, as well as the street lamps, be kept burning nightly, so that those who come will not be disappointed. In future admission to the laboratory to see the light will be only by special invitation or permit from the company's offices in New York.

On October 21, 1932, fifty-third anniversary of the birth of the first successful lamp, Mr. Ford asked us to revive the lost art of making cardboard filament lamps, and to relight

Restored laboratory lighted by cardboard filament lamps,
on October 21, 1932.

the laboratory and grounds as had been done on New Year's
Eve long ago.

Not since 1880 had that thrilling scene been witnessed.
As we reconstructed several hundred of the old horseshoe
filament lamps, we came to realize what difficulties and obstacles Edison had had to overcome. They were so much
greater than ours because he worked in the dark; he had no
guide or precedent to blaze the trail whereas we were able to
follow in his footsteps.

Each of the reconstructed replicas of those old lamps was
tested as in 1879; several were given life tests and found to
range much as in the old days. One or two gave four to five
hours, others thirty to fifty, and some more than three
hundred. We carbonized the fragile filaments down in the
muffle furnace in the restored laboratory, even as our master
did in 1879.

Before the lamp was invented, this laboratory was lighted
with illuminating gas; the second floor still has its piping
and fixtures as on October 21, 1879. Everything on the first
floor has been rearranged to correspond with the exhibition

plan of December 31. Ornamental coverings, made here in Greenfield Village, conceal the pipes. The sockets that hold the globes are exactly like the original ones invented by Edison. Made on a jack switch principle, they consist of two parallel pieces of metal, each connected with the source of current. The metals were inserted in the socket to form the connections for the lamp. The lamp base itself consisted of a piece of foil soldered to the extremities of the lead-wires, bent over on the glass and held in position by thread.

The brackets in the laboratory have been reproduced so faithfully that we have found it impossible to distinguish them from the original one.

The street lamps, which have been restored as they were on New Year's Eve, disclose the type that Edison himself selected for the exhibition. He wanted something different from the old style and found this more attractive one in New York City. Among the relics recovered from the site of the original Menlo Park by Mr. Ford was a complete frame of the original lantern together with the post; these have served as the model for the ones you see in the grounds.

On October 21, 1932, we lighted the cardboard lamps with current furnished from the restored machine shop by dynamos that are exact replicas of the original ones used in 1879 for the same purpose.

As in the old days, we had overhead wires to convey the current; the wires inside the laboratory and elsewhere were insulated in green to mark the positive pole, and red to distinguish the negative.

On the ground floor of the laboratory you may see the restored testing table, where I had charge of regulating the current brought from one of the three dynamos in the shop, which was used as an exciting machine to energize the two current-giving generators. The wires were brought to a regulating resistance box beside my table; here, with the help of a Thomson reflecting galvanometer, I regulated the tension in the manner described in the articles.

Thus Edison showed visitors how he controlled machinery in the distant shop by turning a single wheel in the laboratory. At the same time he thrilled spectators by showing how the lamps could be lowered to dimness and then increased to brilliancy. It was one of the first instances in which electric energy was regulated from a distance. The three generators in the restored machine shop operated on October 21 just as they did in 1879, one as an exciter and the others as current generators; and the wires from the exciter led to the laboratory testing table. Henry Ford started the steam engine in the shop at 8 o'clock that evening and set the belts whirring. Immediately the little lamps began to glow like fireflies and dispelled the darkness.

Ground floor of restored laboratory, Dearborn, lighted
by cardboard filament lamps. October 21, 1932.

INDEX TO ILLUSTRATIONS

INDEX TO ILLUSTRATIONS (Continued)

INDEX TO ILLUSTRATIONS (*Continued*)

INDEX TO VOLUME ONE

INDEX TO VOLUME ONE (*continued*)

INDEX TO VOLUME ONE *(continued)*

133; High-resistance lamp, 250, 254; Incandescent lighting system conceived, 243; Inventions, first, 40, 41; Visits restored laboratory, 340; Lamp: first, 234, second, 235, third, 236; Lamp using vacuum, 250; Law for transmission of electric current, 256; Lighting system shown gas company officials, 397; Lighting system plans, 216, 217; Metals, experiments with, 234; Meter, first, 287; Microphone, first, 134; Motor, Electric, 314, 317; Newark Shop, 50; Occluded gases, discovery of, 250; Phonograph at Washington, 159, 160; Phonograph, demonstration, 170; First demonstration, 165; How invented, 163; Operates, 158, 160; Platinum, experiments with, 236; Pope, Edison & Co., 46; Re-enactment of light's invention, 356; Saves child from train, 36, 37; Sells telephone patents to Western Union, 129; Stock ticker, 43, 50; Suit threatened by Bell, 275; Tar putty experiment, 330; Telegraph, 59, 60; Telephone experiments, 107, 143; Telegraph quadruplex, 75; Telegraph table, 34; Ticker sold for $40,000, 49; Transmitter, 114, 120; Vacuum, lamps in, 250; Vacuum pump, 325; Western trip, 209, 210; Wireless, 89, 90
Electrical World and Engineer—p. 310
Electrician—p. 346
Electric Lighting—By Hippolyte Fontaine—p. 232
Electric pen—p. 10, 13, 20, 94
Embossing telegraph—p. 77
Engineering—p. 217
Etheric force—p. 80
Faraday, Michael—p. 204, 267
Farmer, Moses G.—p. 211; Associate of Wallace, 208, 209
Filaments—p. 330, 337, 347, 348
Fire signal—p. 73
Fish, Frederick—p. 194
Fontaine, Hippolyte—p. 197, 232
Force, Martin—p. 170, 171, 258, 278, 284, 291, 293, 345
Ford, Henry—p. 22, 427, 430
Franklin, Benjamin—p. 200
Franklin Institute—p. 241, 280
Fraser, Michigan town—p. 138
French Academy of Sciences—p. 202
French Exhibition—p. 272
Friction machine—p. 200
Galvani, Prof. Luigi—p. 201
Galvanometer—p. 268
Geissler, Dr. Heinrich—p. 245, 324, 370, 413
Generator test—p. 298, 300, 301
German Edison Co.—p. 408
Glass house—p. 223, 328
Gold and Stock Ticker—p. 42, 43, 47
Gould, Jay—p. 75
Gouraud, George E.—London representative—p. 274, 279, 284
Gramme, Zenobe Theophile—p. 205, 249, 298
Grand Trunk Railroad—p. 36
Graphic, New York daily—p. 179, 223

INDEX TO VOLUME ONE (*continued*)

INDEX TO VOLUME ONE (*continued*)

INDEX TO VOLUME ONE (*continued*)